Driving a Bargain

STUDIES IN INTERNATIONAL POLITICAL ECONOMY
Stephen D. Krasner, Editor
Ernst B. Haas, Consulting Editor

Driving a Bargain

Automobile Industrialization and
Japanese Firms in Southeast Asia

RICHARD F. DONER

UNIVERSITY OF CALIFORNIA PRESS
Berkeley · Los Angeles · Oxford

University of California Press
Berkeley and Los Angeles, California

University of California Press, Ltd.
Oxford, England

© 1991 by
The Regents of the University of California

**Library of Congress
Cataloging-in-Publication Data**

Doner, Richard F.
  Driving a bargain : automobile industrialization
and Japanese firms in Southeast Asia / Richard F.
Doner.
      p.   cm.—(Studies in international political
      economy)
  Includes bibliographical references and index.
  ISBN 0-520-06938-2 (alk. paper)
  1. Automobile industry and trade—Asia,
Southeastern—Foreign ownership.   2. Corpora-
tions, Japanese—Asia, Southeastern.   I. Title.
II. Series.
HD9710.A7852D66   1991
338.8'8952059—dc20   90-40198
                                      CIP

Printed in the United States of America
9 8 7 6 5 4 3 2 1

Contents

Tables

ACKNOWLEDGMENTS

This book draws on the knowledge, generosity, and encouragement of individuals in several countries. I am deeply grateful to those (listed at the back) who granted me some 175 interviews in Japan, the Philippines, Indonesia, Thailand, and Malaysia during the summer of 1983 and most of 1985. I am especially indebted to Kei Ono, Konosuke Odaka, and Ryokichi Hirono in Tokyo; Quintin Tan, Henry Moran, Carlos Sazon, and the staff of *Business Day* newspaper in Manila; Clara Joewono and other members of the staff of the Center for Strategic and International Studies in Jakarta; Ian Chalmers in Australia; Siriboon Nawadhinsukh, Suchart Uthaiwait, and Prakitti Siripraiwan in Bangkok; and Paul Low and the staff of the Institute for Strategic and International Studies in Kuala Lumpur.

In the United States Ernst Haas was and continues to be a vital source of inspiration and discipline to me, as he has been to so many others. My thanks go also to Chalmers Johnson, who provided important comments on all parts of this study; to Joe Grieco, who forced me to confront tough methodological issues; and to Alasdair Bowie, who gave most generously and creatively of his time to read and comment on most of the chapters. Others who read and provided useful comments on parts of the book include Jeff Anderson, Doug Bennett, Stephan Haggard, Anek Laothamatas, Ted Moran, Ansil Ramsay, Randy Strahan, and David Wurfel. Finally, I wish to thank Susan Zaro for her encouragement, her companionship, and her sense of humor.

My research in Asia was funded by a Fulbright Fellowship, a Social Science Research Council Fellowship, and the Political Science Department of the University of California, Berkeley. Subsequent financial support came from the Jewish Community Federation of Cleveland, Ohio, and Emory University. To each of these institutions I offer my deepest thanks.

ABBREVIATIONS AND GLOSSARY

AAE	Asian Automotive Engineering
AB&I	*Asian Business and Industry*
ADC	Automobile Development Committee (Thailand)
AFM	Automotive Federation of Malaysia
AIJV	ASEAN Industrial Joint Venture
AMII	Automotive Manufacturers' Institute Inc. (Philippines)
APIC	Automotive Parts Industry Club (Thailand)
ASEAN	Association of Southeast Asian Nations
ATI	Association of Thai Industries
AWSJ	*Asian Wall Street Journal*
BD	*Business Day* (Manila)
BIES	*Bulletin of Indonesian Economic Studies*
BIT	*Business in Thailand*
BKPM	Badan Koordinasi Penanaman Modal [Capital Investment Coordinating Board] (Indonesia)
BN	*Business News* (Jakarta)
BOI	Board of Investment (Philippines, Malaysia, Thailand)
BP	*Bangkok Post*
BPPT	Badan Penelitian dan Penerapan Teknologi [Office for Research and Application of Technology] (Indonesia)
BT	*Business Times* (Kuala Lumpur)
bumiputra	indigenous Malay
CAPPA	Consolidated Automotive Parts Producers' Association Inc. (Philippines)
Carco	Canlubang Automotive Resources Co. (Mitsubishi affiliate in the Philippines)
CBU	completely built-up vehicle

CKD   completely knocked-down vehicle
CV   commercial vehicle
DE   *Daily Express* (Manila)
DOI   Department of Industry (Indonesia)
EIU   Economist Intelligence Unit
EOI   export-oriented industrialization
EON   Edaran Otomobil Nasional [National Automobile Dis-
                tribution Corporation] (Malaysia)
FDI   foreign direct investment
FEER   *Far Eastern Economic Review*
GAAKINDO   Gabungan Assembler dan Agen Tunggal Kendaraan
                Bermotor Indonesia [Association of Indonesian Auto-
                mobile Assemblers and Sole Agents]
HICOM   Heavy Industries Corporation of Malaysia
ICA   Industrial Coordination Act (Malaysia)
ICN   *Indonesian Commercial Newsletter*
IFCT   Industrial Finance Corporation of Thailand
ISI   import-substitution industrialization
JAMA   Japan Automobile Manufacturers' Association
JCC   Joint Coordinating Committee on Local Content for
                the National Car (Malaysia)
JMB   *Japanese Motor Business*
JPPCC   Joint Public and Private Sector Consultative Committee
                (Thailand)
JTC   Joint Technical Committee for Local Content (Malay-
                sia)
KADIN   Kamar Dagang dan Industry [Chamber of Commerce
                and Industry] (Indonesia)
LC   local content
LDC   less developed country
MACPMA   Malaysian Automotive Components and Parts Manufac-
                turers' Association
MAN   Maschinenfabrik Augsburg-Nürnberg AG
MB   *Malaysian Business*
MC   *Manila Chronicle*
MCA   Malaysian Chinese Association
MIDA   Malaysian Industrial Development Authority

MIDF	Malaysian Industrial Development Finance Corporation
MITI	Ministry of International Trade and Industry (Japan)
MMC	Mitsubishi Motors Corporation
MMVA	Malaysian Motor Vehicle Assemblers' Association
MOI	Ministry of Industry (Thailand)
MTI	Ministry of Trade and Industry (Malaysia)
MVAC	Motor Vehicle Assembly Committee (Malaysia)
NEC	National Economic Council (Philippines)
NEP	New Economic Policy (Malaysia)
NESDB	National Economic and Social Development Board (Thailand)
NIC	newly industrialized country
NST	*New Straits Times* (Kuala Lumpur)
ODA	overseas development assistance
OE	original equipment
OECD	Organization for Economic Cooperation and Development
PAA	Philippine Automotive Association
PCI	Philippine Chamber of Industry
PCMP	Progressive Car Manufacturing Program (Philippines)
PMADE	Progressive Manufacture of Automotive Diesel Engines (Philippines)
PNB	Philippines National Bank
pribumi	indigenous Indonesian
Proton	Perusahaan Otomobil Nasional [National Automobile Industry Corp.] (Malaysia)
PV	passenger vehicle
SIRIM	Standards and Industrial Research Institute of Malaysia
SKD	semi-knocked-down vehicle
SNF	Siam Nawaloha Foundry (Thailand)
TAPMA	Thai Automotive Parts Manufacturers' Association
TDD	Technology Development Division, Astra (Indonesia)
TJ	*Times Journal* (Manila)
TNC	transnational corporation
TS	*The Star* (Kuala Lumpur)
UMNO	United Malay National Organization
UMW	United Motor Works (Malaysia)

1

Introduction

The world's industrialized nations occupy a highly ambiguous position in the eyes of less developed countries (LDCs). Possessor of critically needed resources, the industrialized world is often also perceived as a threat to the sovereignty and industrial growth of LDCs, whose development efforts consequently involve delicate, shifting balancing. Developing countries must press the North for expanded benefits while guarding against pushing so hard that the source of these benefits opts to move elsewhere.[1] This balancing act has been evident over the past fifteen to twenty years as LDCs have sought to strengthen themselves both individually and collectively in overlapping areas such as trade, finance, global commons (e.g., the oceans, Antarctica), and foreign investment.[2] This book examines national efforts to expand benefits from foreign investment. More specifically, it explores the potential for LDC manufacturing in an industry as technologically imposing as automobiles, and the factors affecting the ability of developing host countries to exploit this potential.

I address these questions through a comparative examination of four Southeast Asian cases. The Philippines, Malaysia, Indonesia, and Thailand, all members of the Association of Southeast Asian Nations (ASEAN), have been attempting to establish national automobile industries since the 1960s.[3] Following policies already pursued by Latin American countries, each ASEAN nation has sought to replace imported parts and vehicles with locally manufactured products. Each has believed that local auto manufacture would yield new foundries and machine shops, new jobs and skills, increased foreign-exchange savings, and local control of an industry heretofore dominated by foreign manufacturers. Each has seen the auto industry as both symbol and force in its shift from growth based on primary commodity exports to development through industrialization.

These efforts have encountered daunting obstacles. Rapid innovations in products, materials, and production processes since the early 1970s have raised entry barriers for nascent auto manufacturers. Foreign firms have been reluctant to support manufacturing activities in countries with shallow technological bases and markets too limited for efficient production levels. The ASEAN nations' auto industrialization has consequently involved ongoing negotiations between local officials and entrepreneurs on the one hand, and foreign, largely Japanese, auto firms on the other.

We know from studies of other regions and products that foreign firms do not unilaterally dictate terms to the developing countries in which they invest. Host countries are far from helpless supplicants willing to abandon sovereignty for precious foreign funds, equipment, and skills. Rather, they are active and increasingly capable bargainers, pressing for their own goals through a process that combines conflict and cooperation with foreign firms. Yet literally all studies of bargaining agree that owing to the steep financial and technological requirements of manufacturing, it is more difficult for host countries to achieve leverage in automobile production than in raw materials operations.

One particular view of the bargaining process, here termed the structuralist approach, takes this argument a step further. It asserts that local leverage over manufacturing projects shifts to the foreign investor over time as the host country presses for a shift from simple assembly of imported parts to actual local manufacture. The model attributes this not only to high technological entry barriers but also to the tendency of foreign firms to coopt private interests such as suppliers and consumers with whom they maintain business linkages in the host country. An autonomous state, independent of such coopted actors, is presumed to be vital to a defense of the national interest against foreign capital.

I argue that this approach to bargaining dynamics is flawed. It is overly general with regard to both its predicted bargaining outcomes and the forces it identifies as responsible for those outcomes. I find the view here termed the product-cycle approach more useful and accurate. While acknowledging that LDCs confront imposing entry barriers in their attempts to become manufacturers, this view denies the inevitability of a decline of local leverage over the terms of manufacturing. The entry barriers to manufacturing, even in high technology, are not monolithic. Nor are local businesses necessarily coopted by the foreign firms with whom they work; in certain areas of advanced manufacturing, local entrepreneurs are quite aggressive and capable of competing with foreign actors. An autonomous local state is not necessarily essential for leverage on the part of the host country.

But the product-cycle approach itself requires greater specification. Not all firms in host countries are economic nationalists; and among those that are, not all succeed in expanding at the expense of foreign capital. Explaining variation requires identification of the economic and political contexts in which local capital seeks to expand. Specifically, it requires a focus on the particular product niches of local firms, the characteristics of states in the host country, and the links between states and local firms.

The bargaining focus adopted here bears on the very meaning of dependency and the potential for its reversal. I assume that dependency is a matter of degree, that developing countries operate somewhere between dependency and autonomy, and that increases in local strength are liable to reversal.[4] The question is then how LDCs manage discrete improvements in manufacturing capacity and market structures. In this study I emphasize the contribution of negotiated ties between host countries and local firms to such improvements.

Finally, the study speaks to the issue of who leads in the development process. Recent works on East Asia have emphasized the growth-promoting role of states in protecting, subsidizing, and otherwise encouraging competitive infant industries.[5] Although they do not negate the state's role, the analyses here direct attention to the contributions of a heretofore neglected, but clearly significant, set of actors—Third World capitalists.[6] I do not, however, argue for a firm-centered approach. Rather, I suggest the need to shift the frame of reference from one of state versus private sector to one stressing the *coalitional* bases of industrialization in developing countries.

This study examines the preceding issues in a new geographical context. Analyses of bargaining and development have concentrated on Latin America and, increasingly, on the newly industrialized countries (NICs) of East Asia, such as South Korea and Taiwan. The major external actor covered in most of these works has been Western capital. Conversely, writings on the political economy of capitalist southeast Asia, a region of significant economic growth and global strategic importance, have been rare.[7] Even more neglected have been the interactions between developing countries and Japanese firms. Since Southeast Asia has been the principal focus of Japanese foreign investment,[8] the study can also shed light on the operations of Japanese firms in developing nations.

The study's theoretical context is established in chapter 2, which critically reviews the two competing approaches to bargaining between host countries and transnational corporations (TNCs). Chapter 3 examines the origins, goals, and outcomes of ASEAN automobile policies, focusing on two empirical questions central to the competing approaches to bargaining. Were any of the ASEAN countries able to expand their bargaining leverage over time? If so, which one(s) was (were) most successful? I argue that there has, in fact, been some expansion of local bargaining leverage, and that some countries have done better than others.

Chapter 4 explores the degree to which economic factors, both external and domestic, influenced these outcomes. Through an analysis of the international automobile industry and Japanese auto firms, it first explains how any local achievements occurred at all. It then considers the possibility that cross-national variation in bargaining performance is a function of differences in national economic characteristics. Chapters 5 through 8 pursue a more explicitly political explanation by tracing critical automotive bargaining episodes in each of the ASEAN Four. My primary objective here is to evaluate the impact on bargaining performance of each country's state, private sector, and public-private sector ties.

The broad results of these cases may be stated at the outset: I find differences in relations between governments and business to be the most important explanation of cross-national variation in sectoral bargaining performance. Chapter 9 first reviews these findings in the light of the competing bargaining frameworks and then examines the national context of sectoral arrangements in each of the ASEAN Four. This examination reinforces the point emerging from the case studies: coalitions in which authority is shared by public and private actors rather than monopolized by autonomous state actors can generate significant economic growth in developing countries. In chapter 10 I explore the implications of this for the broader development literature.

2

Contending Approaches to Bargaining

An Accepted Framework

Our understanding of interactions between transnational corporations and LDC host countries has advanced over the past twenty years. It is now clear that foreign direct investment (FDI) is less inherently beneficial to developing countries than presumed by pro-FDI writers, but more potentially useful than assumed by dependency theorists.[1] Detailed case studies have demonstrated the weaknesses in a priori determinations of the outcomes of host country–TNC relations.[2] In their place has emerged a third body of literature: studies that focus on the means available to host countries attempting to expand their power vis-à-vis foreign capital.[3] Host country–TNC relations are now presumed to reflect neither absolute opposition nor mutual benefit. Various sorts of collaborative strategies can expand the pie to be divided and increase absolute returns to all parties.[4] The resolution of divergent preferences occurs through a bargaining process in which each side has particular sources of leverage.

Several characteristics of this process are commonly accepted. Bargaining is, first of all, dynamic. The relative balance of bargaining power shifts over time as a function of changing risk and the uncertainty experienced by each side with regard to investment requirements.[5] Perceptions of risk and uncertainty change in turn as a function of shifts in *potential* power resources—those possessed by one side and required by the other. For foreign investors, firm-specific assets such as technology, management skills, capital, and access to overseas markets yield leverage to the extent that they are critical to an investment project's success but not accessible to the host country. The host country's leverage is a function of its possession of resources required by the foreign investor, such as a large domestic market, inexpensive and/or skilled labor, and plentiful natural resources; the degree of competition among foreign firms for access to these resources; and the host country's ability to develop resources such as technological capacities and overseas market links capable of substituting for those controlled by the foreign firms.

The relative utilities of these factors change with shifts in each side's resources relative to investment requirements. In low technology extractive industries, for example, the foreign investor's leverage is assumed to be high at the beginning of a project owing to steep initial capital costs, uncertainties of production costs and markets, and the weak technology and management skills of the host country. Over time, however, leverage presumably accrues to the host country as risks to the investor decline and local capacities expand: production costs become known and perhaps level off, markets grow, and the host country develops sufficient skills and market linkages to dispense with the foreign investor at little risk. Further, the foreign firm's investment is now sunk and thus more vulnerable to being held hostage; the investor is thus less able to make credible threats of withdrawal in response to expanded local demands.

Conversely, in manufacturing investments, especially in high technology areas, the shift of bargaining power toward developing (and other) host countries is presumed to proceed least rapidly.[6] Technology changes during the life of a project make it more difficult for host countries to accumulate expertise sufficient to dispense with the foreign investor. And unlike raw materials extraction, manufacturing often begins with relatively simple operations requiring minimal sunk investments and thus lower risks for the investor. Demands by the host country for more extensive and complex local operations call for new investments and thus greater risks for the investor. The latter is, in addition, unburdened by prior heavy sunk investments vulnerable to being held hostage by the host country. In sum, the host country's costs of doing without the investor are high, whereas the investor is free to pack up and leave in the face of new and costly local demands.

But the resources listed above do not confer real benefits unless they can be transformed into control over outcomes.[7] A second characteristic of the bargaining process thus concerns the importance of politics and the conversion of potential into actual power. Each side's will and ability to exploit sector-specific resources are influenced by factors such as splits within host governments, the ideological proclivities of local government officials, the corporate cultures and management practices of foreign firms, support from the home country of the TNC, pressure from disgruntled local firms and/or popular sectors, the political significance of a specific industry, and the organizational strength of local entrepreneurs.

Third, the bargaining process actually involves more than two actors.[8] Local negotiators often deal with several foreign firms engaged in competition and collusion among themselves, with foreign banks, and/or with TNC home governments. And a host country may contend with competition from other LDCs participating in a particular TNC's international sourcing arrangement or anxious to do so. In addition, nation-states and transnational firms are themselves complex organizations. Host country policies, rather than being generated by "black box" governments, are in fact partly the outcomes of pressures from various governmental agencies, local capitalists, and popular movements.[9] Similarly, each TNC consists of contending subunits, such as home versus overseas offices and marketing versus production branches.

Finally, bargaining must be understood to include implementation as well as formulation. Foreign firms may accept a proposal only to delay its implementation and thereby redefine the agreement in practice.[10] The implementation process also influences subsequent policy formulation. A host country's inability to compel implementation of an agreement may cause it to tone down its demands in the subsequent stages of bargaining. Conversely, successful implementation can encourage the new local demands and participants noted above.

On this general framework there is relative agreement. Differences emerge over precisely how hard it is for host countries to expand their leverage in manufacturing and why.

Structural Power versus Product Cycles

Structural Power and the Need for State Autonomy

One body of writings—the structuralist approach—argues that entry barriers to high tech manufacturing prevent an expansion of host country leverage. Obsolescence in favor of the foreign investor rather than the host country is to be expected over the course of an investment in manufacturing.[11] Structuralist writers explain this outcome in part as a function of potential power accruing to foreign investors from two characteristics of high technology industries—technological entry barriers and the impact of oligopolistic competition. In industries such as automobiles and computers, constant product and process innovations outstrip the abilities of developing countries to master internationally accepted technologies. LDC reliance on foreign firms is sustained. Rivalry among oligopolistic transnationals does not sufficiently reduce this dependence, since such competition is moderated by a fear of mutual reprisals. Instead of competitive market structures, spheres of influence and "mutual competitive forbearance" emerge, resulting in high concentration. Inter-TNC rivalry takes nonprice forms, such as product differentiation, which in turn fragment markets, reduce economies of scale for local producers, prevents standardization of existing technology, and inhibit local mastery of new technology. Entry barriers for LDC manufacturers remain high and/or grow steeper.

Can host countries muster any political forces to overcome or at least moderate the preceding sources of foreign leverage? Generally not. The structuralist view presumes the cooptation of local businessmen by foreign manufacturers. Manufacturing requires more extensive linkages with host country actors than do foreign firms involved in raw material sectors. Although natural resource projects often operate as isolated enclaves in LDCs, manufacturing firms tend to have relatively large labor forces per unit of capital, extensive networks of white collar employees, a wide constituency of middle-class consumers, at least a few domestic competitors who share broad class interests, and suppliers whose markets depend on the continued operation of foreign firms.[12]

In the auto industry, for example, such groups are presumed to include the workers of, suppliers to, and dealers for the auto TNCs. These domestic groups have much deeper roots in civil society than do elites traditionally associated with raw materials. Foreign manufacturing firms are consequently presumed to be less obvious targets of nationalist forces and more influential in policymaking circles in the host country. In addition to controlling the outcomes of distinct events, foreign firms are consequently able to "structure" the bargaining process itself by imposing certain rules, excluding certain issues, and discouraging the participation of certain actors.[13]

The presumed cooptation of local firms places the responsibility of defending national interests on the shoulders of the host country state—an institutional entity composed of an officially legitimated political leadership and permanent bureaucracy. The state shoulders the burden of policies and mechanisms to obtain from foreign investors whatever minimal benefits are possible. The point is nicely reflected in the title of Douglas Bennett and Kenneth Sharpe's highly useful work on the Mexican auto industry (1985). Bargaining involves not TNCs versus host countries, but *transnational corporations versus the state,* even if it is acknowledged that the state is influenced by societal actors.[14]

What is a strong state? While structuralist writings provide no precise answer, they and more explicitly "statist" writings suggest some useful guidelines. Generally speaking, strong states are autonomous; they can identify their own preferences and translate them into authoritative actions, whether by acting or choosing not to act, without having to compromise with other social and political actors.[15] State strength in particular areas also depends on government orientations—institutionalized policy preferences on issues affecting economic development.[16] Finally, state strength is a function of capacity—the ability to mobilize bargaining resources. This is in turn a function of two further components: a government's organizational "hardness" (its coherence and expertise) and the policy instruments, especially financial ones, at its disposal.[17]

Product Cycles and Host Country Coalitions

Some very different assumptions distinguish the structuralist approach to LDC-TNC relations from the competing product-cycle view.[18] While acknowledging that foreign high technology firms are the least vulnerable to host country pressures, product-cycle writings affirm a potential for a gradual expansion of local leverage even in advanced manufacturing. The expansion predicted is decidedly indeterminate. But relative to structuralist writings, the product-cycle approach is optimistic as to the potential for host country leverage and benefits in manufacturing.

This optimism draws on early writings on the product life cycle whose core belief is in the gradual diffusion of technologies and production processes, allowing the entry of new actors into the marketplace.[19] Rivalry among foreign firms is fundamental to this dynamic: oligopolistic competition, fueled by saturated home markets and overseas tariffs, propels TNCs first into markets in other advanced countries and eventually into LDCs.[20] Product-cycle and related writings do not dispute that entry barriers become steeper owing to changing technology. Nor do they deny that entry barriers are also raised when TNC rivals engage in product differentiation in order to avoid the burden of price competition. But they maintain that inter-TNC rivalry allows for a gradual diffusion of standardized technology to developing countries. This may occur through one or a combination of several processes. Competition can push even giant firms such as GM to accept different types or lower levels of technology in order to adapt to particular national market requirements and regulations. Even where rapid technological change occurs, subsidiaries in LDCs may still be absorbing earlier innovations. New technologies may yield new product niches accessible to LDC producers and new foreign firms willing to share that technology. And, finally, building on imported technologies, LDC firms themselves may innovate in response to their own particular market conditions.

Taking advantage of these potentials depends on the political dynamics of the host country, and here again, product-cycle predictions diverge from structuralist views. Rather than presuming that ties between foreign and local firms lead to the latter's cooptation, more recent and political versions of the product-cycle view argue for the possibility of a more nationalist business response: "The suppliers and auxiliary industries that begin by supporting the foreign multinational will eventually become a main source of competition to it. . . . [For local businessmen] economic nationalism has a permanent attractiveness (and is worth the investment of scarce public resources) while coziness with foreign investors possesses, at best, a tactical appeal limited to when the country needs something from the foreigners that it cannot do without."[21]

Table 2.1.   Contrasting Predictions on Bargaining in Manufacturing

	Structuralist Approach	Product-Cycle Approach
Potential leverage		
Technology	Changing technology outstrips local capacity	Changing technology impedes local mastery, but also provides niches and areas of standardization
Inter-TNC competition	Nonprice; stresses product differentiation and further raises entry barriers	Rivalry intense enough to push TNCs to adapt to local conditions
Host country forces		
Local entrepreneurs	Economic nationalism unlikely, if not impossible, because of links with, and subordination to, foreign manufacturers	Economic nationalism permanently attractive
State	Autonomous, strong state necessary for host country leverage	Role not specified
State/private coalition	Role not specified	Useful for local leverage, but nature of coalition not specified
Outcomes	Local leverage declines; possible local benefits are nonstructural and not representative of local leverage	Potential for increasing local benefits reflecting expansion of local leverage

This perspective is decidedly less state-centric and more coalition-based than the structuralist view. Whereas structuralist assumptions of local business weakness imply the need for a strong, autonomous host state, the product-cycle approach suggests that the strength of the host country may grow out of a domestic coalition in which local businessmen play a central role.[22] Product-cycle and bargaining-school writings are insufficiently specific about the precise nature of this coalition, a point to which we shall return. For now, suffice it to note the important differences between the two competing approaches as summed up in table 2.1.

My purpose in this study is to test these approaches through an examination of four ASEAN automobile industries from the late 1960s through the mid-to-late 1980s. Before we enter the world of Japan-

ASEAN auto relations, however, the two approaches merit evaluation in light of existing case-study materials.

Sources of Bargaining Power: An Empirical Review

An empirical evaluation of the two approaches requires first addressing some methodological weaknesses of the structuralist view. Structuralist assumptions make it difficult to establish benchmarks against which "true" expansion of host country leverage can be evaluated.[23] For while bargaining can yield benefits to host countries, these are presumed to be limited to "conduct dimensions" such as domestic employment and the shift from final assembly to higher value-added manufacture (backward linkages). Structural features such as ownership and market structures are left untouched.

Does this mean that expansion in the "conduct" dimension must be discounted as irrelevant? I believe not. For one thing, while ownership and market structure are important, there is little reason to elevate them to greater significance than backward linkages.[24] Nor should the two dimensions be separated. A project promoting backward linkages and domestic employment can generate local expertise, entrepreneurial interest, and political support sufficient to modify ownership and market structure. Finally, as the structuralist view itself might acknowledge, ownership may not be important for some TNCs (a point to which we shall return with regard to Japanese firms); nor is it necessarily a priority for developing host countries. The Asian NICs, for example, are relatively accommodating with regard to equity ownership restrictions. Yet few would label them weak bargainers, and few would deny that they have derived significant benefits from foreign investment. Thus, while noting outcomes with regard to "structural" shifts, I shall assume that "conduct" changes are also significant and attempt to show where the dimensions interact.

This brings us to a second issue: the structuralist assumption that an expansion of host country benefits reflects TNC-influenced local preferences rather than local leverage. Local demands are assumed not to represent "genuine" local preferences. Conflicts or local victories at the empirical level tend to be interpreted as TNC power at a deeper structural level. The point is a legitimate one, and in some cases this issue can be resolved through an empirical analysis of local bargaining positions. But where tracing the origins of local demands is not possible, any attempt at falsification is blocked.[25] In the absence of evidence to the contrary, I shall thus assume that when demands are initiated by the host country and provoke initial resistance from at least some major foreign firms, these demands constitute a legitimate baseline for measuring bargaining leverage.

What, then, do existing case studies tell us as to bargaining outcomes in manufacturing? Structuralist studies of the auto, tractor, pharmaceutical, and electrical industries in Latin America and Sri Lanka emphasize the gradual weakening of host country leverage over time with regard to market structure, ownership, local value-added, exports, and technology transfer.[26] But some of these same studies indicate considerable growth in local manufacturing capacity and in the political influence of local producers.[27] And still other cases, involving electronics in India and Brazil and automobiles in South Korea, offer more persuasive evidence of host country leverage.[28]

The evidence is thus mixed, but some conclusions can be drawn. The requirements of manufacturing projects do not preclude an expansion of local leverage. Although no Third World country has fully achieved its original goals in pharmaceuticals, auto manufacture, or computers, and all remain dependent on foreign capital, some have moved significantly toward these objectives despite TNC opposition. And while most of these more "successful" nations are classified as "newly industrializing," they reflect a relatively wide variety of sizes and degrees of aggressiveness vis-à-vis foreign investment. This progress has been in part a function of two factors discussed below: most have advanced, at least initially, by producing for particular market niches in which entry barriers were relatively low; and each has benefited from rivalry among foreign firms.

Potential Leverage: Technology and Inter-TNC Competition

Evidence suggests that as predicted by early product-cycle writings, LDCs can expand their benefits even in advanced industries not by immediately attempting to scale the technological heights but by beginning in more manageable niches.[29] The South Korean automobile, Indian computer, and Sri Lankan pharmaceutical industries show that host countries may absorb and begin with earlier technology more consistent with local markets and capacities. The fact that an industry exhibits rapidly changing and complex technologies does not obviate the utility of earlier products, materials, and processes.[30] Relying on more accessible niches, some LDCs have produced and exported their own innovations. These are considerably less publicized and dramatic than the computer and auto cases of Brazil and South Korea, but they are nonetheless significant stepping-stones for the gradual shift of local capacities into high technology areas. Most important, many LDC firms exhibit marked strengths in the innovation of small-scale technology for capital equipment suited for developing countries with small markets.[31]

As the product-cycle approach predicts, competition among foreign investors is vital to LDC access to the above processes. Different firms "make different decisions on the benefits of global optimization."[32] In some auto and electronics cases, rivalry among relatively *established* firms allows host countries to improve general contract terms and to concentrate on manageable market niches by playing firms off against each other.[33] One also finds cases in electronics and pharmaceuticals consistent with what Peter Evans has called "moments of transition"— where technological innovations have enhanced new firms' control over technology.[34]

None of this is to deny the ways in which inter-TNC competition can weaken the host country. Rival TNCs may replicate or even intensify their competitive structure in a host country whose market is significantly smaller than the home market of the foreign firms themselves.[35] The result is extensive brand proliferation. Similarly, inter-TNC competition in industries such as pharmaceuticals, cosmetics, and automobiles does involve the production of large varieties of frequently changing models.[36] The negative impact of such product differentiation on local leverage is strong.[37] Fragmentation undermines local power by impeding long production runs and thus blocking host country mastery of manufacturing processes.

Oligopolistic competition is thus a double-edged sword. Whether it strengthens the local position depends in large part on whether host country actors—entrepreneurs, states, and coalitions—can convert the potential resources inherent in the industry itself into control over outcomes.

Local Entrepreneurs: Coopted Corporate Allies?

Extensive empirical evidence has convinced even those outside the dependency framework that TNC-dominated alliances with local private interests undermine the leverage of the host country.[38] Perhaps the most extensive documentation comes from the automobile industries of Latin America, where massive public relations campaigns by Ford and Chrysler helped defeat crucial rationalization efforts in Venezuela and Colombia respectively.[39] But other cases show that under certain conditions local capitalists act as economic nationalists and enhance local leverage in doing so. Since Bennett and Sharpe use the Mexican auto case to illustrate the cooptability of local capitalists, their own evidence merits special note. Government local-content efforts had encouraged a substantial growth of Mexican parts firms by the late 1960s. But these firms had not yet formed a sufficiently cohesive force to affect the 1968–69 bargaining over export versus import orientation strategies. By 1977 things had changed: parts firms played a key role in maintaining a substantial local-content requirement in an otherwise very export-oriented automotive decree. TNC efforts to gut the decree failed in part owing to the absence of an antigovernment alliance between foreign firms and local auto interests. No such alliance "was possible with domestic entrepreneurs in the supplier industry; the decree was simply too favorable to their interests."[40]

In other cases, local firms have had to oppose government policies. Joseph Grieco argues, for example, that India achieved its nationalist objectives only when domestic private firms successfully opposed the government's procurement policies and its inefficient computer firm.[41] In South Korea during the early 1980s, Hyundai blocked a state-sponsored merger between itself and GM-Daewoo. "GM wanted Korea to be one site for production of GM 'world cars' while Hyundai was adamant on continuing to produce a 'Korean car' for domestic and export markets."[42]

Such aggressive behavior by host country firms is consistent with product-cycle predictions. Yet those predictions remain too general: they fail to explain why some host country entrepreneurs act as economic nationalists whereas others exhibit the coopted qualities predicted by structuralist writings. Differences between industries such as textiles and automobiles can, of course, be explained by different entry barriers. Some cross-national differences can also be attributed to the relative weights and

growth of manufacturing, and to general awareness of the negative consequences of pro-TNC policies.[43] But how do we account for variation
among firms ostensibly within the same industry, cross-nationally, and
over time in one country? Here, as Stephan Haggard argues, we need a
more "internally differentiated view of the domestic private sector."[44]

Several market-related factors can help explain differences in the behavior of local firms. First, different entry barriers and ties between TNCs and
local entrepreneurs exist within the same industry—for example, the more
modest requirements of auto parts manufacture allow LDC parts firms
significantly more independence from foreign investors than most local assemblers. Second, different positions along a producer/end user continuum can also be influential: computer consumers in Brazil, anxious for the
latest and least expensive technology, opposed the country's attempt to
achieve technological autonomy, while nascent producers supported it.[45]
Third, local firms in the same industry may act differently because of contracts and rivalry among the TNCs with which each is associated.[46] And,
finally, differences among South Korean business groups show that variations in the corporate histories, strategies, and resources of local enterprises can lead to different approaches to foreign capital.[47]

Sociopolitical factors such as the political utility of economic nationalism and the collective strength of local firms also count. Local private interests may find TNCs useful scapegoats for domestic socioeconomic
problems.[48] Where the local business community is a relatively insecure
ethnic minority, as is the case with the Chinese in Southeast Asia, economic nationalism may provide an opportunity for domestic firms to
prove their own nationalist loyalty. Business associations can facilitate the
pursuit of such nationalism. Mexican auto and Brazilian computer firms
used increasingly powerful associations to expand markets and control
over conditions of exchange with foreign capital.[49]

Host Country States

State Autonomy versus Public-Private Coalitions.   According to struc-
turalists, the need for an autonomous state in bargaining with manufacturing TNCs increases over time. Two assumptions underlie this argument. First, the growing cooptation of local firms by foreign capital is
assumed.[50] Yet, as we have noted, local entrepreneurs can and do act

against foreign capital, often with a better sense of the national interest than state officials. Dennis Encarnation's 1989 study *Dislodging the Multinationals* goes so far as to conclude that Indian and South Korean business groups "became as likely as state enterprises—indeed, became even more likely—to dislodge multinationals from the domestic market."[51]

The structuralist response is that an expanded state role is still necessary because of a second assumption: entry barriers rise over the life of a manufacturing project. Manufacturing investments in developing countries generally begin with simple assembly and expand, under local pressure, to more expensive and technically demanding processes. Uncertainty and host country learning curves rise. Local firms often lack sufficient technology and financing. They may prefer to remain in areas with more secure and more rapid returns; and/or they may be "users" more interested in obtaining cheaper access to high-quality international products "than in subsidizing a few of their number to develop indigenous products."[52] The state must thus play a larger role in establishing the means of reaching developmental goals as well as in setting them.

Although valid to a point, this argument is flawed because it overlooks two important distinctions: between macroeconomic and more project-specific resources, and between economic resources and political interests. State policies on exchange rates, tariffs, fiscal issues, and property rights can undoubtedly facilitate the movement of private firms into increasingly risky manufacturing processes.[53] But state agencies rarely possess the technological, managerial, and marketing skills necessary to move projects from formulation to implementation and/or to manage the demands of increasingly complex manufacturing.[54] State officials are often compelled to rely on foreign capital for such resources. But the state's own initiatives also create "functional space"[55] for, and thus promote a growth of, project-related skills within firms in the host country. In addition to providing tariff protection under which local firms obtain manufacturing experience, governments often compel the licensing of foreign technology to local firms, and state enterprises generate "breakaway managers" who join or establish private firms.[56]

But "functional space" not only provides local firms with resources critical to a project's success. It can also encourage the growth of sunk investments and in turn generate private pressure to expand a project in ways benefiting local firms. State resources remain important, then, but not necessarily the political influence of an autonomous state. Local leverage can come from local interests attempting to channel state resources in particular directions. It is this combination of project-related knowledge and desire for market expansion that makes local firms such a potentially potent force in bargaining.[57]

If the value of state autonomy is limited, what kind of state-society relationship is more likely to enhance national strength in the long run? Recent work suggests that the precondition for exploiting new market opportunities is less a dominant state than a "supportive" one.[58] In different terms, this refers to what I shall term *concertation*—an arrangement in which "the state and groups borrow from each other the authority to do what they cannot do alone."[59] The empirical emphasis here is on coalitions variously called private-interest governments, policy networks, oligopolistic communities, subgovernments, and so on. These formations obviously differ with regard to their openness and cohesiveness. For my purposes, their shared attribute of what Richard Samuels calls "reciprocal consent" is more important than any difference.[60] The utility of such formations derives from the state's ability to legitimate and to make available public sector assets on the one hand and the private sector's more sector-specific resources on the other. Coalitions become the enabling conditions for local firms to fulfill their national economic potential.[61] A central focus of this study is whether and how such concertation influences LDC-TNC bargaining outcomes. Existing studies do not address this issue explicitly. But Evans has attributed Brazil's success in the petrochemical industry to the operation of a "hybrid sort of oligopolistic community" involving revitalized industry associations and particular state officials.[62] And works by Peter Katzenstein and others strongly suggest the positive impact of such arrangements on national responses to external economic challenges in general.[63]

State Orientations. A state's orientations affect the value of its contribution to local bargaining strength. But the impact of particular preferences is difficult to predict. This can be seen in state preferences on three issues: national self-reliance, or antidependency; import substitution versus export promotion; and consumer choice. The espousal of antidependency generally enhances the degree to which states are willing to bolster local leverage through public resources. The risk here is that such a position can develop into a general anticapitalist stance that drives local capital into a coalition with foreign firms in defense of private property rights. The optimum approach may be what Emanuel Adler calls "pragmatic anti-dependency"—an attempt to correct Brazil's technological weakness, not through the exclusion of foreign firms, but rather through domestic institutions capable of making effective use of foreign resources.[64]

Similarly uncertain is the impact of a government's emphasis on import-substitution industrialization (ISI) versus export-oriented industrialization (EOI). ISI may generate a high level of dependence on foreign investment; but an export strategy can denationalize an industry by forcing local firms to accept reduced local content (in exchange for TNC export commitments) and contend with unstable overseas demand and rapidly changing foreign-held technology.[65] The South Korean auto experience suggests the need for a sequenced mix of the two approaches, one in which exports draw on the prior development of technologically and financially strong local producers.[66]

Finally, state policies on consumer choice can influence bargaining outcomes, especially in high technology consumer industries such as automobiles. The Mexican and South Korean cases provide strong evidence that an absence of make and model limits allows TNC product-differentiation strategies to reduce economies of scale and overwhelm the capacities of local firms.[67] Yet restraints on choice, if maintained too long, can block market pressures for improvements in efficiency. As in the case of ISI versus EOI, the optimum approach to consumer choice seems to involve a judicious and sequenced mix of brands and product variety. Since different preferences benefit different interests, whether such a mix is adopted depends in part on the government's social base.

State Capacities.   Capable or "hard" states feature coherent policies and sector-relevant expertise. There is little debate on the utility of such features, but some question as to their institutional sources. Coherence is often presumed to require centralization. Case studies show that intrastate fragmentation can weaken local abilities to make use of inter-TNC rivalries and to provide incentives for local firms consistent with national objectives.[68] But various forms of decentralization may also prove useful. Technocratic independence from uninformed or otherwise weak elected officials can minimize political interference in otherwise coherent policies.

Breakaway officials may take the lead in pressing for innovative policies, thereby creating constituencies and expertise sufficient to bring the rest of the state along with them.[69] Splits among agencies may provide the opportunity for local entrepreneurs to counter a government policy highly advantageous to foreign capital. Decentralization may avoid excluding and alienating government actors with expertise crucial to policy implementation.[70] Finally, a strong government has instruments to facilitate policy implementation. State financial resources constitute one important class of instrument, but one whose bargaining impact is not always as expected. The logical assumption that increased state revenues enhance local bargaining leverage has been amply borne out.[71] But the history of the Mexican auto industry following the abrupt end of the oil boom in 1982 illustrates that financial *shortages* can also compel nationalist actions on the part of the governments that would not otherwise have been taken.[72] And viewed in hindsight, the South Korean government's financial influence would have weakened local capacities had it been sufficient to compel Hyundai's acceptance of GM-controlled operations.

Cases and Theory

The preceding review questions the accuracy of structuralist arguments on bargaining outcomes, industry entry barriers, inter-TNC competition, cooptation of local firms, and the utility of state autonomy. Although more consistent with case-study evidence on these issues, the product-cycle approach remains too general on at least two counts. Product-cycle writings assert that economic nationalism holds a permanent attraction for local capitalists, but they fail to explain why some entrepreneurs are more nationalistic than others. And while noting the potential contribution of local firms to the bargaining leverage of host countries, the approach fails to specify the kinds of government policies and state-business relations most conducive to host country leverage.

In the following chapters I explore these issues in order to test and refine the product-cycle approach to bargaining. Two questions are central to this effort. Can developing countries expand their bargaining leverage over time in a high technology industry such as automobiles? If so, are some host countries more successful, and why? I address these questions through a comparison of one industry, automobiles, in four Southeast

Asian countries over a similar time period. The countries share some broad characteristics: they have all relied fairly heavily on export of raw materials; they are all more or less free-market economies; they have all enjoyed fairly rapid growth rates over the past twenty years; none of them are governed by regimes exhibiting anything close to the strength of those of the Asian NICs; the auto industries of all four are dominated by Japanese products; and all four have invested significant resources in pressing TNCs to comply with increased automotive local-content and rationalization policies. Yet the domestic political arrangements of these countries differ in some important ways.

These features provide distinct advantages for addressing both questions. First, the relative weakness of the states and high technology nature of the industry examined here mean that our four countries constitute relatively "easy" cases for the structuralist model. The model's prediction of declining host country leverage in a high technology manufacturing industry with a weak host country state should be confirmed with little difficulty. Conversely, the auto industry's technological barriers make these four cases much "harder" ones for the product-cycle view, which acknowledges that high technology TNCs will be the least vulnerable to host country leverage. Evidence that there has been a growth of local power over time for any of the countries would thus constitute strong support for product-cycle views.[73]

Perhaps most important, this study may also reveal and explain cross-national differences in bargaining outcomes. As one of the few examinations of how several countries deal with one international industry, it may avoid the "often implicit counterfactual arguments" of single cases and suggest specific factors accounting for relative differences in bargaining power.[74]

3

ASEAN Automobile Policies: Origins and Achievements

ASEAN and Japan: Growth and Conflict in a Division of Labor

This study's empirical focus, the evolution of the ASEAN auto industries, bears on the future prospects of part of the world's most economically dynamic region—the Pacific Rim. Including Singapore, the ASEAN group has achieved healthy economic growth rates, with the partial exception of the Philippines (table 3.1). Even without Singapore (which is usually grouped among Asia's NICs), the four remaining countries averaged almost 6.5 percent annual GDP growth rate between 1973 and 1984.[1] Significant structural change also took place. Industry grew at over 8 percent annually for three of the four, and industry's share of GDP expanded while the position of agriculture declined for all these countries (table 3.2). Indeed, the four ranked among the top twelve out of forty-three developing countries with regard to industrial performance over the 1973–85 period.[2]

Table 3.1.   Size and Economic Growth Rates of NICs and
              ASEAN Countries, 1985

	Population (millions)	GDP (U.S.$ millions)	GDP (U.S.$ per capita)	Real GDP Per Capita Growth 1960–1985
Indonesia	165.2	86,445	523	3.0
Malaysia	15.7	33,360	2,128	4.2[a]
Philippines	54.7	32,789[b]	600[b]	1.6[b,c]
Thailand	51.3	38,572	752	4.2
Hong Kong	5.4	34,081	6,288	6.3
South Korea	41.1	86,180	2,099	6.4
Singapore	2.6	15,970	6,238	6.7
Taiwan	19.1	59,141	3,095	6.4

SOURCE: Adapted from James et al. 1989, tables 1.3 and 1.4.
[a]1970–85.
[b]GNP.
[c]The Philippines' low cumulative rate reflected the financial crisis and economic downturn of the early to mid 1980s (see table 3.5 below).

Table 3.2.   Changes in Economic Structure (Percentages)

	Agriculture's Share in GDP		Industry's Share in GDP		Industry's Growth Rate	Labor in Agriculture
	1965	1984	1965	1984	1973–84	1980
South Korea	38	14	25	40	10.9	36
Taiwan	24	6	30	46	10.5[a]	20
Hong Kong	2	1	40	22	8.0	2
Singapore	3	1	24	39	8.6	2
Indonesia	59	26	12	40	8.3	57
Philippines	26	25	28	34	5.3	52
Malaysia	30	21	24	35	8.7	42
Thailand	35	20	23	28	8.7	70

SOURCES: World Bank, *World Development Report*, 1986; Taiwan, *Statistical Yearbook*, 1986.
[a]1971–85.

Table 3.3.   ASEAN Export Performance

	Exports as Percentage of GDP		Compounded Growth Rate of Manufactured Exports (%)
	1970	1985	
Indonesia	12.8	22.7	44.9[a]
Malaysia	40.5[a]	54.9	32.3[b]
Philippines	19.1	20.8	24.8[c]
Thailand	16.7	26.3	36.6[a]

SOURCE: Adapted from James et al. 1989, tables 2.1 and 2.3.
[a] 1970 and 1984.
[b] 1971 and 1983.
[c] 1970 and 1983.

These changes have occurred in a context of increasing participation in the world economy. Each individual ASEAN economy has become more open, with exports expanding both absolutely and as a proportion of GDP (table 3.3). The growth rate of the ASEAN Four's exports has been almost as high as that of the Asian NICs.[3] In addition, the structure of these exports has shifted. The four countries are resource-rich[4] and continue to rely heavily on the export of primary commodities. But as seen in table 3.4, the contribution of manufactured goods to total exports has increased in each of the countries. ASEAN exports have, in fact, grown more rapidly than those of middle-income countries outside East Asia.[5] Resource-based goods constituted the largest, but a declining, share of manufactured exports during the 1970s, accounting for 89 percent in 1970 and 63 percent in 1980. In contrast, labor-intensive goods grew from roughly 6 percent of exports in 1970 to 30 percent in 1980. Capital-intensive goods grew absolutely, but remained at under 5 percent throughout the period.[6]

Underlying this structural change may well be what Japanese economists term a "multiple catch-up" process, in which Japan leads the Asian NICs and then the ASEAN Four through stages of comparative advantage. As the NICs follow Japan into capital- and knowledge-intensive products (steel, chemicals, shipbuilding, motor vehicles, electronics, and computers), the ASEAN Four "follow behind with exports from light industries such as food processing, textiles, clothing, and simpler electronics."[7]

Table 3.4.   Structure of ASEAN Merchandise Exports (Percentages)

	Primary Commodities		Machinery and Transport Equipment		Other Manufactures	
	1965	1985	1965	1985	1965	1985
Indonesia	96	89	3	1	1 (0)	10 (2)[a]
Malaysia	94	73	2	19	4 (0)	8 (3)
Philippines	95	49	0	5	6 (1)	46 (7)
Thailand	95	65	0	7	4 (0)	28 (13)

SOURCE: World Bank, *World Development Report*, 1987.
[a]Numbers in parentheses are for textiles and clothing, a subset of "other manufactures."

Sources of ASEAN Growth

This growth and structural change can be attributed to a combination of external and domestic factors. Rising commodity prices provided each of the countries with significant revenues during the 1970s, although the diversity of resource endowments among the countries provided different sets of challenges. The first oil shock benefited the petroleum exporters, Indonesia and Malaysia, but threatened the growth prospects of Thailand and the Philippines, both oil importers. Subsequent healthy prices for their commodities helped Thailand (rice, tapioca, rubber, tin, maize, and sugar) and the Philippines (sugar, coconut oil, copper, timber) recover from high oil prices. Growth was further encouraged by a 250 percent increase of total net capital flows into the ASEAN Four from 1972 to 1979.[8]

The second oil shock had an even greater impact than the first. Oil price increases provided Indonesia and Malaysia with welcome revenues, but also encouraged a slackening of efforts to derive revenues from sectors other than oil, a pattern whose weaknesses became evident when oil and other commodity prices subsequently fell in the early-to-mid 1980s. As heavy oil importers, Thailand and the Philippines faced even greater economic difficulties. Yet except for the Philippines, the ASEAN countries were able to maintain growth from 1982 to 1985, albeit at lower rates than in previous years (table 3.5). As discussed below, Japanese markets,

Table 3.5.   Real ASEAN GDP Growth Rates (Percentages)

	1972–76	1977–81	1982–85
Indonesia	7.8	8.1	3.5
Malaysia	8.4	7.7	5.4
Philippines	6.6	5.4	−1.4
Thailand	7.1	7.1	5.0

SOURCE: Asian Development Bank and World Bank, cited in Campbell 1987, 4.

Table 3.6.   Levels of Savings and Investment

	Gross Domestic Savings as Percentage of GDP		Gross Domestic Investment as Percentage of GDP	
	1965	1985	1965	1985
Indonesia	8	32	8	30
Malaysia	24	33	20	28
Philippines	15	13	21	16
Thailand	21	21	20	23

SOURCE: Adapted from Bhatia 1988, table 11.

imports, and financial support played an important role in sustaining this development.

ASEAN economic expansion can also be attributed to some basic domestic economic and political factors more or less common to all four countries beginning in the mid-to-late 1960s. Capital accumulation was encouraged by an average domestic savings rate of almost 25 percent (compared to an average of 11 percent for South Asia in 1983),[9] while the ratio of investment to GDP expanded in all but the Philippines (table 3.6). The improving quality of the work force, indicated by healthy literacy rates and rising education levels (table 3.7), facilitated the productivity of these investments.

Dynamic local entrepreneurial groups have contributed to capital mobilization and investment. Most notably, ethnic Chinese businessmen, drawing on communal financial and commercial networks, have played crucial roles in each of the four countries.[10] And, finally, economic growth in the ASEAN region has been facilitated by political stability. From 1965

Table 3.7.   Literacy and Education Levels

	Literacy Rate	Number in Secondary School as Percentage of Age Group 12–17		Number in Higher Education as Percentage of Age Group 20–24	
	1980	1960	1983	1960	1983
Indonesia	62	6	37	1	4
Malaysia	60	19	49	1	4
Philippines	83	26	63	13	26
Thailand	86	13	29	2	22

SOURCES: Literacy rates from Clive Hamilton 1984, table 5; secondary and higher education enrollments from James et al. 1989, table 6.7.

until the recent overthrow of President Ferdinand Marcos in the Philippines, there has been no change of government in any of the four countries, with the exception of several military coups and a short-lived democratic regime in Thailand from 1973 to 1976. Nor did the Thai events adversely affect the country's economic performance or modify its basic political arrangements.

This general stability has perhaps compensated for the relatively "soft" organizational capacities of all four states. In 1976 Franklin Weinstein argued that the four were characterized by corruption, inability to extract and mobilize domestic resources, unpredictability of decision making, and generally poor policy implementation.[11] And although there has been (somewhat uneven) progress in administrative capacities since the mid 1970s, one does not find the ASEAN countries characterized as highly capable "developmental states" along with the Asian NICs.[12]

A relatively pragmatic economic nationalism has complemented the structural factors. The policies of these countries are driven by much more than neoclassical market forces. Each government includes "bodies of functionaries or mandarins, often dedicated and technically well-trained, who have strong opinions about what is good for the development of their respective countries, and their policies are often in conflict with what market forces would dictate."[13] The pragmatic side is reflected in the market-conforming nature of public intervention in the ASEAN economies relative to other developing countries.[14]

Furthermore, the extensive entry-control systems operating in the ASEAN Four have traditionally stressed regulation of foreign investment rather than the tendencies toward expropriation more evident in many Latin American countries.[15] There are differences in the restrictiveness of foreign-investment regimes among the four. Indonesia, highly sensitive about TNC threats to its sovereignty, has been "assertive" toward foreign capital relative to its ASEAN neighbors. The other three have pursued more "accommodating," but still selective, strategies.[16]

Indonesia loosened investment regulations immediately following the fall of President Sukarno in the late 1960s. Bolstered by rising oil revenues and pressured by nationalist and ethnic Indonesian (*pribumi*) economic demands, the country shifted to a more restrictive and selective approach during the early-to-mid 1970s. Declining oil revenues and reduced investment flows in 1977 and the early 1980s subsequently led to a moderate loosening of the foreign-investment regime.

Malaysia pursued a highly liberal investment policy until the early 1970s, when the government imposed severe restrictions on foreign and local Chinese capital in an effort to promote ethnic Malay (*bumiputra*) entrepreneurs. With declining investment flows and rising state debts, the government became more flexible vis-à-vis foreign firms. Falling commodity revenues during the late 1980s have intensified this loosening process.

Thailand pursued a relatively laissez-faire approach to foreign capital during the 1960s and early 1970s following a postwar period of economic nationalism. By 1972 large inflows of foreign investment provoked nationalist opposition, contributing to an overthrow of military rule and significantly tighter investment constraints from 1973 to 1976. But capital shortages and a newly established military government led to a liberalized investment code, in force since the late 1970s.

The Philippines is somewhat of an exception to the liberalization, restriction, and reliberalization pattern seen in the other three cases. Following a period of strong postwar protective legislation, the Marcos regime initiated liberalization in the mid 1960s and consolidated it with martial law in 1972.[17]

It is important to emphasize that this relative openness has coexisted with protectionist, generally import-substitution industrialization (ISI), strategies involving import licenses, and extensive tariff protection for a wide range of infant industries, such as automobiles. Beginning in the 1960s, it was assumed that first-stage ISI operations, often limited to assembly, would generate new jobs while gradually reducing reliance on foreign imports.

This infant industry/ISI thrust has not precluded export-promotion efforts. The limits of domestic markets for ISI consumer goods were becoming clear by the 1970s, while declining commodity prices and shrinking overseas commodity markets have cut into the revenues necessary to pay for imported capital goods used in ISI operations. Each of the ASEAN Four has consequently attempted to promote exports—Malaysia and Thailand more extensively and successfully than Indonesia and the Philippines.[18] But the overall incentive structures in all four cases have been biased toward production for domestic markets.[19] Further, industrial deepening has been a critical thrust of ASEAN industrial policies since the late 1970s. Each country has hoped to reduce its reliance on foreign inputs by expanding its manufacture of capital equipment for *both* ISI and exported-oriented (EOI) industries.

In sum, the ASEAN Four have moved a couple of rungs up the comparative advantage ladder behind the Asian NICs. They have expanded manufacturing for both domestic and export markets. But their production remains based in processed raw materials and labor-intensive goods, even as they attempt to follow South Korea and Taiwan into more capital-intensive production. These achievements and continued efforts have drawn Thailand, Malaysia, Indonesia, and the Philippines into close and sometimes conflictual links with the Japanese.

Japan and the Problem of ASEAN Manufactures

The ASEAN economic growth discussed above would have been unlikely at best without the region's dominant external economic partner, Japan. The director of Malaysia's major think tank noted that because "economics *is* security" in Southeast Asia, "what the Japanese have contributed . . . has been nothing short of remarkable . . . [Japan] has helped to underpin in no uncertain terms the structure" of Southeast Asian security.[20] Yet Japan has been a source of obstacles to as well as opportunities for ASEAN expansion.

Japan is ASEAN's principal trading partner, accounting for 28.3 percent of the region's exports and providing 22.9 percent of its imports in 1982.[21] As such, the Japanese have essentially provided a "growth pole" for Southeast Asia. While total world exports grew sixfold from 1969 to 1979, exports from ASEAN to Japan increased almost twelvefold; a com-

Table 3.8.   Major Sources of Overseas Development Assistance and Total
Financial Resources to ASEAN, 1981

(Percentage of net disbursements)

	Japan	West Germany	United States	Multilateral Organizations
Indonesia	30.8	17.8	10.6	16.1
	52.4	10.9	11.9	11.4
Thailand	52.8	11.3	4.4	20.1
	26.8	11.0	3.7	25.1
Philippines	55.7	2.7	13.5	12.2
	24.1	2.7	7.0	44.3
Malaysia	45.8	4.9	0.0	11.3
	7.3	23.6	29.7	12.1
Singapore	50.0	22.7	0.0	15.4
	24.1	10.0	49.5	0.0

SOURCE: Japan, Ministry of Foreign Affairs n.d., 4.

NOTE: Upper row = overseas development assistance; lower row = total net flow of financial
resources, including direct investments, export credits, bilateral securities and claims, loans.

parison of increases in exports of industrial goods shows roughly the same
growth-pole effect.[22] As seen in table 3.8, the picture is the same with regard to financial flows.[23]

Both Japanese funds and markets were critical to the growth strategies
pursued by the ASEAN Four. Each country utilized Japanese investment
for first-stage ISI and the creation of an instant industrial base. The large
sums of foreign exchange required for imports of Japanese capital goods
were obtained by revenues from commodity exports, many of which went
to Japan. In addition, Japan has stood as an Asian model of success whose
work ethic and institutions draw both praise and emulation.[24]

But persistent Southeast Asian frustration with Japan's economic activities has also been in evidence since the early-to-mid 1970s, when Thai
students launched a boycott of Japanese goods and violent anti-Japanese
protests erupted in Indonesia and Thailand during Prime Minister Tanaka
Kakuei's 1974 tour of the region. Building on opposition to Japan's wartime occupation of the region and to local elites believed to be selling out
to the Japanese, popular groups and sections of the elite have attacked
Japan-ASEAN economic ties as exploitative.[25]

Table 3.9.   ASEAN Trade with Japan, 1981 (U.S. $millions)

	Thailand	Philippines	Indonesia	Malaysia
Total exports	6,784	5,756	22,101	11,198
Total imports	10,330	8,864	13,520	11,581
Exports to Japan	1,059	1,712	13,263	2,917
	(15.5%)	(29.8%)	(60.1%)	(26.1%)
Imports from Japan	2,243	1,924	4,115	2,416
	(21.7%)	(21.7%)	(30.4%)	(20.8%)

SOURCE: IMF, *Directory of Trade Statistics, Yearbook*, 1982, cited in Elsbree and Hoong 1985, table 7.1.

Part of the problem has to do with the balance of trade: the ASEAN Four need Japan more than Japan needs them. It is true that the original five ASEAN countries accounted for a significant portion of Japan's exports (10.7 percent) and imports (14.7 percent) in 1982.[26] But calculating dependency as the value of exports in relation to GNP, ASEAN's dependence on Japan is 8 percent, while Japan's dependence is 1 percent.[27] (There are variations in degrees of trade dependency on Japan within ASEAN; table 3.9 shows that Indonesia is the most dependent, followed by the Philippines and Malaysia, and then Thailand.) This asymmetry of needs seems to be worsening in the 1980s, as Japan's slower growth rate and structural shift away from resource-consuming industries during the 1970s have cut into purchases of ASEAN commodities.[28]

Nor does the fact that ASEAN has an overall surplus in its trade with Japan alleviate the problem. Without Tokyo's purchases of energy products from Malaysia, Brunei, and especially Indonesia, the Southeast Asian countries would be running a marked deficit with Japan.[29]

This brings up what is perhaps the more important source of ASEAN frustration with the Japanese—the structure of trade and the belief that Japan has inhibited industrial modernization in the region. ASEAN exports to the Japanese are dominated by primary commodities, while Japan's exports to Southeast Asia largely involve capital goods. Thus in 1982, for example, 84 percent of Malaysia's and 71 percent of the Philippines' total imports from Japan were machinery and metal products.[30] This is, in the Southeast Asian view, the result of a Japanese market largely closed to ASEAN manufactures. A 1983 study of the region's exports showed that only 6.4 percent of ASEAN's earnings from exports to Japan came from manufactured goods. In contrast, the manufactured goods-export ratio between ASEAN and the United States was 48.7 percent.[31] Only as Japanese exports became more expensive with the yen appreciation of the mid 1980s have the Japanese shown enthusiasm for promotion of manufactured exports from ASEAN.[32] These investments have come on the heels of persistent and public ASEAN complaints about the alleged failures of Japanese private investors to promote local employees, to transfer technology, to encourage labor-intensive and export-oriented products, to invest in more sophisticated sectors, and to promote higher local value-added.[33] Along with expanding ASEAN technical capacities, they have resulted in a gradual expansion of ASEAN manufactured exports to Japan. ASEAN's industrial products rose from 7.8 percent of Japan's total imports in 1979 to 10 percent in 1985 and almost 14 percent in 1986.[34]

But these are relatively recent developments in an otherwise troubled set of linkages. For the Japanese, the relationship has been a "virtuous circle," in which Japan's high growth was simultaneously a stimulus to exports from ASEAN and a source of capital goods to ASEAN.[35] For the ASEAN nations, ties with Japan have posed a difficult dilemma. Distancing themselves from Tokyo will result in declining funds, markets, and growth rates. But attempts to expand production within the constraints of existing linkages will entail greater dependence on Japanese capital goods.

In response, each of the ASEAN Four has attempted to transform its ties with the Japanese: each has promoted expansion of local production of capital goods and component parts through measures mandating an expansion of local content; and each has viewed the automobile industry as a major focus for such efforts.

Postwar Changes and the Need for Automobile Industry Reform

The efforts at auto industrialization examined in this study did not begin before the late 1960s. Although they reflected national commitments to indigenous industrialization, these efforts were also seen as solutions to varying combinations of market fragmentation and foreign-exchange losses resulting from prior auto policies.

The Philippines government, for example, had promoted local assembly of completely knocked-down (CKD) vehicles after World War II largely in order to reduce foreign-exchange outflows: the war-caused destruction of the country's vehicle population had created a pent-up demand that was being filled by large-scale imports of completely built-up (CBU) vehicles requiring foreign currency.[36] Government officials presumed that assembling imported components in the Philippines rather than in the country of origin would reduce foreign-exchange losses. New regulations included prohibitions on imports of CBU cars and trucks on a commercial scale, priority dollar allocations, and state-issued licenses to qualified parties for the establishment of auto assembly plants.

The conceptualization and implementation of these policies were weak. While the government fully intended to license only a few operations, lack of a definite policy resulted in a proliferation of assembly plants. High levels of protection[37] led to comfortable profits during the 1960s, which attracted both foreign and local capital: from only one plant in 1951, the industry grew to include nineteen companies assembling over sixty different models of passenger cars in 1968. The number of assembly operations, combined with a limited market (see table 3.10) whose expansion was undercut by illegal imports,[38] meant that no assembler was able to achieve efficient economies of scale. Furthermore, apart from locally produced tires and batteries, the industry remained exclusively an assembly operation through the 1960s. This resulted in part from the opposition of foreign automakers to local production of auto parts. But it also reflected a tariff and tax structure that, for example, discouraged the rebuilding of old automobiles with locally made parts. The industry continued to rely on imported components and remained a major user of foreign exchange. Vehicle imports were a key reason for the country's shift from a rough trade balance in 1960 to a $257 million deficit in 1969.[39]

The country's foreign-exchange problems became particularly acute by 1969 as a result of the reportedly large sums of money spent by Marcos to ensure victory in the 1969 election and a rapid buildup of short-term debt in the economy.[40] As part of its stabilization program, the Central Bank requested that the Philippine Board of Investment (BOI) develop an automotive industrialization program leading to an "economically beneficial use of foreign exchange."[41] The result was the Progressive Car Manufacturing Program, discussed below.

Table 3.10. ASEAN Automobile Assembly
(Thousands of passenger and
commercial vehicles [PV:CV percentage])

Year	Indonesia	Malaysia	Philippines	Thailand
1965	4.0		11.5 (65:35)	10.0 (44:56)
1967	1.0	1.2 (33:67)	18.6 (68:32)	12.7 (49:51)
1969	1.4 (9:91)	25.0 (82:18)	20.1 (66:34)	11.7 (52:48)
1971	17.6 (10:90)		19.0 (49:51)	14.8 (61:39)
1973	37.0 (41:59)	50.4 (84:16)	30.4 (57:43)	27.4 (65:35)
1975	78.8 (39:61)		48.7 (58:42)	31.0 (50:50)
1976	75.5 (32:68)	58.7 (80:20)	50.6 (67:33)	48.3 (33:67)
1977	93.2 (14:86)			65.9 (28:72)
1978	108.6 (14:86)			65.4 (32:68)
1979	98.5 (14:86)	88.6 (79:21)	52.9 (57:43)	88.8 (25:75)
1980	174.7 (13:87)	104.2	41.9 (64:36)	71.7 (32:68)
1981	212.6 (13:87)	111.5	39.8 (63:37)	86.5 (30:70)
1982	188.5 (29:71)	110.9	45.2 (58:42)	81.9 (36:64)
1983	155.2 (16:84)	133.3 (85:15)	41.6 (67:33)	108.8 (31:69)
1984	153.6 (17:83)	124.0 (78:22)		110.7 (32:68)
1985	139.4 (17:83)			81.8 (29:71)
1986				73.3 (29:71)
1987				97.8 (30:70)

SOURCES: Indonesia—1965–67, Central Statistical Bureau and company data in Hansen 1971; 1969–79, GAAKINDO in Witoelar 1984, table 2.4; 1980–85, GAAKINDO in Tang 1988, table 2. Malaysia—1967–83, EIU 1985, tables 3 and 10; 1984, MIDA 1985, appendixes 12 and 13. Philippines—1965–76, Tolentino and Ybanez 1984, table 5.1; 1979–83, EIU 1984, tables 19 and 20. Thailand—1965–78, Nawadhinsukh 1984, table 4.1; 1979, Toyota Motors Thailand; 1980–87, Thailand, BOI n.d., 6.

With minor exceptions, the Thai auto industry emerged in a similar fashion. Foreign auto assemblers and parts firms were attracted to Thailand by the incentives of the 1962 Investment Promotion Act, the growing size of the country's auto market, and the minimal initial investments required.[42] Owing to a very liberal definition of CKD assembly, it was

possible to assemble vehicles with almost no capital investment. Subassemblies can be brought in under the existing CKD regulations to such a degree that only one master assembly jig is required, and that of a minimal nature. The bulk of the labor is performed at the parent or source plant from which the vehicles are shipped. Local plants provide labor mainly for modified assembly, metal finish, paint and trim.[43]

The result was an influx of twelve foreign assemblers into Thailand between 1960 and 1970.[44] The large number of assembly operations, when combined with the fact that CBU imports accounted for almost 80 percent of total sales in 1970[45] limited the market for any one assembler and resulted in high excess capacity and extreme inefficiency. As in the Philippines, the continuing need for imported auto products made the industry a major contributor to Thailand's balance of trade and payments deficits.[46] These weaknesses, in addition to a conflict among assemblers over promotional incentives, prompted the Thai BOI to undertake a major restructuring of the auto industry in 1968.[47]

The initial phase of Malaysia's auto industry was closely connected with the country's early political development.[48] In September 1963 Singapore, along with Sabah and Sarawak, joined Malaya to form Malaysia. That same month, the new government announced its intention to promote an integrated automobile industry to strengthen Malaysian industrialization. In May 1964 nineteen firms, both foreign and local, responded to a government request for applications to begin auto assembly operations and parts production.

But the 1965 separation of Singapore from Malaysia blocked the final selection of applications,[49] and the erstwhile partners became competitors for foreign investment. In 1966 Malaysia restricted auto imports from Singapore, established a quota system for all imports, and forced interested auto concerns to choose between the two countries. The auto firms opposed this division and established the Motor Vehicle Assemblers' Association in 1966 precisely to plead for a common auto market between Malaysia and Singapore. But political differences dominated and the proposal was refused. Confronted with little local assembly activity in 1967 (table 3.10) but a large number of assemblers fighting to gain access to the Malaysian market, the Malaysian government undertook an automotive reform program.

The Indonesian automobile industry was even less developed than those of its ASEAN neighbors by the late 1960s. Following World War II the government initiated a shift from CBU import to CKD assembly with a view to developing labor skills and saving foreign exchange.[50] By the mid 1950s shortages of foreign exchange made even the import of CKD components impossible, and by 1961 almost all production had ceased. Only the assembly of government vehicles, financed by foreign grants, was able to continue. The new Suharto government (1966) made no attempt to promote an expansion of local auto production during its initial years. Reacting to the shortages and inflation of the Sukarno regime's later years,[51] the new government liberalized trade and investment in order to increase the supply of all goods in circulation, including automobiles.[52] The import of four-wheelers was thus permitted in all forms, CBUs, CKDs, and semi-knocked down (SKDs).

The market resulting from these shifts was import-dependent, erratic in its growth, and fragmented. Locally assembled vehicles accounted for less than 25 percent of the country's requirements by the late 1960s.[53] The total number of vehicles imported (both CBU and CKD) fluctuated strongly, although this instability did not prevent an early proliferation of makes and models. Credits from Eastern Europe before 1965 added a wide variety of vehicles from that region to existing Western products. These were joined later in the 1960s by vehicles from the newly expanding Japanese industry. By 1969 sixty makes were approved for import into a market of under 20,000. Most of the assemblers were simply not equipped to handle this variety: in 1970 2,000 CKD vehicles waited in storage areas even though only six of twenty-one assembly firms were actually assembling vehicles.

Each of the four countries viewed assembly as a way to resolve foreign-exchange problems while simultaneously upgrading local labor. In the process, each of the four encouraged the entrance into the market of large numbers of inefficient assemblers, and reliance on imported components and exchange needs remained as great as ever. While local capital was involved in most of these assembly operations, foreign firms supplied essential technology and components. The initial postwar dominance of Western assemblers was quickly eroded by the Japanese, as reflected in the sharp growth of Japanese auto exports to the region (table 3.11). By 1978 Japan accounted for 90 percent of auto sales in Thailand, 92 percent in Indonesia, 70 percent in the Philippines, and 64 percent in Malaysia (tables 3.12–3.15).[54]

ASEAN Automobile Policies in the 1970s and 1980s

The auto industry reforms undertaken by the ASEAN Four were relatively similar. Each aimed at progressively higher local-content (LC)

Table 3.11. U.S. and Japanese Auto Exports to ASEAN Countries
(U.S. $millions)

	1963		1977		Percentage Increase, 1963–77	
	U.S.	Japan	U.S.	Japan	U.S.	Japan
Indonesia	18	21	103	423	469	1,942
Malaysia	1	6	55	210	9,000	3,225
Philippines	33	12	62	190	88	1,485
Singapore	1	4	190	315	14,477	7,219
Thailand	13	32	89	402	563	1,155
Total	66	75	499	1,540	654	1,944

SOURCES: *United Nations Yearbook of International Trade Statistics,* 1963 and 1977, cited in Lim Chee Peng 1982, 44.
NOTE: "Auto Exports" refers to Transport Equipment (SITC 73).

Table 3.12. Thailand: Market Share by Firm According to Yearly Sales
(Percentages)

	1978	1980	1982
Japanese			
Toyota	21.9	26.3	29.2
Nissan	21.5	26.2	24.1
Mitsubishi	6.0	7.9	5.2
Mazda	9.3	9.4	7.3
Isuzu	20.7	10.9	17.7
Daihatsu	1.5	2.2	1.5
Suzuki	1.2	1.0	1.2
Hino	5.8	4.8	3.4
Subtotal	90.7	90.5	90.1
GM	0.2	0.2	0.0
Ford	1.1	2.7	2.7
Mercedes	1.4	1.6	1.2
Miscellaneous	6.5	5.0	6.0
Total	100.0	100.0	100.0

SOURCE: Data taken from Toyota Motor Corp. 1984, 19.

Table 3.13.   Indonesia: Market Share by Firm According to Yearly Sales
               (Percentages)

	1978	1980	1982
Japanese			
Toyota	28.4	29.1	25.8
Nissan	6.2	2.5	0.4
Mitsubishi	34.9	33.3	28.8
Mazda	0.8	0.1	0.7
Honda	3.9	2.8	3.7
Daihatsu	12.5	12.4	16.7
Suzuki	3.5	4.7	7.8
Isuzu	1.1	3.0	3.3
Hino	0.4	0.2	0.5
Subtotal	92.1	88.0	87.7
GM	0.2	5.8	5.9
Ford	0.9	0.2	0.0
VW	1.3	1.0	0.5
Mercedes	2.0	2.5	1.7
Others	3.5	2.5	4.2
Total	100.0	100.0	100.0

SOURCE: Data taken from Toyota Motor Corp. 1984, 15.

Table 3.14.   The Philippines: Market Share by Firm According to Yearly Sales
               (Percentages)

	1978	1980	1982
Toyota	42.1	39.1	35.2
Mitsubishi	21.4	22.2	22.1
Mitsubishi	21.3	22.2	22.1
Chrysler	0.1	0.0	0.0
Ford	20.0	15.9	25.1
Ford	20.0	14.9	11.7
Mazda	0.0	1.0	13.4
GM	10.0	18.2	16.8
GM	1.8	1.8	0.3
Isuzu	8.2	16.4	16.6
VW	6.4	46.0	0.8
Total	100.0	100.0	100.0

SOURCE: Data taken from Toyota Motor Corp. 1984, 17.

Table 3.15.   Malaysia: Market Share by Firm According to Yearly Sales
               (Percentages)

	1978	1980	1982
Japanese			
Toyota	13.9	20.3	20.7
Nissan	21.5	26.4	25.4
Mitsubishi	11.4	11.7	8.1
Mazda	7.6	6.1	9.6
Honda	7.1	8.4	9.2
Daihatsu	1.4	2.5	4.7
Hino	0.8	2.0	1.2
Subtotal	63.9	79.1	80.5
GM	6.1	2.9	2.8
Ford	10.8	3.7	6.9
Mercedes	4.2	4.2	3.1
BL	4.3	2.0	0.7
Fiat	3.1	1.7	1.2
Peugeot	1.1	0.9	0.4
Others	6.5	5.5	4.4
Total	100.0	100.0	100.0

SOURCE: Data taken from Toyota Motor Corp. 1984, 21.

levels; each understood that expanding local manufacture required
greater economies of scale, obtainable only through market rationalization—that is, reducing the number of firms and models available; each attempted to develop an indigenous presence in the industry; and each,
with different degrees of emphasis, has sought to promote exports. These
four goals constitute a composite baseline for assessing the automobile
policy performances of the ASEAN Four, both (nationally) over time and
cross-nationally.

The Philippines

Policy Objectives.   In 1971 the Philippine BOI initiated an extensive
and carefully planned auto reform known as the Progressive Car Manufacturing Program (PCMP).[55] The PCMP was prompted by the desire to
save foreign exchange, to promote Philippine engineering capabilities,

Table 3.16.   Philippine "Local Content" Schedule, 1981

	Overall Percentage of "Local Content"[a]	Actual Physical Domestic Percentage of "Local Content"
1982	45	30
1983	55	40
1984	65	50

SOURCE: Philippines, BOI 1981, 3.
[a] Includes imported components assembled for reexport.

and to strengthen an emerging regional complementarity program in automotive products. But the program's core involved more specific objectives designed to achieve these broader goals.

Local content was initially mandated to expand from 10 percent in 1973, to 25 percent in 1974, to 37.5 percent in 1975, and 62.5 percent in 1976. These levels were not to be a strict reflection of actual local manufacture: auto products exported by an assembler from the Philippines were to count toward LC credit, along with physical local value-added. The Progressive Manufacture of Automotive Diesel Engines (PMADE) program, one of eleven government-promoted industrial projects announced in 1977,[56] supplemented the country's auto-manufacturing capacity.

The original LC targets and formula were gradually modified. After complaints from assemblers about high prices and the low quality of locally produced goods, the 62.5 percent LC goal was "stretched out" from 1976 to 1978.[57] In the late 1970s parts firms complained that the assemblers were not, in fact, procuring parts from local firms, but were instead obtaining LC credit by assembling imported components in-house for reexport. New targets were mandated that distinguished between overall levels of "local content" thus extended and the portion reflecting actual physical domestic content. As seen in table 3.16, these were even more modest than the original PCMP goals.

The BOI's desire to expand auto exports was reflected by the incorporation of exports into LC levels. And while no specific export targets were ever identified, export capacities and commitments were one of the criteria by which the BOI selected assemblers for participation in the PCMP.[58]

The PCMP was also designed to encourage nationalization of the auto industry, especially in production of auto parts. LC increases were to be achieved through horizontal integration of assemblers and parts firms. In-house production by assemblers was to be discouraged; assemblers were instead to "serve as the focal points through which engineering, management and financial assistance would be extended by international companies to domestic part makers."[59] These ancillary industries were eventually to become "the source of the components of other industrial and agricultural equipment needed for the country's economic development."[60] And while the BOI assumed that the auto TNCs would play a major role in this process, it was hoped that the local presence in the assembly process could be maintained and even expanded.[61]

Finally, the BOI recognized that a strengthening of local auto manufacturing required market rationalization—the reduction of types, makes, and models. Types were limited by the fact that the PCMP was to provide incentives only for cars and light commercial vehicles with engines of four cylinders or fewer and 2,000 cc or less displacement. Reduction in makes, the core of the rationalization effort, was to occur through a competitive bidding process: the BOI was to select at least two, and not more than four, assemblers based on willingness and capacity to meet state-mandated LC and export guidelines. In the PMADE program, the BOI similarly intended to limit diesel engine manufacturers to two.[62] The original PCMP guidelines made no provision for model limits or reductions; the BOI assumed that the costs of increasing localization would compel assemblers to reduce the number of models and slow down model changes. But by the late 1970s the number of models available to Philippine consumers had risen. In 1981 the BOI responded with a loose model limit for each assembler of "two and a half" and a prohibition on replacing registered models more frequently than once every three years.[63]

Performance.   With the exception of exports, the results of these efforts were not impressive. The assemblers' association claimed localization levels of 70 percent in 1978, but the actual figure was below 30 percent and has probably never exceeded 35 percent since.[64] Thus, while local value-added did expand from under 10 percent (the PCMP's first-year target) to somewhere around 30 percent, this achievement was significantly short of the original objectives and only barely caught up to the revised 1981 physical LC targets. Nor did diesel engine production enhance the country's manufacturing capacities, since the PMADE program never got off the ground.

The picture with regard to the development of an indigenous automobile presence was equally bleak. The assemblers asserted that the number of local parts firms had grown from 20 in 1972 to 228 in 1978,[65] but an International Labor Organization report found that the true number was closer to 150 firms.[66] This latter figure was all the more disappointing since firms in the parts sector experienced very high rates of failure. Perhaps more discouraging, few of these firms made any significant contribution to local content. What was called "domestic content" consisted largely of (1) the assemblers' own production, (2) parts exchanged among the assemblers, and (3) supplies from foreign subsidiaries and foreign-dominated parts firms. Assemblers' purchases from most local firms were "limited to a small amount of low technology items."[67] Little technology transfer was taking place; what integration did occur was largely vertical, not horizontal.

Nor was the existing indigenous presence maintained in the assembly sector. The PCMP began with four of the five licensed firms operating under majority or significant local ownership (table 3.17). Only Ford Philippines began and remained a wholly foreign-owned subsidiary. GM's assembly operation began in 1972 as a joint venture between GM (60 percent) and two local interests, Yutivo (30 percent) and Francisco (10 percent). Carco began as a joint venture among a local group, the Yulos (65 percent), Nissho Iwai and Mitsubishi (15 percent each), and Chrysler (5 percent). Delta Motors was a 100 percent Filipino-owned company under Ricardo Silverio, operating with a technical tie-up to Toyota. And DMG was a 100 percent Filipino firm owned by the Guevarra family, assembling Volkswagens.

But Yutivo and Francisco sold out to GM in 1976; DMG was taken over by Pilipinas Nissan after going bankrupt in 1982; Nissho Iwai and Mitsubishi bought out the Yulos in 1984; Silverio went bankrupt in 1984, with Toyota and Mitsui taking 35 percent of Delta (the other 65 percent going to the Philippines National Bank) by 1988; and Ford ceased operations in the Philippines in 1984. Simultaneously, Japanese firms completely supplanted American assemblers.[68]

Table 3.17.   Ownership of Major Philippine Assembly Firms

Make	Local Firm	Local Entrepreneur	Local Equity % 1972	Local Equity % 1985	Market Share 1983 (%)
Toyota	Delta Motors	Silverio	100	bankrupt	27
Volkswagen	DMG	Guevarra	100	bankrupt	0
GM	GM Philippines	Francisco/ Yutivo	40	0	17
Mitsubishi/ Chrysler	Carco	Yulo	65	0	22
Ford	Ford Philippines		0	0	29

SOURCES: Interviews; EIU 1984, 68–71; AMII, *Annual Report*, various years; *BD*, various issues, 1984–85.
NOTE: Market share includes commercial and passenger vehicles; the figures do not total 100 percent because poorer selling makes were excluded.

A major impediment to the growth of local auto parts firms was the failure of Philippine rationalization efforts. The number of models produced actually increased from twenty-five in 1973 to forty-eight in 1979 and fifty-one in 1981, while the number of engine types (by displacement) grew from fifteen in 1973 to twenty-five in 1980.[69] Nor was the BOI ever able to reduce the number of makes available. The number of passenger vehicle assemblers never officially went below five, and for much of the 1970s remained at eight, in spite of the PCMP's initial limit of four. By the early 1980s, the country's foreign-exchange crisis, the need for greater efficiency, and the fact that the existing assemblers were bankrupt compelled the government to revive efforts to reduce the number of makes. Two firms, Ford and GM, did leave; but their departure was a function of the Central Bank's refusal to provide foreign exchange and the fact that the market for locally assembled cars had been cut sharply by recession and high levels of smuggling.[70] In 1983 average capacity-utilization rates were low—roughly 40 percent.[71] And while rates were perhaps higher for the industry leaders, Toyota and Mitsubishi (respectively 31 and 32 percent of the PV market),[72] the small size of the overall market made operating levels uneconomical even for these two firms. By the end of the Marcos era, the Philippines auto industry had become dormant. Rationalization efforts under the Aquino administration have encountered similar problems.[73]

Table 3.18.   East Asian Auto Parts Exports (U.S. $millions)

	S. Korea	Indonesia	Malaysia	Philippines	Thailand
1979	14.9	0	3.2	33.9	8.4
1980	20.4	0	2.7	30.3	9.8
1981	29.0	0	3.8	32.8	8.5
1982	30.7	0	5.4	19.1	8.6
1983	37.3	0	6.8	23.2	8.1
1984	52.2	0	4.3	26.3	9.7
1985	92.9	0	4.3	21.1	11.6
1986	127.1	0	3.6	9.8	15.0

SOURCE: United Nations, *Yearbook of International Trade Statistics*, 1983 and 1986, except for Thailand 1986, which is from *FEER*, March 5, 1987, 70.

Exports of auto parts were the one relative bright spot, increasing sharply from less than $1 million in 1975 to over $32 million in 1981, but then dropping back to under $10 million in 1986 (table 3.18).[74] As of the mid 1980s these exports had generated roughly $130 million in revenues.

But according to interviews with Philippine assembly officials, these exports were largely intra-assembler transactions involving major functional components, with little contribution from local parts firms. The industry's import bills also rose—from $174 million in 1976 to $223 million in 1982 owing to the high imported content of locally manufactured parts.[75] By 1983 the auto industry's total import bill was $100 million, compared to export revenues of only $25 million; the auto industry had failed to become a major exporter. By 1983 the government had cut off all foreign-exchange allocations to auto assemblers and banned any auto imports exceeding the value of an individual company's exports. To meet these "no export, no import" constraints (which remain in effect as of 1988), GM exported furniture and Toyota has enlisted the Mitsui Trading Co. to export shrimp.[76]

As President Marcos recognized in 1983,[77] the PCMP was not very successful in terms of its own objectives. LC levels rose, but to barely half the program's initial targets; there was little growth of a national presence in auto parts; auto assembly was denationalized; efforts to consolidate makes and models failed totally; and exports, while expanding, were never great enough to offset import costs. This does not mean that the Philippines exhibited no leverage over the auto TNCs. The country's ability to compel the Japanese assemblers to export is striking in light of those firms' opposition to overseas sourcing, at least throughout the 1970s (discussed in chapter 4). Potential leverage did exist; the PCMP's failure lay in its inability to make use of that leverage.

Thailand

Policy Objectives.   As in the Philippines, Thai auto policies underwent several revisions, although these changes reflected successes as well as persistent obstacles. In 1971 the Ministry of Industry (MOI) set two-year LC targets of 25 percent for passenger vehicles (PVs) and 15–20 percent for commercial vehicles (CVs).[78] Targets were subsequently raised in 1978 to 50 percent, to be achieved within five years.[79] Frozen at 45 percent for PVs and 35 percent for CVs in 1983, LC goals for PVs were subsequently raised to 60 percent in 1987 and 70 percent in 1988, and then frozen at 54 percent in 1987.[80] The Thai BOI has set more ambitious targets—80 percent LC by the fifth year of production—for local manufacture of diesel engines to be used in one-ton pickup trucks.[81]

Thai auto policies do not contain the explicit emphasis on promoting indigenous firms so evident in the PCMP. Thailand does require majority local equity for firms receiving BOI incentives (the case with most auto firms), but foreign ownership is allowed in areas with no indigenous capacity. Nevertheless, interviews with and statements by relevant government officials, as well as persistent increases in LC targets, suggest that strengthening local auto interests has been an important component of Thai policy overall.[82] More explicit promotion of national firms has been evident in the requirements of the diesel engine project that producers promote local parts firms through technology transfer, subcontracting, and the specific use of Thai casting and machining capacity.

Thai auto policy has also consistently stressed the need for market rationalization. The 1971 measures imposed strict limits on vehicle types and on models and engine sizes produced by any one assembly plant.[83] In the face of political opposition, these were dropped by 1972, but in 1978 assembly plants were ordered not to add to or change existing models, and in 1984 the MOI ordered that vehicle models assembled in Thailand be reduced to 168, of which 84 were PVs, grouped in forty-two series (groups of similar models). A separate, but potentially significant, rationalization effort involves the 1984 diesel engine manufacturing project, for which the BOI decided to allow no more than three manufacturers.

Exports emerged as a prominent component of official Thai auto efforts only in the mid 1980s. In 1984, under pressure from the World Bank and Thai neoclassical economists, the government agreed to grant "tradeable export credits to locally established parts firms which sold abroad."[84] This export thrust was more evident in the government's diesel engine project, where aspiring engine producers are required to meet specific export targets.[85] And while Thailand, unlike the Philippines, made no general commitment to allocate LC credit for exports, locally assembled cars slated for export were reportedly allowed to incorporate only 33 percent (as opposed to 54 percent) local content.[86]

Performance.   Localization efforts have been moderately successful. LC rose from 6.6 percent for PVs and 11–15 percent for CVs in late 1973 to around 25 percent in 1977.[87] By 1980 LC for passenger cars had risen to 35 percent and to between 30 and 35 percent for CVs.[88] Presently between 45 and 54 percent, Thai LC is acknowledged to be the highest in Southeast Asia.[89] Even this achievement, however, must be tempered by the high imported content of auto parts made in Thailand, estimated at roughly 60 percent for the early 1980s.[90]

Equally important, these levels have not engendered a denationalization of the Thai industry as occurred in Philippines. Local participation in the assembly sector remains fairly strong and has even expanded, as seen in table 3.19. Thai parts firms increased from several dozen in 1970 to over 200 by the mid 1980s; 150 of these are producers of original equipment (OE) rather than spare parts.[91] The operations and local ownership of most of these firms seem relatively stable, unlike in the Philippines. Most of the firms established during the 1960s were completely Thai-owned and have remained so; and while most of these have technical ties to foreign producers, several of them have also gone on to lead the movement of parts firms for higher LC in the 1970s and 1980s.[92] The country's export performance reinforces the assertion that Thai firms are "significantly ahead of their neighbors."[93] The Thai export surge of the mid 1980s (see table 3.18) is impressive, not only for its rate of growth and volume (exceeding that of the Philippines by 1986), but also because

Table 3.19. Ownership of Major Thai Assembly Firms

Make	Local Firm	Local Entrepreneur	Local Equity (%)		Market Share 1985 (%)
			1972	1985	
Toyota	Toyota Thailand	Bangkok Bank	0	35	27
Mitsubishi	United Development Motor Industry	Lee Inakuul, Boonsoong, and Khan Sue	40	53	7
Isuzu	Isuzu Motors	Boonsoong, Sarasin, and Kahn Sue	50	53	22
Nissan, Datsun, and Suzuki	Siam Motors and Siam Automotive	Thawon Phornprapa	100	100	20
Mazda	Sukosol and Mazda Motor Industry	Sukosol	30	35	7
Opel, Daihatsu, and Honda	Bangchan General Assembly	Yip In Tsoi, Boonsoong, and Sarasin	40	66	—
BMW, Peugeot, and Citroen	YMC Assembly	Leenuttapong	100	100	—
Volvo	Thai Swedish Assembly	Paul Sitti-Amnuay	40	40	—
Fiat, Ford	Karnasuta General Assembly	Chainuwat, Krung Thai Bank, and Kowintha	100	100	—
Hino	Thai Hino	—	30	30	—
Mercedes-Benz	Thonburi Automotive Assembly	Viriyachan	100	100	—

SOURCES: Market shares—EIU 1987, 38; Ownership—*BIT*, September 1983, and interviews by Wiworn Kesavatana.

it has not entailed the denationalization so evident in the Philippines. This is in part because Thai firms began to export parts elsewhere in the region on their own,[94] and because they emphasized the export of lower technology items that are within local production capacities, such as oil tanks, radiators, and wiring harnesses. But the country's recent exports have also involved more complex items, such as brake drums, stamping dies, jigs, and molds. Although undertaken in conjunction with foreign firms (indeed, Thailand is now the favored location for Japanese overseas-production operations), recent exports often come from precisely those local firms that championed previous ISI policies.[95] And while the Thai auto industry remains a large net user of foreign exchange (more so than the Philippines), the industry's trade deficit has slowed considerably since the late 1970s.[96]

Rationalization attempts have been much less successful. In 1983 an estimated 300 models were produced by over fifteen assemblers in Thailand.[97] Overall capacity-utilization rates in 1986 were roughly 60 percent, better than in the Philippines, with rates for the industry leaders probably higher.[98] Toyota, Nissan, and Isuzu accounted for 60 to 70 percent of total sales for the 1978–85 period, and even more of the larger CV market.[99] The results of rationalization efforts in the diesel engine project have been mixed. The BOI finally accepted four manufacturers in 1985 despite its stated preference for no more than three. But a major Thai industrial group—Siam Cement—is the central local partner in three of the projects, and subsequent reports suggest that the foreign automakers heading two of the groups plan to merge their efforts.[100]

Malaysia

Policy Objectives. Whereas Philippine and Thai auto policy goals underwent several modifications, Malaysian auto efforts saw an especially radical break—a move toward a state-led national car project in the early 1980s, after roughly ten years of privately based localization and rationalization efforts. An understanding of the national car project, our principal concern, requires a brief review of the earlier stage. In 1967 the Malaysian government allowed six assembly plants to begin operations as a first step toward an integrated Malaysian auto industry.[101] This was followed by new regulations in 1972 mandating an increase in local content from 10 percent to 35 percent by 1982. Rationalization was to occur through indirect means: assemblers failing to meet LC targets would pay a penalty based on vehicle value. This penalty, along with the costs of localization, was presumed sufficient to weed out low-volume assemblers and models. Finally, the government hoped that the auto industry would provide a channel to expand the economic strength of the majority ethnic Malays (roughly 48 percent of the population). Malay resentment of the business dominance of ethnic Chinese (one-third of the population) had erupted into rioting in 1969, prompting the government to adopt a New Economic Policy (NEP) under which Malay (or *bumiputra*) corporate ownership would expand to 30 percent by 1990 in industries such as automobiles.[102] While an expansion of localization was desired, the growth of Chinese parts firms was not.

Most of these goals had not been attained by the late 1970s: some 11 assemblers were producing 25 makes and 122 models of commercial and passenger vehicles at LC levels of only 8 percent.[103] Ethnic objectives contributed to these problems: five assembly firms were granted entry either because they satisfied the NEP's requirement for *bumiputra* investment participation or because they agreed to locate in stipulated development areas.[104] But real growth of a Malay auto presence in assembly seems to have been minimal, while the number of parts firms with non-Malay owners grew. Between 1970 and 1975 roughly fifty parts firms had begun operation, bringing the total number of firms actually in business to around seventy-five. Most of these had majority local equity, Chinese and Indians being the dominant ethnic groups involved.[105] Malays were active only in auto distribution and reconditioning.[106]

By June 1978 these problems generated government measures to promote the manufacture of an all-Malaysian car.[107] While posing no specific LC targets, the new guidelines imposed mandatory deletions from imported CKD kits; in July 1979 the state began to identify particular components to be removed (deleted) in the country of origin, thus creating market opportunities for local parts firms.

These moves did little to alleviate the industry's weak localization, ethnic imbalance, and inefficiency. Local content had risen to only 18 percent by 1982, although the number of parts firms had grown to roughly two hundred (mostly Chinese-owned firms) by 1983.[108] Malaysian capital had expanded in assembly as the number of assemblers operating in Malaysia with majority foreign equity declined from five out of eleven in the mid 1970s to one in 1983 (see table 3.20).[109] But while *bumiputra* owners held 30 percent of assembly equity (compared to 43 percent for ethnic Chinese), they were found in the weakest firms and acted as little more than silent partners.[110]

The market also remained fragmented, with 11 assembly plants, 22 makes, and 105 models approved for production. These figures exaggerate the degree of fragmentation, since 9 or 10 models of 6 makes constituted 80 percent of the PVs assembled and capacity-utilization rates averaged 64 percent (78 and 84 percent for the two largest plants). Yet even this more moderate variety was intensified by the refusal of assemblers to standardize design, material, and dimensional specifications. Local parts costs remained high, suggesting that higher LC would lead to even higher vehicle costs.[111]

The Malaysian economy's structural weaknesses also began to intensify. With the prices of crucial export commodities falling sharply and import-dependent ISI industries such as auto manufacturing using precious foreign exchange, the country's GDP dropped, while government indebtedness grew in the early 1980s. Even the expanding manufactured-exports sector was plagued by foreign domination, dependence on imports, and a lack of linkages to the rest of the economy.[112] Slower growth in turn made it more difficult to expand *bumiputra* economic opportunities.

The government's response to this dilemma was a series of state-led heavy industry efforts, including a national car project.[113] In late October 1982 Prime Minister Mahathir Mohammad announced that Proton, a joint venture between Mitsubishi (30 percent equity) and a newly established state firm, the Heavy Industry Corporation of Malaysia (HICOM) (70 percent), would produce a Malaysian vehicle known as the Saga (actually a slightly modified Mitsubishi vehicle). The very fact that Malaysia was able to enlist Mitsubishi's support in this effort, considered foolhardy by most foreign auto firms, was a substantial achievement. Bolstered by $168 million in Japanese loans, Proton was to establish a manufacturing operation initially including assembly, stamping, painting, and testing facilities for vehicles powered by 1300 and 1500 cc engines, the model range accounting for 84 percent of the Malaysian market.[114] Production was to begin in 1986, with an output of 5,000 vehicles the first year, increasing to 120,000 annually by the 1990s.

Table 3.20. Ownership of Major Malaysian Assembly Firms

| Make | Local Firm | Equity Ownership 1983 (%) | | | Market Rank, 1983 |
		Foreign	Bumiputra	Other[a]	
Nissan	Tan Chong	—	—	100	1
Toyota	Assembly Services	15	33	52	2
Ford	Associated Motor	—	—	100	3
GM	Oriental Assembly	—	—	100	4
Mitsubishi	Kelangg Pembena Kereta	—	—	100	5
Mazda	Asia Automobiles	80	—	20	6
Volvo	Swedish Motor	50	—	50	7
Hino	Sarawak Motor	—	82	18	8
Mercedes-Benz	Cycle and Carriage Bintang	49	15	36	9
(Commercial vehicles only)	Kinabalu Motor	—	68.5	31.5	10
Toyota (truck)	Tatab Industries	29	60	11	11

SOURCES: EIU 1985, 20; AFM 1984, 3.23.
[a]Ethnic Chinese and Indians. Data do not indicate how much of each group, but anecdotal sources suggest most are Chinese.

LC would begin at 36 percent by utilizing output from the venture's stamping plant, but subsequent local manufacture of engines and transmissions was planned. Benefiting from generous tariff exemptions, the Saga was also designed to rationalize the country's passenger vehicle market by forcing out competing makes in the market's largest model niche.[115] And while the project did not initially envisage exports, market problems (discussed below) soon led government officials to press for the sale of Sagas overseas. Finally, the Saga was intended to promote ethnic restructuring. Since HICOM was officially classified as *bumiputra*-owned, the project could "erode the domination of ethnic Chinese entrepreneurs" while also serving "as training grounds for a new class of bumiputra industrial managers and skilled blue-collar workers."[116]

Performance.   The Saga initially did well. The car rolled off the assembly line almost a year before the original 1986 start-up date, and by late 1986 its LC level was roughly 47 percent, compared to 35 percent for other vehicles.[117] Advance orders initially outpaced production, and in its first full year on the market, the Saga captured over 45 percent of total PV sales.[118] Rationalization seemed to be occurring. Competing assemblers reduced the number of models offered, shifted to other product niches, including auto parts and heavy equipment, or left the market.[119]

This success was short-lived. The car market began to slump in 1985, and Proton's sales amounted to under 20 percent of annual capacity by 1986.[120] The drop in domestic sales, along with a yen revaluation that increased the cost of servicing Japanese loans, put tremendous pressure on the government to export the Saga.[121] But by 1989, only 2,850 Sagas had been exported, although volumes of 8,000 were predicted for England in 1990.[122] Expanded localization was initially hindered by these sales problems and the increased cost of imported items required by locally produced parts. By 1988 local content had reportedly dropped to around 30 percent, but it rose to 50 percent in 1989.[123] Nor did rationalization seem to be moving as fast as it had initially;[124] existing assemblers, seeing Proton's problems, were sticking in the market for the long run.

Ethnic and national goals seemed less and less likely to be met. Existing local content reflected the persistent strength of established Chinese parts firms.[125] And while strong pressure from parts firms for localization increases (discussed below) reflects a strong local, albeit Chinese, presence in parts production, the country's national auto champion was becoming less and less national (and less and less Malay): in what some Malays termed a sellout, the Malaysian finance minister moved in July 1988 to shift Proton's supervision from HICOM (Malay) managers to Mitsubishi out of frustration with HICOM's inefficient management of the firm.[126]

Indonesia

Policy Objectives.   Indonesia modified its specific objectives more frequently than any of its three neighbors (table 3.21). Indonesia's earliest government decree began ambitiously in 1969 by aiming to move from a localization level of near zero to full CV manufacture by 1984.[127] But the decree identified neither specific intermediate LC levels nor particular components to be localized in given years. Rationalization efforts involved prohibiting the import of any new make and encouraging the smaller assemblers to serve as subcontractors for the larger ones. All automotive assemblers were to have a majority of Indonesian equity; established foreign-owned firms were to find local partners and transfer a majority of their shares to them. This initial effort was followed by a more extensive and specific set of objectives for commercial vehicles in 1976, Government Decree No. 307.[128] Assemblers were to procure simple parts and those already produced locally (paint, wheels, batteries) by 1977; items such as windows, seats, wheel rims, and radiators were to be localized by 1978; chassis, fuel tanks, oil and air filters by 1979; and transmissions, engines, axles, and other items by 1984. Following the failure of more aggressive rationalization efforts in 1972 (Decree No. 545), the government adopted the more indirect approach of assuming that the costs of LC increases would gradually exclude the weaker assemblers, brands, and models.

In 1978 LC efforts were temporarily stopped altogether. Decree No. 231 mandated the halt out of concern that localization increases were strengthening the better-financed firms owned by ethnic Chinese.[129] As occurred in Malaysia, auto policy reflected the frustration of indigenous *pribumi* Indonesians by Chinese business dominance. A combination of nationalist and ethnic tensions had exploded in what became known as the 1974 Malari riots: demonstrators mobbed visiting Japanese Prime Minister Tanaka and burned a building belonging to Astra, one of the country's

Table 3.21.   Indonesian Automobile Decrees, 1969–1983

	Decree No.	Localization	Rationalization
1969	—	Full mfg. of CVs by 1984[a]	Reduce makes to 33; consolidate assemblers
1972	545		Merge assemblers and sole agents
1976	307	Gradual deletion schedule leading to localization of major parts by 1984[a]	No specific target
1978	231	Localization halt out of concern for *pribumi* firms	
1979	168	Slower LC schedule with mfg. of major parts by 1990	Model/make reduction
		Establish engine[b] mfg. plants	Limited number of engine plants, probably three
1980	—		Reduce makes from 51 to 42 and models from 147 to 71; group dealers and assemblers into 8 groups
1983	371	Wheel rims, cabins, chassis, frames, axles—1984; engines, shafts—1985; brake, trans., steering, clutch—1986; complete assembly of CV from locally produced or assem. parts—1987	

[a] Majority equity for all local auto firms.
[b] While the engine plants were not officially part of Decree No. 168, they were proposed at the same time and were critical to its implementation.

largest Chinese business groups and the country's major private sector automobile presence.[130]

Decree No. 168 resumed the localization effort in 1979 with more modest targets.[131] Items such as shock absorbers, paint, radiators, and wheel rims were to be procured locally by 1980 instead of 1977–79, and cabins, fuel tanks, and chassis by 1980–81 instead of 1979. The official date for localization of more complex items, such as engines, transmissions, and brake drums, was to be stipulated later; in fact, the minister of industry responsible for the decree assumed that these items would not be assembled locally before 1984 or manufactured locally before 1990. Production of these major components was to be bolstered by state-promoted steel operations and a small number of engine-manufacturing plants, themselves parts of a national move into basic industry involving $11 billion in investments in fifty-two key projects in basic chemicals, basic metals, and engineering.[132]

Decree No. 168 also stressed the need for market efficiency and was supplemented by more specific rationalization targets: brands were to be reduced from 51 to 42 and models from 147 to 71; only a limited number of engine-manufacturing operations were to be promoted;[133] and, most important, the over twenty assemblers and twenty-two distributors were to be merged into eight major groups.[134] In addition to increasing the efficiency of local production, this consolidation had other objectives: the groupings were designed to reinforce national ownership, to promote a Western counterbalance to the dominating Japanese presence, and, above all, to strengthen *pribumi*-owned auto firms.

Finally, implementation problems forced the government to revise its localization schedule once again in 1983. According to Decree No. 371 wheel rims, cabins, and frames were to be produced locally in 1984 as opposed to 1980–81. Specific dates for the assembly of more complex components were also mandated: axles in 1984; engines, shafts, and brake systems in 1985; and steering, transmissions, and clutch systems in 1986. By 1987 CVs were to be completely assembled from locally produced or assembled components.[135] Manufacture of more complex components was to be undertaken by large *pribumi*-owned firms drawing on the resources of foreign parts producers. But the actual deadline for manufacture was left unspecified.

Performance. In spite of the difficulties indicated by Indonesia's frequent revisions of its localization targets, there was limited progress. The local manufacture of auto components more than doubled between 1975 and 1978.[136] Expanding CV sales had encouraged the establishment of some two hundred body part factories throughout the country.[137] By 1982 local firms had begun manufacturing tubular and stamped parts that required neither metal cutting nor much floor inspection. Licenses for more complex parts, such as wheel rims, chassis frames, drive shafts, and rear axles, were issued in 1982, and production of these items began in the mid 1980s.[138] By 1988 Astra affiliates manufactured "everything from chassis to brake systems and car air conditioners" domestically.[139] Indonesia also succeeded in obtaining commitments in 1982 for local engine manufacture from Mitsubishi, Toyota, Daihatsu, Mercedes-Benz, Isuzu, Hino, and Suzuki, with Toyota and Mitsubishi opening their assembly plants in January 1985.[140] All of this amounted to CV local-content levels of some 30–35 percent of actual value-added in mid 1985, and probably around 40 percent by 1988.[141]

This increase in LC has involved vertical integration rather than the strengthening of *pribumi*-owned parts firms as planned by the government. Precise numbers of parts producers are unavailable, but they probably total around one hundred, with forty to fifty producing original equipment and another fifty or so devoted solely to replacement parts.[142] Most of these firms (whose ethnicity is undetermined) are clearly relegated to small quantities of very low technology items. More complex parts, such as wheel rims, leaf springs, and brakes, are handled either directly by the assemblers or by assembler-controlled firms, while much of the original equipment for simpler components, such as seat frames, fuel tanks, and radiators, comes from subsidiaries of foreign parts firms tied in turn to assemblers.[143]

Unlike in the Philippines and, to a lesser extent, in Malaysia, this vertical integration has not weakened local capital in Indonesia's auto assembly industry, although "local" refers here to ethnic Chinese (table 3.22) Assembler equity figures are not available, since each of these groups includes several firms in which precise local/foreign share ratios vary. But interviews and other written sources strongly suggest that the local equity holdings and managerial influence of both Chinese groups, Astra and Liem, have persisted and even grown in relation to their TNC partners (as well as to *pribumi* assemblers).[144] Conversely, Mitsubishi has reportedly expanded its role in the major *pribumi* firm, Krama Yudha, owing to financial problems experienced by the firm's local partners.[145] The only expanding *pribumi* interest in the auto industry was the group headed by Probosutejo—President Suharto's half brother—whose ties to the presidential palace provided leverage with both Chinese and foreign firms.

Rationalization efforts also met with mixed results. The 1980 targets of 42 makes and 71 models were achieved, although in part because market

Table 3.22.   Major Auto Assemblers in Indonesia

	Local Role[a]	Makes	Assemblers of These Makes before 1984–85	Market Share 1976–83 (%)
Astra	High	Toyota	Astra	41[b]
		Daihatsu	Astra	
		Nissan Diesel	Afaan	
		BMW	Ning	
		Peugeot	Probosutejo	
		Renault	Probosutejo	
Krama Yudha Motors	Low	Mitsubishi	Mitsubishi	32
Liem	Medium	Suzuki	Liem	11
		Hino	Ning	
		Mazda	Ning	
		Honda	Ang	
		Nissan	Afaan	
Probosutejo	Low	Chevy Luv	Eman	7
		Holden	Eman	
		Isuzu	Probosutejo	
Joesoef	Low	Mercedes Benz	Star Motors	3
Hasyim Ning	Low	Ford Laser	Ning	2
		Fiat	Ning	
		Jeep	Ning	

SOURCES: For groups and brands, Wibisanto 1984; author interviews. For market shares, Pawitra 1985, 414. Market share percentages are approximate and represent the total shares of the makes in each group.

NOTE: Astra and Liem are Chinese-run firms; all the other assemblers listed are *pribumi*-run.

[a]This is admittedly imprecise. Local involvement was extrapolated from reported equity holdings and managerial control.

[b]According to Friedland 1988, 100, Astra's total market share in 1989 was 45 percent.

forces compelled some assemblers to halt production.[146] By 1983 these had been reduced to some 28 makes and 69 "types and models."[147] And while capacity-utilization rates were roughly 60 percent in 1985 (in part owing to a market decline from 212,000 in 1981 to 153,000 in 1984), the picture was probably somewhat less bleak for commercial than for passenger vehicles, and better for the Chinese-owned than for the smaller *pribumi*-owned firms.[148] Efforts to consolidate assemblers and distributors into a limited number of groups also made progress; but as noted, these entailed even greater dominance of Chinese and foreign over *pribumi* interests. And, finally, the government was compelled to accept seven proposals for engine manufacture as opposed to its original target of three.

Perhaps as a function of the country's huge market (160 million people), export promotion has been noticeably absent over some twenty-five years of Indonesian auto policies, and the country's auto exports are the lowest of the ASEAN Four (see table 3.18).[149] This may change, however. The country's largest auto firm, Astra, increased auto parts exports from $3.4 million in 1986 to $20 million in 1988.[150] And in what would be its first transfer of engines between overseas affiliates, Toyota announced in late 1987 that 50 percent of its Indonesian engine firm's output would be exported to Taiwan and Malaysia, as well as to Japan.[151] This development merits special note, for it suggests that local policies may *indirectly* generate shifts in TNC production strategies. I shall address this point in the following chapter. An overall assessment of the ASEAN Four's auto performances is, however, now in order.

Assessing Performance

Certain measurement difficulties should be acknowledged at the outset. Consistent and comparable data are not available for all four countries over time. This reflects both weakness in ASEAN data-gathering and subtle differences among national goals. Indonesia, for example, has stressed localization of commercial vehicles strongly, and Thailand somewhat less so, while Malaysia and the Philippines have emphasized manufacture of passenger vehicles (although the latter attempted to manufacture diesel engines for commercial vehicles as well). Also, the performance of some countries may reflect broader macroeconomic fluctuations more than local auto industries' ability to produce automobiles and parts (partially the case for Malaysia and the Philippines). Perhaps most important is the problem of moving targets. We are not dealing here with stable sets of national objectives that lend themselves to easy evaluation through comparison with endpoint performance levels. As illustrated in table 3.23, goals have often been revised downward or left unspecified as problems have emerged. These revisions themselves suggest problems in policy implementation.

Table 3.23.   Comparison of ASEAN Four Auto Goals and Achievements

Issue	Goal	Achievement
Local Content (physical)		
Philippines	initially 62.5%, then 30% physical	30–35%
	diesel engine production	never implemented
Thailand	25% for 1976; initially 50% for 1983, then frozen at 45%; raised to 60% in 1987 and 70% in 1988; frozen at 54% in 1988	45–54%; possibly higher for trucks; progress in mfg. of more complex parts
	80% by five years for diesel engines	project just beginning, but TNC commitments obtained
Malaysia	Saga "national champion" auto at least 36%, in 1986, then gradual increase	TNC commitment obtained (Mitsubishi) 47%, then down to 30% but up to 50% in 1989
Indonesia	no specific LC targets; stress on local prod. of more complex parts and components; assem. of CV from locally assem. or mfgred. parts, by 1987—implication of over 70% LC	roughly 40%; higher for Astra
	local engine mfgr; orig. date 1986, subsequently unspecified; engine assem. by 1985	engine assembly begun 1985
Rationalization		
Philippines	not over 4 assemblers; reduce models	8 throughout 1970s model prolif.; c.u.r. 40%[a]
Thailand	reduce models; no more than 3 diesel engine firms	model prolif.; c.u.r. 55–70%;[a] 4 firms, but same Thai firm in 3 of the 4
Malaysia	exclude all makes but Proton from 1,200–1,500 cc niche	47% of niche, but declining market—under 20% c.u.r.[a]
Indonesia	reduce makes and models	moderate success; c.u.r.[a] roughly 60%
	reduce assem. groups to 8	moderate success, but strengthens Chinese; accepted 7 mfgrs.
	limit engine mfgrs. to 3	
Nationalization		
Philippines	explicit emphasis; promote	local parts firms weak; as-

Table 3.23—*Continued*

Issue	Goal	Achievement
	local parts firms and maintain Philippine assemblers	semblers denationalized
Thailand	implicit effort to promote local firms generally; more explicit in engine production	numerical and tech. growth of local firms; central role of large Thai producer in engine project
Malaysia	develop "national champion" (as well as ethnic champion) in assembly	initial success, with foreign support; subsequent Japanese takeover
Indonesia	promote *pribumi* parts firms	fairly weak parts firms; *pribumi* presence overall weak; but local Chinese presence in assem./parts prod. strong
Exports		
Philippines	major emphasis: reduce foreign exchange use; become part of reg. and int'l div. of labor	growth of exports, but of import bill as well
Thailand	moderate and recent efforts; explicit only in engine project	recent export growth; potential for further expansion
Malaysia	recent but desperate efforts	very minor success
Indonesia	not targeted	minimal; but recent (1987) plans for engine export

^ac.u.r. = capacity utilization rates.

But if precise measurement is not possible, some useful general conclusions are.[152] First, as seen in table 3.23, none of the four countries came close to achieving all, or even most of, their initial goals. On the basis of the most recent information, complete localization remained a distant goal, with even locally produced auto parts highly import-dependent. All of the markets were fragmented, with capacity-utilization rates not exceeding 70 percent, and local firms remained highly reliant on foreign capital. Auto part export levels grew significantly only in the Philippines, but even those were rapidly exceeded by South Korean exports (table 3.18)

Second, some progress was made. Locally produced goods made up at least 30 percent of the value of ASEAN autos in niches targeted by

Table 3.24.   Comparative Ranking of ASEAN Four Auto Policy Performance

	Indonesia	Malaysia	Philippines	Thailand
Local Content	2	3	4	1
Rationalization	3	1	4	2
Nationalization	2	3	4	1
Exports	4	3	1	2
Composite	11	10	13	6

NOTE: 1 = best of the four; 4 = worst. The lower the composite score, the better the relative ranking.

government programs; local assembly (and in some cases manufacture) of complex components, including engines, was initiated; some rationalization was achieved; and the ASEAN Four's indigenous auto entrepreneurs grew, as did their total exports of auto parts. Third, whatever progress occurred within each country did so at an uneven pace. Countries were more successful at some times than at others.[153]

And, finally, some did better than others. Table 3.24 presents a comparative ranking of the ASEAN Four, both for each of the four objectives and for all four as a composite. Although admittedly rough, these rankings emphasize quantifiable and easily comparable data (capacity-utilization rates, export totals, LC levels, numbers of local firms, etc.), but also consider "softer" information, including trends noted in the preceding review. For example, Indonesia is ranked second in terms of localization both because of its existing LC levels and Astra's clear capacity for rapid increases. Thailand emerges as the region's best performer, the Philippines as the worst, and Malaysia and Indonesia are together in the middle.

There is nothing surprising about the ASEAN Four's failure to achieve their ambitious initial goals. But interesting questions are raised by the fact that any progress occurred at all. First, did the region's auto policy achievements in fact reflect host country leverage over foreign auto firms opposed to local objectives? Or were they simply a function of converging interests—that is, of market forces and auto-TNC preferences operating independently of host country efforts? Answering this question requires an examination of the external forces facing the ASEAN Four—the international auto industry in general and Japanese auto firms in particular. To the extent that we find the preferences of foreign auto firms to be inconsistent with ASEAN auto objectives, a second question emerges: what aspects of the external auto environment provide potential for local leverage?

These questions are the focus of chapter 4. Their answers will set the stage for an examination of the politics of auto industrialization in each country, and eventually an explanation of variation in ASEAN auto performances.

4

Economic Constraints and Opportunities: Japanese Automobile Firms in Southeast Asia

The Japanese firms dominating the ASEAN auto industries have until recently been international in their markets but largely domestic in their production. Overseas sales accounted for 50 percent of Japanese auto production in 1980, up from 39 percent in 1975.[1] But unlike U.S. firms, the Japanese assemblers strongly preferred to service overseas markets through exports from Japan, not offshore production. While in 1980 the U.S. Big Three averaged almost 35 percent of their production abroad, and the major European firms almost 19 percent, Toyota and Nissan had a combined average of roughly 1 percent.[2] Only in Southeast Asia was there any extensive Japanese production presence. Nor were the Japanese anxious to export (either back to Japan or to third countries) from their existing overseas production sites. By the early 1970s U.S. firms were moving to export from the larger Latin American countries. In 1979, however, 90 percent of the sales of the Japanese transport equipment industry's overseas ventures were aimed at local markets.[3]

Table 4.1.   Japanese Imports of Auto Parts from South Korea, Taiwan, and ASEAN

	(U.S. $millions)			
Exporter	1983	1984	1985	Annual Average Growth Rate, 1983–85 (%)
South Korea	1.8	2.4	3.6	41
Taiwan	0.9	2.1	2.5	67
ASEAN	6.3	13.0	13.5	46

SOURCE: Mitsubishi Research Institute 1987, table 3.10.

By 1984 the Japanese were laying the bases for an international expansion, especially in the United States and in the weaker producing countries of Europe. In Asia, Japanese production patterns were shifting from an emphasis on assembly (production based on imported CKD kits) to greater manufacturing (using significant local content), and to a recognition of the need to export from overseas production sites.[4] In the fall of 1986 a Nissan official predicted that Asian countries would be producing and selling Nissan hardware to each other. Taiwan might be selling Nissan auto bodies to Thailand, while Thai-made Nissan engines would go to Taiwan. Nissan's role would be to "administer the traffic."[5]

Although Japanese firms have still not internationalized to the extent of Western assemblers, the growth is clear. Between 1983 and 1985 Japanese procurement of overseas-sourced parts expanded almost twofold. Much of this shift, both absolutely and relatively, reflected increases in purchases of parts produced in the United States (which jumped from $565 million to $1.5 billion).[6] But Japanese imports of auto parts from the Asian region experienced healthy expansion as well (table 4.1).

This gradual shift, and the competitive international industry of which it is a part, constitute the major external context of ASEAN auto efforts. The first section of this chapter briefly reviews the international auto industry's principal features and impact on LDC auto production. The second section focuses on the Japanese auto firms in Southeast Asia: the extent of their activities in the region, their motivations for ASEAN operations, and the sources of their regional dominance. The third section outlines Japanese auto firms' interests in opposing LDC auto manufacture, their leverage against it, and the industry-specific sources of potential host country leverage for expanding such production. The final section concludes with a provisional look at why some countries have done better than others at exploiting such potential.

International Automobile Production: An Uneven Product Cycle

The potential for auto production by developing countries seemed great when the ASEAN Four initiated their automotive efforts in the late 1960s and early 1970s. In 1966 Raymond Vernon cited the auto industry as an example of a mature industry.[7] After the standardization of engines, chassis, and components between 1900 and 1950, the technical design of automobiles had not changed for several decades. In 1970 the mature auto industry seemed ripe for diffusion to developing countries in line with product-cycle predictions. Indeed, several Latin American countries had initiated ISI-based auto production during the 1960s and were beginning to press the TNCs for more export-oriented production toward the end of the decade.[8]

Then, in the 1970s, the auto industry was "rejuvenated." The nature of automobile production shifted abruptly as higher oil prices and environmental concerns generated a whole range of product and manufacturing innovations: "Essentially every facet of the industry [was] . . . undergoing metamorphosis."[9] Efforts to improve safety, fuel efficiency, comfort, and emissions led to greater use of microelectronics and new materials such as aluminum, plastic resins, and high-strength steel plate.[10]

This technological dynamism did not necessarily preclude an expansion of LDC auto production. In 1979 an MIT-based international research effort on the auto industry assumed that "manufacturing would shift from the developed countries to the less developed countries as automakers took advantage of lower wages to reduce manufacturing costs."[11] Standardization of tastes, rising entry barriers, and competition among a shrinking number of firms were basic to this assumption. Most analysts believed that the need for energy conservation and environmental protection would make the small or light car the standard-sized vehicle throughout the world. Commonization of demand would allow automakers to concentrate on a "world car." U.S. firms in particular believed it possible to develop designs "that are generally acceptable, at least in terms of major

Table 4.2. Rates of Growth for Motor Vehicle Populations, 1960–1980 (Percentages)

	1960–65	1965–70	1970–75	1975–80
World	7.0	6.7	5.9	4.6
United States	4.1	3.7	4.2	3.2
West Germany	13.7	7.8	4.6	5.0
Japan	36.0	22.8	9.8	6.2

SOURCE: Bittlingmayer 1983, table 1.

subassemblies, throughout the world so that the manufacturers can benefit from longer product life cycles." [12] In Asia, Ford was especially eager to promote regional production sharing.[13] But if homogeneous tastes allowed larger economies of scale, only a few "megaproducers" would have the technical and financial resources to stay in the race.[14] The industry was presumably moving toward greater corporate concentration but more geographic dispersal.

Both of these assumptions have proven at least partially wrong.[15] Most important, competition has remained intense, in part because the number of competing assemblers has not dwindled.[16] Tastes have remained highly diversified, allowing specialist producers to create and exploit new niches. In addition, new production hardware and new, flexible methods of organizing production pioneered by the Japanese have lowered the minimum efficient annual scale for individual product lines. Scale requirements no longer drive out established smaller producers. Existing firms have coped with the costs of new technologies in part through new forms of cooperation among competing final assemblers. Support from national governments or financial systems has also kept firms in business.[17] In addition, technological development is increasingly occurring in larger, richer, and more sophisticated parts firms eager to sell to any assembler.[18]

Rivalry among a stable number of firms has been reinforced by growing surplus capacity as declining growth rates in the major auto-producing countries have led to slower growth in global demand (table 4.2).[19] As seen in table 4.3, the major bright spot is the high predicted growth rates for LDC auto markets, especially those in East Asia and Latin America. The desire for footholds in these growing markets has made assemblers in developed countries vulnerable to LDC localization and export plans. The auto TNCs have followed each other first into Latin America and subsequently into East Asia. Most recently, East Asian countries have become attractive (especially to Japanese firms) as production sites from which to avoid protectionism in developed countries and the price burden of a strong yen.

Flexible manufacturing processes have encouraged this "defensive investment" pattern[20] by permitting the TNCs to meet local requirements even in small overseas markets. The result has been an expansion of auto assembly in developing countries from 20 percent of the world total in 1967 to 45 percent in 1980.[21] In addition, the industry's very dynamism has begun to create limited opportunities for LDC parts production in at least two ways. First, rapidly changing parts technologies have resulted in supplies of second-hand parts production equipment no longer needed by parts firms in developed countries but still useful to developing countries' firms.[22] Second, the transfer of some auto parts technology from more to less technologically advanced LDCs has begun to occur.[23]

As a result of the preceding factors, it is now assumed that "the majority of world auto production will at some point take place outside the OECD countries."[24] But that point is very far off. For the foreseeable future, new technologies and oligopolistic competition have limited the spread of auto manufacturing throughout the developing world. High capital intensity, steep start-up costs, and the difficulty of auto design and manufacture preclude the emergence of new auto assemblers without affiliation to existing TNCs.[25] New technologies have cut labor costs to somewhere around 20 percent of a car's ex-factory cost, thus reducing the attraction of LDC cheap labor.[26] Constant innovations require close coordination between R&D, engineering, and production activities. And the expanding technological role of parts firms has encouraged assemblers to expand their reliance on suppliers in developed rather than developing countries.

The fragmentation of LDC auto markets by inter-TNC rivalries has heightened these entry barriers. Driven by the fear of losing foreign markets to competitors, numerous TNCs are willing and able to remain in small LDC markets despite inefficiencies and low profits. Potential losses entailed by such a strategy are minimized by two factors: generally high levels of host country protection and subsidies,[27] and the TNCs' possession of the technology necessary for entry.

Table 4.3.   Predicted Growth of Auto Populations

	Vehicles in 1980 (thousands)	Population per Vehicle in 1980	Predicted Annual Grow of Vehicle Population 1982–95 (%)
Developed countries			
United States	155,890	1.5	1.8
Canada	13,210	1.8	2.0
Japan	37,856	3.1	1.9
France	21,720	2.5	1.4
Italy	19,121	3.0	1.6
United Kingdom	17,358	3.2	1.2
West Germany	24,792	2.5	1.4
European NICs			
Portugal	1,205	8.2	4.9
Spain	8,937	4.2	2.0
Eastern Europe (average)[a]	3,648	24.1	4.4
Asia			
China	905	1,135.0	22.0
Indonesia	1,195	127.0	11.0
Malaysia	730	19.0	7.7
Philippines	1,050	46.0	9.2
Thailand	931	50.0	9.4
South Korea	528	74.0	11.5
Taiwan	420	42.0	9.9
India	1,543	432.0	12.3
Pakistan	361	225.0	12.4
Latin America			
Argentina	4,167	6.5	3.9
Brazil	10,160	12.0	6.5
Chile	588	19.0	7.0
Colombia	753	37.0	10.9
Mexico	4,847	15.0	7.6
Peru	489	36.0	8.7
Venezuela	1,933	7.5	5.2
Middle East			
Egypt	556	76.0	12.8
Israel	465	8.3	3.5
Turkey	1,135	40.0	5.6
South Africa	3,466	9.4	3.7

SOURCE: Bittlingmayer 1983, table 2.
[a] Includes Bulgaria, Czechoslovakia, East Germany, Hungary, Poland, Romania, the USSR, and Yugoslavia.

Through the mid 1980s, then, the preferred strategy of auto assemblers in most LDCs was essentially to do

> quite simply, very little. It follows that [the firms'] behavior will be directed at retaining their positions within the markets, just in case any unexpected developments did occur, at using those positions to reinforce ties with local groups influential both politically and economically, and in general contriving to ensure that no radical policy changes take place.... They have rather few sunk assets in those countries, have no wish to sink any others, but are concerned that the conditions of oligopolistic competition should not swing strongly in favor of any one among them—for that reason those already present want to remain.[28]

This defensive strategy has fragmented LDC markets; it has entailed a significant dispersion of market shares among TNCs, which translates into a proliferation of makes. Competition through new and changing models reinforces this fragmentation. The creation of new product niches through flexible manufacturing is the practice in developing as well as developed auto markets.[29]

The impact of these factors, summed up in table 4.4, has been mixed, encouraging a three-level pyramidlike structure of LDC producers. At the pinnacle is South Korea—the sole case of a nationally controlled assembler (Hyundai) using several sources of foreign technology to manufacture and export its own vehicles. A Taiwan firm's establishment of its own design center may point to a similar, although less independent, producer for that country.[30]

The second level involves extensive parts manufacturing and some automotive exports in what have been called the "semi-industrialized countries"—Spain, Brazil, Mexico, Yugoslavia, Argentina, and India, as well as South Korea. These countries' share of worldwide auto manufacture climbed from zero in 1950 to 2.4 percent in 1960, 5.3 percent in 1970 and 9.5 percent in 1980.[31] The group's collective production was comparable to that of West Germany and France. And while much of this production involves some sort of linkages with the auto TNCs, indigenous capital has maintained a base in the parts sector. Local firms reportedly accounted for around half the local parts production of Argentina, Brazil, and Mexico, and most of such production in South Korea and India.[32]

The ability of these countries to break into export markets has been less impressive. Their share of world trade in automotive products doubled

Table 4.4.   Impact of Automobile Industry Characteristics on Potential for LDC Production

Characteristic	Encourages Production	Discourages Production
Competitive industry structure	Defensive investment	Proliferation of makes
Shrinking global market	Defensive investment in growing LDC markets	
New technologies		
Costs and technological change	Make available used parts and manufacturing equipment	Raise entry barriers for manufacture of new products; tie manufacturing to R&D
Flexible manufacturing	Permits TNC entry into small markets; facilitates ability to meet local conditions	Facilitates model proliferation
Increased importance of parts producers	Developed country parts firms independent, selling to any and all	Promotes tight links between TNC assemblers and developed country parts firms; discourages TNC promotion of, and links to, LDC suppliers
Protectionism	Promotes use of LDCs as production base to circumvent trade barriers	
Exchange rate shifts	Promotes use of LDCs as production base from which to avoid costs of high yen; possible transfer of technology from one LDC to others	

between 1973 and 1979 but still accounted for only 3.1 percent of international exports, while their share of world auto parts exports barely reached 5 percent by 1986.[33] At least through the early 1980s, the "world car" pattern had emerged, but much more slowly than originally expected.[34]

At the pyramid's third tier are the ASEAN Four, as well as Portugal, Greece, Colombia, Chile, Peru, Uruguay, and Venezuela.[35] These are the aspiring auto manufacturers—those countries whose localization and export levels are low and whose degrees of market fragmentation are high relative to those of the "semi-industrialized countries." These countries are at the tail of a product cycle whose evolution has been uneven and slow, at least compared to industries such as electronics or textiles. Yet this third tier is neither static nor monolithic. As seen in the previous chapter, fierce competition for scarce markets has provided opportunities for each ASEAN country to expand its auto-manufacturing activities, and for some to grow more than others.

In sum, until the mid 1980s, the modest expansion of LDC auto industries was a function of politics counteracting economics. LDC industrialization efforts made use of inter-TNC rivalries to offset the automakers' desire to locate production in existing areas of high technology. Since the mid 1980s economic factors—protectionism and exchange-rate shifts—have reinforced politics to encourage the automotive product cycle further.

The Japanese are at the leading edge of technological and competitive developments in the industry. Concerned with new technologies to meet diverse demand, the auto TNCs have only grudgingly supported LDC auto manufacture, and as technological leaders, the Japanese have traditionally been even more grudging than their Western counterparts. Conversely, the industry's competitive structure has provided openings for LDC producers as well as roadblocks; and domestic conditions have generated particularly intense struggles for market share among the Japanese assemblers. Southeast Asia has been a major overseas focus of these rivalries.

The Japanese Presence in Southeast Asia

The dominance of ASEAN auto markets by Japanese vehicles has been accompanied by an extensive growth of Japanese assembly and parts production in the region. Over 40 percent of the Japanese transport equipment industry's cases of direct overseas investment from 1964 to 1980 were in the five ASEAN countries.[36] Of the Japanese assemblers' 138 overseas production bases, 47, or 34 percent, were located in the four ASEAN countries in 1982.[37] This rose to 39 percent in 1985, but then dropped to roughly 20 percent in 1987 with the establishment of new Japanese plants in the United States, Canada, and Western Europe.[38] Further, as seen in table 4.5, each of Japan's eleven auto firms, not simply larger assemblers like Toyota and Nissan, is well represented in the region.

In addition, over 35 percent of Japanese parts producers' 114 overseas manufacturing affiliates and subsidiaries were in the ASEAN Four.[39] The overwhelming majority of these came at the behest of Japanese assemblers attempting to meet ASEAN local-content regulations.[40]

Accounting for this presence requires an understanding of the domestic conditions pushing Japanese firms toward overseas markets, and of the factors drawing them toward Southeast Asia in particular.

Domestic Pressures for Japanese Overseas Expansion

Problems of excess capacity and intense competitive pressures have made expanding exports critical for Japanese assemblers almost since the industry's inception. From 1963 to 1970 Japanese domestic production grew from one million to five million units. Investment in the auto industry rose from one billion yen in 1951 to 14.8 billion in 1957 and 112.8 billion in 1965.[41] These investments, together with the development of new production technologies such as *kan ban* and "just-in-time" production, generated increasing levels of efficiency within the Japanese auto industry.[42]

Simultaneously, the Japanese industry began to face conditions encouraging increased attention to exports. Domestic market growth rates declined from 36 percent in 1960–65 to 6.2 percent in 1975–80 (see table 4.2). In addition, like other large Japanese firms, the auto assemblers relied heavily on debt with high fixed charges, at least during the industry's early years.[43] Together with the practice of permanent employment, these charges constituted strong pressure for capacity utilization.[44]

Perhaps most important, the Japanese auto industry became increasingly crowded and competitive following the Korean War. New firms entered the market from 1958 through the mid 1960s. These included Mitsubishi Motors; Prince Motors (formerly an aircraft maker); Hino (producer of diesel-fueled trucks); Toyo Kogyo—later Mazda (formerly specializing in the production of machine tools and three-wheeled trucks); Honda; and Daihatsu (formerly a marine engine maker).[45] The new entrants were not only attracted by healthy profit rates[46] and a grow-

Table 4.5. Japanese Auto Assemblers in East Asia, 1987

	Taiwan	South Korea	PRC	Malaysia	Philippines	Indonesia	Thailand
Nissan	p/c			p/c	p/c	c	p/c
Nissan Diesel	c	c	c	c	c	c	c
Fuji Heavy	c			c			c
Toyota	c		c	p/c	p/c[a]	p/c	p/c
Hino	c	c	c	c	c	c	c
Daihatsu	p/c		p/c	p/c		p/c	c
Mazda	p/c	p/c		p/c		c	p/c
Mitsubishi	c	p/c	c	p/c	p/c	p/c	p/c
Honda	p			p		p	p
Isuzu		c	c	p/c	c	p/c	p/c
Suzuki	c		c	p/c		p/c	c

SOURCE: Nissan Motor Co. 1987.

NOTE: PRC = China; p = passenger vehicle production; c = commercial vehicle production.

[a] As of 1987 Toyota's plant was not in operation, its local owner having gone bankrupt. Toyota is counted as operating in the Philippines, however, since the firm was involved in negotiations to take over ownership of the plant.

ing domestic market. Firms were also pushed into the market by competitive pressures among the large industrial groups, or *keiretsu,* to which some of them belonged. Such competition took the form of "one set-ism," in which each large industrial group "acquired or created within it a full complement of companies covering all the government-designated growth industries, regardless of whether it made business sense to do so."[47]

Japan's Ministry of International Trade and Industry (MITI) did strive to reduce the number of firms for fear that such a competitive market structure would leave the industry inefficient and weak in the face of newly entering foreign imports.[48] Some mergers occurred in the mid 1960s, but MITI's role was largely irrelevant to the process. Nissan took over Prince in August 1966, when the latter was facing severe financial difficulties. Hino, also financially ailing, concluded a business tie-up with Toyota in September 1966, as did Daihatsu in November 1966. MITI also attempted to strengthen the domestic industry against foreign competition in the late 1960s by inducing the firms to consolidate and reduce prices. These efforts failed, as the smaller firms opposed the ministry's efforts to reorganize the industry around two large groups, probably Toyota and Nissan.[49] Mitsubishi opted to maintain its position by linking up with Chrysler in 1969. Isuzu and Suzuki (with GM) and Toyo Kogyo (with Ford) also followed the path of linking up with foreign capital.

As a result, Japan has ten automakers (table 4.6), more than any other country in the world. These can be divided into the "big two" (Toyota and Nissan, which includes Nissan Diesel), the "medium three" (Mazda, or Toyo Kogyo; Honda; Mitsubishi), and the "small five" (Suzuki; Subaru; Hino; Daihatsu; Isuzu). There is some degree of specialization and coordination among these firms. Hino, Isuzu, and Nissan Diesel specialize in trucks, while Suzuki and Daihatsu emphasize light cars. Groups composed of Toyota, Hino, and Daihatsu on the one hand and Nissan, Nissan Diesel, and Fuji Heavy Industries on the other do engage in some coordination of production and joint research. But the market remains intensely competitive as Nissan fights Toyota for the top spot and the others attempt to move up.

Since the early 1960s this struggle for market share has been reflected in the industry's low number of cartel violations and in its increasing use of product differentiation.[50] Exports, however, were the most important

Table 4.6.   Japanese Automakers, 1983

	Vehicles Produced	Sales (U.S. $billions)	Profits (U.S. $millions)
Toyota	3,272,335	20.6	848
Nissan[a]	2,515,012	14.5	408
Mazda	1,171,350	5.7	108
Honda	1,032,440	7.4	132
Mitsubishi	974,705	4.5	53
Suzuki	631,310	2.3	28
Fuji[b]	540,680	2.4	60
Daihatsu	530,296	1.8	21
Isuzu	390,701	2.9	22
Hino	52,129	1.7	20

SOURCES: JAMA; chart in *Asiaweek*, September 28, 1984, 54.
[a]Includes Nissan Diesel, 45 percent owned.
[b]Produces Subaru.

outlet of interfirm rivalries. The resulting competitive structure drove the companies relentlessly to seek ways to achieve greater efficiency. This intense intergroup competition, supplanted by the entry into the market of companies such as Honda, provided the basis for domestic competition, which spilled over into export competition.[51]

Why, then, did this competition spill over so strongly into Southeast Asia?

The Attraction of Southeast Asia

Southeast Asia's early attraction for Japanese auto firms lay partly in the region's general growth (see table 3.1) and in its auto markets in particular (table 4.7). The ASEAN Four played an important role in the industry's early stages, receiving 22 percent of Japan's vehicle exports from 1960 through 1964. Geography also made Southeast Asia a logical focus of early Japanese automotive expansion. Japan's proximity to, and wartime position as occupier of, Southeast Asia provided contacts and encouraged a view of Southeast Asia as a strategic buffer for Japanese firms. The companies feared that if U.S. and European firms controlled neighboring markets, the Japanese market itself would be endangered.[52]

Table 4.7. Average Annual Growth of Vehicle Ownership,
1970–1980 (Percentages)

Philippines	8.6
Indonesia	13.0
Malaysia	8.3
Thailand	9.1
Singapore	3.9

SOURCE: Sinclair 1982, table 3.

Product compatibility also played a role. The product-cycle theory presumes that an innovating country will export to, and eventually invest in, markets similar to its own. During the 1960s and early 1970s Japanese firms emphasized the production of heavy-duty trucks and small, durable passenger cars (often used as taxis)—precisely the kinds of vehicles needed in Southeast Asia after World War II. In addition, the ASEAN markets constituted a testing and training ground for Japanese vehicles and personnel in preparation for penetration of markets in advanced countries.

These early auto experiences conform to product-cycle descriptions of Japan as a "middle country"—one that exported first to LDCs and not to other advanced countries.[53] But during the 1970s Japan's market strengths, along with its exports and investments, moved more in line with those of developed markets. By 1983 Japanese vehicle exports to the ASEAN Four had declined to roughly 8 percent of the global total.[54] How do we then account for the fact that despite costly local demands for expanding auto manufacture, Japanese firms not only have not quit ASEAN markets, but have grudgingly complied with these demands?

Part of the answer is that the ASEAN countries have continued to be the most important *developing country* markets for Japanese vehicle exports. In 1982 three of the ASEAN Four were the only developing nations among the top twenty export destinations of the Japanese auto industry.[55] From 1980 to 1983 the five ASEAN countries received roughly 13 percent of Japan's total exports of auto parts worldwide.[56] And from 1980 to 1987 East Asia continued to be the largest LDC regional market for Japanese vehicle exports.[57]

The significance of these figures lies in the importance of exports for Japanese auto firms overall. Exports accounted for between 50 and 54 percent of total Japanese production from 1980 to 1987, and in view of the auto industry's central role in Japanese manufacturing,[58] pessimistic predictions for OECD market growth, and the rosy assumptions of East Asian auto expansion noted earlier, the importance of the ASEAN Four for Japanese firms will probably only increase. Thus Toyota, for example, the least international of the Japanese assemblers, moved to expand its ASEAN presence in the early 1980s as a response to declining demand and rising import barriers in Western auto markets.[59]

More specific features of Japanese corporate strategies reinforce the impact of these long-term market considerations. Japanese auto firms incorporate long-range market concerns into short-term investment decisions. An extensive comparative study of Japanese and German auto firms operating in Indonesia concluded that the Japanese time frame for returns on investment is often ten to twenty years, much longer than that of their German counterparts.[60] And when asked how he could justify his firm's production facilities in small Asian markets, a truck firm official responded that Japanese automakers "rejected the strict cost-benefit approach proposed by your former Secretary of Defense Robert McNamara." The level of interfirm competition, he stated, compelled an emphasis on long-term market share, not short-term profits.[61]

This long-term perspective is strengthened by the Japanese view that investments in the individual ASEAN countries are necessary as footholds in a yet unclear regional division of labor. The Japanese firms do not expect each of the ASEAN Four to develop its own independent auto-manufacturing industry. But ASEAN efforts to promote regional complementarity in auto manufacture, initiated in the early 1970s, have recently begun to yield concrete results, with Mitsubishi and Toyota unveiling regional components schemes.[62] In addition, the possibility of Japanese firms' ceding entry-market niches to South Korea and Taiwan opens the possibility that the ASEAN Four, whether individually or through a complementarity scheme, will supply parts for these less costly and less advanced vehicles.

Finally, competition for ASEAN market shares is intensified by the importance of the ASEAN countries to certain Japanese firms, especially the Mitsubishi Motors Corporation (MMC), undoubtedly the most aggressive of the Japanese firms in the region. This is in part because of MMC's desire to compensate for its fifth-place standing in the Japanese domestic market through successful foreign operations. But Mitsubishi has seen its market opportunities in the developed countries reduced by distribution problems with Chrysler and by Voluntary Export Restraint agreements in the United States that have adversely affected the smaller Japanese firms. Consequently, the Far East and Australasia account for between 30 and 37 percent of the company's total exports, second only to those of Isuzu among the Japanese firms with regard to the significance of Asian markets.[63] Finally, the interests of the broader Mitsubishi group may encourage highly aggressive strategies on the part of Mitsubishi Motors.

The Sources of Japanese Auto Success in the ASEAN Countries

Japan's dominance of the ASEAN auto industries has been a function of advantages specific to the region, business strategies, financial strength, and flexible production practices suited to small markets.

Advantages Specific to the Region. ASEAN's proximity to Japan has allowed highly efficient liaison between subsidiaries and parent companies. This has been important because Japanese management practices are "highly centralized and rely extensively on consultation and constant interaction for decision-making".[64] Contacts established during World War II have also helped the firms. For example, the Thai-language abilities and prominent public role of Toyota's manager of Thai operations during the early-to-mid 1980s reflected his wartime experience in Thailand. Finally, "tied" reparations money and other forms of economic aid facilitated early Japanese penetration of certain ASEAN markets.[65]

Business Strategies. One source of Japanese auto success in the ASEAN countries is their willingness and ability to move quickly with investment implementation, even in nations as bureaucratized and nationalist as Indonesia.[66] Japanese firms have also been willing to accept equity restrictions common in ASEAN, whereas U.S. firms have generally strongly preferred majority ownership.[67] These methods have been supplemented by a conscious Japanese effort to develop approaches to auto investment suitable to the industrialization strategies of developing countries. Until the mid 1980s this generally meant adapting to, and attempting to moderate, the ASEAN Four's ISI strategies.[68] But as discussed below, the Japanese were flexible enough to comply with early Philippine export policies, and since the mid 1980s they have moved to accommodate more widespread export efforts in the region.

These strategies have been supplemented by Japanese ties to each of the ASEAN Four's largest economic groups.[69] Links with reliable and powerful local partners, aptly termed "local capital umbrellas" by a former head of Toyota operations in Thailand,[70] are deemed politically and economically indispensable by the Japanese. These linkages are facilitated by impressive Japanese knowledge of local political and economic structures. The auto firms, most of whom maintain Southeast Asian divisions in Tokyo, encourage proficiency in the local language and extended tours of duty by their employees. In addition, the firms have access to an impressive information network composed of Japanese banks and state-backed research organizations.[71] Finally, the ASEAN nations' increasing desire to learn from Japanese industrial successes and the rising number of Southeast Asians educated in Japan provide networks of potential information and influence. Malaysian Prime Minister Mahathir's "Look East" policy, for example, has allegedly provided special opportunities to Japanese investors, including encouraging the government to look to a Japanese firm for its national car plan.[72] The Japanese education of the former Thai Finance Minister Sommai Huntrakul is presumed to have resulted in pro-Japanese decisions in auto policy.[73] And in Indonesia, Persada, an organization of Indonesian graduates of Japanese universities, provides the Japanese community with an expanding network of contacts.

With auto policy in the region renegotiated "on almost a daily basis,"[74] the Japanese have made good legal as well as extralegal use of such networks. While obviously impossible to quantify, the auto firms' willingness and ability to provide funds and blandishments through informal channels is widely, if not publicly, acknowledged.[75] Such offerings take various forms, including simple under-the-table cash payments, trips to and special treatment in Japan, directorships, special stock offerings, presents for wives, and so on. The specific targets vary, but they include American consultants, mid-level local officials, top political leadership, and royalty. In some cases, the objective of such payments is to influence a specific decision by dissuading political decision makers from following the advice of technical staff. In other cases, such as Japanese contributions to charities favored by the queen of Thailand, the purpose is the promotion of general goodwill toward the Japanese firms and their general access to local decision makers.

This is not to deny that U.S. firms have employed similar strategies, at times successfully. As discussed in the next chapter, Christina Ford's relations with Imelda Marcos and the Ford Motor Company's payments to members of the Philippine Congress during the early 1970s were critical to Ford's participation in the Philippine PCMP. But with the 1976 Corrupt Political Practices Act and a much weaker organizational presence, the formal and informal political activities of U.S. firms pale in comparison with those of the Japanese.

Nor is this to deny that the Japanese have encountered their own problems with local partners and politics. Nissan, for example, historically focused its overseas activities on the industrialized countries and devoted relatively little money and manpower to Southeast Asia. The company tended to rely on the Marubeni Trading Company to establish local political and marketing bases. As company officials now acknowledge, trading companies may be well suited for financing, but they do not necessarily adapt well to the requirements of knocked-down assembly and localized manufacturing.[76] Partly as a result, Nissan has found itself with a very weak local base in the Philippines and Indonesia. Nor are more thorough and careful firms entirely safe from the shifting sands of ASEAN domestic politics. Mitsubishi's position in Indonesia was moderately weakened by the downfall of its partner Ibnu Sutowo, former head of Pertamina, the Indonesian state oil company. Toyota suffered a major loss when its formerly powerful Philippine partner Ricardo Silverio lost favor with Marcos and was declared bankrupt. And in linking up with one of Malaysia's larger private groups—United Motor Works—in the early 1980s, Toyota failed to anticipate the government's decision to promote its own national car. But none of these setbacks has resulted in any of the Japanese firms actually quitting the ASEAN markets.

Once established, the Japanese car makers have distinguished themselves by their highly active market research, extensive sales promotion, and rapid responsiveness to customer complaints. Japanese auto salesmen and service staff in Indonesia, for example, visited dealers eight times more frequently than competitors of other nationalities.[77]

Financial Strength. The customer attention discussed above is expensive, especially during initial market penetration, when profits are low. Dealers and subdealers selling Japanese products have been able to sustain short-term losses for long-term gains. Financing has often come through

Table 4.8.   Long-Term Debt as a Percentage of Long-Term Capital

	1971	1973	1975	1977	1979	1981
Honda	57.8	51.4	52.9	39.5	32.3	19.7
Nissan	37.7	24.5	25.4	15.5	14.2	16.1
Toyota	11.0	5.0	2.1	0.0	0.0	0.0
GM	5.1	5.7	8.5	6.3	4.4	17.7
Ford	12.6	13.2	19.4	13.8	10.9	26.9

SOURCES: Anderson 1982; Altshuler et al. 1984, 154.

suppliers' credits extended by a *sogo shosha* (trading company) representing the assembler.[78] Trading companies have also helped to finance initial investments in local production, as reflected in Mitsubishi's partnership with Nissho Iwai in the Philippines.

A second important source of financial support has been the state-affiliated Export-Import Bank (Exim Bank) of Japan. Most (80 percent) of Exim Bank loans are offered to Japanese corporations, with the rest going largely to foreign firms for the purchase of Japanese goods and services. Exim loans totaled almost 30 percent of the transport industry's overseas investment in the 1951–67 period, 24 percent from 1968 to 1973, and 28 percent from 1974 to 1980.[79]

Perhaps most important, the growing financial strength of Japanese auto assemblers themselves has facilitated expansion in Southeast Asia through suppliers' credits and capital investment. Japanese auto firms were burdened with high debt-equity ratios during the industry's early years, but the assemblers' impressive growth resulted in declining debt-equity ratios during the 1970s (table 4.8). Significant variation exists among the firms,[80] yet by the early 1980s the financial resources of the top five Japanese assemblers "allowed them to break loose from the government's dictates."[81] In sharp contrast with the "degradation of the U.S. capital structure," the Japanese firms are now not only the best equipped to endure market fluctuations but "also hold the resources to restructure their operations for multinational production."[82]

It should be noted that such funds are often made available to overseas parts firms as well as to assemblers and dealers. For example, one of the larger Malaysian parts firms required M$40 million to expand from con struction glass into auto safety glass in the early 1970s. Since local funds were unavailable at the time, the firm had no choice but to avail itself of Japanese loans and equity purchases.[83]

Flexible Production and Small Markets. Japan's major contribution to auto manufacture has been in process technology.[84] More specifically, Japanese firms have exhibited an impressive ability to manufacture small numbers of different vehicles and models efficiently. Domestically, through just-in-time and *kan ban* production, as well as the rapid modification of jigs and dies, Japanese auto firms produce nearly three times as many bodies and engines per unit as their U.S. counterparts.[85] Whereas U.S. firms have concentrated on larger LDC markets, the overseas transfer of these innovations has allowed the Japanese to move into smaller, fragmented markets[86] such as those found in the ASEAN region.

In Toyota's Thai assembly plant, for example, a welding jig for main body construction can be changed in 25–30 minutes. Large stamping dies (which stamp or press flat metal into actual body parts) are changed in 10–15 minutes, just slightly more slowly than in Japanese plants. Toyota can consequently change models every twenty units.[87] The range of models assembled is limited not by the plant's capacity but by the availability of components in Japan, the way in which components are shipped, the depreciation of jigs and dies, and the level of localization required. These factors, both individually and in concert, have facilitated Japan's market dominance over its Western competitors. They also bear on the potential for ASEAN bargaining leverage.

Japanese Firms and Potential Bargaining Strength

Japanese Interests through the Mid 1980s: Opposition to Overseas Manufacture

Through the mid 1980s the Japanese automakers have been distinctly "reluctant multinationals."[88] This reluctance can be attributed to three components of the Japanese manufacturing strengths discussed above— capital-intensive production, tight links to component firms, and intense interfirm rivalry—and merits special note. Japanese automakers are highly capital-intensive, even relative to an industry whose overall level of labor utilization is already quite low. By the early 1980s the Japanese auto-makers needed only around 65 percent of the labor required in the U.S. industry to produce a comparable product, and roughly 30 percent fewer hours than the West German average.[89] Such figures do not necessarily in-hibit Japanese overseas assembly, since such activities utilize machinery transported from Japan in which an investment has already been sunk. But they do not encourage increased overseas manufacture in countries whose major attraction is cheap labor. Indeed, since cheap labor generally reflects weak technological infrastructure (numbers of engineers, levels of com-puterization, etc.), low-wage ASEAN countries have held little attraction for Japanese firms.

Japanese automakers are also highly dependent on their parts suppliers. The just-in-time and *kan ban* systems require tight coordination with in-novative outside supplier firms. In Japan, assemblers expect just-in-time parts deliveries based on hourly delivery instructions. Whereas the fre-quency of delivery varies from once to sixteen times daily, the trend has been "toward increasing delivery frequency and shorter lead times from indications of final instructions to delivery."[90]

Such deliveries of newer and increasingly sophisticated parts require that parts makers continually expand their capabilities in production tech-nology. This is encouraged through close geographical, technical, person-nel, and equity linkages between assemblers and parts firms. Such ties are in turn facilitated by cooperative associations of parts makers *(kyoryokukai)* organized by each assembler. The relationship between assemblers and parts firms is not, however, exclusive. The former generally procure each kind of part from more than two suppliers, with one firm coming from outside the *kyoryokukai,* thereby locking parts makers into unending com-petition with each other. Conversely, to promote economies of scale and efficiency, the assemblers encourage affiliated parts makers to produce for other assemblers.

Such close links between automakers and competitive, competent parts makers are difficult to establish in LDCs such as the ASEAN Four. Indig-enous parts firms are often technologically weak, while poor roads and other physical infrastructure impede the kinds of contact and transport re-quired by just-in-time delivery.

Interfirm rivalries exacerbate the impact of highly capital-intensive manufacturing and reliance on strong parts firms. Even if the automakers can be persuaded to relocate manufacturing operations overseas, the generally small and fragmented LDC markets impede large production runs and efficient economies of scale. The market logically requires some cooperative production arrangements. Yet the intensely competitive Japanese firms are loath to accept such joint activities.

From the Japanese automakers' perspective, these factors have meant that expanded auto manufacture in LDCs reduces competitiveness, efficiency, and quality, while raising costs. Increased localization makes it more difficult to duplicate Japanese model changes necessary to compete. Toyota officials estimate that at 20 percent LC levels their operations in Thailand can follow major model changes in Japan by one or two months. At 45 percent localization the time lag increases to around one year because of the need for longer trial runs guided by technical staff sent from Japan.[91] One Japanese firm estimated that engines produced in Southeast Asia were three times the Japanese cost, with production costs for car bodies double those in Japan. Indeed, the same firm said that but for incentives and performance requirements for localization imposed by Indonesia, it would "probably throw the whole [Indonesian] production unit into the Java Sea."[92]

Sources of Japanese Leverage

The kinds of leverage stressed by the structuralist approach to bargaining have effectively reinforced the automakers' opposition to LDC manufacturing. The auto TNCs are able to raise technological and financial entry barriers through a combination of market fragmentation, quality control, and direct cost manipulation. The effective business practices and financial strengths discussed earlier have facilitated the entrenchment of numerous Japanese firms and makes in small markets, even under the most uneconomical conditions. Additionally, their flexible technologies allow the Japanese to create numerous and changing product niches. When one adds to these resources intensive auto advertising in the ASEAN Four,[93] the result is make and model proliferations that inhibit the development of LDC firms. In Thailand, for instance, the Japanese pursue what one assembler termed "day-by-day innovations"—the frequent implementation of changes originating in Japan. In one case, the Japanese introduced plastic bumpers into the Thai market despite the fact that local parts firms could only supply metal bumpers.[94] Two Philippine cases provide further illustration:

• In discussing the problems of local plastic parts producers, a Philippine assembly official "frankly stated that one had to produce probably 1,000 units before one could adjust a mould and start producing plastic parts of satisfactory quality, and yet the actual amount of the assembler's order was often only 150 units or so at a time."[95]

• Francisco Motors was an early Philippine manufacturer of the "jeepney"—a modified U.S. army surplus jeep used as a combination taxi and bus throughout the country. The jeepney's relatively simple technology, its reconditioned engines, and its widespread use seemed to provide the basis for large-scale economies and a gradual expansion of Francisco's manufacturing skills.[96] But the competitive market compelled Francisco to accept foreign partner's suggestion of new engines and power train items (imported from Japan) instead of reconditioned items.[97]

Even if local (or non-Japanese) parts firms believe they have met a wide range of product specifications, Japanese assemblers are in a position to reject such goods on grounds of poor quality and/or high prices. Such rejections are facilitated by Japanese production processes designed specifically for the assembler or its affiliated suppliers.

TNCs are able to resist rationalization and localization by manipulating the direct costs of such efforts. Where local pressure to cut particular models is especially strong, the Japanese have been known to respond with threats of politically costly layoffs (see chapter 6). TNC control of deletion allowances constitutes an especially potent way of making localization uneconomical. The deletion allowance refers to the price reduction allowed by the TNC on an imported CKD pack when certain parts are produced in the host country and thus "deleted" from the imported pack. By refusing to reduce the total CKD price by an amount equal to the price of the original part (thus keeping the deletion allowance low), the Japanese ensure that increased localization leads to higher prices.[98]

All of the preceding practices facilitate what might be termed an "our hands are tied" syndrome consistent with structuralist views. They allow the Japanese to profess support for localization even as the automakers create (and complain about) cost and quality obstacles to that same localization.

While these obstacles are formidable, they coexist with several sources of potential leverage on the part of the host country.

Host Country Leverage

Interfirm competition is, of course, the primary source of LDC bargaining strength vis-à-vis the Japanese auto firms. The need to defend market share in a dynamic and growing region was responsible not only for the aggressive Mitsubishi agreeing to a Malaysian national car effort in the early 1980s. It also accounts for such cases as the highly cautious and domestic-based Toyota building engines in the Philippines for re-export in the early 1970s as part of the Progressive Car Manufacturing Program.[99]

This rivalry does not preclude collusion among the auto TNCs to stave off either the formulation or implementation of localization efforts. Japanese firms acknowledge that issues such as tariffs on machinery, model changes, and LC increases are renegotiated "on almost a daily basis" in the Asia-Pacific region.[100] And as the following chapters demonstrate, interfirm cooperation against host countries does occur during such exchanges. But such TNC collusion is sporadic, ad hoc, and fragile. It is undermined by the same rivalries that make the automakers trade association, the Japan Automobile Manufacturers' Association (JAMA), a timid coordinating body rather than one capable of mobilizing and leading its members.[101]

Interfirm rivalry can serve to compel grudging Japanese acceptance of LDC localization and export measures. But actual *compliance* with such measures involves significant cost increases. And despite their financial strengths and long-term perspectives, the Japanese automakers are under pressure to keep costs down and efficiency levels up. Efforts by the production/engineering divisions of Japanese automakers to reduce the number of models and specifications marketed overseas are one indication of such pressure.[102]

The question then is this: does the auto industry provide opportunities for the Japanese to comply with localization requirements but reduce the cost of doing so? Although limited in number, some such opportunities exist. First, on the demand side.

• Standardized parts usable in different models (such as radiators and brake drums) may be manufactured overseas, while the more "unique" components designed specifically for individual models continue to be produced in Japan.[103] As noted, Mitsubishi has pursued such production on a regional scale: MMC subsidiaries in the Philippines and Malaysia supply transmissions and body parts to Thailand, while Thailand will soon supply bumpers to the Philippines and laminated glass to Malaysia. There also seems to be potential for expanding the definition of *standardized* to include parts exchangeable between makes as well as models. This is reflected in a gradual, but clear, tendency for Japanese firms to share production facilities both at home and overseas.[104]

• LDC sites may also be compatible with the production of major components for older models and/or market-entry models less attractive to Japanese producers. Mitsubishi evidently intends to shift manufacture of some older engine types to Southeast Asia (especially Indonesia), while Toyota's plans call for the manufacture and reexport of a low-cost pickup truck engine in Thailand and a basic utility vehicle from Indonesia.[105]

• There are opportunities for LDCs to manufacture production machinery (such as dies and jigs) either no longer made elsewhere or expensive to produce in small quantities in Japan.[106]

The magnitude of these opportunities is influenced by factors encouraging the supply or diffusion of automotive technology. One is the long-standing and extensive overseas operations of Japanese auto parts firms.[107] Guided, but not dominated, by the assemblers and anxious to expand markets, these parts firms provide an important potential source of information to LDC producers.

These parts firms are contributing to a regional automotive division of labor through which new sources of technology become available to the ASEAN Four. Since the 1970s Japanese firms have supported automotive development in South Korea and Taiwan. As these countries learn from the Japanese and ascend the auto-manufacturing ladder, they become capable of providing the ASEAN Four with less complex automotive technologies. This process shows every sign of accelerating as the Japanese move upmarket, ceding the production of downmarket or entry-level vehicles to the Asian NICs.[108]

The diffusion of production has been promoted not only by mobile parts firms and the increasingly developed Asian NICs but by the Japanese government itself, which since the early-to-mid 1970s has tended to encourage Japanese firms to promote manufacturing in Southeast Asia. The support has intensified in recent years owing to continuing trade disputes with the United States, Tokyo's more general fear that its trade surpluses will destabilize world trade, and the government's calculation that "a given amount of industrial investment in Japan today is likely to generate fewer jobs and thus create less long-term economic welfare than the same amount of money spent almost anywhere else where a Japanese company might choose to build a factory."[109] But even during the 1970s Tokyo responded to ASEAN outbursts of anti-Japanese sentiment with large-scale aid offers and pressure on Japanese firms to adapt to the area's economic nationalism.[110]

I am not arguing here that Tokyo has sided with ASEAN auto efforts against its own automakers. Bennett and Sharpe have noted Tokyo's intervention in favor of Nissan in Mexico.[111] I instead wish to cast doubt on assumptions that Japanese auto firms benefit from extensive state backing in their negotiations with the ASEAN Four. Generally speaking, there is little evidence that the Japanese government throws its weight around in support of its own firms.[112] Such backing is especially unlikely for the automakers.[113] Auto industry—government ties have historically not been harmonious. While benefiting from protection, localization measures, and state-sponsored reorganization of the parts producers, the assembly industry was never targeted by government plans.[114] The industry, as noted, successfully resisted MITI's rationalization efforts; indeed, MITI's policies would probably have dampened the very interfirm competition that accounts for much of the firms' success.[115] The auto industry is consequently something of an outsider with respect to peak business organizations linking state and private sector such as Keidanren. In addition, the large number of intensely competitive assemblers inhibits state support for any particular firm. Several auto executives noted that the government in general and embassies in particular were quite anxious to avoid charges of favoritism.[116] The region's dynamism and economic importance to Japan[117] also discourage Tokyo from interventions likely to generate nationalist outbursts and possibly more general destabilization.

Finally, since the mid 1980s global monetary and trade developments have enhanced Southeast Asia's potential as an automotive export base (and accelerated the growth of a regional division of labor in the process). The yen's appreciation has attracted Japanese parts firms to the ASEAN Four, since their currencies are pegged to the U.S. dollar.[118] U.S. and Canadian trade barriers have encouraged this process. With Japan facing voluntary export restraints and the four Asian NICs no longer benefiting from General System of Preference status,[119] the ASEAN Four are well positioned to serve as bases from which to circumvent protection.[120]

Differentiated and Shifting Structural Leverage

We can now return to one of the questions posed at the end of chapter 3: How do we account for the auto policy achievements of the ASEAN Four? Do they reflect host country leverage over the auto TNCs? Or were they rather a function of shifts in TNC preferences, which then converged with ASEAN auto objectives?

Until the mid 1980s ASEAN auto objectives were strongly inconsistent with the interests of Japanese automakers. These firms were reluctant multinationals because the very ingredients of their global success—capital-intensive production and tightly linked suppliers—encouraged them to manufacture at home. Such preferences were bolstered by resources consistent with structuralist views of bargaining: the capacity to become well entrenched in the ASEAN auto industries at low levels of local content, and the ability to compete through product differentiation so as to raise technological entry barriers to local auto manufacture. The TNCs' structural power lay in their ability to preclude certain options by making them costly. In this context, ASEAN achievements reflect leverage that stems in turn from the intense competition among Japanese firms for market share. Had the TNCs opposed ASEAN auto efforts in unison, local auto policies would have probably disappeared within a few years. But this counterfactual is irrelevant because fierce competition is so central to the international auto industry, and especially the Japanese part of it. Groups of firms may be viewed as a bloc with regard to broad preferences; but it is inappropriate to treat them collectively with regard to their specific market strategies.[121]

But competition is not a sufficient condition for such leverage. Compliance with localization also reflects the auto industry's differentiated demand structure, in which older, standardized parts and production equipment compatible with ASEAN manufacturing capacities remain in the market. The availability of technology for such items is in turn a function of supply factors: the mobility of Japanese parts firms; the ability of South Korea and Taiwan to provide the ASEAN Four with support for less complex auto parts production within a growing automotive division of labor; and the Japanese government's support, however slight, for a shift of auto manufacturing to other parts of East Asia.

Since the mid 1980s, currency shifts and U.S. limits on Japanese auto exports have made the ASEAN Four increasingly attractive to Japanese automakers. Clearly, the size of their markets and their weak technological capacities preclude a full-scale auto industry in any of the ASEAN Four. But their potential for increased localization and exports seems to have expanded.[122] Does this represent a convergence of interests? Will increased auto production and exports from the ASEAN Four be a function of Japanese preferences rather than of ASEAN leverage? To some degree it will. But stressing convergence can hide two other significant points. First, the fact that the Japanese have begun to shift operations to Southeast Asia is in part a consequence of prior ASEAN achievements in promoting local manufacturing capacity. Put another way, previous ASEAN auto efforts have had their own cumulative, structural effect: they have altered the range of options open to the Japanese by giving them manufacturing opportunities they would not otherwise have had.

Emphasizing convergence can also lead us to gloss over the fact that some countries are better able than others to take advantage of these new opportunities. Indeed, as seen in the previous chapter, some have done more than others to create opportunities, having better exploited bargaining potential inherent in the industry since the early 1970s. Some have also done better at one stage in their auto policy efforts than at other stages. Accounting for cross-national and temporal variation in performance now becomes our principal task. An examination of one possible set of explanations for cross-national differences in bargaining performance follows. More specifically, what is the possibility that national abilities to achieve auto policy goals vary with the structural economic features of the ASEAN Four?[123]

Testing Economic Explanations of National Performance

Two possible economic explanations of variation in national performance are intuitively plausible. One holds that large, growing markets and political stability have a special attraction for Japanese auto firms, thus enhancing a host country's potential leverage. The second argues that a host

Table 4.9.   Indicators of Automobile Market Size

	Human Population, 1981 (millions)	Vehicles, 1980 (thousands)	Population per Vehicle, 1980
Indonesia	149.5	1,195	127.0
Malaysia	14.2	730	19.0
Philippines	49.6	1,050	46.0
Thailand	48.0	931	50.0
South Korea	38.9	528	74.0

SOURCES: Human population, World Bank *World Development Report*, 1983; number of vehicles and population per vehicle, Bittlingmayer 1983, 7.

Table 4.10.   Percentage Increase in Motor Vehicle Population

	1960–70	1970–80	1982–95 (projected)
Indonesia	8.3	13.0	11.0
Malaysia	9.8	8.3	7.7
Philippines	10.9	8.6	9.2
Thailand	12.3	9.1	9.4
South Korea	—	15.3	11.5

SOURCE: Bittlingmayer 1983, 5–6, projections of future vehicle population growth based on projected increases in income and current vehicle densities.

country's economic capacities influence its ability to make use of potential leverage.[124]

The size and growth of their markets have been cited as important sources of the automotive bargaining leverage exercised by host countries in Latin America.[125] This does not, however, seem to be the case for Japanese firms operating in East or Southeast Asia.[126]

There is, first of all, no correlation between market size and intensity of inter-TNC competition. Japanese firms involved in Indonesia have not been less numerous or less competitive than those in the other three ASEAN countries, despite the very different sizes of their present automobile markets and predicted growth rates (see tables 4.9 and 4.10). More important, there is no correlation between market size and growth on the one hand and actual automotive performance on the other. Thailand is the strongest of the four with regard to performance, but neither its human and vehicle populations nor its actual or potential growth rates put it first among the ASEAN Four. The point is reinforced by a comparison of Indonesia and South Korea. Both countries enjoyed very high automotive growth rates during the 1970s (over 15 percent for Korea and 13 percent for Indonesia); and both had predicted growth rates of around 11 percent. Indonesia's population is almost four times that of South Korea, and its total number of vehicles in 1980 was twice South Korea's. In fact, South Korea's vehicle population was smaller than those of any of the four ASEAN states in 1980. Yet it was precisely during the 1970s that South Korea clearly outdistanced each of the ASEAN Four with respect to national automobile manufacturing capacity.

This lack of correlation between market size and performance may prove to be a function of the still relatively low localization and export levels among the ASEAN Four. As risks and financial requirements grow, so may the Japanese sensitivity to market size. Yet South Korea's automotive expansion casts strong doubt on this proposition. The features noted earlier—financial strength, long-term vision, and adaptability to smaller markets—would seem to allow Japanese firms the freedom of basing their compliance decisions on factors other than the size of the host country's market. [127]

A host country's level of political risk (i.e., government instability and more micropolitical changes in the regulatory system) might also help explain variation in national abilities to make use of potential bargaining leverage. Micropolitical risks seem to predominate in ASEAN, especially when compared to Latin America, [128] but the Philippines has nonetheless experienced important changes of regime.

Japanese auto firms seem less concerned with political risks than their U.S. counterparts. In terms of macropolitical risks, Japanese firms continue tenaciously to maintain operations in the Philippines where an unstable political context and declining market led to the departure of Ford and GM. GM's concern with micropolitical risks is reflected in its political risk scale emphasizing the predictability of policy and regulatory factors. A GM spokesman, for instance, complained that South Korea's efforts to rationalize the auto industry not only posed "severe problems over the issues of management control" but also represented "a contradiction between GM's 'world car' strategies and South Korea's national goals, and a change in the Korean business environment that may be damaging to

GM's interests."[129] In contrast, Mitsubishi has had no problem adapting to shifts in the Korean policy environment and to Hyundai's managerial control. More generally, a 1983 Japan Automobile Manufacturers' Association evaluation of ASEAN automotive prospects does not even mention political risk factors.[130]

What of the bargaining impact of a host country's economic capacities? It is reasonable, for example, to assume that a host country's industrial expertise may influence its ability to benefit and exact concessions from foreign investors. A country with a well-trained population is presumably best suited to absorb and modify technology from foreign investors, as well as to understand and regulate TNC activities. However, existing information suggests that such expertise is highest in the ASEAN country ranked last in performance—the Philippines. By the early 1960s Philippine engineering and metalworking firms were considered more advanced even than today's Asian NICs and were selling locally made intermediate machinery to Thailand and Pakistan.[131] The country's general managerial capacity was also impressive, at least numerically, with Philippine managers in 1971 accounting for 300,000 of Southeast Asia's total of 748,000.[132] And in 1979 foreign corporations ranked Philippine industrial expertise highest of the ASEAN Four and equal to that of Singapore.[133]

Levels of education might also influence local bargaining leverage. As Stephen Kobrin suggests, education should influence technical, administrative, and managerial capacities, which in turn enhance the confidence and ability of local actors to regulate foreign enterprises.[134] Yet again we find at best only a weak correlation. The Philippines ranked first with regard to secondary and higher education levels for both 1965 and 1984, while Thailand was third and fourth among the ASEAN Four in secondary education but second in higher education (table 4.11). The relative educational levels of Malaysia and Indonesia come closer to their performance rankings.[135]

Finally, a host country's bargaining leverage may be influenced by its long-term financial resources. Contrasting levels of petroleum resources and debt are potentially critical in this regard.[136] The large crude oil and natural gas reserves of Indonesia and Malaysia bring in funds[137] that can reduce local dependence on external sources, help weather short-term inefficiencies, and pay off domestic interests otherwise hurt by particular

Table 4.11.   Education Levels of the ASEAN Four and South Korea

ASEAN Auto Performance Ranking	Enrollment in School as Percentage of Age Group			
	Secondary		Higher Education	
	1965	1984	1965	1984
Thailand (1)	14	30	2	23
Malaysia (2)	28	53	2	6
Indonesia (3)	12	39	1	7
Philippines (4)	41	68	19	29
South Korea	35	91	6	26

SOURCE: World Bank, *World Development Report*, 1987.

policies. Petroleum reserves can also bolster local auto markets by maintaining fuel supplies.

However, only in the case of Malaysia is there a correspondence between petroleum revenues and performance ranking. This does not preclude the possibility of a surge in petroleum-based revenues bolstering host country leverage at a particular time. It suggests rather that, as is the case with other factors discussed above, the long-term cross-national impact of petroleum revenues on bargaining leverage is weak.

The preceding factors—market size, political risk, economic resources—are thus poor predictors of actual bargaining strength. Our focus must shift to political explanations of bargaining leverage, to the factors affecting a host country's willingness and ability to mobilize resources and exploit the auto industry's opportunities: the characteristics of local governments, private sectors, and the relations between the two. The following four chapters evaluate the impact of these factors by tracing the major bargaining episodes in each of the four ASEAN auto industries.

5

Malaysia

Ethnic division is the central characteristic that shapes Malaysia's industrial development efforts. Majority ethnic Malays dominate the state, while minority, but numerically significant, Chinese (over one-third of the population) dominate the economy. Clear social distinctions between the two groups exacerbate this imbalance. The government initiated a major effort to bolster the Malay economic position during the 1970s through the preferential programs of the New Economic Policy (NEP), but its achievements have been disappointing. By the late 1970s Malay frustrations, coupled with concern over the country's continued dependence on imports, spawned a major new industrialization effort. Prime Minister Mahathir initiated a series of state-led heavy industry projects geared to both industrial deepening and ethnic restructuring. One of these projects was the manufacture of a national car—the Saga—through a joint venture between the Malaysian government and Japan's Mitsubishi.

Successful development of the Saga required that the Malaysian state be capable of (1) disregarding the interests of existing Chinese auto entrepreneurs, who had obstructed prior rationalization efforts, and (2) extracting concessions from Mitsubishi. These objectives were to some degree mutually exclusive. The autonomy of Malay political leaders from Chinese firms did make possible a fairly drastic market rationalization. And, freed from interference by a fragmented private sector, the state succeeded in obtaining a foreign backer for a project viewed as economic folly by most auto TNCs. But by themselves government officials were ill equipped to compel Mitsubishi to accept locally made parts for the national car. Only when experienced and organized Chinese auto parts firms became involved in the national car process did Malaysia begin to produce more than just a reassembled Mitsubishi vehicle.

The argument of this chapter is thus that the value, and eventually the degree of government autonomy from certain sectors of business declined as the project progressed. The first section establishes the historical context of this proposition by reviewing the origins of the Chinese parts firms, their role in Malaysia's auto-localization measures prior to the national car project, and the industry conditions leading to the project itself.

The Emergence of Parts Firms, the State as Broker, and the Revival of Localization Efforts, 1978–1982

The State–Private Sector Origins of Mandatory Deletion

As described in chapter 3,[1] Malaysia's initial localization efforts of the late 1960s and early 1970s had limited success. The Ministry of Trade and Industry (MTI) had established a special interdepartmental agency to oversee the auto sector, the Motor Vehicle Assembly Committee (MVAC), whose functions included price administration, import regulation, promotion of local contents, and control of the number of assemblers, makes, and models.[2] But the committee was largely ineffective in the face of assemblers' opposition to localization and market streamlining. The committee's members lacked experience in the auto industry. They were also stymied by a contradictory set of government priorities. The aim of market rationalization was undermined by new, inefficient assembly plants, which the government expected to provide new jobs, investment, and business opportunities for Malays.

But a group of local Chinese parts firms did grow out of these early localization efforts. During the 1976–77 period six parts manufacturers began organizing other firms to lobby government officials for higher local content. The most important of these firms was Malaysian Sheet Glass, a locally owned glass manufacturer based in the construction industry but anxious to gain access to the expanding market for auto safety glass. The firm's non-auto activities provided it with depth of capital and rendered it relatively invulnerable to assemblers' reprisals against its calls for higher local content. But because other Malaysian firms were vulnerable, Malaysian Sheet Glass moved to organize a broader, more coherent organization, and in 1978 the Malaysian Automotive Component Parts Manufacturers' Association (MACPMA) was established.

MACPMA's efforts were strengthened by it members' size, market position, and ethnic homogeneity. By the late 1970s the group included one quarter of the auto parts industry's roughly two hundred firms. Most of these were Chinese-owned and had an average workforce of 100–150 people, and by the early-to-mid 1980s they accounted for approximately 80 percent of the sector's production.[3] Most of the larger firms do have equity or technical tie-ups with foreign, usually Japanese, companies. But foreign equity holdings rarely exceed 30 percent, and Japanese influence in MACPMA has not been significant.[4]

MACPMA's formal establishment in 1978 increased pressure by parts firms on the government to expand localization. Such pressure was a crucial factor in Malaysia's 1979 adoption of a mandatory program requiring foreign assemblers to delete certain components from their imported CKD packs and to procure them locally. The new program included investment incentives and tariff protection for parts makers, duty exemptions and penalties for assemblers, and price, quality, and supply criteria for local firms producing parts listed for mandatory deletion. Local firms had to be capable of producing sufficient parts to cover 80 percent of the vehicles assembled.[5]

Additional factors encouraged the program's adoption. Externally, the Malaysian government was concerned that the country's failure to move ahead in auto manufacturing would result in Malaysia's being excluded from and bypassed by the ASEAN automotive complementarity efforts just getting off the ground.[6] As the ASEAN country with the least developed auto sector, Malaysia found itself faced with the alternatives of either pressing forward in developing its own industry or finding itself locked into purchases from its more advanced ASEAN neighbors.

Domestically, local firms involved in auto assembly mounted little cohesive opposition to MACPMA's localization efforts. This was in part owing to associational weakness. Dominated by strongly competitive foreign firms, most of the assemblers did not take their own trade association, the Malaysian Motor Vehicle Assemblers' Association, seriously. Many viewed it largely as a talking shop and, until the mid 1980s, did not send top decision makers to its meetings. In addition, having themselves begun to produce auto and heavy equipment components, some of the larger local assembly interests (UMW and Tan Chong) expressed some support for MACPMA's objectives.

Finally, the parts firms gradually drew support from within the government itself. The initial target of MACPMA's lobbying efforts for higher localization was MVAC. This committee was largely dominated by officials of the Malaysian Industrial Development Authority (MIDA), many of whom were pessimistic as to the feasibility of local auto manufacture. MACPMA responded by circumventing MIDA's staff and appealing directly to the more receptive minister of trade and industry, Mahathir Mohamad, also deputy prime minister. The committee gradually became more supportive of localization, in part because of Mahathir's influence and in part through the establishment of ties between the committee and the parts firms in the course of discussions on ASEAN auto efforts. Indeed, the degree of Malaysian state–private sector cooperation eventually prompted other ASEAN members to talk of "Malaysia Inc."

Early government initiatives thus created market niches into which Chinese auto parts firms moved and pressed for further market expansion. In so doing, the policies also generated linkages between local firms and relevant government officials. This fledgling public–private sector network, under private sector leadership, significantly strengthened Malaysia's abilities to obtain auto-TNC cooperation in the actual implementation of mandatory deletion.

The Challenge of Implementation

Although Japanese vehicles dominated the Malaysian market by the late 1970s, Japanese automakers had limited input into the decision to begin mandatory deletion. But that decision was simply a prelude to more intense bargaining involving the state (represented by MVAC), the assemblers, and the components firms over the policy's implementation. After preliminary government surveys, tripartite negotiations began in early 1980 over the specific components to be localized.

The talks led to the approval first of safety glass in April 1980 and subsequently of leaf springs and exhaust systems. Existing local production capacity for glass and exhaust systems facilitated approval of these items.[7] But significant resistance by assemblers, especially by the Japanese, emerged as the program was expanded to include other items. The main stumbling block was the requirement that local firms supplying deleted parts be capable of meeting 80 percent of demand at reasonable quality and prices. For most local firms this was a difficult task, especially since the fragmented market demanded the manufacture of products with a wide range of specifications. Local firms thus required technical support from the Japanese.

The Case of Wire Harnesses.   This issue emerged most sharply when a Malaysian wire-harness manufacturer sought to substitute its products for imported items. The firm first attempted to link up with an experienced Japanese supplier in order to expand production capacity and improve technology. This effort failed when the Malaysian firm refused the Japanese demand for 70 percent equity control. The Malaysians then established a technical tie-up with a New Zealand firm that had various production licenses for wire harnesses, including one from Yazaki, the most important of the Japanese producers.

The Japanese refused to cooperate. Yazaki not only claimed that parts produced with the New Zealand firm were not genuine; it also refused to supply drawings necessary to identify which specific terminals were used in which of the many models assembled for the Malaysian market. The Japanese assemblers then claimed that the Malaysian firm was incapable of meeting original equipment (OE) requirements. Model proliferation thus enhanced the importance of Japanese control over essential technology.

Concerned that this conflict would endanger the entire program, government officials turned to MACPMA for advice. The association urged them to maintain pressure on the Japanese to comply with the deletion requirement. State support was especially needed, MACPMA argued, in light of Malaysian regulations that placed local parts firms at a disadvantage. Because Malaysia imposed no particular localization deadline on the auto TNCs, it was the responsibility of the local parts firms to demonstrate production capacity *before* obtaining the market. The assemblers were thus able to undermine localization by citing the lack of existing local capacities. In other ASEAN programs, assemblers were to localize certain percentages of a vehicle's cost or value by a certain date. This compelled the assemblers to search out and even help create qualified local parts producers.

MVAC officials compromised. They ordered the wire harnesses deleted from imported CKD packs. But, swayed by Yazaki's claims of technical inferiority on the part of the local firm's New Zealand partner, the officials set only a tentative deadline for deletion. The Malaysian firm then purchased the necessary equipment for large-scale assembly of wire-harness parts from New Zealand in hopes that the investment would compel the state to enforce the deadline. But the firm still lacked sufficient technical capacity to produce the required variety of products at acceptable prices and quality. The Japanese again refused to commit themselves to purchases. The Malaysian firm then brought together a group of retired English, Scottish, and Australian technicians.

As the tentative deletion date approached, the state affirmed that the deadline would be enforced, largely because of the wire-harness firm's investments and preparations. Yet the firm needed definite purchase orders from all of the assemblers in order to arrange inventory and establish production schedules for the various specifications required. It had instead received only vague production forecasts and was consequently unable to meet the demand by the deletion date. When assembly of new models was to begin, none of the assemblers had sufficient wire harnesses. Each rushed down to the local firm, insisting that its own order be processed first. Attempting to accommodate all, the firm literally got its wires crossed, thereby undercutting the quality of the product it did manage to assemble. All of this occurred, moreover, during a period of brisk auto sales. The assemblers had to fly units in from Japan, which was very expensive because of the high duties on imported auto parts not included in CKD packs.

The fiasco allowed the assemblers to claim that the deletion of harnesses had been overly hasty. The parts firms pointed to a total lack of sup-

port from assemblers. MVAC then initiated an inquiry that both strengthened the parts firms and led to a regularization of localization processes.

The Joint Technical Committee.   The inquiry became a three-day judi-
cial process, during which MACPMA, acting as the parts firms' advocate,
pressed the assemblers for proof that they had in fact provided adequate
production information. The Japanese were unable even to produce any
telexes notifying their home offices of the mandatory deletion date.
MVAC found that the majority of assemblers simply did not believe that
the deletion would occur.

Yazaki continued to balk at providing prototypes even after the inquiry.
But some of the assemblers were now convinced of the state's commitment to mandatory deletion and were anxious to avoid further production
problems. Toyota officials agreed to press Yazaki for the necessary samples. In return, the Malaysian wire-harness firm agreed to establish an advanced production schedule and to reimburse the assemblers for duties on
parts flown in.

The case had important consequences. In highlighting the state's lack
of expertise with regard to crucial aspects of the localization process, it
prompted MVAC to request institutional help from the private sector.
The result was the establishment of a Joint Technical Committee for Local
Content (JTC) consisting of four parties: MACPMA representing the
components firms; MMVAA representing the assemblers; the Malaysian
Motor Traders' Association for the dealers; and the state, represented by
the Ministry of Trade and Industry and SIRIM, the industrial standards
agency.

The JTC became the central clearinghouse and state-backed arena for
bargaining over local content, eventually taking over some of the functions of MVAC itself. Local parts firms seeking to supply deleted parts applied to MVAC, which then referred the case to the JTC. The latter made
on-site visits, mediated between conflicting parties, recommended specific
deletion timetables,[8] and suggested guidelines for improving the industry's efficiency through standardization of parts.

The operations of the JTC also had broader consequences. By institu-
tionalizing bargaining over LC, the committee legitimized localization itself. As a monitoring agency, the JTC has generated expertise among both
state officials and local firms. The committee also strengthened the compo-

nents firms both as participants in the bargaining process and in terms of production capacity. The JTC chair has been the head of MACPMA.[9] Because the JTC is the arena in which the assemblers raise problems of local quality and delivery, the committee's chair is compelled to press MACPMA members on production issues. As the body responsible for monitoring and nurturing local parts firms, the committee has also generated closer public–private sector linkages. And, finally, as discussed in subsequent sections, the committee has constituted a base from which both parts firms and established state agencies can influence the national car project.

Persistent Problems: Prelude to the National Car

Despite the efforts of the Joint Technical Committee, the Malaysian auto industry exhibited persistent and serious weaknesses in the early 1980s. High prices were endemic, with locally assembled vehicles costing as much as 50 percent more than imported CBUs.[10] Many felt these costs reflected what has become known as the "deletion allowance" problem—the failure of Japanese assemblers to reduce the price of their imported CKD packs by the same amount as the price charged by local producers of parts deleted from the packs.[11] Also contributing to the problem were extensive market fragmentation (see chapter 3) and costly auto parts, whose prices were bolstered by various forms of protection and the lobbying strength of the local parts firms.[12]

Ineffective state oversight was also a problem.[13] The government issued directives (forty-nine for the assemblers alone in 1980–85),[14] but state policy lacked long-range clarity and consistency. The mandatory deletion policy contained neither target levels nor any definite system for weighting the importance of various parts to determine LC levels.[15] Conflicting state objectives further weakened policy. The state continued its efforts to rationalize the industry while simultaneously attempting to support *bumiputra* economic development by allowing an increase in the number of assembly plants. It also tried to raise local content while attempting to increase state revenues through high taxes on imported raw materials essential to locally produced components.

Finally, the automobile industry shared the weaknesses of Malaysia's economy more generally. Guided by a New Economic Policy that failed to provide consistent sector-specific policies,[16] the industry remained Chinese-dominated, import-dependent, and generally disappointing to government leaders in terms of its contribution to national industrialization.[17] These problems, combined with the national economy's stagnation and poor performance, led to the Mahathir administration's espousal of projects like the national car as the key to Malay-led, second-stage import substitution.

Coming to Terms: Negotiating with Mitsubishi

In May 1983 the state-owned Heavy Industries Corporation of Malaysia (HICOM) signed a contract with Mitsubishi to establish Proton, a joint venture responsible for the production of Malaysia's national car. The precise terms of the final agreement had not been divulged as of late 1985. Mitsubishi had reportedly agreed to the following: construction of assembly, stamping, painting, and testing facilities for vehicles powered by 1,300 and 1,500 cc engines; starting dates; equity shares; training of Malaysian personnel; and new design changes every two years, with model changes every five years.[18] According to interviews, several areas were left vague and seemed to provide Mitsubishi with significant advantages. These included future LC levels, CKD prices, royalty payments, the use of non-Japanese technology and parts, technology transfer, and exports.

The results of the Malaysian state's initial negotiations were thus mixed. Government negotiators were able to secure foreign support for a national car with the potential to streamline the industry—something no other ASEAN country achieved. But the initial contract had distinct weaknesses. At best it laid the basis for further bargaining. At worst, the possibilities of gain appeared "far more secure for Japan and Mitsubishi than for Malaysia."[19]

Political factors help account for these mixed results. As discussed below, negotiations were essentially led by one man, Prime Minister Mahathir, with the ability to adopt policies sharply at odds with existing auto interests. This autonomy accounted for the project's initial achievements. But the national car's problems reflected the degree to which that autonomy involved isolation from the private sector as well as from other government representatives.

Negotiations under Mahathir: Running a Tight Ship

The concept of a Malaysian national car first emerged in 1980 when Mahathir, then minister of trade and industry, requested a study of the feasibility of such a vehicle and ordered the Malaysian Industrial Development Authority to hold exploratory discussions with the Japanese automaker Daihatsu.[20] The talks were discontinued when Daihatsu agreed to build a body-stamping plant but balked at meeting Malaysian demands for a "Malaysian" car. Following Mahathir's (1981) rise to prime minister, a senior Mitsubishi official visited Malaysia in the fall of 1981 and submitted a comprehensive proposal. Serious negotiations began in February 1982, led to the October 1982 unveiling of the national car project, and culminated in the 1983 contract.

The talks were conducted under strict secrecy and tight time constraints. When talks with Daihatsu broke down and Mitsubishi made its initial offer in the fall of 1981, Mahathir placed the negotiations under HICOM, a newly established agency reporting directly to the prime minister. Negotiators were ordered by Mahathir to reach an agreement rapidly and to negotiate only with Mitsubishi. In effect, Mahathir "accepted Mitsubishi without the company having to go through competitive bidding."[21] But not all those in HICOM were even aware of the talks; most of the work was done by HICOM officials in or close to the Prime Minister's Office itself.

Secrecy was further enhanced by the private sector's complete unawareness of, let alone participation in, the negotiations. Following the October 1982 announcement of the car project, Malaysian assemblers and parts firms expressed concern over the arrangement's secrecy, attempted vainly to obtain information, and sought state–private sector discussions on the industry's future.[22]

The secrecy was strikingly illustrated by the experience of Eric Chia, a HICOM board member and prominent Chinese industrialist recognized by the government for his support of NEP policies promoting Malay entrepreneurs.[23] In September 1981 Chia's firm, United Motor Works, succeeded in obtaining the Toyota franchise after five months of intensive negotiations that pitted UMW against three of Malaysia's largest business groups. The agreement involved a UMW investment of M$160 million and occurred just as HICOM and Mahathir were beginning to negotiate with Mitsubishi. Chia was "shocked" by the announcement of a project whose national car status and special state-mandated protection threatened the value of his own investment. There is perhaps no better illustration of the Malaysian government's autonomy at this time than Mahathir's willingness and ability to contravene the interests of a politically and economically powerful Chinese industrialist.

Why the strict centralization, the time pressures, and the exclusion of local business interests? The exclusion of most government officials in part reflected Mahathir's anticipation of widespread skepticism of the project's feasibility and resulting heavy flak. Mahathir's deputy, Musa Hitam, was decidedly cool toward the project, echoing opposition to the national car from within the United Malay Nationalist Organization (UMNO), the dominant Malay political body and the dominant party in the governing coalition.[24] Skepticism was also expressed privately by economists in the government and publicly by those in academia over the project's failure to make use of Malaysia's comparative advantage, its waste of sunk investments by existing assemblers, and its benefits to Mitsubishi. Never, according to one source, had an intended projected "been so lambasted as the Malaysian car project."[25] Ethnic considerations also encouraged Mahathir's reliance on a trusted few within the government. Many mid-level technical officials from agencies such as MIDA were Chinese and, as described earlier in this chapter, had developed close ties with Chinese auto firms. These officials might alert Chinese assemblers and their foreign partners, thus provoking the kind of competitive free-for-all Mahathir hoped to avoid (see below).

The local private sector's exclusion was in part a function of the project's effort to circumvent existing Chinese auto interests. Mahathir decided not to use existing (Chinese-owned) assembly facilities in the new project, while HICOM had no plans to involve existing (Chinese-owned) components firms in supplying the national car. But secrecy was also based on the potential for obstruction of the government's rationalization objectives by the private sector. Local assembly interests, most of whom were Chinese, had impeded attempts to rationalize the industry in the past. Involving them in negotiations would alert all automobile interests, both local and foreign, to this most ambitious rationalization effort. Indeed, attempts to build one efficient motorcycle-engine plant foundered precisely on defensive investments by Japanese engine makers. In 1981 HICOM signed a letter of intent to build a M$60 million engine manufacturing plant in partnership with Yamaha. The plan fell apart when Honda and Suzuki learned of it and demanded that they, too, be able to begin engine ventures with HICOM. HICOM was compelled to reopen talks with all the motorcycle makers and in October 1983 announced three separate joint projects. Concerns emerged within the industry that splitting the project among the three makers would render all the ventures less viable and more costly.[26] Interfirm competition thus posed tangible dangers as well as opportunities. Given the government's proven inability to handle these dangers, attempts to preclude rivalries made sense.

Concern that lengthy negotiations would lead to a competitive free-for-all undoubtedly contributed to efforts to conclude the talks rapidly.[27] Progress on regional auto initiatives also required speed. The ASEAN Automotive Federation had begun to explore the concept of "brand to brand" (firm-based) regional complementarity in the summer of 1982. Linking up with one firm would position Malaysia to participate in the regional effort if it did occur, but to go it alone if it did not.[28] Finally, Mahathir was under domestic political pressures. The prime minister had ascended the political ladder in part by calling for heavy industrialization. Complex haggling with no concrete results would undermine Mahathir's political position in general and within UMNO in particular.

The need for quick results and the fear of fragmenting competition also contributed to the government's limiting its talks to one firm. That firm was unlikely to be Western. Mahathir's desire that Malaysia adapt the disciplined work habits of Northeast Asia, expressed through the "Look East" policy, guaranteed that the foreign backer of the national car would be Japanese. But why Mitsubishi? Why didn't "we look further east?" one MIDA engineer wondered after the contract with MMC had been signed.[29]

The decision to link up with Mitsubishi reflected the structure of competition among Japanese auto firms and Mahathir's assessment of that structure. Mahathir believed that a national car project had regional export potential, especially given the ASEAN complementarity initiative. Of all the Japanese firms, MMC had been the most supportive of the ASEAN plan. Mahathir was also impressed with MMC's support for Hyundai during a visit to the latter firm's operations in South Korea. And of all the Japanese firms, only Mitsubishi initiated contacts with Malaysia and offered a proposal. It remains for us to explain how competitive pressures led Mitsubishi to extend such support.

Mitsubishi's Interests

Mitsubishi's decision to back the Malaysian car can be traced in part to pressures from within the Mitsubishi group as a whole.[30] Production departments within the Mitsubishi Motors Corporation reportedly opposed the project, based on simple economic feasibility. But Mitsubishi Corp. (the group's trading company) and the marketing forces within the larger Mitsubishi conglomerate, strongly urged participation. These forces had gained significant influence as a result of the success in Indonesia of the Mitsubishi Colt, a pickup truck claimed as the marketing department's brainchild. From their perspective, the car project offered an opportunity to expand Mitsubishi's share of the Malaysian auto market from roughly 8 percent in 1982 to perhaps 60 percent of a growing market by 1991.[31] Malaysian operations represented a foothold from which MMC might be able to dominate the ASEAN complementarity scheme through the production of commercial vehicles in Indonesia and passenger vehicles in Malaysia.

Participation in the car project would promote the group's interest in other sectors of the Malaysian economy as well. Various Mitsubishi firms were already involved in HICOM's iron and steel projects, as well as in various Malaysian resource extraction efforts. Participation in a project of such obvious political importance as the national car could only enhance the group's chances for involvement in other state-supported ventures.

As negotiations proceeded, skeptics within MMC saw the project in a more favorable light. Initial increases in the national car's local content would be supplied by the products of the stamping plant run and built by Mitsubishi. MMC's initial outlay for a project promising the lion's share of a growing market was not much more than the total investment required for local engine operations in Indonesia and Thailand. Since the Malaysian car was to be a copy of an existing MMC model, design costs were minimal. And, finally, the firm planned to supply many of the national car's components at cost from its plants outside Malaysia. MMC thought it might make a small profit as early as 1986, and a Toyota official admitted that Mitsubishi "took a difficult position by the Malaysians and made it into something feasible."[32]

MMC faced little if any competition from other firms. While many knew of Mahathir's interest in a national car project,[33] most assumed that Malaysia would not pursue such an ambitious project given its weak components sector and that, if it did, Mitsubishi would not support the plan. The firms were also influenced by Mahathir's moderate stance toward the private sector in the early 1980s. The prime minister had stressed the need for privatization and a Malaysia Inc. approach to industrialization.[34] Few believed that Mahathir would go through with negotiations that excluded competitive bidding and involved such a dominant role for the state.

In sum, the other automakers would not have jumped at the chance to participate in the national car program. But their total lack of involvement was essentially a function of the state's decision to exclude them on grounds of efficiency and political necessity. That decision was facilitated by the automakers' perceptions of government goals and Mitsubishi's desire for a larger share of the market.

Autonomy and Centralization: Benefits and Costs

As subsequent chapters show, no other ASEAN state was able to promulgate such a significant reform with the minimal business input seen in the early stages of Malaysia's national car program. Nor was any other government leader able to centralize and energize a bargaining process the way Mahathir did. This autonomy and centralization served Malaysia well in several respects. The government did succeed in obtaining a foreign partner for a venture that most foreign firms considered unfeasible. In so doing, Mahathir laid the basis for a thorough rationalization of the auto market's largest niche. And because Proton's staff were largely Malay, the project had the potential to strengthen the *bumiputra* automotive presence.

But autonomy was significantly less useful in the case of contract issues such as localization and technology transfer. The problem here was that the government's autonomy was not accompanied by any great capacity on its part for organization. Mahathir's extensive centralization and secrecy may have prevented disruptive efforts by competing foreign firms and their local supporters, but they also deprived the state of important expertise accumulated by others in government and the private sector. The government did use a British consulting firm at certain points in the negotiations. But, as one HICOM consultant noted, it was "difficult to know how much initial investigation was undertaken prior to the agreement."[35] Expertise was, in fact, available. MIDA and various Malaysian firms had experience with CKD pricing, technology transfer, and local-content negotiations, which could have been used to strengthen Malaysia's hand in talks with Mitsubishi. But with Mahathir's mistrust of established state firms and state agencies, this did not occur. The result was an agreement whose benefits for Malaysia were mixed.

That agreement was not, of course, set in stone. With its ink barely dry, the contract became the focus of intense negotiations, which soon expanded to include some of the same Chinese auto firms the government car project had sought to bypass.

Initial Success: The Dual Role of the Chinese

The national car project was at first quite successful. The first Saga came off the Proton assembly line at the end of August 1985, nearly a year before the date originally projected. Local content amounted to 47 percent of its value (compared to 35 percent for other vehicles), and the new car captured 45 percent of all passenger car sales and large advance orders.

Government support, especially extensive tariff exemptions, encouraged this initial growth. The Mahathir administration's efforts to make the car a symbol of Malaysian nationalism and its attempts to placate domestic critics through tours of Japan and pledges of openness to constructive criticism of the project also promoted sales of the car.[36] But these measures would not have been possible without the government's ability to moderate competition from the existing assemblers.

Rationalization and Autonomy

The government moved rapidly to squeeze competing assemblers through formal and informal means. Import permits for new vehicles were frozen at existing levels, and it was announced that only a certain range of foreign makes would be licensed for assembly once the Saga was in full production.[37] MIDA began to force other assemblers to reduce the number of models offered, while some assemblers were told unofficially that their efforts to engage in serious price competition with the Saga could be construed as undermining the national interests.[38] Government representatives affirmed that existing assemblers had the option of merging into larger and more efficient plants, reconditioning old cars, or diversifying into the production of auto parts.[39]

The government largely ignored the adverse impact on the assemblers of these measures. The latter reacted to the Saga by acknowledging its overall utility but expressing concern over the future of existing facilities, requesting temporary tax relief, and presenting a detailed plan for a more gradual expansion of Proton's production.[40]

As the government's determination to proceed with its plan became clear, the assemblers, both foreign and local, moved to adapt. As noted in chapter 3, some simply reduced output and indicated plans to leave the market (Ford; Mazda). Some shifted production to commercial vehicles and/or higher priced passenger cars that did not compete with the Saga. Some emphasized other product lines, such as heavy equipment, real estate, and finance (UMW; Tan Chong; Boon Siew–Honda). The larger firms also sought to get a piece of the national car project itself, either through cooperation in the Saga's production (Nissan), production of components for the car (UMW-Toyota and Tan Chong–Nissan), or help in the Saga's distribution (about which more below).[41] Interviews and published reports indicate few, if any, efforts to undermine or circumvent the Saga through payoffs, mobilization of the political opposition, or major publicity campaigns.

This was a very benign response to a project that threatened to destroy what had been a profitable industry.[42] It is partially explained by the larger assemblers' opportunities to fall back on other product lines by virtue of their membership in diversified economic groups.[43] The assemblers themselves also believed that the industry was indeed too fragmented and required rationalization. Opportunities for diversification and belief in the need to streamline auto markets were nonetheless also to be found in other ASEAN countries, where they did not prevent effective, often behind-the-scenes, efforts at obstructing rationalization.

Factors of a more political nature can thus help explain the weak response of assemblers in Malaysia. Local assemblers were discouraged from mounting strong opposition to the Saga by the threat of state sanctions, possibly through invocation of the Internal Security Act. Nor was opposition to the Saga by bribing top Malays a viable alternative. As discussed in chapter 9, UMNO, the communal political base of Malay government leaders, has its own sources of largesse; and the polarized nature of Malaysian ethnic politics raises the risk for a Malay politician of being seen to be in the pocket of a Chinese businessman. Such transactions do occur, but they are less widespread than elsewhere in ASEAN.

In addition, some assemblers felt that the car project's success could help stabilize an otherwise volatile ethnic situation. Conversely, the failure of the Saga, if perceived as resulting from Chinese opposition, could result in increased racial polarization and even more difficult conditions for Malaysian Chinese business.

The Mahathir administration, in sum, enjoyed and made use of significant autonomy from Chinese assemblers to sideline competition for the Saga. With no local representatives, the foreign automakers were generally quiet as well. But the government's independence from Chinese auto parts firms was not very useful for promoting the national car's localization. Part of this was a function of Malaysia's initial success. Having reduced foreign interests to one, namely Mitsubishi, the state could no longer draw on the reality or even the threat of competition from other assemblers to induce Mitsubishi's support for localization. Confronted with Mitsubishi's control of prices, technology, and quality decisions, attempts to make the Saga national required input from national, albeit Chinese, firms.

Local Contents and Japanese Market Domination

The Malaysian government intended its national car to be something more than a Mitsubishi vehicle with body parts stamped in a Malaysian plant established and supplied by Mitsubishi. Yet, according to one HICOM official, the initial contract between HICOM and Mitsubishi spoke only of both parties' commitment to the "spirit of increased localization."[44] This "oversight," as the official called it, left room for conflict over three localization issues: whether components already localized through the mandatory deletion program would be used in the Saga; how rapidly new locally produced components would be incorporated into the

Saga; and whether and to what extent local and foreign firms not allied with Mitsubishi would supply components to the car.

Incorporation of Already Deleted Components.   Before the advent of the national car, all of the assemblers in Malaysia, including Mitsubishi, had been using parts included in the 1979 mandatory deletion program. After the national car project was unveiled, Malaysian parts firms were shocked to learn that the initial contract with MMC did not provide for the Saga's incorporation of these parts. The firms lodged immediate appeals with HICOM and the Ministry of Trade and Industry arguing that there was no reason to exclude components already accepted by the assemblers as original equipment.

HICOM refused to make this decision on its own and had to consult with its Japanese partner, MMC. This was to be the first of several cases in which a state agency involved in the national car project would find itself pulled between local private business interests and those of the Saga's Japanese manufacturer. In the event, demands from the parts firms provided HICOM with justification for pressing MMC hard on the issue. The parts firms were conscious of being used as a source of state bargaining leverage and were quite willing to play this role.[45] As a result, in early 1985 the ministry announced the awarding of HICOM contracts to local parts firms; Proton began production with sixteen local parts, of which fourteen were already produced locally under the mandatory deletion program.[46]

This was an important Malaysian accomplishment, for it undermined Mitsubishi's intention to dominate the Malaysian market without extensive local manufacture. It thus indicated an expansion of local leverage, but an expansion reflecting input from the private as well as the public sector.

Local-Content Increases and Initial Consolidation of Local Forces.   Incorporating progressively higher levels of locally produced parts into the Saga proved more difficult than obtaining commitments to incorporate existing levels of localization. As a MIDA official noted, Mitsubishi had accepted Malaysia's demands for stamping and assembly facilities fairly easily, but was clearly dragging its feet on expanded localization.[47]

MMC's strategy of opposition was to proclaim its commitment in princi-
ple to higher localization, but to emphasize the poor quality of local
products.[48] As in the conflict over incorporating already localized parts,
localization pressure on the Japanese came from private Malaysian interests, mediated through state agencies. But in the case of incorporating
new items, the state proved to be significantly less unified than it had been
over the initial Saga contract.

The issue emerged first and most prominently in the case of locally
made rubber components. Malaysian rubber makers argued that the state
should consciously use assurances of dominant market share to compel the
use of locally made rubber components in the Saga. MMC responded that
local rubber products, being natural, did not have the reliability and ver-
satility of synthetic materials essential to items such as radiator hoses.[49]
MTI eventually ruled that Saga radiator hoses were to be made from local
rubber.

But Proton, more strongly influenced by Mitsubishi than the ministry
was, criticized the decision. This conflict prompted MTI to set up an interagency group—the Joint Coordinating Committee on Local Content
for the National Car (JCC)—from which to press the Japanese on localization. As originally constituted, JCC did not include representatives
of the private sector.[50] Pressed by this group to provide a list of parts
to be purchased in Malaysia for the national car, Proton identified 280
in 1985. JCC, and especially MIDA, found that this list inflated the
true localization levels and reclassified the items into a new list of 147.
These were to be localized in six stages, to be completed by the end of
1988.[51]

Mitsubishi responded by exercising two sources of leverage. One was
its control over deletion allowances. By not reducing the price of an imported CKD pack by the full cost of the particular item to be purchased
locally and thus "deleted" or removed from the pack, Mitsubishi was able
to raise the cost of localization. This was an area, in the view of HICOM's
chief, where state intervention was necessary and justified.[52] The other
source of leverage was Mitsubishi's technological superiority. Local parts
firms were to submit samples to Proton in order to qualify as suppliers of
original equipment for the Saga. But since neither Proton nor SIRIM had
appropriate testing facilities, MMC itself conducted most of the tests and
determined whether local parts were of sufficient quality to be adopted.

Mitsubishi then used its own test results to justify not including locally made parts.

This issue highlighted the government's lack of automotive expertise and the lack of unity among government agencies involved. SIRIM moved to upgrade its capacities, and Proton pressed Mitsubishi for increased training of its staff.[53] But neither of these agencies had much automotive experience. MIDA, with responsibility for several industrial sectors, was spread very thin; and economists whose expertise was in price administration, model definition, and tariffs rather than in engineering dominated its staff. Nor could the government draw on private sector expertise. Local firms were not represented on the JCC.

Serious differences also emerged within and among government agencies as to the national car's overall feasibility, the degree to which the Saga should benefit *bumiputra* interests, and control over Saga-related issues. Although several members of their staff were recruited from MIDA, Proton's and HICOM's responsibilities as leaders of the drive for heavy industry clashed with MIDA's long-established function as major state promoter of industrial development.[54] Fragmentation was reinforced by the fact that Proton and MIDA were administering separate LC programs—MIDA through MVAC in the JTC, and Proton in the JCC.

There was also conflict between Proton and HICOM. The former increasingly asserted its autonomy from its majority shareholder (HICOM) as it developed closer ties to Mahathir and became preoccupied with the Saga's immediate commercial success. Meanwhile, planning for long-term localization, originally HICOM's responsibility, passed on to Proton, where it was largely ignored owing to the pressures of marketing and other details necessary for the vehicle's initial introduction.[55]

But as the national car project proceeded, coordination and contact grew among state agencies and also between the public and private sectors. Proton was forced to interact with other agencies on issues such as tax exemptions, manufacturing licenses, and incentives. It also found itself working more with, and more influenced by, local parts firms as a result of the parts association's efforts to include mandatory deleted parts in the Saga. This was reflected institutionally in a summer 1985 decision mandating Proton's participation in the JTC.[56] Largely a result of pressure from MIDA, this placed Proton in consistent contact with Chinese auto interests. Acting through MACPMA, the latter successfully argued for a consolidation of Proton's departments responsible for local procurement. Until late 1986 local firms trying to sell parts to Proton had to deal with two, often competing, Proton departments. A direct MACPMA appeal to Mahathir resulted in the merger of the two departments, into one—the Department of Procurement and Vendor Development—more sympathetic to the parts firms.

Proton's acceptance of more locally produced parts led to its support for a long-standing MACPMA goal: the promotion of larger firms able to guarantee acceptable quality. Increased obligopoly and even monopoly in the parts sector thus emerged as by-products of Proton's concern for the Saga's commercial success and MACPMA's effort to secure and expand markets.

The Acceptability of Parts from Firms Other Than Mitsubishi. Local actors may have been able to compel MMC's acceptance of locally produced parts. But by early 1985, representatives of both the government and the private sector were expressing fears that "local" parts would come only from transplanted operations of Mitsubishi itself or those of its affiliated suppliers. The danger was that "the Mitsubishi monopoly on quality control could lead to the eradication of some firms and their replacement by entirely Japanese controlled entities."[57]

Also concerned with Malaysia's huge trade deficit with Japan, Proton and HICOM publicly committed themselves to increasing the roles both of independent local firms in localization and of non-Japanese as sources of technology and other inputs for the Saga.[58] The government pledged to act as a middleman in linking Malaysian firms with non-Japanese suppliers and organized delegations to other countries in search of foreign parts makers.[59]

But the government's concern for the project's commercial viability forced it to be cautious in opposing MMC's advice as to suitable suppliers. Consequently, pressure from both local and non-Japanese firms was crucial in supporting, and where necessary compelling, government approval of non-Japanese suppliers. As the following cases illustrate,[60] these efforts met with only partial success, as the Japanese responded with a combination of underpricing, specially constructed proposals, and complaints about poor quality:

1. *Wheel Rims*. Tan Chong, the large local firm assembling Nissans, intended to produce wheel rims for the Saga as one way of adapting to the car project. The firm linked up with Taiwanese interests to acquire the necessary technology and applied to the government industrial bank, the Malaysian Industrial Development Finance Corporation (MIDF), for the necessary funds. In its application Tan Chong quoted what was considered to be a fairly reasonable price for wheel rims. Mitsubishi responded with a claim that it could procure rims through its own facilities at a significantly lower price, thus forcing MIDF officials to reject Tan Chong's bid for funding. MIDF officials were convinced that the Mitsubishi price was unrealistic, and that the Japanese would make up the loss by raising the price of another component. But neither MIDF nor other government officials had the expertise to prove and act on this. Nor did Tan Chong have the sunk investment and proven manufacturing capacity that might have otherwise swayed the officials.

2. *Painting*. Stronger foreign support facilitated relatively greater Malaysian success in obtaining non-Japanese participation in painting. Automobile painting involves three general stages: pre-treatment, priming, and final coating. MMC's original proposal to Proton was designed specifically for its affiliated firms to cover all three stages: Nihon Pockerizing for the first and Nippon Paints for the other two.

HICOM subsequently received strong offers from two firms—ICI and Berger—whose registered capital was Malaysian but whose expertise was largely Western. Mitsubishi strongly opposed the other bids. HICOM's acceptance of ICI or Berger, it claimed, would slow down the entire project, since MMC would be forced to redesign the painting processes. Nor could Mitsubishi guarantee the quality of the Saga's paint if the Japanese firms were not involved.

The HICOM staff, after extensive examination of the relevant technology and proposals, were convinced that ICI and/or Berger could handle all three stages. But the final decision was made by higher level political officials, who were alarmed by Japanese threats of quality problems.[61] The decision was a compromise: the first stage went to Nihon Pockerizing, with ICI and Berger splitting the other two stages. Nippon Paints reportedly salvaged some of the business by linking up with Berger.

3. *Steering Gears, Lights, and Instruments*. Even more successful were the joint efforts of regional private interests and West German firms. One

project involved a cooperative venture among German, Malaysian, Thai, and Philippine interests established under the ASEAN Industrial Joint Venture (AIJV) program to produce steering gears for the regional market. The venture, known as Asian Automotive Engineering (AAE), included the technologically strong German firm ZF and Thailand's giant Siam Cement group.[62] Mitsubishi's efforts to block AAE's bid were undermined by the venture's proven technological capacity, its export potential (since AIJV products benefit from preferential tariffs in other ASEAN countries), its willingness to produce for many makes, and a commitment to use high percentages of local materials. AAE subsequently linked up with another German firm, as well as with Philippine interests active in the ASEAN auto-complementarity effort, to produce vehicle lights for the Saga.[63] Finally, the German firm VDO secured the contract to provide the Saga with instrument panels. Initiatives by these foreign firms led to both steering gears and instrument clusters being included among the first items to be manufactured locally for the Saga.[64]

CKD Prices and Royalties

Progress on localization was not simply a function of getting MMC to agree on the use of local or non-Mitsubishi parts for the Saga. It was also influenced by the Saga's price and the degree to which increased localization raised that price. At least three issues were relevant here: the original price Mitsubishi charged for the Saga CKD pack imported by Malaysia; the deletion allowance; and the royalties Mitsubishi charged Proton for use of Japanese technology.

Government negotiators reportedly fought hard with some success for price limits on original CKD packs.[65] Malaysia's leverage on this issue reflected Mitsubishi's concern that the Saga be cheap enough to sell well. "Once Mitsubishi was hooked into the project, it had to go along and help make it a success," one official noted.

But the initial agreement was far from conclusive, and the government's ability to exact further price concessions from Mitsubishi was limited. As the Malaysian auto market contracted in 1985, Proton pressed for further price reductions. In talks with both MMC and Nissho Iwai, (the trading company handling MMC auto sales in ASEAN), Malaysia was informed that further CKD price reductions were impossible.[66] The message was clear: any further reductions in the Saga's price would have to be borne by Malaysia, through either increased government subsidies or reduced tariffs on the Saga.

Malaysia's leverage on this issue was in part undermined by Mahathir's hasty decision to allow further reductions in import duties on the Saga. This allowed MMC to argue that the car's price would already be sufficiently low.[67] In addition, the state's commitment to the Saga and the exclusion of other makes precluded Mahathir's using the threat of competitive price cuts by other assemblers to push for reductions by MMC. Finally, the government's bargaining position on price issues was undermined by the absence of representatives from the private sector capable of bringing to the negotiations a level of detailed expertise on parts prices not available within Proton itself.

The lack of private sector expertise also placed Proton at a disadvantage on the issue of royalties. According to one MIDA official, Proton's royalty payments to Mitsubishi are excessive, given the low level of true technology transfer, even compared to arrangements between Japanese automakers and other Malaysian assemblers.[68] Specific information on the deletion allowance issue was not available when research for this study was completed. But local weakness on general price issues suggests only minimal Malaysian success in compelling its foreign partner to reduce the CKD price when a local part was substituted for an imported item.

Underlying the above account is a pattern that is ironic given the ethnic realities of Malaysian politics: avoiding complete dependence on its foreign partner required closer ties between the Malaysian government and the largely Chinese interests dominating the pre-Saga auto industry. Expanding Malaysian leverage, although difficult, was far from impossible if private sector resources, and eventually influence, became part of the process. The government's need for Chinese expertise was even more striking in the area of marketing and distribution.

Marketing the National Car: The Politics of Ethnic Benefits

Malaysia was hit by a commodities slump in the latter half of 1985 that led to a general economic decline and a serious drop in auto sales. Advance orders for the Saga dropped from six thousand in September to one thousand in December 1985.[69] With Proton sustaining substantial losses, the possibility of the project's failure and associated negative political consequences for the Mahathir administration began to grow. These concerns intensified government efforts to ensure the project's commercial viability through efficient marketing and distribution.

HICOM believed that such efficiency could only be achieved through reliance on proven businessmen. It therefore encouraged extensive Chinese participation in EON, the state-backed firm established in 1984 with sole rights to distribute the Saga. A subsidiary of Eric Chia's United Motor Works (UMW) held 35 percent of EON, while Tan Chong was also involved through dealership holdings. HICOM itself held 45 percent, and two *bumiputra*-controlled private firms held the rest: 15 percent was in the hands of United Assembly Services, a diversified operation with interests in finance, property, commercial vehicle assembly, and chemicals; and 5 percent was held by Pekema, a firm representing the Bumiputra Motor Traders' Association. The latter represented firms whose Malay members monopolized the import of built-up vehicles by virtue of New Economic Policy preferences.[70]

Opposition to the extensive Chinese role in EON came from Pekema and its supporters within the state itself. The former viewed EON as a vehicle for Malay market expansion. The local car, they asserted, must be sold by a "local company."[71] The Ministry of Trade and Industry backed Pekema by arguing that awarding EON dealerships to UMW and Tan Chong was premature; as a national car, the Saga had to comply with NEP goals.

Opposing this MTI–Pekema alliance was HICOM, for whom the Saga's commercial (as opposed to ethnic) success was imperative. From HICOM's point of view, the state itself was the long-term guarantor of *bumiputra* interests. The national car itself, "in one form or another," was a "mighty stroke for the NEP sword."[72] It was not appropriate to undermine the success of such an important project by pandering to the particular interests of certain entrepreneurs, many of whom were considered lacking in business acumen. In addition, HICOM was well aware that a major marketing and distribution role for Pekema might alienate Chinese consumers critical to the Saga's success.

HICOM and EON attempted to diffuse the dispute through pro-Malay statements[73] and encouragement of Malay participation in parts production for the Saga, while not giving any ground to the Pekema po-

sition. Private Malay entrepreneurs were urged to consolidate their operations and engage in component distribution and production for the Saga
through tie-ups with Japanese parts firms. HICOM intensified earlier
attempts to act as a broker between Malay businessmen and Japanese suppliers. This effort was designed to ensure that *bumiputra* firms would
eventually supply 30 percent of the Saga's components.[74]

Problems with this approach appeared immediately.[75] Chinese assemblers, themselves anxious to diversify into parts production, complained
that Malay interests obtained, but then failed to exercise, licenses to produce Saga components. There was also a rush to Japan of what one Japanese called "*bumiputra* politicians" seeking to link up with Japanese parts
firms on the basis of often false claims of market position and government
support. The process became so unmanageable that the government felt
pressured to accept Mitsubishi's demand for control of any link-ups between Malaysians and Japanese parts firms.[76]

HICOM stood firm in asserting the necessity of Chinese participation
in the Saga's distribution. It did so by publicly welcoming *bumiputra* dealers but simultaneously establishing terms for participating EON dealers
that clearly exceeded the capacities of most Malays.[77] In response, Pekema
established a consortium to compete with EON itself.[78] But these efforts
seem to have been in vain. By the beginning of October 1985 the tariff increases on non-Saga CBUs had resulted in the demise of ten *bumiputra*
distributors.[79] And in 1988, while Proton continued to suffer significant
losses, EON, under Chinese leadership, did well, profiting handsomely
from sales commissions and installations of accessories (chapter 3). In fact,
a cold war emerged between Proton and EON over the latter's profits
from accessories.[80] The NEP-inspired national car project thus began to
crowd out some of the *bumiputra* interests it was meant to promote.

Exporting the National Car

Pressures for Export

The original agreement with Mitsubishi incorporated a de facto restriction on exports of the Saga.[81] The contract stated simply that for five years
MMC would help produce a car for the domestic Malaysian market. Focusing on the political impact of the car and assuming that the domestic

market's rapid growth would absorb most of the Sagas, Mahathir simply did not press Mitsubishi on exports. Moreover, unlike many in the private sector, government negotiators were unaware of the variety of export options available.[82]

The necessity for exports became clear to Mahathir with the auto market's collapse in 1985 and a general deterioration of his own political base.[83] In 1985 the prime minister suddenly ordered government officials to develop exports within five years of the project's inception. Then, as the depth of the market decline became clear and the costs of Malaysia's yen-dominated loans jumped owing to the yen's appreciation, he demanded exports within two years of the vehicle's appearance. Spurred on by Mahathir's own salesmanship,[84] Proton's initial exports focused on other LDC markets that would not require expensive emission and safety controls. But as Proton's losses mounted and the Malaysian dollar's 78 percent depreciation against the yen increased the costs of the project's $168 million yen-denominated loans, it became clear that the Saga needed access to the larger, developed-country markets.[85]

In fact, there was intense debate among government officials as to the advisability of attempting exports to developed-country markets. Britain, for example, was the first major export target as one of the world's largest markets for right-hand-drive vehicles,[86] but opponents emphasized the risks of an early export effort to England—failure would constitute a significant setback for the Saga at home as well as in future export markets. Others, concerned by the slump in auto sales, argued that the car's success in the United Kingdom would lend it instant international legitimacy. This debate resulted in a stalemate that paralyzed government export initiatives to Britain until the intervention of a *bumiputra* businessman, Mohamed Ramli Kushairi.

Kushairi, an important Malay business figure, helped establish Edarlaus Enterprises in order to export Sagas. Although his first target seems to have been China, he quickly turned his attention to the United Kingdom with the reported support of Proton itself.[87] Thus began Malaysia's attempts to break into developed-country markets.

Exports to England.   By the end of 1985 Proton and HICOM announced their intention of exporting six thousand Sagas to England in roughly two years.[88] Export promotion so soon after the vehicle's introduction in Malaysia depended on the availability of a marketing channel independent of Mitsubishi, and in late 1984 Proton (presumably through the efforts of Edarlaus) signed an agreement with an English firm, Mainland Investment, which already held exclusive franchise rights for the distribution of eleven makes in England and was reportedly backed by leading British finance companies.[89] Mainland was reported to have great ambitions for the car, believing it could upstage Colt Car Co., holder of the English franchise for Mitsubishi vehicles.[90]

Concerned, MMC dispatched senior officials to Kuala Lumpur for renegotiation of the original agreement's export clause.[91] The firm clearly feared the possibility that exports from Malaysia would outsell the Lonsdale, a modified Mitsubishi Galant manufactured in Australia for export to England, which represented MMC's efforts to avoid English quotas on Japanese exports. The Lonsdale had not been selling well and would be underpriced by the Saga if the latter qualified for General System of Preference status.[92] Moreover, since the Saga would have to incorporate at least 60 percent local content to qualify for GSP status, Mitsubishi would face increased Malaysian pressure for localization in addition to competition for its Australian exports.

Mitsubishi attempted to control this export effort through two simultaneous approaches. One involved convincing Proton that entry barriers to the British market rendered Saga exports unfeasible. Countering Edarlaus's claims that the necessary modifications would require no more than M$1.5 million and less than twelve months, MMC argued that the changes would cost significantly more and require three years. If Proton followed the Mitsubishi schedule, however, MMC would already have come out with a new model for European distribution by the time the Saga entered the British market.[93]

Mitsubishi's second approach involved ensuring its own control over the Saga's exports if it failed to prevent them. The firm attempted to undercut Edarlaus by pressuring the Japanese shipping company K Line to stop negotiations with Edarlaus on arrangements for shipping the car to overseas markets.[94] Mitsubishi also began direct negotiations with Proton to win the export business. These negotiations were evidently successful, since Proton set up its own export-marketing division in early 1986 and subsequently denied any agreement or understanding with Edarlaus over the export of the Saga to Britain or any other country. This prompted

strong protests by Kushairi, the Edarlaus chairman, and increased Proton's vulnerability to charges of being anti-*bumiputra*. These conflicts delayed any auto exports to Britain until the end of January.[95]

Exports to the United States.   Annual sales of three and a half million
new subcompacts in the United States seemed to be a major opportunity
for Malaysia to achieve both necessary economies of scale and eventual
profitability. Again, the existence of a marketing channel independent of
Mitsubishi proved critical in the initial stages. Acting without consulting
Mitsubishi, Proton signed a letter of intent with Malcolm Bricklin in December 1986 to establish a company called Proton America.[96] Bricklin, a
maverick in the North American car business who was responsible for
U.S. distribution of the Yugo, publicly announced hopes of selling
100,000 Sagas in its first year of export and 250,000 in its fifth year.[97]
MMC was, of course, opposed to such a move, since the problem of competition among Mitsubishi products in the American market was even
worse than in England.[98]

An agreement was reportedly reached between Proton and Bricklin in
November 1987 that was to result in U.S. sales of the Saga by late 1988.
Few of the accord's details are known, but the negotiations foundered
over several issues. One involved responsibility for the costs of modifying
the Saga to meet U.S. safety and emission-control regulations.[99] Such expenses were certain to be high, since the Mitsubishi engines used in the
Saga were based on a ten-year-old design that produced considerably
more emissions than more recent designs. [100] Bricklin initially pledged to
bear the estimated $10 million costs of modifying the car, possibly by
teaming up with Japan's Mitsui Trading Company to obtain alternative
sources of components and spare parts from outside Japan if necessary to
lower overall costs.[101]

Malaysia's link with Bricklin did give Malaysia some leverage vis-à-vis
Mitsubishi. The real possibility that the Saga might be exported to the
United States compelled MMC to negotiate with Proton over the cheap-
est method of modifying Saga engines.[102] But Malaysia's U.S. marketing
channel proved unreliable. In 1988 Bricklin sold his franchise business,
and the new owners were unenthusiastic about taking on the Saga.[103] Unable to meet U.S. safety standards by the end of 1988, Proton failed to export any vehicles to the United States in 1988.[104]

This development provided Mitsubishi with significant potential leverage over the car project at a time when the government was already thinking of transferring Proton's management from the inefficient HICOM to Mitsubishi itself (see chapter 3). Mitsubishi's ability to provide "a solution to languishing exports" and potential readiness to reschedule Malaysia's loans were certain to encourage such a shift.[105]

The preceding account suggests a definite, but somewhat uneven, strengthening of Malaysia's automotive bargaining position from the early 1970s through early 1985. The 1972 measures failed in many respects, generating make and model proliferation but minimal increases in local content. These measures did, however, promote the growth of local auto parts firms that subsequently spurred on both the formulation and implementation of mandatory deletion measures. These were followed by a state-led national car program involving radical and effective rationalization of the auto industry; and an initially effective effort, led by the private sector, to expand the national car's use of local parts. But Malaysia's economic slump and auto market decline of 1985 stymied these efforts. The initial results of Mahathir's subsequent attempts to export the Saga reflected the limits on Malaysia's bargaining resources.

6

Indonesia

As in Malaysia, sharp ethnic divisions have shaped Indonesia's ability to induce TNC support for local auto manufacture. Indonesia's economic resources tend to be in the hands of ethnic Chinese, while the state is dominated by indigenous (*pribumi*) Indonesians. Like its Malaysian counterpart, the Indonesian government has been torn between the goals of ethnic redistribution to reduce Chinese wealth and of national industrial growth relying on and strengthening Chinese business interests. And as in Malaysia, Indonesia's bargaining leverage has been bolstered by ties between Chinese firms and the state, just as the automotive bargaining process has expanded those ties.

There are, however, important differences between the two countries.[1] With regard to the private sector, the extreme numerical inferiority of the Indonesian Chinese (5 percent of the population) and the *pribumi* majority's sensitivity to Chinese economic strength have discouraged Chinese associational growth. Yet Chinese businesses tend to be larger and more vertically integrated than in Malaysia, and Indonesia also has a more developed *pribumi* entrepreneurial class than is the case with the *bumiputra* majority in Malaysia. Politically, the Indonesian state is more overtly nationalist than its Malaysian counterpart. But ironically (given the Chinese community's small relative size), the New Order state is more reliant on Chinese business than are Malay political leaders. Although formally unrepresented in the government and with few associations, Chinese entrepreneurs are themselves, however, highly dependent on the Indonesian state. Indonesia is, in sum, characterized by informal, but highly symbiotic, ties between the state and Chinese business.

These differences have influenced Indonesia's approach to, and capacity for, bargaining with foreign auto firms. First, public–private sector ties, while important to the country's bargaining leverage, have not been as consistently association-based as in Malaysia. Links between individual firms and government agencies have instead played a prominent role. Second, government rationalization measures have been impeded by attempts to expand the market on the part of numerous *pribumi* and Chinese entrepreneurs, as well as by the government's vulnerability to charges of selling out *pribumi* interests. But competition for state support between *pribumi* and Chinese businesses (as well as rivalries among all the firms) have given government officials some degree of autonomy and the ability to draw on the resources of the private sector in dealings with foreign firms. Finally, the technical and financial resources of large Chinese firms have enabled Indonesia to move, albeit slowly, into the manufacture of parts with higher value-added than was the case in Malaysia.

Developmental Nationalism versus Ethnic Favoritism, 1966–1976

Political Change, Clientelism and Rising Entrepreneurs

By the late 1960s Indonesia's auto market was even more fragmented and import-dependent than those of its ASEAN neighbors. The new (1966) Suharto government had relieved shortages and inflation through liberalization of trade and investment, facilitating an influx of many makes of CBUs and semi-knocked-down vehicles into Indonesia. But the

fragmentation also reflected a multiplicity of local actors anxious to participate in the lucrative auto industry and willing to serve as local partners
for foreign assemblers.

   The first Indonesians involved in the auto industry were *pribumi* businessmen distributing and selling Western makes. Often Sumatran traders,
these entrepreneurs obtained access to the necessary foreign exchange and
auto import licenses by virtue of their contributions to party factions that
controlled the Department of Transportation prior to 1966.[2] The benefi-
ciaries of this clientelist arrangement lost considerable influence with the
rise of Suharto's military-dominated New Order.[3] Some simply lost their
market positions; others, such as Hashim Ning and Fritz Eman, were able
to continue operations by developing ties with the Suharto leadership and
the new auto interests emerging in the mid-to-late 1960s.

   One group of new entrants included Indonesian Chinese, especially the
highly diversified Liem and Astra groups. The Liem group built an early
base on state-granted monopolies in clove imports and flour milling,
linked up with Suharto by providing goods to the military, and eventually
became a giant conglomerate under the New Order.[4] In automobiles,
Liem first supplied Volvos to state officials, and gradually moved into the
assembly of various Japanese vehicles (see table 3.22). Astra entered the
auto sector in 1968, when the firm's founder, William Suryajaya, obtained
eight hundred Chevy trucks.[5] This purchase, which generated a substantial profit owing to exchange-rate shifts, allowed Astra to pay back central
bank loans and supply the heavy vehicles needed for the New Order's effort to rebuild roads and irrigation systems. Astra tightened its links with
the New Order when it took over an old GM plant that had been nation-
alized and was considered a financial burden by the government. Eventually linking up with Toyota and other companies (table 3.22), Astra emphasized auto assembly and parts production, while also expanding into
trade, finance, real estate, and other types of manufacturing, often in partnership with foreign firms.[6]

   Political-military officials in the new Suharto administration, often tied
directly to foreign and/or Indonesian Chinese, constituted a second group
of new auto interests. In addition to other activities, the Army Strategic
Reserve (Kostrad) took over Volkswagen operations in partnership with
Chinese businessmen.[7] The presidential palace developed an interest in
automobiles when Suharto's brother, Probosutejo, became part owner of

import and distribution operations for Peugeot, Renault, Isuzu, and others (table 3.22). Perhaps most important, Indonesia's giant state oil company, Pertamina, developed an extensive automobile presence through Ibnu Sutowo, its chief until 1975, and his two major associates, Mohamad Joesoef and Sjarnubi Said. Sutowo linked up with Mitsubishi to form Krama Yudha Motors in 1971, joined Hashim Ning in National Motors (Mazda and Hino), and held 50 percent of Star Motors (Benz).

Finally, linkages developed between these two new groups. Sutowo, for example, became a shareholder in some of Astra's operations. Astra in turn held shares in Sutowo's holding company, while involving Probo sutejo in the ownership of its Peugeot and Renault operations.[8]

These new automobile interests were only just getting established in the late 1960s. The industry's ownership structure was in transition as old guard *pribumi* businessmen tied to European and U.S. makes fought to maintain a presence against a new guard working with aggressive Japanese firms. This fragmented entrepreneurial structure thus strengthened a fragmented market structure. But in the short term, it also prompted the country's first set of auto-localization measures.

Initial Auto Reforms: Localization and Pribumi Protection

By late 1960s the New Order's initial liberalization came under general attack from two forces active in the automobile industry. Managers and generals within state power centers, such as Ibnu Sutowo in Pertamina, found that open trade and loose investment policies undermined their opportunities to obtain contracts, credits, licenses, and lucrative partnerships with foreign firms.[9] In addition, long-established entrepreneurs like Ning argued that policies such as unrestricted CBU and SKD imports after 1966 had caused severe excess capacity and economic losses.[10] When combined with an easing of inflation in 1969, these pressures strengthened the deep-seated Indonesian mistrust of market forces and emphasis on national resilience through backward linkages.[11]

Within the bureaucracy, this traditional tendency was reinforced by two officials responsible for auto policy: Sumitro Djojohadikusumo, minister of trade from 1968 to 1973, and Ir. Suhartoyo, director general of the Directorate of Basic Industries in the Department of Industry from the late 1960s to 1978.[12] These two men differed on some important issues. Sumitro emphasized the need to protect *pribumi* capital and resist TNC domination. Suhartoyo was more developmental than protectionist; his concern was with the creation of vertical linkages among Indonesian, rather than specifically *pribumi*, capitalists.[13] But in 1969 these differences were overshadowed by agreement on the country's need to shift from importing automobiles to manufacturing them.

This consensus resulted in a 1969 set of auto policies aimed at localization, protection of local ownership, and industrial rationalization (see chapter 3), which in turn triggered an influx of Japanese assemblers seeking legally mandated groups for joint assembly and distribution operations. But the auto TNCs could largely ignore Indonesian demands for greater localization. Local technical capacities, even among the larger and newer groups were minimal, while the smaller old guard assemblers opposed rationalization efforts necessary for increased local contents.[14] Yet the 1969 measures did help to plant the bureaucratic and private sector seeds of a more aggressive and elaborate localization effort.

Bureaucratic Initiative and Private Sector Support, 1970–1972

The emergence of Suhartoyo (and the Directorate of Basic Industries) as a clear locus of state initiative was a crucial factor in Indonesia's persistent auto industrialization efforts. Bolstered by an official economic nationalism concerned less with protecting *pribumi* capital than with promoting an integrated national industrial capacity, the directorate was given complete responsibility for regulating the auto industry. [15]

But bureaucratic initiative required private sector support. In 1971 Suhartoyo involved Hashim Ning in the process of designing a new localization program. Ning, still the dominant local automotive interest, was assumed to be powerful enough to compel his foreign principals to make major new investments in local auto manufacturing. He did, in fact, publicly urge Fiat and Ford to back localization,[16] thereby helping to stimulate competitive support from other local firms, both old guard survivors and potential new entrants. When GM Holden refused to commit itself to local manufacture in 1971, its local partner, Fritz Eman, decided to launch an ambitious scheme for component manufacture without auto-TNC support. Between 1972 and 1974 subsidiaries were established in East Java for the assembly of air conditioning units, batteries, exhaust systems, and shock absorbers.[17] Kostrad's director put considerable pressure on Volkswagen to begin production of a basic transport vehicle, and Ibnu Sutowo urged Mitsubishi to begin local assembly and parts manufacture. Indeed, Sutowo and his Pertamina lieutenant, Sjarnubi Said, styled themselves the major backers of state auto policy.

Both urging and responding to this pressure, Suhartoyo began to make elaborate plans for a deletion program that would gradually move from minor to major functional parts.[18] And in 1972 he renewed efforts to promote economics of scale by mandating the merger of assemblers and distributors into a few large efficient groups (Decree No. 545).[19] Nor was this rationalization effort purely a government initiative; according to Ian Chalmers, much of its impetus came from private sector mergers that had already begun by 1972.[20]

These efforts achieved little in the short term. GM, for example, effectively blocked increased local procurement by holding back investments.[21] In addition, the emerging Chinese groups, Liem and Astra, had not yet lent their active support to localization efforts. But an official locus of auto reform had emerged in conjunction with private sector initiative.

Developmental Nationalism, Policy Networks, and Comprehensive Auto Policy, 1972–1976

An expansion of Indonesian resources and willingness to put pressure on the auto TNCs reinforced the developments outlined above, resulting in a more ambitious and effective set of regulations by 1976. The oil price hikes of the early 1970s generated sharp increases in both Indonesian oil revenues and in the country's auto market (see table 3.10).[22] One consequence of this was to intensify interfirm rivalry among the Japanese for access to the Indonesian auto industry.[23] Another was to expand the financial capacities of local auto interests, both public and private. Pertamina, the national oil company, had become an autonomous source of capitalist accumulation, which had important consequences for the auto industry. The oil firm was not only a large purchaser of local vehicles,[24] it also began to invest in a wide range of domestic activities, including the government-owned Krakatau Steel. Krakatau soon became a critical component in Suhartoyo's plans for an integrated iron and steel industry that would in turn contribute to the manufacture of major auto parts.[25]

If financial strength made state-led nationalism a feasible option, rising opposition to New Order policies made it a politically necessary one.[26] From 1970 through 1974, students, intellectuals, and small *pribumi* capitalists accused the government of exploiting Indonesia in cooperation with foreign capital and ethnic Chinese. Fueled by differences among state factions, these frustrations exploded in the 1974 Malari riots. The rioters' protests against visiting Japanese Prime Minister Tanaka and their burning of the Astra building neatly symbolized the perceived links between foreign capital and Chinese economic domination under the New Order.

The government responded with a series of ineffectual measures to promote *pribumi* firms. The more significant components of the state's response were constraints on foreign investment and support of big capital groups, including Chinese businesses. This was largely a function of the dramatic increase in Indonesia's oil revenues during the 1970s. Crude oil prices jumped 430 percent between 1972 and 1974, with oil income rising from 25 percent of total government revenues in 1971–72 to 48 percent in 1974–75.[27] It also reflected the weight of big capital in Indonesia. By the mid 1970s large Chinese and state groups constituted critical sources of funds for individual military and political leaders. In terms of structural importance to the economy, state capital accounted for probably 50 percent of domestic capital investment, especially in large projects. Chinese firms accounted for roughly 75 percent of private domestic investment.[28] As will be discussed in chapter 9, support for large capital also had a nationalist intellectual justification: prominent officials developed the view that large-scale, integrated Indonesian capital constituted the only force capable of counterbalancing foreign TNCs.

The most important consequence of these developments in the auto industry was the emergence of an effective, public-private sector policy network led by Suhartoyo. In addition, the Directorate of Basic Industries was able to shape the industry by channeling government vehicle orders to particular makes.[29] Suhartoyo also had greater cooperation from large Chinese firms. Astra in particular felt compelled by the Malari riots and related opposition to prove its nationalist credentials by expanding investment in domestic production, including automotive localization.[30] The larger firms saw in Suhartoyo, as evidenced by his 1972 rationalization measures, a key backer for their own attempts at market expansion.

Suhartoyo in turn encouraged greater cohesion in the private sector. Policy coordination between the two major auto industry associations began in 1973 under his urging, and in 1975 the two groups merged to form GAAKINDO, the Indonesian Association of Automobile Sole Agents and Assemblers.[31] The new group, at least for the short term, effectively combined smaller *pribumi* firms with the larger government and Chinese interests. The former dominated the association numerically and, guided by Suhartoyo and not yet threatened by the costs of higher localization, backed the general principles of nonethnic industrialism.[32]

These developments in the private sector strengthened Suhartoyo's ability to formulate a new localization policy in at least two important ways. Individually, several private firms increased localization pressure on their foreign partners. Ibnu Sutowo's firm, Krama Yudha, reportedly "pioneered the manufacturing of auto components in 1974."[33] Astra, in "an early sign of its alliance with the Directorate, decided to move into commercial vehicle production despite Toyota's opposition."[34] And several TNCs followed Volkswagen's example and indicated intentions to introduce basic transportation vehicles.[35]

Collectively, associational linkages facilitated consultations between Suhartoyo and the associations. In 1973 Suhartoyo initiated talks to draft a comprehensive automobile reform policy. The joint nature of the process provided benefits for both sides: the directorate obtained technical information and public backing for its plan, while GAAKINDO and its members gained status as national industrial pioneers as well as opportunities for vehicle sales to the government.[36] The talks resulted in draft measures that became the core of Government Decree No. 307 in 1976.

Its weaknesses (discussed below) notwithstanding, the decree was a much more sophisticated document than its predecessors and reflected the expanded expertise of public and private sector auto interests. There was, for example, a new product emphasis. The Department of Industry mandated localization only for commercial vehicles (CVs) because Indonesia's huge, but largely rural, market provided potential for commonization and economies of scale in trucks and buses. The CV emphasis was part of a trade-off with the auto TNCs, which were to be permitted to sell passenger vehicles with minimal local contents in exchange for agreeing to localization of CVs. The government also calibrated its tariff structure to encourage CV sales.[37]

The decree also reflected Suhartoyo's understanding of the need for a division of labor in localization.[38] The assemblers themselves would manufacture pressed parts such as chassis and fuel tanks; two or three parts firms would produce more complex items such as wheel rims; and the government itself would promote the manufacture of power-train components through investments in steel production and close coordination of foreign investment.

Finally, the decree incorporated a new approach to rationalization. Indonesia's initial strategy of reducing the number of firms and models *before* increasing localization had not succeeded. The 1969 measures had attempted to stop approval of new makes and end sales of unapproved makes. Yet licenses continued to be approved after 1969.[39] The 1972 efforts to create a few large groupings generated strong domestic conflict. With tight links to foreign assemblers and a limited number of makes, the newer assemblers had no trouble organizing themselves into groups. But the measures were opposed by smaller *pribumi* firms, which often handled several makes and had difficulty consolidating operations among several foreign assemblers.[40] Together, Indonesia's attraction for foreign assemblers and the influence of locals willing to serve as the TNCs' "capital umbrellas" precluded any real rationalization.

With this failure in mind, the Directorate of Basic Industries reversed its approach to industrial streamlining: under Decree No. 307, localization would *precede* and *drive* rationalization. The directorate did plan to deny import licenses to any model not meeting minimum sales volumes, but relied mainly on the cost of rising local contents to weed out those assemblers whose volumes were too small to spread out such costs.[41] Underlying this assumption was an untested belief in the government's ability to enforce its localization levels.

By the mid 1970s Indonesian automobile policy had passed through two stages. From the late 1960s to 1972 a combination of state initiative and pressure for protection by established *pribumi* firms had legitimized the objective of local auto manufacture and generated local-contents targets. But weak local technical capacities and a lack of active Chinese support allowed the foreign firms simply to disregard localization measures. From 1972 to 1976 Indonesia generally possessed greater financial resources and a clearer commitment to making use of foreign capital for nationalist purposes. In the auto industry more concrete and ambitious localization efforts gradually emerged from a consciously crafted auto policy network composed of a more programmatically cohesive, better-financed state and a private sector incorporating newer, larger capital groups as well as old guard firms.[42] Necessary though it was, this policy network was clearly temporary, since it had developed under the guidelines of nonethnic developmental nationalism and involved only minimal local content. *Pribumi* firms supported localization without ever having to pay its costs. In 1976 a central question was whether the smaller *pribumi* firms would be financially and technically capable of meeting the new localization targets. If not, what would become of the developmental nationalist network?

The Political Costs of Localization: Fragmentation of Domestic Capital, 1976–1978

Clearer TNC opposition to Indonesia's localization efforts emerged in response to the increasingly specific and ambitious LC targets of Decree No. 307. This rarely involved public refusals by TNCs to comply with the new measures, but rather the more subtle manipulation of deletion allowances: several firms raised the costs of localization to Indonesian consumers by setting the prices of "deleted" CKD packs higher than those of equivalent CBU units.[43] Yet, as noted in chapter 3, there was a two-fold rise in local-content levels between 1975 and 1978 and an expansion of body parts factories throughout the country.

The economic strength, but political Achilles' heel, of this localization was that the newer, large firms encouraged and accounted for most of it. Following a financial scandal in Pertamina, Sjarnubi Said replaced Ibnu Sutowo as the principal local interest in Krama Yudha but continued to press Mitsubishi on localization.[44] Astra, however, was the local leader in parts production. Having convinced Toyota that a failure to expand localization would result in market losses to other makes, Astra aggressively expanded in-house parts production in cooperation with Toyota and various parts firms (table 6.1). Since Astra and Krama Yudha accounted for over 70 percent of the commercial vehicles assembled in 1977,[45] this expansion of in-house operations meant that the Indonesian auto industry was becoming vertically integrated as well as oligopolistic.[46]

Table 6.1.   Astra Joint Ventures in Parts Production, 1975–1978

Firm	Date Established	Product(s)	Foreign Partner(s)
PT Nippondenso Indonesia	May 1975	Air conditioners, electric motors, starters, etc.	Nippondenso
PT Kayaba Indonesia	1975	Shock absorbers	Kayaba, Toyota
PT Toyota Mobilindo	November 1976	Body parts, metal stampings	Toyota
PT Tri Satria Utama	June 1978	Leaf springs, chassis, etc.	U.S. firms, names unknown
PT Superior Coach Indonesia	June 1978	Bus bodies, load boxes	U.S. firm, name unknown

SOURCE: Edward Suryajaya (the son of Astra's founder), M.A. thesis, Asian Institute of Technology, Manila, n.d., title not noted.

As deadlines approached for the localization of more complex components, foreign assemblers intensified their complaints about local quality[47] and the entry barriers to the older *pribumi* firms grew. The case of the country's only independent wheel-rim producer, PT Inkoasku, owned by Fritz Eman, is illustrative in this regard. Wheel rims, along with shocks, cabins, and mufflers were slated for mandatory deletion in 1978.[48] Ir. Soehoed, who had become minister of industry in 1978, made several attempts to convince Toyota to accept wheel rims from Eman's plant, but after testing the product in Japan, Toyota consistently refused it on the basis of poor quality. Exasperated, Soehoed finally sent Toyota one of its own original wheel rims for testing, only to have it refused on the same grounds. This provided the DOI with some leverage to accuse Toyota of bad faith and demand that the firm accept the local product. Toyota eventually did so, but only when Soehoed pledged to invite a Japanese wheel-rim producer to help Eman's firm. Technical and perhaps financial requirements eventually compelled Eman to give up management and a major portion of shares to Astra, thus reinforcing the trend toward vertical integration.

By 1977 the costs of localization were straining the cohesion of Suhartoyo's private sector supporters. The threatened *pribumi* firms began to oppose localization openly, with important consequences for GAAKINDO and its ties with the directorate. After 1976 the group began to divide along what one former DOI official called "strong brothers" and "weak brothers."[49] Emphasizing the costs of localization, the group began to function as the organ of the smaller, but numerically dominant, old guard firms.

There were attempts to bridge the strong-weak gap, notably a proposal by the smaller firms for "commonizing" component production.[50] The proposal was consistent with the directorate's view of rationalization and was reflected in subsequent plans for standardizing the manufacture of major components. But it conflicted with the auto TNCs' competitive strategies, and, more important, it drew little support from Astra and Krama Yudha, which intended to pursue localization in-house.

In a 1977 effort to accelerate the localization process, Suhartoyo moved to abandon the old network. Bypassing GAAKINDO, he appealed to independent parts producers, pledged state support for the development of local foundry and forging capacity, and mounted a public relations campaign to promote local production of auto parts.[51] The larger firms similarly moved to "neutralize" GAAKINDO by establishing more direct links to government officials such as Suhartoyo.[52] They also continued to press their foreign partners for localization support. Indeed, the "directorate's campaign really only gathered steam after a number of major firms were able to convince their principals to invest in manufacturing."[53]

In sum, the state–private sector auto alliance had shifted from one involving both old and new guard businessmen during the pre-1976 formulation stage to a tightening of links between the directorate and the larger new firms during the initial 1976–78 implementation stage. This modified coalition and the initiatives taken by the newer firms were central to the increased LC levels achieved by 1978. But they also weakened Suhartoyo's position in the face of those more concerned with the fate of *pribumi* firms and less confident of Indonesia's benefits from foreign investment. Indeed, by 1978 Indonesian government officials responsible for negotiations with the auto TNCs were widely divided on the issue. Yet an underlying economic nationalism and growing private sector resources meant that Indonesia was far from impotent vis-à-vis the TNCs, even as the country's demands for localization required greater risks and investments by the foreign automakers.

Intrastate Conflicts and Competitive Nationalism, 1978–1983

Ir. Soehoed: Policy Differences and Institutional Changes

Throughout most of the 1970s Suhartoyo's Directorate of Basic Industries had functioned as a sort of auto ministry unto itself.[54] In 1978, however, its autonomy was severely reduced by a new, more aggressive minister of industry, Ir. Soehoed. Formerly chair of the Capital Investment Coordinating Board (BKPM), Soehoed concurred with the need for industrial deepening, but differed sharply with Suhartoyo on several related points.[55]

First, he believed that Indonesia's industrial policies had "contributed to a widening rather than a deepening of the industrial structure."[56] The auto industry was a perfect example of this problem: Suhartoyo's close ties with local firms (especially Astra) and the TNCs (especially Toyota) had allowed the foreign automakers to drag their feet on localization. Second, laxity on the part of government officials had facilitated Japanese domination. Although foreign capital was certainly necessary, greater efforts were necessary to draw on Western as well as Japanese firms. In his suspicion of Japanese capital, Soehoed had an important ally in B. J. Habibie, a German-trained engineer called home by President Suharto in 1976 to establish the very well funded Agency for Research and Application of Technology (BPPT) and prepare Indonesia to compete technologically with the rest of the world by the next century.[57] Third, Soehoed echoed the belief that previous auto policies had unnecessarily weakened *pribumi* entrepreneurs. The "Dilemma of Business Growth and Oligopoly"[58]— the sharpening of divisions between strong, mostly Chinese firms and weak *pribumi* business—was perceived as increasingly serious. The auto industry, where Liem and Astra dominated and indigenous entrepreneurs like Ning deteriorated, was perhaps the most obvious case of expanding Chinese oligopolies.[59] Indeed, by the summer of 1978 localization seemed to be stalled precisely owing to the problems of *pribumi* firms.[60] These firms "lobbied for a suspension of the programme, their trump card being that 'forced localization' would spell the end of these predominantly pribumi business groups."[61] Soehoed was compelled to grant numerous individual exceptions for even minor LC requirements to *pribumi* firms, much to the annoyance of the larger firms that had complied.[62]

The new minister thus faced the challenge of meeting redistributional objectives at home while achieving greater industrial independence vis-à-vis the outside world. His solution combined a more ambitious role for the state in promoting second-stage ISI with the concept of large firms supporting smaller ones. Strong state coordination and even participation were required to channel capital into sectors yielding major developmental spin-offs.[63] This effort was reflected in the Third Development Plan's stress on capital goods industries. One of the plan's projects was a factory producing diesel and gasoline engines for agricultural and automotive use. Because of its potential for generating industrial spin-offs, the auto industry was one of Soehoed's major concerns. These large projects would also, he believed, help narrow the gap between small *pribumi* and larger Chinese firms. The larger projects would generate spillover effects such as technology and subcontracting beneficial to smaller firms. The state would, of course, play an important role in brokering ties between small and large firms.

This strategy led Soehoed to initiate institutional changes within the government itself. In late 1978 he restructured the DOI's directorates, replacing *sectoral-based* (e.g., Textiles) units with *functional* ones (e.g., Allied Manufactures). The intent was twofold: to consolidate government operations around products sharing similar market characteristics, profit margins, and requirements for state support; and to dilute the influence of large conglomerates on the DOI, while undercutting the leverage of Suhartoyo's directorate, which lost responsibility for inessential auto parts.[64]

He also shifted the locus of auto policy formulation from the DOI to an "Inter-departmental Permanent Committee on the Sector of the Automobile Industry." This was clearly one more step toward diluting Suhartoyo's influence. But it was also an effort to forge a new bureaucratic consensus on auto policy independent of private sector influence (the group had no member representing the private sector).[65] The committee immediately urged a temporary halt to localization (Decree No. 231). The issue was ethnic equality. Prior efforts had opened the original-equipment market only to the strongest firms. Localization would continue now only when "the small industry" was ready.[66]

To reconcile *pribumi* interests with expanding and efficient local auto manufacture, and to achieve a national balance of foreign capital, Soehoed designed a new decree in 1979 (No. 168) with two basic components: an ambitious rationalization program to streamline the industry while maintaining *pribumi* interests; and a less ambitious deletion schedule to ensure that the smaller firms would not be fatally weakened by the financial and technological requirements of rapid localization. Chapter 3 outlines the basic provisions, problems, and achievements of Decree No. 168. The sources of its failures and successes are examined below.

Decree No. 168: Dilemmas of Rationalization

Groupings.   For Soehoed, rationalization had other functions beside increasing the industry's efficiency. It could involve groupings that strengthened the position of both *pribumi* interests and Western firms capable of counterbalancing the Japanese. This belief was bolstered by a series of studies by BPPT and Stanford Research Institute proposing a truly "multinational" strategy in which the Indonesian industry's long-term rationalization would blend into the needs of the world industry. Three to five TNCs would be chosen through a bidding procedure based on (1) willingness and ability to launch an investment program utilizing Indonesia as a source of exports, and (2) geographic balance.[67] This was essentially the strategy attempted by the Philippines in the early 1970s.

But in Indonesia the approach was never adopted. The strategy lacked support from the presidential palace, the private sector, and most of the bureaucracy concerned with industrial policy. Unlike in the Philippines, engineers emphasizing the virtues of ISI dominated export-oriented technocrats in Indonesia. Suhartoyo opposed the strategy on the additional grounds that it would create a level of complexity exceeding the bureaucracy's administrative capacities.[68]

But while the bidding and export components were dropped, Soehoed's belief in the need for a broad rationalization was reinforced. His major effort in this regard was a state-mandated grouping of all assemblers and distributors (sole agents) into eight major groups designed to strengthen national ownership, *pribumi* interests, and the presence of non-Japanese automakers.[69] A group consolidation did occur, but one involving the very weakening of *pribumi* firms Soehoed sought to prevent. Ning, long known as the "king of the Indonesian auto industry," sold the Mazda and Hino franchises to Liem, and BMW to Astra, while Nissan Diesel and Datsun moved from Afaan to Astra and to Liem respectively. In addition, Mitsubishi expanded its voice in the management of Krama Yudha, while ethnic Chinese expanded their dominance of the firm's dealerships.[70] The only expanding *pribumi* interest was Probosutejo, whose ties to the presidential palace yielded waivers from government localization requirements.[71]

Soehoed's approach simply legitimized an existing market-induced process. Some smaller firms, conscious of their inability to meet future localization levels, were happy to be incorporated by the larger groups, which in turn gained an opportunity to enter new market niches.[72] The latter were able to determine the allocation of financial resources and product mixes, with profits accruing to the group's core companies through transfer pricing. At least one *pribumi* group, the Afaan brothers, however, strove mightily to remain independent but failed. Nissan, their foreign partner, accused the Afaans of gross mismanagement and demanded a new local partner. In a highly publicized fight, the Afaan group called for government support in defending the integrity of local, especially *pribumi*, firms. The government, possibly impressed by Nissan's offer of an investment in engine production, named a new local partner—a firm representing Indonesian military interests. At the time this research was completed, the joint venture was coming under the management control of the Liem group.[73]

Makes and Models.   In addition to consolidating groups, Decree No. 168 proposed to reduce makes and models through the cancellation of licenses for low-volume items, the exclusion of new makes, and the cost pressure of increased localization on low-volume makes and models. This was followed by a 1980 ministerial decision mandating the reduction of makes and models (see table 3.21).

As noted in chapter 3, the results of these efforts were better for commercial than for passenger vehicles. The absence of localization requirements for passenger cars reduced technical and financial entry barriers for these vehicles, especially for *pribumi* firms without significant capital. Thus a sort of "dual market" was emerging in the Indonesian auto industry: a passenger car market dominated by smaller, highly inefficient *pribumi* firms, and the commercial vehicle market, in which larger groups—Astra, Liem, and Krama Yudha—operated more efficiently with fewer makes and models.

Yet even in the commercial vehicle niche there remained some seventeen makes and thirty-one models (twenty-five and thirty-nine if jeeps are included).[74] The factors accounting for this phenomenon were broadly examined in chapter 4, but a more detailed explanation of proliferation in the Indonesian context is useful at this point. One factor involved the promise of future market growth. From the Japanese perspective, even if a make or model accounted for only a small portion of the market, the possibility of increased sales in a market whose production grew from 22,000 in 1972 to over 200,000 in 1981 justified maintaining operations. This was especially the case for firms like Suzuki, Daihatsu, Hino, and Mitsubishi, for whom Indonesia is a major export market.[75]

The competitive market structure also encouraged production of many models. Given the sophisticated nature of Indonesian auto demand, the auto TNCs presumed that a failure to fill every niche would undermine a make's overall market position. And, finally, the short-term costs of producing many models were reduced by "intra-group offsets." More specifically, some large groups and their foreign principals used a mixed cost calculation in determining sales prices so that high volume sales in one vehicle category supported much lower volumes in another.[76]

When faced with determined government efforts to exclude makes or models, the foreign firms also had important sources of leverage. "Loading," an especially potent instrument used during Soehoed's tenure as minister of industry, involved threats of layoffs. If the government refused a firm's request to produce a model for which it had no license, the firm responded with promises of layoffs well in excess of those justified by the failure to produce the vehicle in question.[77]

Ties to politically influential local partners were the most important source of TNC resistance to rationalization. The government was willing to refuse support to certain *pribumi* firms (e.g., the Afaans), especially if there were military clients to serve. But its vulnerability to accusations of reliance on the Chinese precluded market pressures, especially localization costs, from weeding out all of the weaker makes and models. The prime example of this pattern was Probosutejo, whose Chevy Luv consistently benefited from exceptions to localization requirements. It should also be emphasized that state favors were not the exclusive domain of *pribumi* firms. Owing to his close ties to the president, Liem reportedly also obtained exemptions from localization requirements for certain Hino products handled by his group.[78]

Rationalization measures were not limited to restricting existing products and firms. The government also attempted to streamline the industry through its particular approach to localization—that is, by limiting the number of firms manufacturing newly localized parts.

Localization

Divisions among State Officials.   Progress in localization was both slow and uneven. Local production of minor assemblies stipulated by Decree No. 168 was carried out relatively smoothly, albeit mostly by the larger firms, such as Astra and affiliated TNCs (table 6.2). Localizing the manufacture of engines and other complex parts was significantly more difficult. By 1982 such production had barely begun.[79] Indeed, much of the period between 1978 and 1983 involved securing TNC commitments of support and/or identifying the local interests to be involved with such projects.

Slow progress was largely a function of the foreign automakers' reluctance to undertake the significant costs involved in producing more complex components, but it also reflected the splits among Indonesian government officials. The actual division of responsibility between the Department of Industry and the Capital Investment Coordinating Board was blurred.[80] Within the DOI cooperation was rare between Minister Soehoed and Director General Suhartoyo. The latter had the power to initiate policy but not to follow through. In 1978, for instance, Suhartoyo asked the TNCs and their local partners to submit letters of intent to localize major components.[81] The foreign firms sent top officials from their home offices to engage in what turned out to be largely abstract discussions. The firms submitted letters of intent and complied with a 1980 request for feasibility studies from Suhartoyo, but while both Soehoed and Suhartoyo agreed on the need to move into more complex components, their conflicts precluded focused pressure on the TNCs to undertake actual investments.

Table 6.2.   Components Manufactured in Indonesia, 1982

Parts	Suppliers
Shock absorbers	PT Kayaba,[a] PT Ionuda
Leaf springs	Indonesian Spring Co.[a]
Radiators	Auto Diesel Radiator, Nippondenso[a]
Mufflers	PT Ionuda, PT Krama Yudha, others
Safety glass	Asahimsa[a]
Seat frames	PT Krama Yudha, PT Mobilindo[a]
Fuel tanks	PT Mobilindo,[a] Imorahonda, others
Cabins	Various assemblers
Frame assemblies	PT Mobilindo[a]
Brake linings	Akibono
Spark plugs	IMC, Nippondenso[a]
Tires	Bridgestone, Dunlop, General Tire
Batteries	GS Battery[a]
Paint	ICI,[a] Nippon
Exhaust systems	Ionuda, PT Mobilindo[a]

SOURCE: Swaminathan 1982, 25.
[a]Firm linked or subcontracting to Astra.

Although it was to persist throughout the early 1980s, this fragmentation was alleviated somewhat in 1981, when Suhartoyo became chairman of the BKPM and gradually reemerged as the primary formulator of auto policy. The impact of this change was seen most clearly in government efforts to promote the beginning of local engine assembly.

Engine Manufacture.   In February 1981 Suhartoyo requested that the foreign automakers submit a new letter of intent. Some five months later the BKPM sent the assemblers terms of reference for engine production and gave them one month to submit applications for manufacture. There had been little consultation over the terms of reference between government officials and private firms, foreign or local. The terms were designed within the bureaucracy based on the operations of a partially state-owned plant producing Deutz diesel engines.[82]

Despite the lack of consultation, applications flowed in during 1981. The new locus of state initiative was reinforced by strong inter-TNC rivalry and pressure from local interests. Spurred on by its own aggressive interests in the ASEAN region and by pressure from its partner, Sjarnubi Said,[83] Mitsubishi led the way in 1981 with a proposal for a $120 million plant to begin operations in 1984.[84]

But if interfirm competition was useful in obtaining commitments to engine manufacture, it undermined government efforts to promote a *limited number* of engine plants, each producing a standardized engine.[85] Astra had backed this objective by (unsuccessfully) urging Toyota and Daihatsu to share an engine plant.[86] The Japanese refused to share any production facilities, arguing that technical specifications and quality control made such commonization impossible. There was also the fear that Mitsubishi's early move would force Toyota, Hino, Daihatsu, and others to rely on a Mitsubishi plant.[87]

Unable to induce TNC cooperation on engine production, Suhartoyo eventually accepted seven proposals (see chapter 3). But he did so on the condition that the automakers agree to standardize the other aspects of major component production: parts, such as transaxles and clutches (to be discussed below), and upstream steel production and machining operations. On this issue the state was able to hold firm, in part because Suhartoyo had conceded on the engine-plant issue, but in part owing to a generalized nationalism within the bureaucracy backed by local financial resources.

While Suhartoyo and Soehoed may have disagreed over preferences for *pribumi* firms, they were part of a nationalist consensus, strongly supported by President Suharto, on the necessity for local production of engines and major components.[88] The TNCs thus had few bureaucratic supporters in their efforts to obstruct production of major components in Indonesia.[89]

This bureaucratic consensus had access to both official and private funds. The government had initially requested funds for a standardized foundry and forging operation from Japan's MITI. When the Japanese refused, the government opted to promote steel production through the Krakatau Steel plant, financed in part through rising state oil revenues.[90] But these funds were insufficient to turn Krakatau, a notoriously inefficient money-loser, into a more reliable operation, and it was here that private sector resources came into play. Liem was induced to enter Krakatau as an active partner. As "the only capitalist with the resources and influence for such a task," Liem was "able to raise $552 million in foreign loans and arrange for US Steel to become the consultant and manager."[91] The availability of such backing was essential to the project's implementation after MITI's refusal of support.[92]

But engine production and upstream processes required large, integrated operations dominated by Japanese, state, and Chinese capital. Greater emphasis on ethnic and geographic balance was evident in the state's approach to the local manufacture of "non-engine" major components.

Major Components. Both Soehoed and Suhartoyo put great stock in Western firms as sources of ethnic and national balancing as well as localization. Firms such as Dana-Spicer (drive shafts and rear axles), Champion (spark plugs), Bosch (electrical parts), and Borg-Warner (transmissions) would not only offset Japanese strength but also prove more amenable to transferring technology to local entrepreneurs. And because the Western firms were not tied to market-leading assemblers, they would presumably be interested in producing parts suitable for several different makes. Finally, it was hoped that these firms would develop a stake in strengthening the *pribumi* role in parts manufacture.

To encourage this *pribumi*-Western partnership, Soehoed and Suhartoyo attempted to broker joint ventures between indigenous auto entrepreneurs and Western auto parts firms searching for access to the growing Indonesian market.[93] As of the mid 1980s this effort had essentially failed. While most of the new components firms had a *pribumi* partner, they were far from the independent spin-offs envisaged by the government. One state-sponsored survey of suppliers to the two largest assemblers found that major components were manufactured either in-house by the assemblers or by large supplier firms affiliated with foreign capital. Indigenous subcontractors from "economically weak groups" were benefiting little, if at all, from localization.[94] Nor did Western suppliers develop a significant presence in production of major components (see table 6.3).

The Dana-Spicer Case. Detailed information on these efforts to promote joint ventures was difficult to obtain. But a brief examination of Dana-Spicer's experience shows how a combination of Western corporate weakness, *pribumi* unreliability, and Japanese market position undermined these ventures.[95] Strongly supported by Suhartoyo, Dana first linked up

Table 6.3.   Production of Major Components in Indonesia

Component	Assembler Linkage	Nationality of "Parent" Supplier	Small Firm Indigenous Presence
Brakes, clutches, transmissions	Astra	Japanese	Wanandi (Chinese)[a]
Leaf springs	Astra	Japanese	Sugio
Wheel rims	Astra	Japanese	Eman
Transmissions, axles	Astra/Krama Yudha (IGP)	Japanese	
Steering gears	All in-house		

SOURCE: Author interviews.
[a]The name of the firm is WEP. The German firm ZF also operates, but only through imports.

with a *pribumi* businessman of fairly solid reputation, Sugio, in a venture to produce leaf springs. This operation seemed eminently feasible, since leaf springs were one of the earlier components to be localized and Dana had a used U.S. factory it was prepared to set up in Indonesia. The obstacle was quality. The springs would be used largely by Japanese makes, but Dana, which reportedly had only one person stationed in Indonesia, designed a sample in the United States without consulting the Japanese themselves. The product failed to meet Japanese standards. Dana's local partner, discouraged at the firm's failure to intensify its quality-improvement efforts, linked up with a supplier firm in the Toyota group, which immediately sent a complete technical team to Indonesia for engineering support.

Quality problems, as well as an unreliable local partner, fatally damaged Dana's subsequent efforts to produce drive shafts and rear axles. Dana initially declined to make an investment before the government required the Japanese assemblers to accept its products. The Japanese refused, since Dana's only sample was produced in the Philippines, and the Japanese wanted something manufactured in Indonesia. Nor did this position necessarily reflect deliberate efforts to exclude Western suppliers. Toyota, anxious to avoid total reliance on the only other axle producer (IGP, a firm established by Mitsubishi), provided Dana with specifications and offers of help with testing equipment. But the Japanese eventually

withdrew their support owing to the severe financial and political problems of Dana's local partner, Mohamad Joesoef, an individual Dana had
been warned to avoid.[96] In an effort to obtain a more reliable partner,
Dana approached Astra, but was met with the demand that Dana take responsibility for most, if not all, of the investment. Astra was using the
U.S. firm's problem as an inexpensive avenue into axle production. Dana,
however, decided that the financial risks were too high.[97]

Dana's failure to provide strong on-site support, its ignorance of local
political conditions, and its unwillingness to shoulder heavy investments
for long-run gains were weaknesses of U.S. component firms more
generally.[98] Nor are these factors a sufficient explanation for the absence
of *pribumi*-Western ventures. The financial and managerial weaknesses of
pribumi entrepreneurs such as Joesoef also contributed to the problem. In
another case of *pribumi* weakness, Probosutejo simply failed to follow up
queries by a Japanese producer of steering gears arranged by Suhartoyo.
When it became clear that its effort to promote an independent firm was
failing, the BKPM came under strong pressure from assemblers to ap-
prove in-house production of these items. Lacking alternatives and faced
with assemblers' arguments that steering mechanisms were brand-specific,
the state conceded.

Finally, without alternative technical support, government officials
found it difficult to counter Japanese claims that the products of non-
Japanese suppliers were of poor quality. Nor were the officials always
united on the legitimacy of such claims. Soehoed's attempt to promote a
transmission firm between Ning and Peugeot was stymied by Suhartoyo's
demand that Peugeot obtain letters of intent to purchase its products from
the Japanese assemblers. Given Peugeot's reputation for quality, this was
viewed by Soehoed and *pribumi* businessmen as an example of Suhartoyo's
special bias toward the Japanese.[99]

Indonesian Leverage: A Preliminary Review

These problems did not preclude progress on localization. During the
late 1970s and the early 1980s Indonesia obtained TNC commitments for
upstream activities as well as the local manufacture of engines and major
components. Firms producing these components had been established
(with construction of the engine plants initiated) and, by 1985, local en-

gine assembly and production of the simpler nonengine components such as wheel rims, chassis frames, and axles had begun (see chapter 3). But the agents of this localization were not evenly distributed among Indonesian entrepreneurs and TNCs of various nationalities. This was emerging as a vertically integrated process dominated by large Indonesian groups tied to Japanese automakers. And that vertical integration implied a gradual and partial streamlining of commercial vehicle production.

Would progress on localization have been more rapid had the government been successful in enlisting foreign components firms? Probably, although we have no counterfactual situation to support this assumption. The more critical question is how Indonesia managed to get as far as it did with localization despite TNC opposition (recall the desire of one Japanese firm to throw its Indonesian engine operation into the Java Sea).

Somewhat surprisingly, one source of Indonesian leverage was precisely the fragmentation of state authority usually assumed to weaken a government's capacity. Chalmers lays particular stress on this point: the redirection of auto-TNC investment began to be monitored with renewed vigour precisely when government authority over the industry was most fractured.[100]

The key to this apparent anomaly is that underlying the differences between Soehoed and Suhartoyo was a rejection of neoclassical/comparative advantage thinking and a consensus on the need for backward linkages (e.g., promoting local steel production for the auto industry) and active state guidance of foreign capital. Once Decree No. 168 was promulgated, intrastate rivalry "was expressed in ideological terms, in competition to gain the political kudos associated with localization."[101]

The orientations and capacities of the new guard auto entrepreneurs reinforced the government's developmental nationalism, albeit somewhat unevenly. Sjarnubi Said pressed Mitsubishi to comply with localization requirements or risk losing market share. Liem played a dual role by backing government steel production efforts at Krakatau while using links to the president to avoid certain localization requirements. Astra was the most consistent and thorough local LC supporter, as reflected in its dominant role in the production of major components (see table 6.3) and general willingness to comply with and even anticipate government localization requirements. With regard to the LC levels stipulated in Decree No. 168, Astra "sniffed the way the wind was blowing and prepared itself accordingly. At the time the policy was announced, Astra's Toyotas could already boast as high as 50% locally produced components."[102]

We see, then, that the new guard auto assemblers were far from being a monolithic group. Sjarnubi Said, who had built a private fortune on the basis of his prior position in Pertamina, was essentially a rentier with little industrial expertise or organization. But Said's pressure on Mitsubishi for localization also showed that rentiers, when it is in their own interests, can strengthen national pressure on foreign capital. Astra, the primary agent of localization, was the most industry-oriented of the major auto interests. This firm's expansion owed less to clientelist ties to the presidential palace than to a deliberate expansion of industrial capacity. The Liem group falls somewhere between the two; Liem profited by his extensive ties to Suharto,[103] but also developed an empire whose primary strengths seem to be financial and commercial.

In sum, the constellation of public and private sector forces in the Indonesian auto industry did not facilitate an effective antilocalization coalition in which the auto TNCs could participate. Such a coalition did exist in the early 1980s; if anything, it became even more active toward the middle of the decade and continued to slow the pace of localization. But its resources and cohesion were inferior to those in favor of localization. Nor were the latter manifested exclusively through state pressures on foreign capital. Important bargaining also occurred between TNCs and their Indonesian partners with little if any government input.

State, Networks, and Bargaining at the Firm-Level, 1983–1985

Antilocalization Forces

Worsening macroeconomic conditions strengthened opposition to Indonesian auto manufacturing during the 1983–85 period. Poor sales caused production levels to fall from roughly 212,000 units in 1981 to 188,500 in 1983 and then 152,300 in 1984. Combined with a 1983 devaluation that raised the costs of imported parts for locally made components, the weak market provided ammunition for public efforts by the auto TNCs to delay localization.[104]

TNC pressure was accompanied by calls for a halt to localization by the smaller *pribumi* assemblers through the auto assemblers' association, GAAKINDO.[105] From 1981 to 1984 GAAKINDO was headed by a subordinate of Probosutejo—perhaps the most outspoken and anti-Chinese opponent of expanded localization. In 1985 the group's leadership was taken over by the managing director of one of the Liem firms,[106] who managed to moderate the association's anti-Chinese rhetoric, but sided with GAAKINDO's *pribumi* majority in opposition to what was seen as the government's intention to sweep away the smaller *pribumi* firms. The tendency, noted earlier, for the Department of Industry to bypass GAAKINDO and deal directly with the larger assemblers became even more pronounced.

GAAKINDO's smaller members did more than protest. In some cases they simply refused to comply with existing localization requirements.[107] Since the government was politically incapable of cancelling the assembly licenses of such firms, this noncompliance allowed the Japanese partners of the larger local groups to argue that no further local manufacture should occur until all local firms met state requirements. Forces in favor of export-led growth (such as the Department of Finance and the World Bank) added to this pressure by arguing that the state's auto industry generated negative value-added while hindering *pribumi* entrepreneurs.[108] There was no evidence of concerted action among these actors. But their separate pressures were sufficient to compel a reconsideration of auto objectives by the Department of Industry.[109] That the policy did not substantively change was a function of the persistence and, in some cases, the strengthening of the forces sustaining localization.

Government Personnel Changes and Policy Continuities

In 1983 Soehoed lost his position as minister of industry, and in 1984 Suhartoyo was forced to resign as BKPM chief after his monopolization of contact with foreign investors had alienated more powerful elements, such as the State Secretariat.[110] The persistence of state pressures for localization even after the dismissal of the policy's two most ardent advocates highlighted the Indonesian political elite's deep ideological and political commitment to auto manufacture. Suhartoyo was replaced by an individual whose close ties to the State Secretariat and general views made him a supporter of local auto manufacture.[111] Soehoed's position was taken over by Ir. Hartarto, an individual with little of either Soehoed's or Suhartoyo's broad industrial experience. Hartarto was, on the other hand, politically ambitious and eager to make good on a commitment to fulfill the manufacturing goals of the Fourth Development Plan.

Hartarto's support for localization was seen in his efforts to tighten up Decree No. 168's localization schedule through a revised decree in 1983 (No. 371).[112] In 1984 Hartarto shifted auto policy initiative back to the DOI and restored its directorates to a sectoral basis. He continued efforts to forge a broad intrabureaucratic consensus on auto policy through an interdepartmental team, but its chief was the director general of basic metals, a man largely sympathetic to Suhartoyo's industrial approach.

Finally, the DOI reportedly expanded its monitoring capacity. Building on a process initiated by Suhartoyo, the department required assemblers to submit biannual localization reports in order to screen out dummy companies and prod the others into implementing previous commitments.[113] This monitoring capacity did not translate into penalties for those failing to comply with government requirements.[114] The political costs of overt moves against small *pribumi* firms were still too high. The approach was instead an indirect one that combined pressure for localization with more general efforts to suppress *pribumi* opposition to the larger Chinese firms.[115]

Private Sector Interests, Private Sector Bargaining, and Public–Private Sector Alliances

All of this begs the question (only briefly addressed up to now) of why some Indonesian entrepreneurs opted to back government localization plans even as it involved them in larger and riskier investments. No concise, systematic answer is possible. The explanations, which vary across firms, include the New Order's value to large firms as a sociopolitical arrangement, the state's ability to furnish firms with particular benefits, and the pressures of sunk investments on particular firms.

The New Order provided the new guard auto interests with a relatively stable institutional and political context in which to expand. Most important, it has furnished Astra and Liem with political protection against opposition from small *pribumi* firms. There is a widespread feeling within these groups (albeit clearly more prevalent for Astra than Liem) that a failure to comply with government policies could endanger the New Order and/or entail a loss of state protection from destabilizing populist *pribumi* forces.[116]

It should be noted that the threat of populist reaction also acted as a constraint on Japanese automakers. A number of Japanese officials emphasized their reluctance to take an openly hard line against localization for fear of portraying the government as subservient to foreign capital, an image that could weaken the New Order's often taxing, but generally profitable, investment climate.[117]

For local firms, compliance with localization could also mean, to use Chalmers's phrase, "nationalist kudos." These in turn could be cashed in for significant (if unquantifiable) auto sales to the state, as well as government support for other economic activities. Chalmers has identified three "automotive power centers" whose rivalry for state resources helped drive forward localization, even when government initiative was weak: (1) Liem, the presidential palace, Volvo, Suzuki, and presumably Hino; (2) Astra, the DOI, and Toyota; and (3) Joesocf, Sutowo, BPPT, Mercedes-Benz, and Mitsubishi.[118]

The impact and dynamics of these centers, while important, must also be qualified in three important ways. They are not mutually exclusive. Astra has sought "political insurance" through ties to a wide range of public and private sector actors.[119] Nor are the power centers internally harmonious or monolithic. Rather than "triple alliances" in which the state plays the role of arbiter, they are often the arenas in which local firms promote local auto manufacture through a combination of pressure on government officials and direct bargaining with foreign principals.

Understanding power centers as bargaining arenas requires a recognition that while local and foreign firms share the need for New Order protection and more tangible benefits, they also operate under somewhat different political and economic constraints. Local entrepreneurs are more vulnerable to domestic political shifts and more in need of state resources than are their foreign principals. Their economic inferiority (relative to the auto TNCs) also means that local firms are under greater pressure to utilize sunk investments and even expand domestic market activities.

The experiences of Joesoef and Astra illustrate the ways in which intra-group maneuvers can strengthen the state against both foreign capital and local firms opposed to localization.

Joesoef and Cabin/Frame Localization.   Actual localization of cabins and frames for certain commercial vehicles had been delayed in the early 1980s. Mitsubishi had the largest market share (30–40 percent) in this niche, followed by Mercedes-Benz. Although usually aggressive, Mitsubishi had refused to localize these parts, perhaps because of its fears of poor-quality steel from Krakatau. With no initiative from Mitsubishi, Mercedes-Benz was content to follow a similar pattern of passive noncompliance.

In 1983 Mohamad Joesoef, Mercedes-Benz's local partner (and the individual involved in Dana's ill-fated effort) upset this approach.[120] To secure political support in his struggle with Sutowo (noted earlier), Joesoef approached Minister of Industry Hartarto and offered to move ahead on implementation of cabin and frame localization. The commitment was made without the knowledge or approval of Mercedes-Benz officials, who were subsequently informed of it by the DOI and BKPM. Mercedes-Benz officials strongly opposed the move, since they doubted the quality of Krakatau steel (some of which eventually cracked when placed in the firm's presses). But they complied with Joesoef's commitment, convinced that a failure to do so would cede market share to more aggressive moves by Astra and Liem. Armed with the agreement, the DOI informed the Japanese that their failure to localize the parts would lead to Mercedes-Benz's domination of the market niche. The Japanese went along as well.

This was a case in which an industrially weak entrepreneur had little to lose and much to gain by circumventing his foreign partner with direct offers of cooperation to the state. Industrial cost and efficiency calculations did not enter into Joesoef's calculation. We see a different pattern in the activities of Astra. Here an industrially capable firm bargained directly with foreign partners to encourage localization through the more efficient use of sunk investments and the reduction of foreign input costs.

Astra and the Quest for Efficiency.   In 1983 Astra officials acknowledged the economic burden imposed by government localization policies, but also noted that the firm had no choice but to comply with those policies.[121] Such compliance was politically necessary. It was also encouraged by the constraints of sunk investments. Astra had "moved aggressively into value-added production"[122] and had to make efficient use of equipment and facilities already built. It was thus necessary to pursue localization while attempting to reduce costs. More specifically, this involved increasing the firm's general level of technical capacity, and directing that capacity toward countering two of the auto TNCs' major strategies for undermining localization—product differentiation and expensive foreign inputs.

On a general level, this has involved expanding the firm's level of managerial and technological skills.[123] In the early 1980s the firm established a Technology Development Division (TDD) at the urging of its operations directors. Largely composed of engineers, this division's function has been to promote autonomous and less expensive technical capacities. Because Astra's board of directors was less informed and thus more vulnerable to Japanese auto-TNC pressures than TDD engineers, the division has found it necessary to educate the board as to the benefits and feasibility of initiatives deemed unworkable by foreign partners.

An important general strategy of cost cutting involves reducing or preventing the duplication and excess capacity generated by TNC refusal to share operations and standardize parts. Because it ran up against the Japanese practice of product differentiation, such a strategy was likely to encounter stiff TNC resistance. We have already noted Astra's unsuccessful effort to persuade Daihatsu and Toyota to share an engine plant. But the firm was able to compel the two to share machining operations. The TDD also engineered joint engine operations among Perkins, Komatsu, and Nissan Diesel, although TDD officials stressed that they first had to convince their own board of directors that this was indeed feasible.

Astra has also attempted (so far with minimal success) to initiate production-sharing between makes internally. It had intended to use its motorcycle shock absorber facilities for the manufacture of four-wheeler shocks as well. But the motorcycle facility operated under license from the Showa Company for Honda motorcycles, while the automobile shocks were to be manufactured with Kayaba. In spite of the fact that the sharing of facilities would have resulted in a 30 percent saving on locally produced shocks, Kayaba refused to accept the parts because of its ties to Yamaha, a Honda competitor.

Finally, Astra's attempts to expand capacity utilization have involved market expansion through exports. A relatively recent initiative (see chapter 3), Astra's export efforts have encountered resistance from its Japanese partners because the auto TNCs "don't like the fact that Astra will share in the profits."[124]

Because of Astra's extensive in-house production of components, most of its efforts to reduce the cost of parts have involved direct negotiations with foreign firms. At least three related types of strategies have been pursued with varying success. One has involved gathering comparative price information from other LDCs such as Thailand and Taiwan in order to induce an increase in the deletion allowances permitted by firms such as Toyota and Daihatsu. Astra has also pressed Toyota and Daihatsu to reduce component prices by arguing that Mitsubishi's lower prices threatened the market positions of other firms.

Third, Astra searched for an alternative source and/or produced a component itself when the firm believed the price of the imported item to be unjustifiably high. This has involved promoting technology transfer through ties to non-Japanese manufacturers. The Technology Development Division, for instance, obtained capital equipment from Taiwan for mirror production and has begun to copy the Taiwan firms' practice of "depackaging" Japanese technology.[125]

The preceding cases are not meant to illustrate Astra's dominance of its foreign partners on issues such as import costs and facility-sharing. They do suggest that bargaining between local and foreign firms (with little or no government participation) influences the implementation, and thus the success, of a country's auto policies. Such bargaining does not, of course, preclude greater cooperation between local private and public actors.

Astra and the Department of Industry.   Astra's policy role has also included providing support for the Department of Industry against antilocalization attacks from both public and private sector interests. In one instance, the DOI asked Astra for a response to assertions from the Departments of Trade and Finance that Indonesian auto policies were overly costly for consumers. Astra researchers furnished data that turned the issue into a nationalist one; high vehicle prices, they argued, reflected the Japanese practice of jacking up input prices, not the inefficiencies of Indonesian auto firms.

A more public Astra effort occurred in response to a 1985 GAA-KINDO attack on localization policies. Speaking in the Indonesian Parliament, the association's head argued for a halt to localization on the grounds of higher vehicle prices, market contraction, and destruction of the smaller assemblers. In response, Astra officials held a press conference in which they presented evidence of low Indonesian prices (relative to the other ASEAN countries) and the auto industry's general contribution to the nation's industrial growth.[126]

Interviews suggest that the preceding cases involving Astra are representative of many others driving the country's auto initiatives. And while they concern only one firm, it accounted for over 40 percent of Indonesia's auto market, initiated Indonesian auto exports, and represented the country's leading private sector source of industrial expertise. Finally, the cases highlight the importance of economically driven bargaining between local and foreign firms over implementation, as well as of more direct private sector support for public officials.

The results of Indonesia's auto industrialization efforts have come nowhere close to the goals stipulated in the country's numerous auto decrees. The ability of the auto TNCs to impede local auto manufacture was evident throughout the period covered in this study. But the localization increases, the modest shift into products with higher value-added, the gradual rationalization of commercial vehicles, the modest beginning of exports, and the strengthening of local auto interests all reflect gradual, although uneven, expansion of local leverage. Just as important, these developments seem to have laid the basis for subsequent progress in local auto manufacture.

7

The Philippines

The Philippines began its Progressive Car Manufacturing Project (PCMP) with what seemed to be distinct advantages over Malaysia and Indonesia. There were no pressures for ethnic restructuring to undermine the goals of efficiency and development of a national auto industry. True, the Philippines is generally a "racially sensitive" society, in which Chinese business interests retain their own representative associations and informal networks,[1] and nationalist economic policies did push the Chinese out of retail sectors during the 1950s. But those same Chinese were subsequently able to enter manufacturing through joint ventures with non-Chinese.[2] This career mobility, combined with extensive intermarriage by early Chinese settlers, encouraged a more extensive and harmonious integration of Chinese into Philippine society than was the case in either Malaysia or Indonesia. Most Chinese were not "a special subgroup of Chinese. They were a special kind of native."[3]

The Philippines also seemed superior to Malaysia and Indonesia with regard to private and public sector expertise. In addition to the Philippines' strengths in metalworking and engineering, noted in chapter 4, the country's auto efforts were led by an experienced and highly regarded group of "technocrats." Highly educated men like Vicente Paterno and Roberto Ongpin headed the Board of Investments (BOI) in an effort to modernize and deepen the country's industrial structure.[4] They were committed to Western scientific management and open markets, but they were also aware of the necessity for industrial rationalization and the potential benefits from competition among TNCs. The Philippines, argued Paterno,

> should deliberately create wide interest in and competition of foreign investments for participation in our larger industrial projects on the principle that competition will result in terms most advantageous for us.... We could follow a process of inviting competitive foreign investment proposals for particular projects desired for the economy, to be pursued in directions which we ourselves preset, such as we did in the car manufacturing program.[5]

Finally, these technocrats seemed politically well equipped to implement the PCMP. President Marcos saw in them a means of circumventing traditional interests impeding national industrialization. And after martial law was proclaimed in 1972, the Philippine bureaucracy seemed as autonomous from stubborn local firms as its Malaysian and Indonesian counterparts, if not more so.

But, as discussed in chapter 3, the PCMP's achievements were not impressive. Local-content levels were disappointing, and rationalization efforts failed. And while auto exports grew, they did so under TNC auspices, doing little to strengthen local firms. The Philippines was unable to transform competition among the auto TNCs into actual bargaining leverage.

The argument of this chapter follows the emphasis of chapters 5 and 6 on domestic coalitions as fundamental explanations of automobile leverage and performance. Despite the ostensibly favorable characteristics noted above, the emergence of an industrializing coalition was discouraged by the structural weaknesses and problematic policy orientations of the Marcos state. Intrastate cleavages, state autonomy from the "wrong" (i.e., more industrially oriented) entrepreneurs, and technocratic belief in the priority of products with high value-added undermined the country's leverage over foreign auto firms.

Table 7.1.   Major Entrepreneurs in the Philippine Automobile Industry,
              Early 1970s

Entrepreneur	Firm Name	Foreign Partner
Silverio	Delta	Toyota
Guevarra	DMG	Volkswagen
Francisco	GM Philippines	General Motors
Yutivo/Sycip	GM Philippines	General Motors
Yulo	Carco	Chrysler/Mitsubishi

The PCMP: Participants and Policies

The Progressive Car Manufacturing Program promised an expansion of
auto parts manufacturing under the auspices of local firms (see chapter 3).
This was to be achieved through horizontal, rather than vertical, integration; industrial rationalization; and exports to promote greater economies
of scale and foreign-exchange savings. The policy aimed at strengthening
the country's small and medium-sized engineering firms. But its initial
agents were local assemblers, a limited number of whom, in conjunction
with foreign partners, were to be chosen through a bidding process.

Philippine Auto Firms in the Early 1970s

Philippine import-substitution policies of the 1950s and 1960s gave
rise to a set of local assemblers—part of a generally strong engineering
and metalworking sector—who were anxious to participate in the PCMP.
An examination of the most important of these (table 7.1) provides a first
glimpse into the economic orientations, political links, and policy preferences of local auto entrepreneurs. It also, as will be seen, helps explain the
origins of important policy components of the PCMP.

Silverio.   Ricardo Silverio was the major Filipino presence in the auto
industry from the late 1960s through the early-to-mid 1980s.[6] Having begun as a textile merchant in the 1950s, Silverio shifted to automobiles after somewhat accidentally obtaining a shipload of CKD Toyotas.[7] After
some difficulty in gaining market acceptance for Toyotas, Silverio successfully tested the vehicles as taxis, and by the late 1960s Toyotas were the
country's best-selling make.

In addition to marketing skills, links to Marcos and the Japanese encouraged the market dominance of Silverio's company, Delta. The quintessential "crony," Silverio had ties to the president that dated from his substantial financial support for Marcos's 1965 election campaign. Presidential support facilitated ties to the Japanese. Prior to the PCMP Marcos funneled two Japanese reparations loans to Silverio, allowing Delta to initiate a seat and trim plant and a $3.5 million foundry, the latter secured over the objections of Marcos's own advisory board, the National Economic Council.[8] Delta's automotive growth led to Silverio's expansion into thirty-eight firms, mostly joint ventures with the Japanese, in heavy machinery, ceramics, banking, insurance, real estate, air transport, logging, mining, and consumer electronics as well as automobiles.

Guevarra.   Domingo Guevarra began in the radio repair and import business in the early 1930s. When the imported supply of surplus radios dried up in the 1950s, Guevarra began to assemble electronic and electrical products, as well as general machinery. His machinery division expanded into trucks, farm equipment, and industrial machinery during the mid 1950s, eventually obtaining the Volkswagen franchise in the late 1950s, and devoted itself exclusively to the assembly and distribution of Volkswagen products. The Guevarra family also became the core of a diversified business group (although it was not as large as Silverio's).[9] However, the family's relations with the palace were weak as a result of Guevarra's reported refusal to provide Marcos with vehicles for the 1965 election campaign.[10]

Yulo.   The Yulos may be the least industrial of the Philippine interests involved in the automobile industry. Essentially a sugar-based group,[11] the family has a role in twenty-seven major corporations, twelve of them among the top one thousand, that include finance, wholesaling/ retailing, and a variety of manufacturing sectors. The group's entrance into the automotive industry through a tie-up with Chrysler in the late 1960s did not signify a commitment to the local manufacture of motor vehicles. Instead, the family's interest was based in part on the hope that Chrysler's plan for a PCMP-related transmission plant might solve unemployment problems on their sugar estate, and in part on the high-status nature of automobile production.

Francisco.   In terms of technical expertise and industrial orientation, Francisco Motors was the most promising. The family's founder began as an auto painter in the late 1940s, expanded into general automotive repair, and then moved into building jeepney bodies in 1955. Jeepneys were basic transportation vehicles made of reconditioned engines and other modified components from surplus U.S. army jeeps after World War II. The actual production of jeepneys began a year later, and in 1965 Francisco obtained the assembly license for Isuzu vehicles.[12] The jeepney operation remained independent, and its potential as a focus of local auto manufacturing seemed great. The extensive use of jeepneys throughout the country (there were over 15,000 in Manila alone in 1976) provided significant economies of scale. And the jeepney's relative simplicity made it suitable as a base for the gradual expansion of local manufacturing capacities.

Yutivo and Sycip.   Building on its base as the Philippines' largest retailer of hardware and construction materials during the 1930s, the Yutivo family obtained distributorship rights for General Motors products before and after World War II. When foreign exchange for the import of assembled vehicles became scarce in the 1950s, the Yutivos moved into assembly.

David Sycip, a member of an economically prominent family in its own right,[13] married into the Yutivo family and became heavily involved in the family's distribution of GM cars and trucks until the early 1970s. Sycip was the Philippine private sector's primary and most sophisticated proponent of a long-term auto rationalization and industrialization policy. His concern for local control was reflected in his departure from the Yutivos' auto operations when the family accepted a minority position in the new assembly firm that GM established with Francisco Motors following GM's successful bid for participation in the PCMP. In losing control of assembly, Sycip believed, the Yutivos were abandoning a crucial chance to affect the local auto industry.[14] As president of the Philippine Automotive Association (PAA) during the mid 1960s and head of the PAA's Industrialization Study Committee in the late 1960s, Sycip developed a detailed, sophisticated approach to the localization of auto manufacture, stressing the need for gradual localization compatible with the capacities of Philippine firms (about which more below).

The assemblers' collective voice was the PAA until the PCMP's inception, when the Automotive Manufacturers' Institute Inc. (AMII) was established. Judging from Sycip's leadership role and the PAA's early policy positions, foreign influence was important but did not dominate the group. The PAA was consulted by the BOI during the process of designing the PCMP and urged both an increase in localization and a reduction in the number of auto firms.[15]

One group of local firms was conspicuously absent from the auto industry, however. These were the great entrepreneurs of Spanish origin, such as the Ayalas and Zobels, who began in commercial agriculture and moved into food production, finance, insurance, and real estate. Although noted for their financial and managerial strengths, these firms tended to remain apolitical. This probably led them to avoid the auto industry, in which favoritism was becoming increasingly important. As a result, the industry was deprived of what were probably the most economically efficient group of local capitalists.[16]

Nevertheless, the Philippine private sector seemed to provide a promising base for auto industrialization. There existed a fledgling auto-manufacturing base (Guevarra and Francisco), the potential for large-scale economies in a vehicle whose basic technology was compatible with local capacities, a long-range industrial vision (on the part of Sycip), and strong technical and managerial skills within the Philippine private sector more generally.

Problems in Policy Formulation

Even before its initial implementation, critical features of the PCMP undermined the project's stated support for localization and strengthening of indigenous firms. First, the BOI came under strong political pressure to moderate its commitment to horizontal integration. Whereas the board's original position strongly emphasized the benefits of horizontal integration, but allowed some flexibility, the final guidelines allowed for a case-by-case determination of the optimal type of integration.[17] The BOI modified its position under presidential pressure.[18] Marcos believed that vertical integration would compel the assemblers to make stronger commitments to the car program. Even more important was the fit between vertical integration and Silverio's ready-made capacity for production of engine parts resulting from the Japanese reparations loans previously mentioned. Neither Silverio nor Marcos wanted this capacity to remain idle.

The PCMP's support for indigenous firms was also undermined by the BOI's emphasis on immediate manufacture of major functional parts. This was more the result of technocratic assumptions about the localization process than of overt political pressure.[19] Paterno estimated that the limited size of the domestic market would not generate significant localization potential without immediate manufacture of parts with high value-added. The BOI also believed that technology transfer and export earnings would best be served by the production of major functional parts. Finally, the board seemed to place greater faith in the abilities of the larger assemblers, which tended to prefer in-house production. The PCMP applications of the smaller firms, on the other hand, were generally assumed to place significant emphasis on horizontal integration given their relatively limited facilities and capital.[20] But the BOI neglected the fact that the tight specifications required for major components could only encourage in-house production dominated by foreign firms.

As noted, Sycip had proposed an alternative.[21] This involved initial localization of components with high replacement rates (e.g., clutch facings, brake linings, fan belts, filters, and radiators), the use of basic products rather than semifinished products, (e.g., gray iron rather than rough castings) to help promote industrial linkages and increased value-added, the rebuilding of parts by using "cores" from originally imported parts, and standardization and commonization of locally produced parts and components. If GM was producing transmissions, Chrysler/Mitsubishi could produce transaxles. The goal was to reduce the high tooling costs of local parts firms resulting from the large number of different specifications they had to meet. If the major assemblers would not cooperate, Sycip urged, the government should bring in an independent producer such as Dana for transaxles or Borg Warner for transmissions. Like the Indonesians, Sycip assumed that such independents would be more amenable to commonization.

Paterno rejected this alternative because of his belief in the technology-transfer potential of major components, his fear that imports from Taiwan and India would undersell locally made replacement parts, and potential problems of quality and safety with locally made parts. The foreign assemblers also opposed Sycip's plan, which would have cut into their highly profitable sale of original equipment parts. Sycip had no political base from which to impose his views. The parts firms, as we shall see, were underdeveloped and poorly organized, while the strongest local assembler, Silverio, had little interest in diffusing localization.

Finally, the PCMP's localization requirements were full of loopholes.[22] A "carry over" provision allowed assemblers to build up LC credit for one year and then not source locally the next year for a specific model since, on a model-mix basis, the average was still within acceptable limits. Penalties for failure to meet LC requirements were insufficient to deter assemblers from simply refusing to localize. Finally, and most important, the government told the TNCs that component exports would offset the requirement to procure parts made by local firms. As a result, official localization levels did not represent the amount of goods actually purchased from local suppliers.

In sum, the PCMP's initial formulation reflected Marcos's willingness and ability to override the BOI technocrats, the technocrats' own bias toward more complex, capital-intensive operations, and the political weaknesses of the older Philippine assemblers. These and other problems weakened the country's position toward foreign auto firms during the PCMP's initial—and as it turned out, critical—implementation period.

Implementation Problems, 1970–1976

How Many Assemblers?

Initial Maneuvers.   The BOI was well aware that limits on the number of assemblers participating in the PCMP were crucial to the economies of scale necessary for PCMP success. As discussed in chapter 3, the BOI intended to select the participants through a competitive bidding process. Paterno's original preference, supported by the views of the Philippine Automobile Association, was for only two participants.[23] But when the program went into operation in 1973 the BOI had accepted five firms as participants. Three others were to be phased out, but in fact continued operations for several years. This failure merits detailed examination inasmuch as it undermined economies of scale for local parts firms and reflected the broader weaknesses of the country's auto policy forces.

Paterno believed that the size of the Philippine market allowed efficient economies of scale for only two assemblers, but he feared the political consequences of excluding either a Japanese, a European, or a U.S. firm. He thus settled on three, favoring GM, Toyota (Delta), and Volkswagen, and submitted this proposal to Marcos through the National Economic Council (NEC). Evidently supported by Marcos, the NEC recommended raising the number to four on the basis of its more optimistic demand forecasts, perhaps not unrelated to its greater vulnerability to pressure from firms anxious to participate in the program.[24]

With four PCMP entrants now permitted, the BOI began to evaluate seven proposals submitted by the assemblers before the end of 1971. The period from early 1972 to the BOI's final decision in mid April of that year was marked by intense maneuvering by foreign assemblers and their local partners to ensure participation in the PCMP. This was signaled even before the end of December 1971 by the PAA's own fragmentation over the issue of how many firms should be allowed in. The organization's previous support for rationalization became academic. Its members now worried about their own businesses.[25]

The firms also began to exert direct pressure. In January and February of 1972 Paterno warned the assemblers against pressuring the BOI by holding out promises of large capital investments.[26] This marked the beginning of what was to be a losing battle for the BOI against Ford's (and to a lesser extent Mitsubishi's) efforts to make size of investment the determinant of who should be allowed into the program. At the same time, Paterno accused the firms of submitting bloated data on local-content potential.[27] Meanwhile, the PAA officially requested an outright lifting of the limit on the number of firms, directing its request not to the BOI but to the more accessible National Executive Council.[28]

These pressures led to a delay in the board's decision on participants from the end of February to mid April. As the BOI deliberated, all of the firms launched intense advertising campaigns extolling their particular products and proposals, while the PAA organized a major exhibition of the assemblers' vehicles.[29] Top GM officials came to the Philippines to talk with President Marcos and other high-ranking government officials both to stress the company's commitment to the PCMP and to highlight the importance of GM participation for the country's overall ability to attract foreign investment.[30]

In response Paterno accused the firms of using "intrigues and veiled blackmail on the BOI to be approved as participants in the program,"[31] and rejected assemblers' proposals for what he called self-serving modifications in the evaluation criteria.[32] But pressure from assemblers severely complicated the board's deliberations, and it was only in mid March that the BOI approved even the precise weight to be accorded various criteria in the bidding process.[33]

Ford's Intervention.   It had become clear that Ford was running in fifth place in the BOI deliberations during this time.[34] The company responded by dispatching Henry Ford's wife, Christina, to Manila to confer with Mrs. Marcos, whom she had previously befriended. Ford also stressed the importance of its proposed stamping plant to the Philippines' newly established Mariveles Export Processing Zone and promised to more than double its investment in the zone if admitted to the PCMP.[35]

The strategy worked. In mid April the BOI announced that five firms, not four, had been accepted, and Ford was the fifth. But the decision did not settle the issue. From April through the end of August 1972 the two major excluded firms, Universal Motor Corporation (UMC), producing Nissan vehicles, and Renault, strongly attacked the BOI's decision in a dispute marked by nationalist overtones and continued manipulation by Ford, now a backer of the BOI.

Seven Participants?   Just after the BOI's selections were announced, the head of UMC submitted an appeal to Marcos alleging that the BOI had exaggerated Ford's ability to meet local content requirements. UMC was joined by Renault in an appeal to the NEC, which in turn recommended UMC's inclusion.[36] The BOI was thus attacked for going over its original number in a decision that the board itself had not made but had to support. Paterno responded that five was the final number, that any additions would result in a loss of the government's credibility as well as an overcrowded market.[37]

Between May and August the issue took on national prominence and the whole program threatened to unravel as the focus shifted to the Philippine Congress. Accusations of selling out the national interest[38] led to an inquiry of BOI malfeasance by the House Committee on Government Enterprises and a review by Marcos, who was to have the last word. Un-

Table 7.2.   PCMP Assemblers

Participants	Major Components	Investment
Chrysler/Mitsubishi	Transmissions	—
DMG/Volkswagen	Car bodies, tops	—
Delta/Toyota	Engine blocks	$8 million
Ford Philippines	Car body stampings	$36 million
GM Philippines	Transmissions	$17 million

der pressure from the excluded firms and the French government (in support of Renault),[39] Marcos hinted that he might allow seven firms, but on August 31 he finally backed the BOI's limit of five (listed with the major components they pledged to produce in table 7.2).

Threats by Paterno to resign if more firms were admitted influenced Marcos's decision to keep the number to five.[40] Probably more important was the pressure mobilized by the five firms that had been accepted, especially Ford. Under Ford's leadership, the five claimed that an increase in the number of participants would lead to a 5–20 percent rise in car prices[41] and threatened to withdraw from the program altogether.[42] The company also provided funds to defray the costs of the BOI's legal defense during the congressional hearings and to secure support for its position within an otherwise nationalist Congress. Finally, in a classic illustration of the tactics stressed by structuralist bargaining views, the company mobilized allies by emphasizing its contribution to the economy,[43] announcing its intention to place orders with local parts firms,[44] and, two weeks before Marcos made his final decision, declaring its choice of local companies accredited for the financing of installment purchases of its new models.[45] A large number of parts firms did come out in support of only five firms,[46] but this had more to do with the firms' genuine support for a limited number of assemblers than any pressure from Ford.

Still Three More?   The victory of Ford and the other four selected firms was far from complete, however. While Marcos stated that the excluded firms were to withdraw after a one-year grace period, three of them—Commercial Motors (producing Benz vehicles), UMC (Nissan), and Renault—were able to continue operations into the late 1970s/early

1980s under a special "fold-in" arrangement.[47] As of 1981 these three firms accounted for 10–15 percent of the middle-range and luxury car market.[48]

How were these firms able to continue operations in spite of an official decision to limit the number to five? The most credible explanations have to do with foreign governments' exercise of influence in unrelated areas.[49] German loans were coming due, and Mercedes-Benz's participation in the market was reportedly a condition for their renewal. The government allowed Renault's participation after French customs imposed cumbersome documentary conditions on Philippine exports to France.[50]

The preceding emphasis on Philippine weaknesses should not lead us to ignore the nation's success in obtaining TNC commitments to the manufacture and export of major auto components. Such investments were consistent with Ford's regional strategy, but they contrasted sharply with Japanese objectives and thus constituted no small accomplishment. Yet the government's success was marred by an inability to encourage the efficiency of such production, a failure all the more crucial given the large investments involved.

By 1973, for example, Delta's engine operation was functioning at only around 25 percent of capacity. Toyota attempted to cope with the problem by implementing small-scale production techniques,[51] and was considering exports to Toyota in Japan and sales to GM's Philippine operation. The latter possibilities were, however, subject to Toyota's stringent time and quality requirements and GM's international sourcing decisions.[52] Added to these problems of economies of scale was the state's inability, evident during the first few years of the PCMP's operation, to promote a true diffusion of localization operations and benefits.

Modest Localization and Vertical Integration

As described in chapter 3, modest localization increases occurred during the PCMP's initial years. But even this reflected more an expansion of TNC activities than a growth in indigenous parts firms' capacity. The large assemblers' abilities to initiate and implement in-house production of parts exceeded the BOI's administrative, technical, and political monitoring capacities. For instance, the board was powerless to close down

seat and trim plants established by Ford and Delta before the PCMP began. This was a significant failure because many soft trim items were precisely those most suitable for early localization. Yet many of the local parts
firms were only getting started in the industry and were too weak to
protest.[53] Only where local firms were well established and organized, as
when local battery producers protested against Ford's construction of an
integrated battery plant in direct violation of PCMP guidelines, was it
possible to prevent in-house manufacture.[54]

The BOI also had difficulty in limiting makes and models, despite pleas
from precisely the kinds of engineering firms ostensibly targeted by the
PCMP. For example, just a few weeks after Marcos's final decision on the
number of participants, an official of the Philparts Manufacturing Company, the country's only independent manufacturer of engine bearings,
pistons, and cylinder linings, asked for limits on changes in power-train
parts. The variety of makes existing at that time, he argued, made local
manufacture of automotive parts unfeasible.[55] Yet proliferation continued, even involving a growth in the number of competing Asian Utility
Vehicles. (These were vehicles, similar to the jeepney, whose low technology and absence of frills made them suitable for standardization.)

Part of the problem lay in the BOI's basic industrial orientations: its refusal to impede the operation of a market in which the consumption patterns of an aspiring middle class encouraged a highly differentiated auto
market. Even more serious, the BOI assumed that the expenses involved
in meeting rising local-content requirements would force the assemblers
to cut costs by reducing the number of models. But the BOI was incapable
of enforcing its own local-content regulations.

This was in part because of loopholes provided by the PCMP's export,
"carry over," and penalty provisions. More important, however, were the
board's technical and political weaknesses.

Expertise.   The BOI did not have an official running the auto program whose background was in the auto industry itself. Most of those
involved in the program's formulation had only general mechanical engineering backgrounds. There were also personnel shifts out of the BOI between the formation of the guidelines and the beginning of the program's
implementation. Three of four of the board's best people went to nonautomotive private sectors, while the fourth was hired by the automobile as-

semblers' association, AMII. As a result, no one who had been involved in the original planning and knew the assemblers' original commitments was left except Paterno.[56]

Consequently, the board lacked the technical expertise and information on CKD component prices essential to identify the assemblers' actual local-content level. In fact, the BOI actually relied on the assemblers to design and develop the PCMP reporting, monitoring, and auditing systems.[57]

The BOI's Isolation.   Still more important than the board's technical deficiencies was its lack of political clout.[58] Its dilemma was reflected in the failure to provide macroeconomic incentives for the promotion of small and medium-sized manufacturing firms. Tariff preferences (favoring capital imports, but discouraging those of the raw materials used for auto parts), along with low interest rates and an overvalued peso, encouraged capital-intensive integrated operations during the early 1970s.[59] But the low technology items initially produced by local firms were not included in the BOI's Investment Priorities Plan list. While Paterno was aware of the need to restructure tariffs,[60] tariff changes on raw materials and intermediate goods conflicted with the interests of domestic producers of products such as foundries. As a result, the BOI felt it would be open to charges of favoritism if it took the initiative to push for the changes itself.[61]

Nor was the board's position on incentives and other issues strengthened by the promulgation of martial law in 1972. Most of those interviewed, including Paterno, felt that the impact of martial law was largely to disrupt routine procedures and institutions.

The board was also unable or unwilling to draw support from various sectors of local capital. This was in part owing to the technocrats' strong commitment to free markets and their general aversion to the rising tide of "crony capitalism" under Marcos. The board never thought of building up any of the local assemblers as a "national champion," even though Marcos spoke of cronies such as Silverio as potential "zaibatsu."[62] The board may have been amenable to a Philippine version of "Japan Inc.," but not if it were to be achieved with Silverio. Silverio did manage to become the dominant force in auto production. But, as discussed below, he did so by using political influence to avoid LC while covering losses through cheap government loans.

Why, then, did the board not encourage and use pressure from local parts firms? The answer lies partly in the economic, organizational, and political weakness of these firms. Many were new to the auto industry, and organizationally the sector was split into three sometimes overlapping groups: the Philippine Automotive Parts Manufacturers' Association, composed mostly of small-to-medium Chinese firms producing for the replacement market; the PAA, dominated by the assemblers; and the Philippine Chamber of Industry (PCI), a general industry association.[63]

The BOI did make limited attempts to strengthen the parts sector. Right after deciding to allow five PCMP participants, Paterno urged the car parts firms to organize themselves into one group to gain better leverage in bargaining with the assemblers.[64] In 1972 this led to the establishment of what was to become the major voice of the parts firms, the Consolidated Auto Parts Producers' Association (CAPPA). The BOI recognized CAPPA as the official representative of the parts firms for purposes of program review. This did strengthen these firms' ability to argue for a tightening of localization measures. Under pressure from the parts firms, and to the assemblers' consternation, the government decided that component exports could offset only 15 percent of local content.[65]

But CAPPA's growth was stymied by internal and external forces. In 1973 the group expanded to include the manufacturers of truck and motorcycle components, a move that left car parts firms as only 30 percent of CAPPA's membership.[66] A more significant obstacle was Paterno's refusal to recognize CAPPA members as the only firms certified to supply the PCMP assemblers. When there were some moves in this direction, the more powerful PCI objected in defense of those of its members who did not belong to CAPPA. Granting a supply monopoly to CAPPA would have required a presidential directive and forced the board to grant monopolies in other sectors. Its own policy orientations biased the board against such a move. Corporatist linkages of the sort established between organized Malaysian parts firms and their government counterparts were unlikely in the Philippines.

Finally, the more potent links in the Philippine case, those between Marcos and Silverio, served to offset whatever leverage the parts firms could muster. A good illustration: the government decided to exempt Delta from the 15 percent limit on LC offsets through component exports.[67] The firm holding the dominant market share was thus allowed to reduce its local procurement more than its competitors.

Domestically, then, the BOI found itself in a political "no man's land." This was in part because of its own orientations. But without strong support from Marcos or close ties to the private sector, the board was vulnerable to TNC pressures on the basic issue of the number of PCMP participants, overruled on horizontal integration, incapable of promulgating macroeconomic incentives, and hamstrung in efforts to expand local procurement.

Localization, 1976–1986

Pressures for Mandatory Deletion

By 1976 the PCMP was proving to be a disappointment. Although cumulative fixed investments by passenger car firms had grown nearly fourfold since 1973,[68] physical local content was nowhere near stipulated levels, and the growth of local parts firms had been disappointing. In 1976 the assemblers asked to delay or "stretch out" the LC targets for that year. Despite opposition to the request from the BOI and local parts firms whose tooling plans would be thrown off by the changes,[69] the assemblers prevailed.

This, however, intensified complaints from parts firms that the assemblers were building up their official localization levels either by simply falsifying localization reports or by using export earnings in place of actual local procurement. A further incentive to model proliferation (and thus impediment to localization) also emerged during the mid-to-late 1970s. The PCMP contained a provision that foreign-exchange allocations would increase with market share. The problem here was that the firms were operating in a highly competitive environment; dollar allocations were necessary to bring in new models with which to compete, while market share (through model variation and change) was critical for obtaining more foreign exchange.[70]

These issues were the object of public attention in the late 1970s, and by 1978 the idea of mandatory deletion (the obligatory deletion of certain parts from imported CKD packs so as to necessitate their local purchase) had appeared in the press.[71] In 1981 the BOI actually approved such measures. But these were watered down and poorly implemented. Indeed, the process through which they were formulated and implemented merits further attention. Although it demonstrates the potential local leverage resulting from inter-TNC rivalry and the competitive efforts of local parts firms, it also reveals the inability of Philippine domestic policy to turn such potential into actual power.

Bargaining on Mandatory Deletion

Pressures for New Regulation.   A combination of circumstances led to the BOI's adoption of mandatory deletion. But the precipitating factor was, ironically, a split among the assemblers over localization burdens. Carco (the Yulo-Mitsubishi joint venture), believing it was purchasing a number of parts locally that the other firms were not, pressed for forced deletion on the assumption that increased localization would force the other firms to raise their prices and thus reduce their market shares.[72] Of special concern to Mitsubishi was Delta's evasion of existing LC regulations. According to one former Carco official, Delta's connections with Marcos allowed it to produce five models with no physical local content.[73]

Carco's views were well received in the BOI because of the firm's close ties with the BOI official directly responsible for PCMP implementation. Paterno's replacement by Roberto Ongpin in the summer of 1980 also helped. Paterno had objected to mandatory deletions as counterproductive and antithetical to the market incentives on which the PCMP was based,[74] but Ongpin was open to a more interventionist stance by the BOI. There developed within the board the belief that mandatory deletion would promote increased commonization of local parts and therefore assure the parts firms of greater economies of scale.

Supplementing these factors was the organizational strengthening of the parts firms' association, CAPPA.[75] In 1976 the association elected a new president, Joe Concepcion, a self-made industrialist based in the food-processing industry (who later became minister of industry under President Aquino). Concepcion, who was anxious to get involved in auto parts production, was chosen largely because of his stature and his presumed clout with the BOI. The new president was careful to avoid antagonizing Paterno over the local-content issue. When Ongpin replaced Paterno, however, Concepcion pressed his case strongly.

His ability to do so was bolstered by the transfer of personnel from his own food firm to CAPPA. In addition to this administrative strengthening, the parts group also received a lesson in the utility of a more activist state from a somewhat unexpected source—the Japanese parts producers' association. In 1978 CAPPA had asked the Japanese Auto Parts Industries Association for a presentation on the political and economic bases of parts firms' growth in Japan. The report evidently spurred CAPPA to press the BOI to adopt a more active role. And, finally, CAPPA benefited from the links between Marcos and Republic Glass, one of the group's largest and most enthusiastic supporters of mandatory deletion.[76]

Finally, CAPPA's public role expanded in part under pressure from the BOI itself.[77] Although the board felt that mandatory deletion was necessary, it could not take such a position publicly for fear of alienating certain assemblers benefiting from the PCMP loopholes, especially Delta. It therefore unofficially asked CAPPA to press for mandatory deletion. The group responded with suggestions for sixty-four parts to be sourced locally and incentives for increased local content.[78]CAPPA also raised complaints, echoing an exhaustive ILO study, that the assemblers had failed to comply with their original commitments of support for local firms, including free prototypes, guaranteed payments in thirty days, and advanced down payments to parts firms.[79]

What seemed to be emerging here for the first time since the PCMP's inception was an informal local coalition in favor of greater and more efficient localization. The parts firms were benefiting from a division among the assemblers, changes in BOI leadership and philosophy, and their own associational growth. However, these factors proved to be a fragile political base.

Formulating the Policy.   In March 1980 the BOI publicly questioned the advisability of using export earnings for LC credit, and in July the BOI actually came out with a tentative localization schedule that mandated *physical* LC levels of 43.8 percent for 1981, gradually rising to 75 percent in 1985.[80] In fact, the schedule was clearly unrealistic, as the BOI acknowledged by calling the proposal simply an opening bid, stating its (the board's) openness to different proposals from the assemblers and assuring the assemblers that localized parts would have to be produced by at least two domestic firms, be used by at least two assemblers over the past twelve months, and be of reasonable quality and price.[81]

A process of negotiations then began between the BOI and the assemblers, in which the board backed down extensively from its original positions on when mandatory deletion would become effective and the specifics of the new regulations. The BOI agreed to delay any changes until 1981 because of a "series of requests" from the assemblers.[82] The board opted to await the assemblers' suggestions before deciding on the final percentages,[83] and in fact it relied quite heavily on the assemblers themselves for advice on mandatory deletion rates.

The problem lay partly in the BOI's persistently low and even declining level of expertise.[84] After almost eight years of PCMP operation, the board had not yet developed a cadre of automotive experts, although its overall responsibilities had been extended to several other sectors. With Paterno's departure there was really only one responsible BOI official with several years of automobile experience by the early 1980s. The BOI did bring in an outside consultant to help sort out the 1981 mandatory deletion revisions. But the individual left in frustration after failing to clarify the board's monitoring procedures. Nor did the BOI consult with CAPPA on the particulars of mandatory deletion or its enforcement.

Relying largely on the assemblers, then, the BOI produced new, more moderate, guidelines in July 1981, which it promised not to implement until April 1982. The new guidelines mandated physical LC levels of 30 percent in 1982, rising to 50 percent in 1984. The guidelines also contained important loopholes—namely, that mandatorily deleted parts had to be "economically feasible" to manufacture, be produced by two firms, and be used by at least two assemblers over the preceding twelve months. This last condition allowed the assemblers to drag their feet on several components that were not, they claimed, used by two assemblers.[85] This was, of course, a vicious circle, for the industry's proliferation of makes and models inhibited the use of particular parts by more than one assembler.

In addition to the BOI's lack of technical expertise, the ostensibly strong push for mandatory deletion was undermined by a shift in patterns of competition among assemblers and a weakening of CAPPA. Carco reversed its position and joined the opposition to mandatory deletion upon finding that it, too, was vulnerable to the higher prices charged by local parts firms producing mandatorily deleted parts. Moreover, Carco doubted its own ability to meet the originally proposed mandatory deletion levels and was concerned that it would be forced to rely on foreign suppliers linked to rival Japanese assemblers.[86]

Pressure from CAPPA for a tougher mandatory deletion program also diminished. Concepcion, who subsequently became quite active in plans for an ASEAN regional auto scheme, stepped down as the association's president in 1981. And, unlike in the Malaysian case, the assemblers' influence in the group expanded, as Ford and GM representatives were elected to the CAPPA board.[87] Active private sector support for BOI efforts was thus disintegrating, a fact reflected in the board's ill-fated efforts to implement the watered-down mandatory deletion regulations.

The Compliance Committee and the Problem of Silverio

Once the new mandatory deletion schedule was established, the BOI had to rely on individuals working for the assemblers themselves for help in monitoring and stopping noncompliance by assemblers. But cheating clearly continued, as reflected by the complaints of both the parts makers and various assemblers. Of particular importance was the frustration of other assemblers over Delta's ability to circumvent BOI local content rules and consequently to produce vehicles with cheaper and higher-quality (imported) parts.

The result of this grumbling was the establishment of a Compliance Committee in late 1982.[88] This committee represented the BOI's effort to turn competition among the assemblers into an organized self-policing mechanism. But the committee was headed by a BOI official with little automobile experience and even less desire to step on assemblers' toes, especially those of so politically well placed a firm as Delta. Moreover, the board excluded CAPPA from the committee's deliberations, arguing that the BOI itself could effectively represent the interests of the parts firms, and that CAPPA was not a responsible partner in industry deliberations.[89]

CAPPA argued that the BOI was unable to defend the interests of the parts firms on the Compliance Committee.[90] The board was, in fact, plagued by more than simply technical inadequacies. In a number of cases its hands were tied by connections between assemblers, especially Delta, and higher political officials. Silverio's firm was consistently able to import mandatorily deleted parts, avoid payment of duties and tariffs, and generally exaggerate its actual degree of localization. In a particularly flagrant case, Silverio received 15 percent LC credit for "complete engine assembly" whereas the actual operation did not involve over 5 percent of local products or labor.

There were limits to Silverio's ability to circumvent regulations, but these were imposed more by competition from another crony than by BOI procedures or even the complaints of other assemblers.[91] For example, Delta decided it was feasible to stop purchasing locally produced glass on obtaining 15 percent LC credit for its engine assembly. This hurt the country's only glass producer, Republic Glass, whose owner, as noted earlier, had close links to Marcos. Republic's complaints to the BOI resulted in the board's pressuring Delta, as well as other firms who were not using local glass for some of their models, to resume its purchases of local glass. But such success in forcing Silverio to comply with regulations was rare.

In sum, the BOI's efforts at correcting the weaknesses in its LC program were weak in both formulation and implementation. Competition among the assemblers had much to do with the attempt's even getting off the ground. But this rivalry was unstable in its intensity. And because neither the parts firms nor the BOI was able to make effective use of the competition when it did exist, pressure for higher local content rapidly disappeared. At the same time, the BOI's oversight capacity had not grown. Rather than strengthening and utilizing the admittedly fragmented parts firms for monitoring assistance, the board opted to rely largely on the assemblers themselves.

In theory this approach made sense. Each firm wanted to make sure the others did not gain a market advantage by cheating, and there were some individuals within the firms who wanted the program to operate fairly. But the political connections and market strength of Delta, the major offender, made such a strategy unworkable in practice.

A Crony Nationalist.   It should be emphasized, however, that Silverio's negative contribution to Philippine auto policy lay not in his lack of nationalist ambitions, but in his irresponsible business practices, made possible by ties to Marcos.[92] Far from being a TNC puppet, Silverio was highly committed to expansion of the Philippine auto industry. Delta had probably the most advanced and complete tool and die shop in the country. The firm, which dominated the market up to 1980, maintained a fairly competent R&D center and even began to develop an export market for a Philippine-made vehicle in competition with Toyota itself.[93]

But his ambitions were undermined by extensive corruption and short-range vision. Silverio and many of his major officers bled the auto operation of large sums of money, which went into individual pockets and ventures, such as home appliances, that exceeded the Silverio group's resources. Silverio's own management team, especially the financial group, was ill-equipped to handle large-scale operations. The team itself exerted little or no control on Silverio's investment decisions, while Silverio himself refused to let the firm go public. His ability to remain private depended on his links to Marcos, through which Delta obtained large state loans from the Philippine National Bank, beginning in 1981.[94] These loans were made despite PCMP guidelines prohibiting participants from obtaining government loans and opposition to such rescues from both the technocrats and the World Bank.[95]

Nor was Toyota able to control its local partner, despite Silverio's large debt to the Japanese firm (mostly in suppliers' credits). Toyota had failed in attempts to streamline Delta's operations during the early 1970s. Toyota then attempted to gain some control by granting Delta a ten-year loan of $3 million in exchange for collateral of 40 percent voting rights. But Silverio obtained presidential directives prohibiting foreign equity in a firm that had received reparations money, and the Japanese were never able to exercise their rights. Nor did Toyota representatives working inside the company have much influence.[96] It was only with Delta's financial crunch in the 1980s that the Japanese were sufficiently part of Delta's management to countersign checks.

Silverio's crony status thus allowed him to operate independently of foreign capital, but it also removed him from the discipline of either the BOI or the market. The impact of this arrangement can be seen in an important area of Philippine auto policy not directly linked to the PCMP—the BOI's 1977 effort to promote local manufacture of diesel engines.

The Instability of Local Capital and Foreign Domination in Diesel Engine Production

Maneuvering for Position.   In 1977 the BOI announced its Progressive Manufacture of Automotive Diesel Engines (PMADE).[97] Convinced

that local truck assemblers would be compelled to use the locally manufactured engines, Silverio moved to become one of the PMADE manufacturers by linking up with a German firm, Maschinenfabrik Augsburg-
Nürnberg (MAN).[98] Having seen its South Korean and Japanese
operations reduced by strong local partners and effective government localization policies, MAN was anxious to gain access to expanding ASEAN
markets such as the Philippines. The company's officials were impressed
by Delta's political, financial, and managerial resources, and agreed to a
Silverio proposal through which Delta would assemble MAN commercial
vehicles on the condition that MAN produced diesel engines with Delta
under the PMADE program.

The problem of limiting program participants, so critical in the PCMP,
once again emerged. Eight manufacturers submitted applications for
participation in the diesel engine project, for which the BOI had stipulated only one, "but in any event no more than two."[99] Surprised by the
large number of contenders, the BOI was not able to make an initial reduction of the applicants until May 1978. The short-listed firms included
MAN/Delta; Perkins in cooperation with the Herdis group;[100] Leyland
with Marsteel; and Isuzu with C. Itoh, one of Japan's largest trading
companies.

By the end of 1978 the BOI indicated unofficially that MAN would be
selected for engines above 150 hp, and Perkins for those between 90–150
hp. Bargaining over two contentious issues followed. The BOI insisted,
based on its PCMP experience, that the foreign licensor carry the full financial risk during an initial five-year period, that no licensing fees or royalties be paid to the parent company during the initial period, and that 60
percent of the shares be transferred to Philippine hands after twenty years
of operation. The short-listed competitors initially resisted these conditions, but they eventually agreed under mutual pressure. Faced with the
need to allocate substantial funds for the engine operation, MAN decided
to use money it was owed by Silverio from the already-established commercial vehicle assembly operation as its investment in diesel engine
production.[101]

The second problem involved levels of protection. The BOI awarded
MAN production of 170 to 320 hp engines in February 1979, but failed
to make the use of these engines mandatory in locally assembled trucks.
The protected market did not exist. After strenuous protests by MAN and

Silverio, the BOI allowed MAN to supplement its market by producing engines for the more popular 90–150 hp niche. While this decision created an overlap in production between MAN and Perkins and ran counter to the BOI's original 1977 guidelines,[102] it was accepted grudgingly by all parties.

But MAN and Perkins, both disappointed with their potential market shares, then requested more favorable government incentives: no export obligations, a ban on the import of engines for CKD vehicles, and a ban on imports of second-hand commercial vehicles. Although the BOI agreed to consider the import restrictions, it insisted on LC levels ranging from 30 percent at the beginning to 60 percent after five years, and export requirements of $60 million over the first five years for Perkins, and DM 30 million for MAN.[103] The firms responded to the BOI's stance by hedging on their commitments.

But they soon came under strong pressure from Isuzu to comply with BOI terms. Isuzu had lost out in the first bid, but mounted a strong public campaign for readmission, even without a politically influential local partner. The majority of diesel engines in the Philippines were, in fact, Isuzu-made, and many of them needed replacement. The Japanese firm called in support from users of its engines—namely, jeepney drivers, bus operators, and trucking companies, who even placed advertisements in the newspapers demanding Isuzu's inclusion. Most critically, Isuzu stated its willingness to accept all BOI conditions.

Isuzu's campaign had the desired effect; the BOI told Perkins to withdraw at the end of 1979, and in January 1980 Isuzu agreed to produce 50–150 hp engines under the BOI's export and LC requirements. BOI officials promptly pressed MAN to accept a similar deal. The BOI received strong support in this effort from MAN's local partner, Silverio, who was now concerned about his own position in the engine project. Lengthy negotiations followed, which seem to have resulted in a compromise by August 1980: in exchange for an agreement to meet somewhat modified LC and export requirements, MAN obtained BOI assurance that by mid 1981 locally assembled trucks would have to use its locally produced engines. Effectively drawing on private sector pressure from Silverio, and using competition among foreign firms, the BOI seemed to have driven a good bargain in exchange for guaranteed market access.

Delta's Financial Problems.   But the bargain was undermined by Silverio's financial setbacks. In 1980 it became evident that Delta's sales targets for commercial vehicles produced with MAN had been wildly over-ambitious. All five major car manufacturers were losing money, Delta for the first time in its history.[104] Silverio's position deteriorated even more in early 1981 in the wake of the bankruptcy and flight from the Philippines of Dewey Dee, a textile and banking crony of Marcos's, who left behind over $80 million in largely unsecured debts. Dee's disappearance created a temporary financial panic that caused the collapse of numerous institutions, including Silverio's own finance house, Philfinance.

Silverio then obtained rescue funds from state banks. MAN hoped that these loans would allow Delta to repay its long overdue debts to the German firm.[105] MAN intended to use this money as its investment in the diesel engine operation. But the financial crisis provided new leverage for the technocrats, never great friends of Silverio's. Backed by the World Bank and the IMF, the BOI's head, Roberto Ongpin, compelled Silverio to drop its commercial vehicle operations with MAN in order to qualify for continued state loans.

Under these conditions MAN refused to sign an agreement on the diesel engine project. Isuzu, meanwhile, offered to step in should the German firm withdraw. The BOI accepted this offer, and its revised guidelines stipulated that diesel engines from 50 to 150 hp must be purchased from Isuzu's Pilipinas Engine Corp.[106] Isuzu's success was short-lived, however, since the diesel engine project never got off the ground. The government essentially let it die a slow death in the face of strong World Bank opposition and a very weak domestic market. Other Japanese truck manufacturers were also prepared to circumvent Isuzu's monopoly by using engines with slightly different specifications than Isuzu products.[107]

These factors might well have killed the project regardless of Delta's financial problems. But Silverio's unrealistic market projections, his willingness to assume huge debts, and his assumption of constant support from the Marcos government certainly helped delay the project until the market dropped. In doing so, Silverio not only undermined a relatively successful BOI effort to learn from its PCMP experience and make effective use of inter-TNC rivalry; he also paved the way for the project's denationalization.

Problems of Rationalization, 1976–1986

Model Proliferation and the Attempted Correctives

Pressures for Model Limits. The combination of unstable local capital, inter-TNC rivalry, and BOI weaknesses seen in the preceding section also plagued efforts to rationalize the auto industry. The BOI had assumed that formal limits on the number of models were not necessary, reasoning that the costs involved in increased LC levels would induce a reduction. But intense competition in a sophisticated market, and the PCMP's allowance of foreign exchange based on market share (with market share requiring numerous models) encouraged persistent fragmentation.

By 1976 this fragmentation was clearly hindering plans for increased local auto parts manufacture.[108] Consumers, parts makers, and even some of the assemblers themselves began to press for state-mandated model limits. Consumers' belief that a reduction in the number of models offered would lower costs and prices pushed Marcos to order a BOI study of the problem.[109] The parts firms argued that the large numbers of models translated into small, uneconomical production volumes for them. But CAPPA did not present a unified position on this issue, in part because of threats from assemblers to avoid purchases from firms pressing for model reductions.[110]

But as in the mandatory deletion issue, the critical source of pressure for model limits involved inter-TNC competition. Some assemblers argued that the ability of competitors to offer a wide variety of new models provided an unfair market advantage. Specifically, most firms attacked Delta's ability to offer a wide range of models while disregarding local content levels. Several firms were also concerned with Ford's importation of six-cylinder models (since the PCMP only covered production of four-cylinder vehicles).[111] By November 1979 pressure for model limits prodded the BOI to initiate a review of the situation and pledge to settle the issue once and for all by the end of the year.[112]

Formulation of Model Limits. In 1981, after initial differences on model numbers, the BOI and the assemblers agreed on a formula of "two and a half": two basic models with one variant each, and one basic model with no variant.[113] The real bargaining turned on the definition of *vari-*

ant. The board had originally understood a variant to have the same engine, wheelbase and chassis, but to differ as to number of doors or being a sedan as opposed to a station wagon. But after intense negotiations, the BOI agreed to a much more permissive definition. Under the revised formula of the 1981 guidelines, a variant could have an entirely different engine from the basic model.[114]

The BOI's surrender on this issue was in part a result of pressure from Carco and Delta, the two firms offering the largest numbers of models.[115] Silverio was especially insistent, charging that a stringent definition of variants would only help the multinationals. The state, he asserted, should help Philippine companies to promote technological development, since foreign firms "are here only to sell products and have no interest in developing indigenous technology."[116]

The shift also reflected changing government energy policies and a strong desire by TNCs for access to the country's large taxi market. When the government promoted a switch to diesel fuel in the mid-to-late 1970s (as reflected in the PMADE project), GM almost doubled its market share from 1980 to 1981 by quickly coming out with a diesel version of its Gemini aimed especially at the taxi market.[117] But by 1980–81 the country's diesel supplies were significantly less than originally projected, prompting the BOI to limit the use of diesel fuel to commercial (i.e., non-PCMP) vehicles.[118] This policy change threatened GM's new market gains as well as other firms' chances of competing with GM for the diesel niche in the small car market.

While the new definition of variant did provide flexibility for including new diesel models within the two-and-a-half limit, the BOI resisted actually allowing diesels in the program as late as early 1982.[119] But under strong pressure from the assemblers, especially Delta, the board took the easy way out and opted to judge the issue on a case-by-case basis.[120] The door was open for GM to retain its successful model and for Delta and Carco to move in and compete for the taxi market.

Implementation Problems.   Carrying out these already weakened regulations proved extremely difficult. In what the Manila papers called "snubs" and "defiance" of the BOI, some of the firms simply failed to meet two 1981 deadlines for registration of their new models.[121] And when the firms did register their models, they essentially overwhelmed the BOI by including all their existing models and variants plus a diesel-powered model to contest GM's market position. This allowed them to gain leverage, as one paper noted, when they began to "haggle" with the board over model numbers.[122]

The BOI remained technically and politically unprepared to contend with the issues involved. In many instances the board had to seek clarification from individuals within the assembly firms on model definitions.[123] As with respect to the LC issue, these weaknesses emerged most glaringly in its inability to control excesses by Silverio. The monitoring of the LC levels required to bring in two extra models proved especially difficult. The other assemblers accused Delta of importing extra models with nowhere near the required domestic components. But the BOI was technically incapable of checking, and if it had been, Delta's political ties probably would have precluded effective action.

Delta's competitors did try to use the Compliance Committee to restrain the firm, but Silverio's political ties to the presidential palace generally neutralized the committee.[124] When it was reported in June 1982 that Delta was disregarding official model limits a government official admitted that the company had the "blessings of the government since Delta has led the market in terms of sales for the past few years and it would be ungrateful to penalize the company with the new PCMP rules."[125] By May 1982 it had become clear that the broad model limits that had evolved were ineffective. Models were "flooding" the market in excess of BOI limits.[126] The final (1984) set of PCMP guidelines allowed the firms to produce any models they chose as long as LC, foreign-exchange, and price requirements were met.[127]

The technicalities and political problems of identifying and monitoring model limits overwhelmed the BOI, especially in the context of intensifying corporate competition and an absence of support from Marcos or local firms. There remained, however, one area where the issues were a bit simpler, where a combination of macroeconomic pressures, interfirm rivalry, and broad public support for the BOI seemed likely to unite the domestic forces necessary for reform.

Reducing the Number of Assemblers: Last Efforts

The final efforts to streamline the auto industry during the Marcos period began with BOI efforts to resolve the country's worsening balance of payments deficit.[128] In April 1983 BOI chairman Ongpin publicly noted rising automobile costs and attributed them to artificial pricing and insufficient deletion allowances on the part of Japanese assemblers. Arguing that these practices were a form of transfer pricing leading to tax losses and unnecessary outflows of foreign exchange,[129] Ongpin announced that CKD prices were to be frozen at a level no higher than 85 percent of the CBU price.

Only one assembler, Carco (Mitsubishi), was willing to comply with Ongpin's price limit. Both Carco's local chief and the Mitsubishi home office hoped that a cooperative attitude would earn Mitsubishi closer ties to and better leverage with the Philippine government.[130] The other firms took a strong stand against the board's plans, asserting in mid July that they would have to close down operations if forced to limit their prices. Accepting Ongpin's proposal would not only constitute an implicit admission that their deletion allowances had, in fact, been too small; it would also possibly open the door to similar measures in other countries.[131]

Ongpin responded by wondering if this 85 percent rule might not be a good way to achieve reduction to the number of firms originally planned for the industry.[132] He had several sources of leverage with which to meet the assemblers' threats of withdrawal. One was the willingness of South Korean firms, as well as Mitsubishi, to comply with the new rules. Ongpin noted that the South Korean minister of commerce and industry had discussed with him the possibility of introducing the Pony into the Philippines. This, for Ongpin, would be healthier than a situation where the Japanese firms operated like a cartel in threatening to cut off operations. "The Philippines," he proclaimed, had "been taken for a ride too long."[133]

Ongpin also had support from within the government because of the automobile industry's contribution to the Philippines' trade deficit with Japan.[134] And, finally, because the BOI was clearly fighting for price reductions and taking an overtly nationalist stand, various consumer organizations urged the government to pursue its course even if it meant the exclusion of Japanese suppliers.[135]

Riding this nationalist wave, the BOI found itself in direct negotiations with the Japan Automobile Manufacturers' Association (JAMA). The latter was unable to implement its central strategy—namely, to present a united front against the 85 percent ruling by bringing Mitsubishi back into line. Mitsubishi's expression of compliance with the BOI's announcement "shook the industry."[136] When the Japanese embassy and MITI refused to intervene,[137] the BOI seemed to have the upper hand. In the beginning of August, GM and Nissan joined Carco in agreeing to the price levels, and by the end of that month JAMA gave up.[138]

But the tactics adopted by the assemblers during the bargaining process exacerbated the foreign-exchange problem. During the course of their dispute with Ongpin, most of the assemblers had, in fact, stopped deliveries from Japan; dollars would have to be provided to renew the previous high level of imports. It was at this point, in early August, that Marcos issued Executive Order No. 906 mandating the BOI to come up with new PCMP guidelines to limit the participants to not more than two assemblers.

Assembler Reduction . . . and Addition.   The BOI failed in a series of attempts to carry out Marcos's mandate. The board sought to encourage voluntary mergers that would include both truck and car operations. Ongpin hoped to end up with two firms that would reduce the number of makes and models, increase local content, bring in more sophisticated manufacturing techniques, and move away from exclusive reliance on Japanese suppliers.[139] The plan failed when the assemblers refused to merge into what the BOI considered single operations.[140]

The board's next approach was to let the firms fight it out by competitive bidding based on self-sufficiency in foreign exchange, reasonable prices, local content, and willingness to buy out those firms not accepted for the program. The firms resisted, arguing that huge investments of between $200 and $600 million would be necessary to generate the kind of exports necessary for self-sufficiency in foreign exchange.[141]

The BOI's response was a proposed "knockout" scheme—a natural elimination process in which foreign-exchange allocations would be reduced over three years, so that 1987 allocations would be 25 percent of 1983 levels. By 1987 the firms would submit bids based on past and future foreign-exchange earnings capacity, from which the BOI would select two participants.[142] Again, the firms objected to the expense and risks involved.[143] As the structuralist approach would predict, heavy investments required of the TNCs weakened the BOI's ability to proceed with the last of the Marcos-era rationalization efforts.

These failures did not mean that the existing industry structure remained stable. As noted in chapter 3, several firms stopped operations between 1982 and 1985. DMG, plagued by mismanagement and an uncompetitive brand (Volkswagen), went out of business in 1982. Ford announced its closing in March 1984, and GM a year later, both presumably owing to reluctance to make new investments in a country of questionable political stability. And Delta, heavily indebted, stopped operations in the summer of 1984 when the Philippines National Bank (PNB) refused to provide rescue loans and decided to foreclose.[144]

Other things being equal, these closings would have led to precisely the market streamlining desired by the BOI. But other things were not equal; competitive Japanese TNCs and Philippine "capital umbrellas" ensured that numerous firms would continue to contend for a small market. Pilipinas Nissan Inc. joined the PCMP after taking over DMG's assets in 1982. In 1984 Mazda Philippines Inc. was formed in hopes of taking over Ford's facilities. Both used ties to Imelda Marcos's family (the Romualdez group) to bolster their chances of market access.[145] And while the Romualdez group was offering to take over Ford's facilities with Mazda, it was also eyeing Delta's facilities. Two other prominent families, Floirendo and Cojuangco, were also interested in joining Mazda. Finally, even as the PNB was foreclosing on Delta, Toyota was asking the BOI for permission to retain Delta's PCMP slot through a joint venture with the PNB itself.

The BOI struggled to maintain some control over this process. It insisted that Mazda's and Nissan's local operations merge before beginning operation; and it refused Mazda the right to buy Ford's stamping plant without coming through on a previous commitment to set up a transaxle assembly plant whose output would service other Nissan assemblers in the region.[146] But with Marcos's power crumbling and powerful local interests willing to play host to the Japanese, the board had little leverage. The PCMP ended in the kind of stalemate generally preferred by the Japanese. Except for Mitsubishi (which had expanded its commitment to Carco), the Japanese were successfully keeping their fingers in the market with minimum investment.

Philippine efforts to develop an efficient national auto industry by manipulating inter-TNC rivalry were only minimally successful. The BOI did attract significant foreign investments into the manufacture of major car components both for export and for local use. But auto parts production was a vertically integrated process in an increasingly fragmented market where aggressive TNCs, a nationalist but inefficient local assembler, and other "capital umbrellas" overwhelmed the BOI. Most damaging, the PCMP's performance declined after initial success at obtaining large TNC investments. By the end of the Marcos era, the industry was largely denationalized, and localization levels were disappointingly low.

Judged by these overall results, the Philippine auto experience seems to support the structuralist view of host country–TNC bargaining. Such a conclusion would be mistaken. While the structuralist approach accurately predicts many of the obstacles to Philippine auto-manufacturing efforts, it does not account for the significant initial successes. Nor does it show why poor performance and decreasing local leverage were inevitable outcomes. Specifically, it fails to account for the country's potential leverage, the complexities of private sector support for local auto manufacture, and the importance of the Philippine political economy in discouraging the promotion and utilization of these factors for local advantage.

8

Thailand

Thailand undertook auto industrialization under a set of domestic political conditions that differed from those in each of its three ASEAN neighbors. The Thai state did not exhibit the high degree of centralized political leadership and/or the clientelist links to specific entrepreneurs seen under Marcos. And, unlike in Malaysia and Indonesia, Thai auto policy did not have to balance its industrialization project with ethnic redistribution efforts. The result was a growth of local firms attempting to increase local auto manufacture and a strengthening of functional ties between these firms and their public sector counterparts. These developments in turn facilitated the region's strongest auto policy achievements. But the process, as elsewhere, was far from even.

Defeat of State Reform, 1971

The Origins of Automotive Reform

As elsewhere in ASEAN, Thai auto efforts of the late 1960s and early 1970s were a response to the problems engendered by prior industrialization policies. Government incentives of the 1960s had helped create a fragmented industry dominated by numerous foreign assemblers (see chapter 3). Foreign domination did not, however, mean an absence of local capital. Western and Japanese assemblers, and in some cases Japanese parts firms, had entered the Thai market via links with large local conglomerates. These Thai groups, themselves close to important Thai banking interests, saw ties with foreign capital as opportunities to shift from import and distribution into assembly and eventually manufacture.[1]

Local capital also emerged in parts production, at least initially to supply the replacement parts market. One partial list identifies thirty local parts firms established between 1962 and 1975. Ten of the twelve firms established during the 1960s were completely Thai-owned.[2] And, as discussed below, while most of these firms had technical tie-ups to foreign producers, several would also go on to lead the movement of parts firms for higher localization in subsequent years.

By the late 1960s the lack of controls on new foreign entrants and their linkages to influential local capital resulted in a proliferation of inefficient, import-dependent assembly operations that contributed to serious balance of trade and payments deficits. When a conflict broke out between assembly firms whose promotional incentives were due to expire and those just entering the market and due to receive new incentives, the Thai Board of Investments (BOI) decided to reassess the country's approach to auto localization. As the agency responsible for granting incentives, the BOI commissioned a survey of the industry by an American expert, J. B. Organ.

While the resulting report in 1968 urged increased investments in local parts production, the "most critical and decisive step" it proposed was rationalization through a limitation on the number of authorized assemblers.[3] The report argued that the Thai market could justify at most only six assembly operations and urged a reduction of assemblers, not through arbitrary selection, but through minimum requirements for invested capital, annual production levels, and size and productive capacity of facilities. This was, moreover, to be a "quick and decisive" transition; the weeding out of the weaker firms over time simply through competition would be too slow and politically painful. It was essential for the government to "enforce rigid regulations now . . . and not be tempted to show timidity" in doing so.[4]

The report reinforced similar views of Thai public and private sector officials. The BOI stopped granting promotional status to new firms in 1969[5] in conjunction with a review process undertaken by the Ministry of Industry (MOI), the agency responsible for issuing factory licenses. The initiative of the MOI's Department of Industrial Economics was critical. The department chief, Dr. Wichitwong Na Pomphet, set up an interagency Automobile Development Committee (ADC) and proposed a number of policy guidelines paralleling those of the 1968 Organ report. Supported by the cabinet, Wichitwong initiated a two-year process of investigation both within the bureaucracy and, most important, with business.

The process began with an MOI-organized seminar, "Solutions for the Problems and Obstacles to Industrial Development," in which Thai business's leading association, the Association of Thai Industries (ATI), played a central role.[6] Led by former government officials who had moved into the private sector, the ATI criticized the government for its tax policies, incentives, and failure to develop a long-term industrial strategy. Reinforcing the earlier BOI Organ report on the need for industrial rationalization, the association denounced the government's "liberal industrial policy" of unrestricted entry, which had led to overcompetition, surplus capacity, and the crowding out of small businesses in industries such as textiles, electrical appliances, and automobiles.

The ATI's role in the making of auto policy grew. Early in 1971 the association followed up its initial proposals by stressing that government auto strategy be clear-cut and consistent, protect local industries from foreign competition, and restrict the number of newcomers. The ATI was especially insistent on this last point. While government officials argued that new entrants brought with them needed marketing skills, the ATI stressed that localization was not possible without efficiency, and efficiency required limits on new entrants.[7]

On the basis of subsequent negotiations and its own investigation, the MOI announced a comprehensive plan for reform of the auto industry in July 1971. Reflecting the ATI's views, the new policy mandated both an expansion of local content and a series of rationalization measures (limits on vehicle types, limits on models and engine sizes, and minimum capacity and investment).

There were pockets of opposition to this policy. U.S. firms, concerned that the proposed limits on engine sizes would place them at a disadvantage in relation to the Japanese, sent top officials from home offices to lobby against the new regulations.[8] But the most serious opposition was to come from one of the newer entrants, Bangchan General Assembly, a Japanese-Thai joint venture to assemble Volkswagens, Opels, Austins, and Mazdas. Bangchan had obtained a license in 1970 and was hoping to assemble nine models of several different makes, well in excess of the two allowable models permitted under the proposed regulations. Backed by its foreign principals, Bangchan pressed government officials to relax the restrictions. With cabinet backing,[9] the MOI refused the request and the new regulations were announced in July 1971.

Thailand's new auto policy indeed seemed to have sufficient political basis for successful implementation. Despite the opposition noted above, most foreign and domestic firms supported the measures.[10] Thai and foreign assemblers generally recognized the need for streamlining and were pleased with the limits on new competitors. The Japanese in particular knew that the model-reduction process would favor small cars, in which they had a marked advantage over Western firms. The increased number of Japanese component firms moving into Thailand during the early 1970s was evidence of Japanese willingness to comply with new localization plans.[11] And, finally, Thai auto parts firms were encouraged by the markets promised by new LC requirements.

The policy also benefited from a clear locus of initiative within the state bureaucracy—the MOI's Department of Industrial Economics. State agencies were not united over levels of protection and tariffs.[12] But the department was generally able to count on the support of other units working through the ADC. Wichitwong stressed that the policy was a package of measures requiring interministerial coordination,[13] and successfully emphasized the nationalist benefits of auto industrialization in appeals for support from both government officials and the public. The response was quite positive, with one Bangkok daily urging the government to create a national car.[14]

Conspicuous by its absence from the entire auto policy process was the Thai military. Although the military had accepted a constitution in 1968 after a decade of authoritarian control, it maintained significant general influence through its majority in the 1969 parliamentary elections and thus in the cabinet. Its support for the MOI and general absence from the auto policy arena was in part a reflection of the auto industry's increasingly technical requirements.

But it also reflected the strengthening of the private sector and the changing nature of public–private sector relations. The military governments of the late 1950s and early 1960s presided over an increasingly laissez-faire system that, together with ethnic harmony, facilitated the economic and associational strengthening of generally Sino-Thai local capital. The ATI was the most visible symbol of this growth. And as national goals became more ambitious, the state's need for, and openness to, private sector support grew. As Patcharee Thanamai notes, the "government was relatively more responsive to the business group because it wanted their cooperation to implement industrial policy (such as in local content requirements)."[15]

In sum, the 1971 auto measures reflected a shift from a top-down, largely clientelist process to a more functionally based network concerned with orderly marketing and production arrangements. As it turned out, however, these more corporatist arrangements were still rather fragile.

Patronage Reasserted and Rationalization Blocked

In November 1971 political support for the new auto measures weakened. The Thai military drew on public dissatisfaction with what was perceived as an irresponsible parliamentary opposition and dissolved the country's two-year-old legislature.[16] Although the military claimed to proceed with reforms, the coup did not lead to a regularization of administrative structures and procedures. It instead entailed a reassertion of patronage politics over an increasingly professionalized bureaucracy, albeit in a more centralized form than was possible with parliamentary intrusion into the economic policy process.

Career bureaucratic officials like those who had designed the 1971 auto policy saw their influence reduced. Bangchan, which began producing more than the allowable number of models after the coup,[17] circumvented these officials and made direct appeals for a revision of the rationalization measures to one of the top military leaders and the new minister of economic affairs, Pote Sarasin. Sarasin, a major business figure who eventually became an important shareholder in Bangchan, backed the request and ordered the MOI to remove the model restrictions.[18] MOI officials protested the change to the new leadership group, the National Executive Council, but were met with what one official termed "an ignorance of the industry's economic requirements."[19] Unsuccessful appeals were also lodged by other auto firms, both individually and through the ATI.[20] The government announced a modified policy in February 1972. Limitations of vehicle type, model, and engine size were dropped. The other assemblers, having first opposed such a change, felt compelled to join the competitive bandwagon by requesting and obtaining "equal rights" with Bangchan in terms of numbers of models.[21] Responding to widespread nationalist sentiment, however, the new government maintained the 1971 LC requirements. Broad support for localization before the coup intensified with a student-led boycott of Japanese goods in November 1972. While such sentiment was not shared by the new government, the military viewed the maintenance of 25 percent LC levels as visible proof of its nationalist credentials.[22]

This new policy was double-edged. Its localization requirements expanded opportunities for local parts firms, who would eventually reinforce pressure for rationalization. But in the short run its lack of model and plant restrictions laid the groundwork for a competitive free-for-all. Domestic Thai politics—the undermining of career bureaucrats and the weakening of links between them and organized business—broke the restraints on the more destructive aspects of inter-TNC rivalry. As firms fought to fill every market niche, the stage was set for increased market fragmentation.

Market Fragmentation, State Inaction, and Forces for a New Policy, 1972–1979

Industry Problems and Industrial Policy Problems

New makes exacerbated the impact of model proliferation. Eight additional assemblers, attracted by the lack of model restrictions and rumors of a CBU ban, sought and obtained licenses between 1972 and 1977. By 1975 Thai assembly plants had a combined capacity six times higher than annual vehicle sales.[23] LC levels did increase to roughly 25 percent by

1977, but costs were high and complaints about poor quality frequent.[24] One manufacturer had to produce over 200 specifications for radiators, while the leading shock absorber firm produced 130 types.[25]

These weaknesses were a function of chaos and contradictions in state auto policies during most of the decade. There were no controls on make and model proliferation, and no restrictions on new entrants.[26] The government's rationalization strategy was, like that of the Philippines, one of attrition: market competition and rising LC requirements were expected to weed out the weaker firms. Yet officials admitted to having no plans beyond 1976—the highly unrealistic target date for local manufacture of major components.[27] Even existing localization plans were hampered by a series of other problems: (1) the government failed to ban CBU imports (which accounted for well over 50 percent of vehicles sold until 1978), thus limiting the market for local goods; (2) tariff incentives for CKD assembly versus CBU import were weak;[28] and (3) the government's LC formula allowed assemblers to inflate the value of locally purchased components.[29]

This paralysis of state auto efforts reflected broader problems in the policy environment. Interagency differences impeded policy coordination. MOI plans for tariff differentials to promote local manufacture were resisted by the Finance Ministry, which feared revenue losses.[30] And, because of poor coordination between the MOI and the Customs Department, a "not insignificant" quantity of CKD kits entered the country without the required percentage of deleted parts.[31]

Political instability impeded organizational learning and the use of accumulated knowledge within the bureaucracy. From 1972 to 1977 Thailand had six different prime ministers, ruling with different cabinets and degrees of authoritarianism.[32] These changing governments with incumbent changes of ministers limited the value and effect of the MOI's Automobile Development Committee. The MOI had accumulated the information, personnel, and policies "that could rationalize this increasingly chaotic but expanding" sector. But suggestions and appeals from within the MOI were "ignored by those in government positions."[33]

Long-term auto policy was also discouraged by the prevailing political atmosphere of the 1973–76 "democratic period." With successive governments attempting to meet demands for improvements in the plight of labor and the rural poor, little energy was devoted to negotiations with foreign firms and long-term industrial development. The political tone of the period tended more to the exclusion of foreign capital than to complex negotiations with it. Wichitwong, the architect of the 1971 measures, left the government, convinced that popular pressures had so weakened the state that a consistent industrial policy was impossible. Political changes also discouraged inflows of foreign capital, while encouraging capital flight.[34] Financial scarcities inhibited government efforts to exact any specific conditions on TNC operations.

Finally, the structure and leverage of private auto interests did not encourage a strong auto policy. The assemblers were concerned with low efficiency, but their belief that model restrictions would entail a loss in overall market share led them to oppose rationalization.[35] The assemblers were not highly organized, but they were politically well represented in the ATI's Automobile Assembly Club. The club's leadership was often in the hands of Japanese assemblers, while the association's leader during much of this period was the former minister who had approved the gutting of the 1971 rationalization measures.

The major private sector voice for rationalization and increased local content was that of the parts firms. And while some of these firms were highly vocal in their demands, the sector was weakened by differences between the 20 or so larger firms producing original equipment and the over 150 smaller firms producing substandard and counterfeit parts.[36] In addition, there was no formal organization of parts firms until 1976–77, when those perceived by the assemblers as most "responsible" (i.e., least politically aggressive) were brought into an assembler-dominated joint group within the ATI, the Automotive Parts Industry Club (APIC). The function of this group was to forge a common approach toward the ASEAN auto-complementarity project, not to press for a more aggressive and efficient localization policy. Yet in Thailand, as in Malaysia, regional challenges and prior localization efforts created market and organizational opportunities for a growing and assertive parts sector.

Sources of Change

Despite their weak incentives, the 1972 LC requirements provided "substantial business for large sized, independent ancillary firms which [relied] on the supply of original equipment."[37] By 1977 the range of components manufactured in Thailand was becoming "increasingly comprehensive."[38] The number of Thai parts firms seemed to be growing. They totaled roughly 180 by 1977[39] and were relatively immune to bankruptcy and other forms of turnover seen in the Philippines. This growth was in part a function of the country's rising auto sales (from roughly 46,000 in 1971 to over 100,000 in 1977). But it also reflected more available financing as well as more consistent support by assemblers for parts firms than was the case in the Philippines, a point to which we shall return.

This expanding parts sector provided pressure for a more aggressive localization and rationalization policy as early as 1975.[40] The most openly vociferous advocates of a new auto policy were the smaller companies that either produced spare parts or were involved in other activities but anxious to gain entrance to the expanding auto market. It was the strident agitation of these smaller firms that kept issues of auto industry reform on the policy agenda and helped push the larger companies toward a more activist position by the late 1970s. Although initially reluctant to attack the assemblers and thus endanger their status as growing suppliers of original equipment, the larger firms gradually began to use APIC as an arena to develop their own independent positions. By 1977 pressure from the parts sector, along with state initiative and support from the larger Japanese firms, gave rise to the first of a series of auto reform measures.

Government Initiatives and Private Sector Pressure, 1978–1980

Policy Formulation

After almost five years of policy paralysis, the government adopted several new auto measures between 1978 and 1980. These included a partial ban on CBU imports and tariff revisions; a gradual increase and change in the method for computing local content; a ban on new assembly plants and vehicle models; and a diesel engine manufacturing project. None was completely successful, but each reflected more aggressive and organized Thai firms, as well as stronger links between these firms and government officials.

CBU Ban and Tariff Reform. In early 1978 the government imposed a long-awaited CBU ban for most kinds of passenger vehicles and adjusted import duties to encourage localization.[41] The initiative for these measures came from government officials, who viewed them as necessary to reinvigorate the rationalization process and to reverse a deepening trade deficit.[42] But the ban would not have occurred without pressure from local parts firms[43] and splits among the foreign assemblers. While the smaller assemblers (for whom CBUs were important) strongly protested the ban,[44] the larger Japanese firms generally backed it. Nissan and Toyota, each of which had upped its auto investments in Thailand in anticipation of the CBU ban, hoped that the measures would force the weaker firms out of the market. Hillman, Simca, Dodge, and Holden did in fact quit the market.[45]

Local Content, Rationalization, and the Organized Parts Sector. The CBU ban and tariff changes reinforced pressures from within the bureaucracy and private sector for more localization and model restrictions. After a two-year study by the MOI and extensive negotiations with assemblers and parts firms, local content for passenger vehicles was mandated to increase from 25 to 50 percent between 1978 and 1983, and from 15 to 50 percent for various types of commercial vehicles.[46] A new LC formula was adopted to compel the assemblers to procure more important parts locally. The new rules computed local content by assigning points for each part based not only on existing and expected local technical capacity but also on the part's contribution to the growth of such capacity.[47] Thus, more LC points were given to more important parts, although the formula did leave open the possibility that "locally" made components might simply be imported parts assembled in Thailand. The emphasis on requiring assemblers to localize specific parts was reinforced by a third measure, "the mandatory deletion" of a small number of parts deemed compatible with local production capacities (e.g., radiators, exhaust systems, leaf springs, safety glass, and brake drums).

The parts firms played critical roles in the adoption of these measures. In general, "local parts manufacturers put considerable pressure on the government for assistance. The 201 registered parts manufacturers represent a powerful lobby in their own right, with high ranking political connections and key figures in the Japanese joint-venture companies."[48] And while the assemblers (in consultation with the ADC) designed the new LC formula, they did so only upon realizing that pressure from the parts firms would inevitably result in higher LC requirements. The formula was the assemblers' attempt to make the new requirements as palatable and feasible as possible. As one Thai assembly executive noted, "We didn't want the parts firms to run the whole thing."[49]

Mandatory deletion directly reflected efforts of the larger firms producing those items with relatively broad markets, ease of standardization, and local comparative advantage. But political influence, both collective and firm-specific, was as important to the adoption of mandatory deletion as economic capacity. In 1978, having become dissatisfied with assemblers' resistance to higher local content in the Automotive Parts Industry Club, the larger parts firms established a separate association solely for parts firms. Known as the Thai Automotive Parts Manufacturers' Association (TAPMA), the new group provided reduced initiation and membership fees designed to attract small as well as larger parts makers.

In one case, however, mandatory deletion resulted from the direct exercise of political influence by one firm—Siam Nawaloha Foundry (SNF), a part of the giant Siam Cement Group. Benefiting from Siam Cement's subsidies and its experience in producing spare parts for the parent group,[50] SNF linked up with Japan's Kubota to produce parts for agricultural diesel engines in a BOI project, to be discussed below. Based on this experience in machining and casting, SNF began to produce brake drums as original equipment for the auto industry in 1979. The firm subsequently appealed directly to the MOI for mandatory localization of brake drums. In light of the firm's proven capacity and its significant political clout (Siam Cement is private but closely tied to the Royal Crown Property Bureau), the MOI granted the request without consulting the assemblers. The Japanese and their local partners were furious, complaining privately that SNF had acted as a "monopolist" and publicly that the assemblers had no chance to express their views on fundamental issues such as price controls and alternative suppliers.[51] TNC power had indeed been undermined by growing links between the bureaucracy and the local firm.

Diesel Engines, the BOI, and Industrial Deepening.   SNF expanded its machining and casting capacity through participation in a government-sponsored plan to manufacture large automotive diesel engines (50–300 hp) and smaller agricultural diesels (under 20 hp). The project was designed and implemented by the newly strengthened BOI,[52] which was anxious to push Thailand toward second-stage import substitution. Responding to the saturation of the country's ISI consumer industries, the BOI initiated several large scale agro-industrial and industrial projects, one of which involved diesel engines. The project was given further impetus by progress in the ASEAN complementarity package, in which diesel production was allocated to Singapore and Indonesia. Thailand, like the Philippines, which initiated a similar project at the same time, refused to cede a product with such high value-added to an ASEAN neighbor.

The BOI required that interested producers invest at least 25 million baht, begin production by early 1981, and increase local content by 20 percent for the first four years of plant operations in order to shift from assembly to casting and forging and finally to machining.[53] Despite these ambitious and relatively expensive goals, the board had no trouble attracting foreign participants. Twelve foreign firms applied, and in January 1978 the BOI accepted six proposals: Hino, Isuzu, and Nissan for automotive diesels, and three others, including a joint venture between Kubota and SNF, for agricultural engines. However, the leverage required to obtain formal commitments was not necessarily sufficient to induce actual compliance.

Problems of Policy Implementation

Local Content and Rationalization.   Carrying out the new measures proved difficult. The assemblers asked for and obtained a de facto delay in imposing the freeze on new models stipulated under the rationalization measures, claiming that the freeze unfairly benefited those already handling a large number of models.[54] Initial localization efforts were slightly more successful. Local content for passenger vehicles rose from 25 to 35 percent by 1980, with few protests from assemblers, and while the required minimum local content for commercial vehicles was 25 percent in 1981, many assemblers exceeded levels of 35 percent.[55]

The growing volume of commercial vehicle sales (60,000 in 1981) encouraged this development. Also, it was possible for the assemblers to meet LC requirements of up to 35–40 percent through the local production and purchase of inessential parts and gadgets.[56] Finally, existing sunk investments allowed Japanese assemblers to increase local purchases at relatively little added expense. Japanese vehicle manufacturers were already "heavily committed" in Thailand and had been "forced to bring supporting industries to operate in Thailand rather than ship the necessary inputs from Japan."[57]

But when the industry moved beyond the 35–40 percent levels, the assemblers faced greater costs and risks necessary in purchasing more expensive and technically demanding components. This was especially true for commercial vehicles, which began with relatively few accessories. Thus, as the structuralist view would predict, foreign firms lobbied to "delay or eliminate the local content regulations after 35% was achieved."[58] The TNCs found temporary allies within a relatively fragmented Thai state. The BOI's thrust into heavy industry was coming under attack from government economists pressing for an industrialization strategy that was more export-oriented.[59] Overall bureaucratic leadership was weak, as frequent changes in government entailed the "appointment of ministers who, initially at least, knew little about their portfolios."[60]

Local parts firms responded to these efforts with press conferences and radio announcements urging localization increases beyond even those provided for in government regulations.[61] While the Automobile Development Committee tended to back this position, it could take no initiative without ministerial leadership. A resolution of differences, the ADC announced, would "have to await a compromise worked out by the Thai Industries Association." [62] The private sector would have to resolve its own conflicts as the state's role shifted from initiator to broker. The resolution was a compromise: the sunk investments and political leverage of local parts firms pushed actual levels up to roughly 45 percent for passenger cars by 1983, but LC targets did not exceed the target of 50 percent mandated by the 1978 measures.

Diesel Engine Manufacture.   The manufacture of automotive diesels proved even more difficult. Inexperienced, divided, and deprived of active private sector support, the BOI was so incapable of overcoming TNC resistance that the automotive diesel project was temporarily abandoned in the early 1980s. Since it highlights the structural obstacles to local leverage in efforts requiring large costs and risks, this initial failure merits our detailed attention.

As noted above, the BOI had no problem in attracting foreign bids for local auto engine manufacture. Indeed, by effective use of interfirm rivalry, the board was actually able to improve the terms agreed to by the final three applicants. Hino first refused to participate, but subsequently rushed to submit the first bid on learning of Isuzu's interest.[63] Hino's first offer was followed by bids from four other firms during the February–August 1977 period—MAN, Leyland, Isuzu, and Nissan Diesel. The board then suggested improvements in the terms of proposals with respect to investment levels, degrees of subcontracting, and local manufacture.[64] After "heavy bargaining,"[65] the three Japanese firms largely incorporated the BOI's terms in new proposals, which were formally accepted in January 1978.

But the board's leverage was less than implied by these initial successes because it failed to begin the project with what BOI officials knew was necessary for its success—a limit of one participant producing a standardized engine usable by all the TNCs. Local political support for this was not wanting. Both the press and the parts firms warned that an inability to impose strict make and model limits would undermine diesel manufacturing just as it had weakened auto assembly.[66]

The BOI's position was weakened in part by the absence of competitive strength on the part of the Western firms, precisely those willing to manufacture standardized engines to expand a relatively small market share. In fact, the European firms were never really in the race. They lacked the corporate logistical capacity, political base, and overall commitment necessary for a rapidly changing bidding process.[67]

The BOI was also plagued by internal technical and political weaknesses. Its lack of automotive experience was reflected in the final project terms, which allowed bids to include eight different sizes, thus reducing the potential for standardization.[68] Perhaps most significant was the split between the BOI technical staff and its governing board. The former pressed hard for only one approved manufacturer, but the governing board, composed of top economic ministers and representatives of leading private sector associations, proved less cohesive than the technical staff and more vulnerable to pressures from foreign interests and their local partners anxious to avoid exclusion from the Thai market. As one member of the BOI staff noted, owing to the automakers' "access to top decision makers, we had to settle for three."[69] And with three, no model would be likely to exceed 1,500 units per year.[70]

But the auto-TNC bids were more a tactic to defeat the project than to participate in or monopolize it. Hino actually supported the inclusion of several firms to reduce the project's feasibility and thus block its implementation.[71] Nor did Hino believe in the Thai government's ability to enforce a monopoly even if it had granted production rights to only one firm. The "losing" engine manufacturers would circumvent a monopoly either by appealing to the government to relax original restrictions after the winning firm had begun to invest or by making slight engine modifications that could be imported in different categories not covered by LC restrictions. The best strategy was thus to support the project in words but undermine its economic logic.

This strategy was strengthened by a drop in sales for large automotive diesels and shortages of diesel fuel in 1978 and 1979.[72] The three Japanese firms then dragged their collective feet. In late summer 1978 the firms were working out a joint strategy to delay implementation of the program and to exact better terms from the state.[73] By October 1980 none of the larger engine firms had even begun factory construction.[74] The firms requested and were granted two postponements. They also asked for increased tariff protection, a slowdown in the rate of engine localization, guaranteed limits on fuel price increases, and expanded tax privileges. The BOI was willing to grant only the last request. Work on the project stopped by 1981–82 in the face of a third postponement request and a united position among the three firms.

This failure showed how an ambitious and complex project can enhance the leverage of auto TNCs possessing the necessary funds and technology. But bargaining can be a cumulative process in which even a defeated policy gives rise to private and public sector forces capable of strengthening local leverage in a subsequent effort. The process described above was in fact only the first phase of what was to become a more successful effort. A critical source of this success was the emergence of a private sector force—SNF and the Siam Cement Group—with the political, managerial, and financial capacities to support and even push state officials toward stronger positions. For while the automotive diesel project lay moribund, the smaller agricultural diesel component of the project proceeded smoothly.[75] Its less rigorous technical requirements and large rural markets encouraged a steady growth in SNF capacities. And as seen below, SNF subsequently sought to apply these capacities to the manufacture of automotive diesels.

Expansion and Sources of Host Country Leverage, 1981–1986

By the early 1980s the Thai auto industry was faced with serious opposition to further reform and deepening. In 1983 the government proclaimed a freeze on local content for passenger vehicles, and the diesel engine project lay dead in the water. Yet from late 1983 to the present the list of auto parts for compulsory localization has grown, local investments have been made in engine manufacture, and the number and range of auto exports has expanded.

These developments reflect both the cumulative impact of previous shifts and certain factors new to the Thai auto industry. They also reinforce the view that the bargaining power of host countries is an attribute of the country as such and not simply of its government. Important though they are, government measures incorporate private as well as public sector goals and capacities.

Localization: The Politics of Import Substitution

Local content had continued its gradual rise, reaching approximately 45 percent by 1983. At that point the MOI froze local content for passenger vehicles, 5 percent below the target mandated by the 1978 measures. This action was the result of an unlikely alliance between Japanese assemblers and EOI forces within the Thai government. The liberal Thai economists who had pressed for a shift to automotive exports a few years earlier now mounted a major effort to restructure ten excessively protected industries, including auto assembly.[76] This included proposals to cut LC requirements, force out low-volume assemblers, and end the ban on CBU imports in exchange for a commitment by the auto TNCs to use Thailand as an export base for auto parts. Backed by the World Bank and developed by a U.S. consultant, the approach was a conscious adaptation of Mexico's emphasis on auto exports in the 1970s.[77]

In general, these proposals were viewed skeptically by the ISI-based assemblers and the parts firms, as well as by those state agencies historically responsible for auto policy—the MOI and BOI. For one thing, the proposals were developed in isolation from public and private sector forces long active in the industry and then abruptly sprung on them.[78] More important, the Japanese assemblers disliked the export emphasis and saw it as a wedge enabling Western firms to move into the Thai market.[79] Nor, given their sunk investments in Thailand, were they interested in doing away with existing LC regulations.

But the Japanese opposition to *further* localization overlapped with the EOI position. Since Thailand had reached the highest LC levels in Southeast Asia (45 percent for passenger and 35 percent for commercial vehicles), any further local increases would require assemblers to procure locally made power-train components, especially for commercial vehicles. The assemblers' pressure for a freeze thus intensified, with the Japanese issuing public reports and speaking in open meetings.[80] When combined with EOI pressure and a relatively passive minister of industry, the assemblers convinced the MOI to halt further localization increases.

But the freeze proved temporary. In September 1983 a new minister of industry announced his intention to expand localization through the mandatory common use of all parts already produced in Thailand. Despite intense opposition from the assemblers as well as government economists (some within the MOI),[81] this was followed in 1984 and 1985 by MOI announcements that (1) local content would reach 70 percent by 1988 and 100 percent thereafter; (2) it would be based on a list of 155 specific components available in Thailand, and (3) assemblers were required to provide the government with their CKD price lists.[82]

Each of these measures was galling to both the assemblers and the EOI forces. The LC targets would clearly involve local manufacture of major components such as transmissions and engines. The list-based LC formula contained no provision for a gradual movement from simpler, less expensive parts to more complex, expensive ones as urged by the government's liberal economists. Finally, the assemblers strenuously resisted providing price lists, claiming that such information would become public and prove useful to competitors. From the MOI's perspective, however, such information was essential to resolving the "deletion allowance" problem.

The measures were adopted. And although Thai local content had not reached 70 percent by 1988, LC levels and the number of parts firms continued to grow, exceeding those of Thailand's ASEAN neighbors.

Sources of Local Leverage. The measures outlined above reflected a number of mutually reinforcing developments in the auto industry and the broader Thai political economy. One was a ministerial change. In May 1983 Ob Vasuratna, a self-made businessman based largely in import-export and construction activities and prominent in one of the government coalition parties, became minister of industry. Ob embodied a major trend in Thai politics in which "members of the business elite . . . have come to play a major role in Thai cabinets and in economic decision making."[83] He also represented a distinctly nationalist trend within the business community. A former head of the Board of Trade (the Thai commercial sector's peak business association) and minister of commerce, Ob had reportedly developed a strong suspicion of Japanese firms and was clearly committed to a nationalist ISI policy. In auto assembly, his position directly contradicted the policy of his predecessor to freeze LC at 45 percent.[84]

But given the intense opposition to the new measures, Ob's personal views are not a sufficient explanation for their adoption. Reinforcing his position was a more assertive Thai economic stance vis-à-vis Japan. Reacting to a deteriorating trade balance, the government established a Subcommittee on Restructuring Thai-Japanese Economic Relations in 1984, the first high level body of its kind.[85] At a 1984 joint Thai-Japan meeting at which the government reduced cultural and sporting exchanges with Japan, Ob pointedly reminded the Japanese of the need to redress imbalances in the trade in auto parts between the two countries.[86]

A third factor, competition among assemblers, weakened opposition to Ob's plans for localization increases. This rivalry was most prominently seen in an ambitious 1984 bid by Peugeot and its local representative, Yontrakit, to manufacture "Thai vehicles"—24,000 sedans and pickups annually, with a local content of 95 percent, including major components for both the domestic market and export.[87] The Yontrakit group has been especially aggressive in its willingness to expand in-house production of auto parts, while Peugeot is anxious to expand its regional presence in

Southeast Asia. The project was eventually vetoed, in part because of the Finance Ministry's objections to its incentive costs to the government, and in part owing to strong opposition from Toyota.[88]

But before its defeat the proposal drew "me-too" bids from Nissan and Mitsubishi,[89] both of which saw overseas markets as a major channel for overtaking Toyota, the firm generally most opposed to any overseas sourcing.[90] Nissan, moreover, is tied to Siam Motors, a highly aggressive Thai industrial group not averse to taking a nationalist position when it seems advantageous. "MNCs who chose not to participate in this program may eventually lose their foothold here," Siam Motors' vice president argued.[91]

Finally, the growing political influence of local parts firms reflected and reinforced Ob's views. As the head of the Assemblers' Association complained:

> I dare not ask them to wait. The parts manufacturers are pushing so hard. But I also worry—can the parts manufacturers take all this on at once and deliver on time? If they cannot fulfill our requirements—we have to buy and they cannot supply us—what will happen? I think they are too greedy, too ambitious.[92]

These firms were greedy and ambitious; they were also fairly effective in their policy efforts. As one of the more striking aspects of the Thai auto case, the parts sector's expansion merits detailed examination.

The Parts Producers' Strength: A Review

During the early-to-mid 1980s Thai parts producers managed to expand their organizational base and policy influence along several dimensions:[93]

1. *Associational Base.* Unlike their Philippine counterparts, assemblers operating in Thailand agreed that original equipment (OE) parts suppliers must be members of either TAPMA or APIC, the parts association incorporated in the Association of Thai Industries.

2. *Compulsory Localization Approval.* As in the Malaysian case, decisions on localized parts must now be approved by two-thirds of TAPMA's directors, none of whom are Japanese. Such collective deliberation will provide an important forum for consideration and resolution of assemblers' complaints with regard to safety or quality problems with local parts.

3. *Information and Standards*. Both TAPMA and APIC have worked with the assemblers to develop required standards for OE parts suppliers. This has involved lobbying for an expansion of staff in the Thai Industrial Standards Institute and the development of comprehensive information, using SNF computer facilities, about all OE parts, their producers and buyers.

4. *Agenda Setting*. Both collectively and individually, parts firms have raised a number of issues pertaining to the long-term structure and characteristics of the industry. They have pushed the government to determine what types and rates of technological changes are appropriate for the Thai market.[94] They have also pressed for state limits on vertical integration. More specifically, the firms have asked that the assemblers not be permitted to produce items already manufactured by local producers, unless local capacity is clearly insufficient. This is a reaction to assemblers letting local parts firms manufacture a product until demand increases, and then producing it in-house. Parts firms have also protested their previous lack of political access to government officials compared with that of the assemblers. And, while stressing their willingness to cooperate with the assemblers in ironing out quality and price issues, the parts firms have portrayed themselves as nationalist industrializers deserving support from the Thai state in their constant conflicts with foreign-dominated assemblers. Without such support, they argue, Thailand's citizens will "be relegated to tilling fields and growing rice."[95]

The preceding initiatives suggest a degree of industrial orientation and policy influence well in excess of structuralist assumptions. How do we account for the obvious desire to shift from the simple assembly of imported parts into components toward the actual manufacture of such parts? Altruistic nationalism may provide some of the answer, but interviews with representatives of parts firms suggest the weight of more prosaic market constraints and opportunities. Increasing the number of localized parts widens markets and potential profits. It also helps alleviate the problem of excess capacity; declining demand for some items has occasionally led firms to begin producing related auto products through modification of existing technology or acquisition of new machines.

Increased local manufacture can also be a response to temporary shortages of imported items. Needed parts from overseas may be held up by customs inefficiency or shortages in Japan itself. The resulting losses have encouraged some firms to begin the manufacture of these parts to ensure their ability to meet assemblers' orders. The inability to procure sufficient spare parts was the Siam Cement Group's original motivation for establishing its own foundry and machining operations. Thailand's tax structure may provide further encouragement to localize. Imported parts that make up components are taxed at high spare-parts rates that make it economically advisable for local firms to produce them themselves.[96]

Finally, increased localization has been a response to pressure from the government and assemblers to "put up or shut up" about the need for higher LC levels. In 1984–85 the government began requiring parts firms to submit process charts showing precisely how a component is made— that is, whether the local operation involves only simple assembly or extends to significant value-added. According to one source, the charts were seen as a response to assemblers' complaints about high prices and/or different prices for the same parts. Submission of the charts would presumably make the operations of parts firms more transparent, thus facilitating government and/or assembler pressure for standardized and more efficient processes. One effect has been to pressure some parts firms into carrying out more extensive local manufacturing, presumably to justify the prices they charge.

The Thai case provides an especially useful picture of the sources of these orientations, but we have seen similar localizing efforts by parts firms in Malaysia and the Philippines. The more striking and puzzling aspect of the Thai parts firms is their relative superiority in translating these objectives into reality. What explains this relative success? Part of the explanation lies in the firms' associational strength. But we must turn to other factors for the sources of such strength.

Ethnicity.   Thailand's particular combination of ethnic distinctiveness and integration has contributed to the growth of local parts firms. The fact that most local parts firms are Chinese-owned suggests that ethnic homogeneity has facilitated organizational cohesion, as in Malaysia. At the same time, the country's extensive ethnic mixing has facilitated TAPMA's legitimacy and the links it has established with government officials. As officials and owners of the larger parts firms stress, they are not first-generation merchants or artisans operating out of their own houses; they are highly educated, often speak English and/or Japanese, have full political rights, and frequently share basic background experiences (such as university) with government officials.[97]

But if being Chinese is not a political disadvantage, being Thai has some benefits. The (1987) president of TAPMA is an ethnic Thai whose father's past role as under secretary in the MOI has resulted in useful information and contacts. SNF's position as part of Thailand's major industrial force with close ties to the royal family has also been important to the development of a collective parts firm presence.

Financing.   No systematic study of comparative industrial financing is yet available, but interviews suggest that several aspects of the Thai financial system benefit local parts firms. The Thai financial system is dominated by private Chinese capital and features numerous banking institutions in addition to large financial groups.[98] This has allowed the parts firms relatively easy access to financing, in some cases based on ethnic and family ties. And while the Thai government has played an important macroeconomic role, Thailand has neither large development banks nor massive state-funded heavy industry projects.[99] This has reinforced the financial sector's relative independence from politics and prevented the degree of political favoritism seen in Philippine lending.

This has meant that, unlike in the case of Silverio in the Philippines, most industrial borrowers are vulnerable to the financial system's monitoring and discipline. Excessive diversification and milking of firms for individual gain seem to be moderated.[100] The one local firm involved in the auto sector with sufficient political clout to flout the market—Siam Cement—does not do so. Its close ties to the Crown Property Bureau have encouraged aggressive, but careful, diversification. The pattern is much closer to Indonesia's Astra than to the Philippines' Silverio.

The financial system's lack of favoritism has also benefited the parts firms by discouraging late payments by assemblers to parts suppliers. Interest penalties levied on late payments to suppliers are relatively high. A parts firm suffering from late payments has access to litigation, which usually favors the creditor. And late payments can reduce an assembler's credit rating, since news of them spreads rapidly throughout the banking community.

These factors, and the sociopolitical order of which they were a part,[101] facilitated the economic and political strengthening of Thai parts firms. In so doing they encouraged a rise in the LC level of the country's auto industry. On localization the auto TNCs were thus confronted with a relatively solid de facto local coalition. Local forces in favor of rationalizing the Thai auto industry were, however, significantly more fragile.

Rationalization Efforts: The Persistence of Market Fragmentation

When Ob took office in the spring of 1983, the Thai motor vehicles market included roughly twenty makes and over a hundred models. The weaker assemblers, forced out by the 1978–79 measures, were replaced by the Yontrakit group, backed by aggressive European firms.[102] Other small firms managed to stay in the market by moving into truck production (Daihatsu) or switching to smaller Japanese vehicles. Most important, the larger Japanese firms, such as Toyota and Nissan, produced vehicles in every category, and only one model (known in the industry as a "ghost") in some. The goal, as elsewhere in ASEAN, was to respond to market shifts with different models and to use profitable models to make up losses in less profitable categories.

Arguing that such proliferation had led Thailand to become "luxurious while the country is still suffering from poverty,"[103] Ob argued for an eventual limit of twenty models.[104] In the short term, however, he proposed that vehicles be limited to eighty-four models and that no new licenses be granted. The National Economic and Social Development Board (NESDB) strengthened Ob's position by suggesting that the license of any series with sales of fewer than six hundred units in one year be terminated.[105]

But even these modest goals proved politically impossible to achieve. Ob resisted the NESDB's proposal on the grounds that it would have led to the termination of fully twenty-seven of the forty-two series produced, a figure whose political repercussions he considered too great.[106] The assemblers also resisted implementation. In June 1985 eleven of sixteen assembly plants successfully appealed for deferment, claiming that only Toyota, Nissan, and Yontrakit could survive without extreme difficulties.[107] And in a final demonstration of the weakness of any local coalition backing market rationalization, Honda entered the market through links to Bangchan.

Ministerial Changes and "Realistic" LC Expansion

The possibility of achieving increased localization was undermined not only by the industry's persistent fragmentation but also by the departure of Ob himself following a brief and unsuccessful coup attempt involving one of Ob's political allies. Dr. Chirayu Issarangkuh na Ayuthaya, an EOI supporter and MOI under secretary to Ob, was named as the new minister. Bolstered by Chirayu's new role and a drop in market sales, the EOI obtained cabinet mandate for a newly formed Industrial Policy Committee to review the country's industrial development policy, with auto production as a primary focus.[108]

The new committee, which was dominated by EOI forces, constituted a separate institutional locus of auto policy with the potential to undermine the role of the MOI and Board of Investments and roll back existing measures. By and large this did not happen, in part owing to sunk investments. Other things being equal, the new committee would have preferred to reduce localization levels. But with existing investments by both parts firms and assemblers, and with parts firms investing "huge sums" in preparation for the new LC goals set by Ob, such a move was politically impossible.[109]

A freeze was, however, possible and even welcomed by many parts producers, who believed that the sharp declines in auto sales made it "too expensive for the local content manufacturers to produce needed parts."[110] Tripartite negotiations followed. In August 1986, after extensive consultation between the Automobile Development Committee, assemblers and parts firms, local content was frozen for two years at 54 percent.[111]

This did not signal the end of pressure for LC increases. By March 1987 a group of parts firms argued that levels exceeding 54 percent could be achieved if the assemblers would slow down vehicle changes and place longer-term orders. Refusing the request, the assemblers claimed that competition required constant modifications in parts and components.[112]

But the parts firms did demand a long-term TNC commitment to localization in exchange for their willingness to accept the freeze. Their ability to obtain such a commitment was bolstered by a stronger associational base. SNF was not only pressing hard for localization increases but was doing so in closer coordination with the other firms. SNF's managing director had become the head of APIC and a leader of TAPMA.[113] The parts firms also benefited from the actions of a new actor within the MOI—the ministry's chief engineer, Preecha Attavipat. With a concern for efficiency that complemented his minister's approach, but with a clear desire for expanded local manufacture that pleased the parts firms, Preecha was able to broker a new LC formula: instead of compelling assemblers to localize *all* parts available locally (as Ob's formula had done), the new measures required the automakers to install at least 27 designated locally made items and to select a gradually increasing number of parts, beginning at 27, from a list of 127 other items.[114] The mandatory, but gradual, localization of major components such as steering systems, gear boxes, and suspension systems was a central goal of the new policy.

But the successful implementation of these new goals would clearly require a market in which large economies of scale were possible. With even further additions to the already crowded passenger market,[115] MOI officials began to focus on the less fragmented commercial vehicle sector— especially one-ton pickup trucks, whose sales volume of 60,000 units in 1983 accounted for almost 50 percent of the entire Thai market. By April 1986 Preecha headed a task force to consider ways in which the MOI could encourage a "national pick-up truck."[116] Since such a vehicle could incorporate locally made engines, the MOI was drawn into active support for the Board of Investment's diesel engine project.

The effort to increase both efficiency and localization thus entailed a tightening of links between the BOI and the Ministry of Industry. But this did not mean a state-dominated coalition in favor of local content. As will be seen below, private sector initiative and resources were critical to the very revival of the diesel engine project and subsequently to the country's leverage vis-à-vis the previously recalcitrant foreign engine makers. Indeed, this study offers no better illustration of local capital's potentially nationalist bargaining role than the recent phase of Thailand's auto engine project.

Diesel Engines: The Recent Phase

In 1985 the automotive diesel engine project reemerged with a specific focus on engines for one-ton pickup trucks. And while the project was perceived by the BOI as the solution to the dual problems of low localization and market fragmentation, the board took action largely because of pressure from the private sector—specifically, Siam Nawaloha Foundry.[117] Along with NESDB officials, SNF representatives sat on a BOI subcommittee on diesel engines organized soon after the first plan was dropped. SNF argued that having successfully manufactured agricultural diesel engines with Kubota, it was capable of meeting production requirements for one-ton pickup engines.[118] SNF further promoted the project by organizing a trip to Japanese engine facilities for BOI and MOI officials to give them a sense of the manufacturing realities and to show the Japanese the seriousness with which Thailand was treating engine production.

Government officials, already favorably disposed to the project, began to draw up new project requirements. Negotiations between the BOI and prospective foreign participants ensued.[119] One contentious issue was the Thai insistence that foreign engine makers use existing Thai casting capacity. The requirement, written with SNF in mind, drew Japanese opposition. But SNF's successful experience with agricultural engines undermined Japanese claims of poor quality. The requirement was thus included. It is worth note, however, that in return for its support, the BOI successfully obtained a commitment by SNF to farm out work to smaller Thai companies.[120]

As in the late 1970s, the number of manufacturers also emerged as an important bargaining issue. The BOI technical staff fought hard for a limit of one but was willing to settle for two. The MOI's Preecha also urged two engine makers, one European and one Japanese, arguing that this arrangement would "give Thailand better bargaining power."[121] But again, the BOI governing board was influenced by Japanese claims that standardization among makes was not possible and that a limit of one firm would discourage competition. The final terms allowed "no more than three" firms.

A third contentious issue concerned exports. The Japanese initially insisted that the project's terms include explicit export restrictions. But when the BOI insisted that the size of the Thai market made exports obligatory, especially with several manufacturers, the Japanese agreed to terms encouraging exports on a case-by-case basis. The fact that Thai parts firms were beginning to show their ability to export strengthened the BOI's hand here. But the most important factor was competition among the Japanese. Toyota's president visited Bangkok to express his interest in the project, for example, and raised the possibility of exporting Thai-made stamping dies for truck bodies in Indonesia.[122] This move reflected the seriousness with which the Japanese, even home-based Toyota, took the renewed project, for it came before the yen's appreciation encouraged Japanese interest in manufacture for export.

The actual application process was highly competitive. After press conferences and visits from TNC executives, the board received bids from four groups in August 1985: (1) Toyota, with equity divided among Toyota-Japan, Nippondenso, Siam Cement, and the IFCT; (2) Siam Motors/Nissan, with equity divided among Siam Motors, Nissan, Bangkok Bank, SNF, and the IFCT; (3) Isuzu, Mitsubishi, and Mazda, with equity divided among the three Japanese firms, the IFCT, the Crown Property Bureau, SNF, and other local business interests; and (4) Peugeot/Yontrakit (data not available on equity shares).

The participation of SNF or a related entity (Siam Cement, Crown Property Bureau) in three of the four bids strongly suggested the potential for standardization. SNF clearly did not intend to play a passive role in these projects. Even before the project took shape, SNF expanded its own engineering capacities through acquisitions and development of new subsidiaries.[123] Another striking aspect of the bids was the equity role of the IFCT,[124] an agency dominated by export-oriented economists and traditionally hostile to the expansion of local auto manufacture. But before the board could choose the winning firms, the plan was halted in early 1986 by another wave of diesel fuel shortages and opposition from the Finance Ministry to any project encouraging the use of diesel fuel.[125] As a number of officials noted, however, SNF had invested too much money in the project for the halt to be permanent. SNF pressure, along with the BOI's own commitment, resulted in the project's renewal in May, along with a further initiative, local production of motorcycle engines.[126] The two projects involved overlapping technology and investments, just as agricultural diesel production had promoted local capacity to meet automotive engine requirements. Not surprisingly, the Siam Cement Group announced large investments in production of motorcycle parts, utilizing the companies it had previously acquired or established in anticipation of the automotive diesel project.[127]

The renewed bidding process was as competitive as before. "Strong lobbying by the four groups began when it was known that the BOI held to its limit of three manufacturers."[128] Efforts to sway the Thai government included visits to the prime minister, press conferences by top Japanese corporate officials, pressure from each group's local partner, and a new element: strong Japanese export commitments.[129] And while the yen's appreciation was clearly a key factor in this development, it is not a sufficient explanation for what seems to be a particular attraction to Thailand as a production base.[130] In the case of auto production, the manufacturing capacity promoted by prior government localization policies and private sector responses seems to have been critical. This is indicated by the fact that much of the export activity now beginning involves Japanese cooperation with precisely those local firms that emerged from and fought for the ISI policies described in this chapter.[131]

Once again, the intensity of TNC efforts to take part in the project precluded any limits on participating firms. In September 1987 the BOI awarded promotional certificates to the four original firms, albeit with one change—Mitsubishi broke away from the Isuzu group and joined Nissan's project.[132] But SNF's participation was maintained, as were export commitments and promises to expand local content from 20 percent in the first year to 80 percent by the fifth year of operation. More basically, there seems to have been little of the collusive TNC foot-dragging that marked the BOI's first attempt. By the beginning of 1988 each of the firms had begun actual plant construction, and they were to start manufacture by mid-to-late 1989.[133]

There is, of course, the danger that exports may undermine Thailand's bargaining leverage on localization, as occurred in Mexico.[134] For example, at the time of this writing discussions were under way as to whether LC credit would be given for exports, thus reducing domestic value-added.[135] Indications are, however, that while Thailand will offer some compromises in the case of exports, the political and economic resources of established Thai firms will preclude any significant rollback in local procurement.

The extensive participation by both local capital and a new state actor suggests that Thailand's localization coalition expanded even as Thai localization efforts began to stress efficiency and incorporate an export component. This coalition was insufficiently cohesive to induce direct rationalization (i.e., through preferred limits on project participants). But in engine manufacture it did obtain real commitments of significant investments with clear benefits for local firms. And by compelling the TNCs to accept both a major role for one local firm and some inter-TNC cooperation, it laid the basis for a longer-term standardization of components and processes.

9

Bargaining and State-Society Relations in Southeast Asia

The analysis of this book has shown that developing countries, even those without strong states, can expand their automobile industries despite initial auto-TNC opposition. They can do so, moreover, in several ways consistent with product-cycle assumptions. Yet the ASEAN cases also show the gaps in the product-cycle view. In the present chapter I draw on the evidence presented in the preceding pages to evaluate the two approaches. The first section reviews the potential bargaining resources of the ASEAN Four in auto manufacturing and identifies sources of their neglect by structuralist writers. The second section explores differences in private sector motivations and/or government policies as a source of cross-national differences in bargaining leverage. The third section focuses on relations between state and society, arguing that for the ASEAN Four, variation in local leverage has been a function of coalitional strength at the sectoral level. The final section takes the analysis one step further and explores the national contexts of sector-specific coalitional strength.

Structural Power in the ASEAN Auto Industry

The Japanese automakers rarely, if ever, stated outright opposition to ASEAN auto-industrialization policies. Their response was instead one of "our hands are tied"—that is, an emphasis on the existing obstacles to efficient increases in local auto manufacture in Southeast Asia. Underlying this approach was the TNCs' ability to define the range of feasible alternatives through control of new technology and market-fragmenting strategies. By refusing to accept standardized components, refusing to slow down model changes, maintaining low deletion allowances, and designing projects that precluded obtaining parts from outside producers, the Japanese could convincingly claim that ASEAN policy objectives were just not viable economically. The structuralist approach effectively captures this aspect of automobile bargaining in Southeast Asia. But the approach underestimates the potential for host country leverage. It oversimplifies the nature and impact of entry barriers, sunk investments, and rivalry among TNCs. These flaws contribute to a markedly one-sided concept of structural power.

Technological Entry Barriers.   Central to the structuralist view is the assumption that an industry such as auto manufacturing presents monolithic and impenetrable entry barriers to local firms. Underplayed here is any sense of the unevenness of the international product cycle. The fact that international automobile manufacturing moved out of its mature standardized phase during the early 1970s did not eliminate market niches compatible with ASEAN capacities. As most fully elaborated by David Sycip in the Philippines, these include rebuilding the used "cores" of imported components and manufacturing simpler items with high replacement rates, through which most ASEAN parts firms entered the market. They also include parts and even relatively complex vehicles that lend themselves to standardization by virtue of compatibility with local market requirements. The opportunities presented by other types of manufacturing have also been important to ASEAN producers. The leading Malaysian producer of safety glass began in the construction business. The manufacture of motorcycle parts has provided a bridge for a number of ASEAN firms—most notably Astra and SNF—into the manufacture of more demanding automobile components. Finally, Thai manufacture and export of stamping dies reflect the potential for ASEAN production of certain types of production machinery either no longer made elsewhere or too expensive to produce in small quantities in the developed countries.

Sunk Investment.   The structuralist concept of sunk investment stresses the physical property of foreign firms: the inexpensive and/or movable assets required by initial stages of a manufacturing investment are seen as providing host countries with high leverage but no property to hold hostage for subsequent demands involving greater risks and expense to the foreign investor. This view accurately describes ASEAN automotive bargaining dynamics in many instances. The minimal costs of establishing CKD assembly plants permitted each of the ASEAN Four to draw large numbers of auto TNCs into the first stage of auto production. But as demands by the host country for higher local content called for more capital investment, the opposition of the foreign firms became more determined and effective. As illustrated most clearly by Thai and Indonesian efforts to produce major components, this opposition took the form of consistent foot-dragging in implementing formal commitments.

But the ASEAN experiences reflect other dimensions of sunk investment more in line with product-cycle predictions. First, sunk investments by host country firms also influenced the bargaining process. Malaysian Sheet Glass's investment in production of auto safety glass constituted an important factor in the government's decision to name glass as the first item for mandatory localization. In Thailand, a critical source of pressure for implementation of diesel engine production was SNF's prior investment in plant and equipment for brake drums and agricultural diesels. In Indonesia, Liem's resources facilitated the government's decision to move into the manufacture of engine components. And in some instances the need to render prior investments more efficient prompted the Astra group to press for increased in-house manufacture and the reduction of product differentiation.

Second, even modest TNC investments involved a greater stake in the ASEAN markets than implied by structural assumptions. While these investments did not have the "hostage" quality of a mine or a plantation, they did represent commitments that the Japanese were loath to abandon. In Thailand, for example, TNC investments in existing local-content programs led the Japanese to *oppose* the dismantling of localization advocated by advocates of auto exports. Two characteristics of Japanese firms seem to encourage this tendency for market commitments to solidify quickly. One is the Japanese emphasis on long-term (regional as well as local) market share. The other is the nonautomotive nature of sunk investment. Mitsubishi's willingness to back the Malaysian national car was at least in part a result of the long-term needs and commitments of the overall Mitsubishi group in Malaysia and the region.

TNC Collusion.   The ASEAN cases provide extensive support for structuralist predictions that competitive strategies of products differentiation would fragment local markets. ASEAN efforts to expand economies of scale have generally foundered on efforts by numerous TNCs to maintain a market presence and to fill every model niche. Structuralist predictions of TNC collusion are much less accurate, however. Instances of "mutual competitive forbearance" were quite rare and, as in the case of the Thai diesel engine project, generally temporary.

Much more common was unrelenting pressure to compete, even when such competition required investments in the manufacture of major components. The activities of one firm, Mitsubishi, intensified the levels of rivalry beyond those predicted by the structural approach. In the Philippines, Mitsubishi not only broke rank and agreed to raise the deletion allowance but also increased its investment in transmission production in the face of a precipitous market decline and growing political instability. In Indonesia Mitsubishi moved quickly to support and implement government localization plans. In Thailand, the firm's offer of support for the diesel engine project prompted the government to disregard commitments by foot-dragging firms and reformulate the project. And in Malaysia, Mitsubishi shocked its competitors by agreeing to participate in the national car project.

This pressure to compete may even lead to indirect rationalization. Each firm's desire to maintain market access has allowed for higher localization levels. To minimize the costs of local manufacture, the TNCs have begun to accept standardization and common facilities in Thailand and Indonesia.

One-Sided Structuralism and Changing TNC Preferences: The Perceived Hegemony of Foreign Capital.   The structuralist approach views foreign capital as the deus ex machina influencing the range of feasible options, agenda items, and actors. Yet host countries influenced the structure of opportunities as well. ASEAN auto policies provided market opportunities for local firms whose growth generated new local demands and actors. In Malaysia, parts firms whose origin lay in prior localization efforts demanded participation in the national car project. In Indonesia, the expansion of production capacity by firms such as Liem and Astra allowed the MOI to promulgate and begin to implement requirements for the local production of major components. And in Thailand, production experience in parts such as brake drums and agricultural engine components provided the base on which SNF and the BOI pressed for TNC commitments to automotive diesel manufacture.

The accumulation of local resources also influenced the structure of opportunities available to the TNCs themselves. In so doing, it helped modify the preferences of foreign investors themselves. This point is important with regard to the recent willingness of Japanese firms to relocate manufacturing activities, including manufacture for export, in Southeast Asia. Exchange-rate shifts and increasing protectionism obviously account for much of this change, but it was encouraged by the existence of reliable overseas production facilities, themselves the result of previous LC (and regional complementarity) efforts.

Equally important, the Japanese tendency to relocate more in Thailand than elsewhere reflects that country's achievements relative to its neighbors. In sum, while features of the automobile industry certainly do not encourage host country strength, neither do they preclude it. The international auto industry provided each of the ASEAN Four with the same potential to modify and manipulate industry obstacles. But cross-national differences in performance suggest that the capacity to translate such potential into actual leverage varied. In chapter 4 we saw that national economic features such as market size, education levels, and numbers of managers do not explain the variation in such capacity. How, then, to take the extreme case, did the Philippine car industry end up "at the bottom of the ASEAN heap"[1] despite the fact that it began with a group of highly educated technocrats, a large number of skilled managers, and a large existing market for unsophisticated vehicles?

One set of answers, discussed in the following section, focuses on host country firms and states. A second, covered in the third section, emphasizes relations between the two.

Capitalists and State Orientations

The Conditions of Self-Interest

Some ASEAN entrepreneurs have provided support for the auto TNCs in line with structuralist predictions, yet many others have attempted to increase market share at the expense of foreign capital. Did firms find nationalism less attractive in some countries than in others? If so, do these differences help explain variation in bargaining achievements?

The cases described in this study do not suggest any such cross-national differences in private sector motivations. In each country we have found firms pressing publicly and privately for higher local content and greater rationalization. However, we did find what might be termed a subsectoral difference within countries. With some important exceptions (discussed below), local parts firms exhibited orientations that were consistently more industrial, and thus at odds with TNC preferences, than were those of local entrepreneurs in auto assembly. Judging by their roles in the policy process, the former were more committed to an expansion of manufacturing and economies of scale, while the latter took positions reflecting satisfaction with more commercial activities—that is, the assembly, distribution, and marketing of a wide variety of foreign-made goods.

Given the importance of private actors to the local bargaining position, an explanation of behavioral variation among local firms is necessary. Yet neither the structuralist nor the product-cycle approach is of great help. The former fails to specify causal linkages involved and simply assumes that the dominant resources of foreign capital facilitate domination of affiliated local firms. The product-cycle emphasis on local capital's "self-interested attraction to nationalism" provides more long-term predictive accuracy, but it fails to identify the factors conditioning self-interest and encouraging nationalism in some but not in others. We require, in sum, a more market- or product-based approach to the varying motivations of local firms. Based on the ASEAN cases, this would need to take into account (1) entry barriers, (2) foreign inputs, (3) profitability of local value-added, and (4) TNC leverage (table 9.1).[2]

Entry Barriers.   The technological and financial requirements for local entry into and/or control of assembly activities are significantly greater than those for parts production. Firms meeting the demands of Southeast Asia's sophisticated vehicle market must use expensive, capital-intensive, flexible assembly equipment. Breaking into assembly often means entering at the top floor.

By contrast, local firms can begin the manufacture of auto parts and components requiring less capital and advanced technology. The wide range of parts incorporated in a motor vehicle and the opportunity for spare-parts production allow local firms the option of beginning with simple operations and gradually moving up. These avenues of market entry and skill development are also open to assemblers extensively involved in parts production, such as Indonesia's Astra and, to a lesser degree, Thailand's Siam Motors.

Foreign Inputs. ASEAN parts firms began by assembling and processing imported subcomponents. But in Thailand (and presumably elsewhere), delivery delays and high import taxes have prompted local parts firms to make them instead of continuing to buy them. In addition, these firms' relatively narrow financial margins encourage them to explore methods of cost reduction, including the use of cheaper local labor and more appropriate production processes.

Delivery problems and cost increases are less of an incentive to make instead of buy for ASEAN assemblers. Their tight links to foreign assembly lines tend to ensure timely deliveries, while their generally stronger financial base and backing from the auto TNCs themselves allow them to absorb input cost increases more easily than local parts firms. But in those ASEAN assembly operations with both extensive in-house parts production and a strong, cost-conscious local capital presence, delivery and cost do encourage increased manufacture. Astra is the outstanding example of this pattern, but it also seems to occur in Thailand's Yontrakit and perhaps Siam Motors.

Profitability of Local Value-Added. The incentive structure of ASEAN parts firms has encouraged support for localization and rationalization. Low local content meant no market and no profits, but greater localization was easier to achieve with less product variety. For assemblers, on the other hand, assembly of knocked-down models often yielded generous and fairly safe profits. Increased local content implied generally lower

Table 9.1. Market Conditions, Linkages, and Orientations of Local Capital in Auto Manufacture

Producer Category	Conditions/Linkages				
	Entry Barrier	Stability of Inputs	Profitability at Low Value-Added	TNC Leverage	Orientations[a]
Local assemblers	High	High	High	High	Commercial
Local parts producers	Low rising to high	Moderate	Low	Medium to high	Industrial

[a]Commercial orientations imply support for and/or subordination to auto TNCs. Industrial orientations imply more competitive efforts and policy positions vis-à-vis auto TNCs.

quality and higher costs. Only where governments provided special financing (e.g., for Delta), or where the danger of an ethnic outbreak required active compliance with state localization measures did assembly firms (e.g., Astra, Tan Chong) move to increase (in-house) localization.

TNC Leverage. At least two factors provide foreign firms with greater leverage over local assemblers than over local parts firms. We have already discussed the impact of one, contrasting entry barriers. The second has to do with the ratio of foreign to local actors. Most ASEAN assemblers are locked into tie-ups with one particular auto TNC. They are committed to a single make and are thus severely limited in their ability to take advantage of inter-TNC rivalry. It is significant in this regard that the assembler exhibiting the most active support for local manufacture, Astra, is linked to a number of different makes.[3]

Given the fragmented nature of the ASEAN auto industries, parts firms must maintain ties with a more diversified set of assemblers. This reduces the parts makers' vulnerability to any particular assembler's retaliation (e.g., through late payments, changing product specifications, and order cancellations).[4] In addition to the number of buyers, local parts firms usually also enjoy a broader range of foreign sources from which to obtain raw materials, subcomponents, equipment, and technology than is the case for local assemblers. This was reflected in the ability of Thai parts firms to obtain and modify used foreign equipment from diverse sources, and the availability of foreign engineers to support the Malaysian wire-harness firm's initial manufacture of original equipment. Similar patterns were seen in some (Astra, Yontrakit) but not all of the local assemblers handling more than one make.

Where the ASEAN Four differed was not in the private sector's tendency to economic nationalism, but rather in the ability of local firms to translate such motivations into both economic strength and political influence. How do we account for the impressive market expansion and policy contribution of parts firms in Malaysia and Thailand relative to those in the Philippines? How do we explain the economic fragility of the "crony nationalist" Silverio compared to the corporate strength of Astra?

The Impact of State Orientations

The answer to both questions lies partly in the adoption of different development strategies. The contrast between the Philippines and the other three countries with regard to two policy directions merits special note. One involves the sequence of import substitution versus export promotion. The Philippine BOI's early advocacy of an export-promotion component encouraged (1) vertical integration by assemblers *prior to* the growth of local firms and (2) reliance on TNC networks by both parts firms and local assemblers. By contrast, early and consistent ISI thrusts in Thailand and Indonesia encouraged the independent growth of local firms based on lower-technology products for the domestic market. Given their more solid internal technical capacities, these firms seemed better poised to take advantage of recent export opportunities than to be absorbed by them.[5]

The timing of attempts to manufacture major functional components was also important. Where this decision was made early in the industry's growth, as in the Philippines, the technology required to meet foreign markets exceeded the capacities of local firms, whose dependence on foreign inputs thus grew. Where efforts to produce major components occurred more gradually, as in the other three countries, local firms had more opportunity to build up and avoid extensive foreign control.

Because pressure on TNCs for expanded local auto manufacture often came from local firms, explaining variation in the economic strength of such firms through reference to state orientations can help explain cross-national bargaining leverage. But state industrial policies are an insufficient explanation of local corporate strength and national bargaining leverage. For Thailand exceeded Malaysia and Indonesia with regard to general policy performance and the growth of local firms even though all three nations shared similar orientations.

A more fundamental explanation of performance lies in relations between the state and private auto interests. Rather than Bennett and Sharpe's "transnational corporations versus the state," the most common source of host country success involved arrangements of the type identified by Theodore Moran and Joseph Grieco: networks of public officials and aggressive local firms at the sectoral or firm levels. I shall address soft and hard variants of this hypothesis. The former simply asserts that such networks can strengthen the host country's bargaining position; the latter, that such arrangements promote local strength more effectively than an autonomous state.

Concertation and Bargaining Leverage

The Argument

Although the ASEAN auto cases do not provide definitive evidence on this question, this study lends support to the view that functional concertation between public and private actors at the sectoral level can enhance the host country's leverage in manufacturing, and under certain conditions can do so more effectively than state autonomy.[6]

The central component of concertationist arrangements is shared authority based on presumed limits to state capacities.[7] The concept of concertation employed here emphasizes negotiations and collaboration between public authorities responsible for a particular sector on the one hand and organized private actors in that sector on the other. Close to being a loose form of corporatism,[8] concertation in this sense is an ideal type that is useful to distinguish policy processes in which functional coalitions based on shared authority are strong from those in which such coalitions are weak or nonexistent. The latter include cases of state autonomy, where states can plan and implement policy without having to compromise with other social and political actors; and of pluralism, in which neither the state nor private actors possess sufficient identity or coherence to form stable functional networks. I understand concertation to involve a state that is, on the one hand,

> autonomous enough in the policy arena at issue not to be "colonisable" by the interest or interests involved, and credible enough to threaten these interests with a worse possible outcome—usually direct regulation—if they do not agree to respect the "public-regarding" provisions it imposes. On the other hand, the state must be weak enough to recognize that the costs of implementing a given policy authoritatively will exceed its likely benefits.[9]

Three dimensions can help us to distinguish between concertation, state autonomy, and pluralism (see table 9.2). First, concertation involves formally organized business interests, typically in the form of a small number

Table 9.2.   Characteristics of State-Society Relations

	State Autonomy	Concertation	Pluralism
Business organization	Generally low; if high, penetrated by state officials	High	Low, fragmented
State preferences	Very high, developed without reference to views of private sector	High	Low, more derivative of private views
Consultation/ collaboration	Low; relations top-down	High	Low, emphasizes lobbying

of business associations monopolizing the representation of interests in specific functional areas. These groups may have emerged with state encouragement, but, unlike in a situation of state autonomy, they are not subordinated to state control or penetrated by official bureaucratic and party organizations. These interests are commonly organized at the macro (peak) level or at the meso (sectoral) level. Pluralist arrangements involve less formal or institutionalized private sector organization, with at best a large number of competitive associations with overlapping interests.

Second, if concertation is present, the state's bureaucracy is presumed to have a relatively identifiable and independent set of policy preferences.[10] The issue here is not the degree of state intervention. The state under concertation may opt to eschew a high-profile role. But it ideally contains functional agencies whose policy initiatives are relatively depoliticized. They are sufficiently insulated from popular movements (below) and from particularistic elite pressures (above) to sustain "an independent and adversarial relationship"[11] with private actors. These agencies are not, as would be the case under state autonomy, able to develop and act on such preferences without reference to the needs and preferences of private actors. Nor, as would be the case under pluralism, are state preferences derivative of societal interests. In extreme situations of "pluralist colonization" or "capture,"[12] the state's interests are essentially identical with those of particular interests.

We encounter here the difficulty of determining whether state preferences that overlap with those of private actors are the preferences of independent state actors[13] or private sector preferences imposed on a captured state. Often state preferences are a mixture. But the degree to which they lean to one side or another is important and can only be resolved empirically. One (admittedly imperfect) indicator of the strength of state preferences is personnel stability in agencies responsible for auto policy. A second is the consistency and cohesion of those preferences.

Finally, and most important, concertation presumes frequent, if not institutionalized, negotiations or collaboration between private interests and their functional counterparts in the state. Although usually found at the macro and/or meso levels, such functional ties can also occur on what Alan Cawson calls the micro level—that is, "collaborative policy-making between a single firm and a state agency."[14] Whatever the level, this negotiation presumes that "affected interests become incorporated within the policy process as recognized indispensable negotiators and are made co-responsible (and occasionally completely responsible) for the implementation of policy decisions."[15] Institutionalized linkages between government and business can also occur under state autonomy. But the authoritarian, top-down nature of the process means that organized business acts more to absorb and contain demands than to collaborate in the policy process. Under pluralism, business influence is commonly exerted through lobbying of a representative body or political leadership rather than direct negotiations with relevant government officials.

Again, however, we must address a difficult distinction—namely, that between shared authority and private dominance. How are we to distinguish what Cawson calls a micro-corporatist (i.e., "micro-concertationist") arrangement from one in which the state or some of its representatives essentially belong to a faction of local capital, a case of pluralist colonization or capture? Conceptually the difference harkens back to whether the links are functionally based and whether influence flows in both directions or only from firms to government officials. Actual empirical distinctions are obviously difficult to draw, but two indicators are useful. I shall assume that more pluralist arrangements exist if (1) a firm's links are primarily with political leaders rather than with career officials responsible for the firm's sector, and (2) the firm is consistently able to avoid government regulations imposed on other firms in the sector.

What are the potential causal links between concertation and local bargaining strength? Existing writings (cited in chapter 2) are designed to explain national abilities to contend with foreign markets rather than with foreign investors. But two general patterns found in this literature seem at least heuristically useful for our present concerns. First, concertation can regularize the policy process by rendering it "less subject to changing political fashion."[16] Second, concertation among organized private and public sector interests can "enlarge a country's repertoire of policy alternatives."[17] More specifically, an association of firms and/or a large industrial group can facilitate the gathering of information on production techniques, input sources, domestic market conditions, and so on. An organized private sector can also improve market conditions through regulation of competition and development of industrial standards. Concertation can facilitate the provision of such information to government officials, thus both improving the quality of state policies and moving them in directions consistent with the goals and capacities of private actors. And, finally, improving the quality of state policies can "increase the acceptance of regulation by those affected by it."[18]

Evidence

Table 9.3 places each of the ASEAN Four on a state autonomy–concertation–pluralist continuum based on a review of the three dimensions discussed above. The nature of the rankings suggests greater gaps between the countries than may be warranted. But they do capture basic variations with regard to state-society arrangements at the sectoral level. Thailand is the most concertationist, the Philippines the most pluralist, and Malaysia and Indonesia closer to the state autonomy pole. As the table shows, these rankings are consistent with relative policy performance/bargaining leverage. After reviewing the differences with regard to relevant dimensions, we address the ways in which these features influenced bargaining strength.

Organized business.   We are concerned here with the degree of associational strength of firms supporting local auto manufacture (including production for export) and market rationalization. Thailand and Malaysia both featured formally organized and consistently influential auto interests. Organized Thai assembly firms played an active policy role as early as 1969–71, when the Association of Thai Industries pressed the MOI to streamline and deepen local auto manufacture. TAPMA, an association devoted to parts firms, emerged in 1977 and went on to play a major role in the promulgation of mandatory deletion in the late 1970s, in preventing a rollback of localization in the early 1980s, in pressing for local content levels to exceed 54% in the mid-1980s, in promoting the diesel engine project, and in attempting to reduce the rate of model changes. SNF played a major role both by itself and as a leader of the parts firm association.

A Malaysian auto association of assemblers and distributors existed as early as the 1960s but did not play as active a role as its Thai counterpart. MACPMA, a homogeneous parts firm group, emerged in 1978, and immediately became a major force in pressing for and designing the mandatory deletion program, as well as ensuring that the national car would incorporate locally (and privately) made parts.

An Indonesian parts firm association did exist, but its level of organization and policy role were negligible.[19] More prominent was the association of assemblers, GAAKINDO, itself the result of a state-initiated fusion between two other groups. Critical to the policy process through the mid 1970s, GAAKINDO fragmented in 1977–78 as higher localization levels pitted the "weak brothers" against the "strong." Organizationally weakest in the ASEAN Four were the Philippine firms. Divided into three separate groups prior to the PCMP, Philippine parts firms merged into one association, CAPPA, in 1972. But apart from three or four years of moderate organizational strength under Joe Concepcion, the association had little cohesion or policy role.

Independence of bureaucratic preferences.   To what extent did the policies of ASEAN government officials actually reflect state preferences? In Thailand, strong advocacy of increased localization and market streamlining characterized the Ministry of Industry and Board of Investments throughout the period covered by this study. These views did overlap with those of many private firms. But the reform initiative taken by Wichitwong in the early 1970s prior to the emergence of an organized parts sector, the organizational integrity and consistency of the MOI[20] and the Automobile Development Committee, and the consistency of the

Table 9.3. State-Society Arrangements and Auto Policy Performance in the ASEAN Four

| | Dimensions of State-Society Arrangements | | | | |
	Organized Business	State Preferences	Negotiation/ Consultation	State-Society Arrangements	Relative Auto Performance[a]
Indonesia	Mixed; GAAKINDO strong to mid 1970s, then fragmented; replaced, to some degree by Astra	Strong; stable personnel, agency bases, and policy; but policy weakened by need for ethnic equality	Strong from early to mid 1970s; then partially replaced by micro-level ties between DOI/Astra; persistent clientele/pluralistic ties between palace/Liem/Probo.	Greater state autonomy	3
Malaysia	Strong; MACPMA well organized, but not as comprehensive as Thai association	Fairly strong; personnel stable, policy consistent but weakened by need for ethnic equality	Strong, then moderate; well institutionalized in JTC since late 1970s; but JTC circumvented by direct Mahathir-Mitsubishi links		2

Thailand	Strong; ATI active in early stages; TAPMA estab. in 1977; cohesive and comprehensive; backed by large group, SNF	Fairly strong; personnel stable; policy consistent; minor opposition from EOI backers; some private influence, but influence dispersed	Strong in late 1960s/early 1970s; weak in mid 1970s; strengthened with TAPMA links to ADC; also, micro-level ties between SNF and BOI	Greater concentration	1
Philippines	Overall weak; moderate in early 1970s; parts association moderately active in mid 1970s, then weak	Initially strong, then weakened; personnel unstable; technological policy dominated by Marcos intervention	Weak; initial consultants between Paterno and local firms (PAA/Sycip); BOI later isolated; weak ties to CAPPA; major ties of a "colonized" nature between Marcos and Silverio	Greater pluralism	4

[a]Based on table 3.23.

views suggest that government preferences reinforced or promoted similar views in the private sector rather than deriving from them. These views did not represent a consensus within the government. They were criticized by proponents of export-led growth from the late 1970s on, and, in the case of rationalization, overruled by political leaders influenced by local and foreign assemblers. But they did constitute a stable basis of the government's "authoritative actions and inactions" with regard to auto policy.

In Indonesia, distinct government preferences were reflected in the emergence of Suhartoyo's Directorate in the Department of Industry as a consistent source of auto policy initiatives, his continued role on the Capital Investment Coordinating Board, and even the policies espoused by Soehoed. If anything, the localization preferences of the Indonesian government were more pronounced than in Thailand. The Malaysian Industrial Development Authority, HICOM, and Prime Minister Mahathir himself constituted a similarly consistent base of policy preferences for localization and rationalization. But even more than in the Thai case, the cohesion of government preferences in Indonesia and Malaysia was undermined by a competing set of concerns. The need for ethnic equality, imposed by political leaders sensitive to the danger of outbreaks of *pribumi* and *bumiputra* extremism, compelled officials in both countries to moderate their basic preferences.

In the Philippines, Paterno's advocacy of rationalization, exports, and manufacture of complex components represented a major independent government initiative. But if government preferences in Indonesia and Malaysia were undermined in part by ethnic pressures from "below," in the Philippines they were even more muddled by politics from "above." Silverio's links to Marcos, his access to preferential financing, and his ability to avoid localization requirements and model restrictions represented the dominance of particular interests over the BOI's concerns with the development of the entire sector. The problem was exacerbated (or perhaps reflected) by personnel turnovers within the BOI itself.

Negotiations/consultation.   How regularized (institutionalized) were the policy links between organized private actors favoring local auto manufacture and government officials responsible for auto policy? Thailand emerges as the strongest of the ASEAN Four on this dimension. An initially constructive process of joint discussions, which led to the 1971 reforms, was aborted by the military takeover of late 1971. The Automobile Development Committee did subsequently solicit input from the private sector. But until 1977–78 consistent ties were hindered by the generally volatile political environment, the ADC's own lack of bureaucratic clout, and the relative weakness of the parts firms. By 1977, however, the emergence of TAPMA and the need for national positions on the ASEAN complementarity project facilitated more consistent contacts. Initially ad hoc, these became more regularized through the ADC's consultation with TAPMA and its individual members over localization initiatives.[21] A second important channel was a microcorporatist one involving Siam Nawaloha Foundry and the Board of Investments. Following the failure of the initial engine effort, SNF became a regular member of the Board of Investment's subcommittee on diesel engines. Nor, despite SNF's ties to the Crown Property Bureau, did this relationship involve the firm's capture of the BOI. For just as SNF encouraged the board to revive the engine project, the latter impeded SNF's monopolization of the project by compelling the firm to expand its subcontracting.

By the late 1970s public-private sector negotiations in Malaysia were probably the most institutionalized in the region. As in Thailand, links between the parts firms and government officials were encouraged by the ASEAN complementarity efforts. With the adoption of mandatory deletion, these links became institutionalized in the Joint Technical Committee. But unlike in Thailand, these links were bypassed and weakened by an automotive initiative from above—Mahathir's national car project.

The concertation process in Indonesia grew stronger over time, but gradually shifted from a meso to a more micro level. Under Sukarno the process had been almost classically pluralist, with individual firms obtaining benefits through party ties to frequently changing ministers. With the New Order, Suhartoyo encouraged private sector cohesion and worked closely with GAAKINDO in the development of the 1976 auto policy. But with the opposition to increased local content of the "weak brothers," Suhartoyo and subsequently Hartato relied principally on large, individual firms, especially the country's largest automotive entity, Astra. Astra's links were primarily and consistently with the Department of Industry, and the firm did not generally avoid the burden of government localization requirements. Astra's LC levels were, if anything, higher than those of other firms.

Indonesia was far from the concertationist ideal, however. Probosutejo falls at the pluralist end because of his personal ties with the president and his consistent evasion of government measures. Liem, with his significant corporate resources but low localization levels and close ties to Suharto, falls somewhere in the middle, but closer to the pluralist ties exhibited by Probosutejo than to the more functionalist links between Astra and officials in the DOI. What we have here is a balance between concertationist and pluralist arrangements.

No such equilibrium existed in the Philippines. True, the PCMP did emerge out of consultations between the Philippine Automobile Association and BOI technocrats like Paterno. But as the policy was implemented and martial law proclaimed, the BOI found itself isolated from the dominant auto policy link—that between Marcos and Silverio. Unlike in Indonesia (where Astra balances off Liem), there was no offsetting arrangement between the BOI and a major firm complying with and even strengthening government policy efforts.

Politics, Information, and Bargaining

Let us turn then to causal links. Did concertation actually strengthen local bargaining leverage by buffering the process from "changing political fashion" and expanding the country's repertoire of policy alternatives as proposed earlier? Evidence in support of these propositions is mixed.

Backing for them may be found even in the Philippines, where CAPPA's support was a necessary condition to the Board of Investment reducing the localization credit obtained through exports and adopting mandatory deletion.[22] As illustrated by SNF's guiding BOI and MOI officials on a tour of Japanese engine facilities, the development of links between SNF and Thai officials allowed Thailand to build and maintain pressure for engine-component standardization. The Thai parts firms' association, including SNF, also provided information and pressure critical to the adoption and subsequent modification of mandatory deletion. The same pattern was seen in Malaysia, where MACPMA also pressed for the improvement of production standards among local parts firms through its role on the Joint Technical Committee and its support for the government's industrial standards institute. Indonesia's Astra, through its links to the Department of Industry, has not only provided information essential to sustained localization policy; it has also supported the government through its own direct bargaining with foreign partners.

Perhaps most striking is the fact that in both Indonesia and Malaysia, the *functional* links between Chinese firms and government officials have moderated the impact of increased popular ethnic animosity to overall Chinese dominance and to those Chinese more clearly benefiting from special state favors. While no clear counterfactual situation exists, it is safe to say that attacks by *pribumi* firms on Indonesian localization policies would have been much stronger and more effective without what Chalmers calls a "power center" composed of the DOI and Astra, the nationalist industrializer.[23]

There is, of course, plenty of evidence that the absence of concertation undermines strength by politicizing the policy process and depriving government officials of critical support, pressure, and information. The Philippines is the outstanding negative case. As the BOI's Paterno noted, martial law disrupted routine procedures and institutions. The board's efforts at implementing the PCMP were overwhelmed by the injection of particularistic interests channeled through the presidential palace. The BOI's general isolation from the parts firms deprived it not only of information on CKD prices, deletion allowances, and model changes, but also of political support essential to the formulation and implementation of its basic policies. Similarly, Thai government policy, especially on model and make limits, underwent harmful fluctuations owing to the 1971 coup, government sensitivity to popular demands during the 1973–76 democratic period, and the vulnerability of BOI leaders (as opposed to staff) to Japanese appeals. Mahathir's circumvention of MIDA, the Malaysian parts firms, and even HICOM, resulted in a weaker contract with Mitsubishi than presumably would have been the case with other sources of information and pressure. And in Indonesia, despite Astra's role, ethnic concerns and the needs of firms close to the president resulted in frequent shifts in localization requirements.

Good Politics/Bad Politics?

The preceding paragraphs stress the weakening of bargaining leverage by political factors (i.e., those external to the functional ties between organized firms and relevant officials), be they particularistic ties within the elite (links between Marcos and Silverio, Liem and Suharto), pressures from popular movements (Thailand's democratic period, anti-Chinese pressure), or some combination. It would, however, be a serious error to lose sight of the potential benefits of such factors. As noted in chapter 2, popular demands can result in foreign investment becoming an issue whose political salience actually increases the willingness of host countries to mobilize bargaining resources.

How are we then to distinguish between political influences that enhance local leverage and those that undermine it? One useful point of departure is whether such factors strengthen or weaken the functional ties between government officials and local firms. Indonesia's Malari riots enhanced the country's ability to play Japanese firms off against each other. Although these riots were in part aimed at local Chinese merchants, they actually strengthened the nationalist policy network of which Astra was a critical component. Yet anti-Japanese activities and subsequent popular movements in Thailand through the mid 1970s destabilized bureaucratic procedures, undermined an emerging network, and resulted in several years of policy inactivity. Marcos's declaration of martial law had a similar impact, undermining the authority of the BOI. The consequences of ethnic frustrations in Malaysia were more mixed. The threat of recurrent riots of the 1969 type constituted an intangible, yet recognized, pressure on foreign as well as Chinese assemblers to accept the national car. Yet in large part because of these pressures, Mahathir circumvented existing national auto interests and, at least initially, put Malaysia at the mercy of Mitsubishi.

Negotiated Authority versus State Autonomy

What of the "harder" version of the concertation hypothesis? Do the ASEAN cases back the contention that shared, negotiated authority enhances a host country's leverage more than state autonomy? Because none of the cases involved the actions of a highly autonomous government, a simple answer is impossible. But the Mahathir-led Malaysian government was better able to act independently of local private actors than its neighbors. Auto efforts in Malaysia thus provide some basis for judging the costs and benefits of state autonomy.

The benefits were strikingly illustrated in Mahathir's ability to impose a market-rationalization plan. Concerned with anti-Chinese reactions and unable to buy off a prime minister chosen by an organized and well-financed *bumiputra* base, Chinese assemblers made no moves to sabotage the car project. Instead of the behind-the-scenes maneuvers adopted by Bangchan in Thailand and Probosutejo in Indonesia, Malaysian assemblers complained but adapted by moving into different vehicle niches, parts production, and/or nonautomotive activities. Deprived of capital umbrellas under which they could maintain market share, the auto TNC had no choice but to adapt as well.

But the costs of autonomy rapidly became clear. Mahathir's contract with Mitsubishi provided only the weakest basis for actual local manufacture. Only with intervention by local Chinese parts firms was Mitsubishi compelled to accept existing localization levels. And to the dismay of *bumiputra* motor traders, the national car's commercial success meant relying on Chinese retail and service networks. The state simply did not possess sufficient resources to do more than establish Proton with incentives not available to others. Promotion of local manufacture, distribution, and, as illustrated by Mitsubishi's recent takeover of the firm, even management of Proton itself were beyond state means. Continued refusal to utilize Chinese resources and existing public-private networks meant relying on Mitsubishi and thus reproducing dependency.

The Malaysian national car experience thus suggests that the bargaining utility of state autonomy is issue-dependent—greater for market rationalization than for directly promoting local contents. The case does not, however, suggest the utility of a passive state even in localization. Mahathir's initiative provided the basis for greater economies of scale in parts production, while agencies such as MIDA helped to maintain pressure for local manufacture in local hands. But these efforts bore fruit only when married to activities in the private sector.

State-Society Relations in Southeast Asia

Economic sectors have characteristics transcending national boundaries. But the configurations of each country's political economy shape sectoral policy arrangements. My primary aim in this section is to explore the national political economies in which the ASEAN auto industries are embedded.

More broadly, I am also interested in whether these national arrangements constitute what J. A. C. Mackie has called "growth coalitions"—

that is, "tacit alliances" between the state and local firms promoting national industrialization.[24] Viewed as key to economic growth in the Asian NICs, such coalitions are often presumed to require a relatively autonomous state in which political leaders insulate bureaucratic actors from "extra-bureaucratic and extra-elite pressures."[25] This chapter's examination of the ASEAN context sets the stage for us to shift the analysis of sectoral sources of host country strength to the national level. More specifically, in chapter 10 I shall draw on the concept of functional concertation to suggest that national "growth coalitions" are possible even if we sharply modify the assumption of state autonomy.

The Philippines

The idea of a "growth coalition" was a particularly attractive one for Ferdinand Marcos. With extensive power following the 1972 imposition of martial law, Marcos proclaimed his intention to build a Filipino version of Japan Inc.—a public-private sector partnership capable of moving the country forward.[26] But rather than a partnership, what emerged was an increasingly narrow pact of domination in which one clique, organized around Marcos, came to exercise almost total control over the civil bureaucracies, the military, most major banks, most major businesses, and all of the press.[27]

This process of clique-based government involved several phenomena also found in the Philippine auto industry: inefficiency in business, deinstitutionalization, elite divisions, and general weakness vis-à-vis external actors.

The origins of these developments lay in the conditions encouraging Marcos's assumption of martial law power. By the late 1960s the Philippines faced structural economic problems and growing political fragmentation. A divided, but still powerful, landowning elite successfully resisted national efforts to take control of local and regional politics;[28] a Congress of elected landlords dragged its feet on desperately needed land reform;[29] and the country's postwar ISI-based economic growth was slackening.[30]

The result was a policy stalemate reminiscent of the conditions provoking bureaucratic authoritarianism in Latin America.[31] Prior elite cohesion had broken down. Nationalist forces found in the Philippine Congress, in the increasingly radicalized student movement, and among ISI-based entrepreneurs backed protection for domestically owned industry and limits on foreign investment. The technocrat-led BOI championed a more efficient state-led ISI strategy. Thus, in defending his plan for eleven major industrial projects, BOI Chief Roberto Ongpin argued that reliance on labor-intensive activities would leave the Philippines "a country of sweatshops, processing through our cheap labor the produce of the industrialized countries around us."[32] But the BOI's approach involved a bias against small and medium-sized firms, greater openness in the country's trade and foreign-investment regimes, and rationalization of the fragmented and inefficient economy. Finally, it required "constitutional authoritarianism" to control the unruly political forces opposing economic reforms.[33]

The technocrats and Marcos did not lack support. Many in the Filipino business community, including those with nationalistic leanings, had come to agree that "the total system needed rationalization based on greater discipline, leadership, and less interference by politicians, especially those in Congress."[34] The country's auto industry fit nicely into this mold. The PCMP, devised by technocrat Paterno, was seen as the means by which to rationalize this fragmented and inefficient industry. Businessmen like Sycip who were not Marcos cronies may have disagreed with the program's immediate stress on high value-added production. But Sycip's belief that the Philippines could not "develop as a nation by becoming a sweatshop" meshed well with the thrust of BOI efforts.[35]

Marcos seemed to move quickly and effectively on many fronts. He expanded the country's infrastructure, weakened the landed oligarchy, reduced anti-Chinese discrimination, rationalized key bureaucratic agencies, and improved public safety.[36] He also followed the East Asian NICs by promoting the Philippine equivalent of Japan's zaibatsu and South Korea's *chaebol*—government-favored conglomerates capable of implementing the technocrats' industrialization strategies. With state guidance, Ricardo Silverio was to be the Philippines' Hyundai.

What emerged instead were robber barons, cronies who were "more interested in enriching themselves in the short run than in building lasting industrial empires."[37] Under the guise of rationalization, Marcos created crony-controlled and horribly mismanaged monopolies in crucial agricultural markets.[38] Powerful crony conglomerates also emerged in the manufacturing and service sectors through preferential finance, monopolies over basic imports, and special exemptions from government regulations. Among several examples are Silverio's access to Philippines National Bank loans and his avoidance of LC and rationalization rules.[39]

To this was added a penchant for expensive projects. The government spent huge sums on hotels and international assemblages. In industrial policy, the presidential palace's desire to benefit cronies such as Silverio through vertically integrated operations reinforced the BOI's antipathy to small and medium-sized firms and its preference for high tech ventures involving high value-added such as the eleven industrial projects. Finally, the regime was characterized by significant levels of outright theft. For example, the diversion of precious metals by Marcos and his associates reportedly led to a 45 percent drop in the country's gold reserves during 1973, the first full year of martial law.[40]

These practices removed the crony firms from any serious discipline imposed by competitors or the financial system. Overextension and inefficiency were encouraged. Inefficiency was reflected in the incremental capital-output ratio, the amount of money required to raise annual national output by one dollar. In the early 1980s the figure for Indonesia was $4, for India $6, and for the Philippines $9.[41] Inefficiency combined with high debt levels led to national financial fragility. In 1981 the departure of the Chinese businessman Dewey Dee with 635 million pesos required massive state rescues of several overextended crony firms, including Silverio's Philfinance. The government's bailout of one large crony firm, the Construction and Development Corporation of the Philippines, for example, involved a sum equal to 20 percent of the country's money supply and 10 percent of the entire government expenditure for 1982.[42] The crisis did lead to the downfall of several cronies, including Silverio, but at tremendous financial cost. The assassination of Benigno Aquino on August 21, 1983, exacerbating an already serious crisis of confidence, set off a balance of payments crisis. In mid October the country declared a ninety-day moratorium on debt payments.

Underlying these developments was the deinstitutionalization of the Philippines. Although the initial martial law measures hinted at a "possible institutionalization of corporativism," the regime "effectively destroyed old institutions" but did not move to create new supporting ones.[43] In economic policy, a "dualistic economic policy-making structure" emerged generally as well as in sectors such as auto manufacture.[44]

Prime Minister Cesar Virata was unable to implement cabinet decisions because of objections from non-technocrats in the cabinet, especially Mrs. Marcos, who controlled public and private funds equal to 50 percent of the total government budget.[45] Through Presidential Decrees, Letters of Instruction, and personal appointees, Marcos also circumvented technocratic influence in financial institutions such as the Central Bank and the Monetary Board. Virata, for example, opposed Philippine National Bank guarantees to another crony, Herminio Disini, for overseas loans necessary to a takeover of the Caterpillar Tractor distributorship. He was overruled by Marcos on grounds of national security.[46]

Under political pressure, and with the country in economic decline, competence deteriorated. The most egregious example of this was the Central Bank's use of overnight borrowings to cover external payments shortfalls. Coordination among agencies responsible for industrial policy, finance, and long-term planning was almost nonexistent. The Board of Investments came into frequent conflict with the Philippine National Bank's preferential lending and the liberal views of the National Economic Development Authority (a body one BOI official termed "a group of statisticians").[47]

Deinstitutionalization occurred in other areas as well. In business, the advantages given to rent-seeking crony firms and the technocrats' antipathy to nationalist ISI entrepreneurs resulted in a weakening of previously dynamic associational activity.[48] A regular framework of consultation between business and government was undermined by the concentration of decisions in the presidential palace, the weakening of existing business associations, and the BOI's bias against small- and medium-sized firms. Although the BOI had "close links with the private sector,"[49] these were with disorganized non-crony firms with little political clout.

The system that emerged during the 1970s was thus not a "growth coalition." Martial law insulated the technocrats from troublesome nationalists, but it also encouraged political interference from the palace and related interests. In the end, economic policy officials were irrelevant, more isolated than insulated. Nor did this arrangement strengthen the country's position vis-à-vis external forces. The auto industry's denationalization reflected a broader weakening of Philippine firms relative to foreign capital[50] as well as the country's overall financial collapse in the 1980s.

Indonesia

The Philippine auto industry evolved in a national environment in which the policymaking establishment became increasingly narrow in its interests and ad hoc in its decisions. Indonesia has moved in the opposite direction, tending toward a broadening of interests and regularization of procedures. Indonesia is, of course, far from being a dynamic bourgeois order. But it has begun to shake off its status as a "bureaucratic polity" in which important decisions are the exclusive domain of the state.[51]

This began during the 1970s, when government officials on their own initiative presided over a dramatic strengthening of large business groups. The process was accelerated and complicated in the 1980s. Falling oil prices have reduced both state revenues and state leverage over private firms, including previously passive smaller firms. Yet the state has maintained a strongly tributary character and political leaders are at best ambivalent toward capitalism. As a result, Indonesia is "a tantalizing combination of authoritarianism at the political level and liberalism at the economic."[52] In terms of state-society relations, this has meant a gradual move away from state autonomy toward a much more fluid, but balanced, set of links between private firms and government officials.

We can identify four broad stages in this shift, the first of which ran from independence in 1949 up to the overthrow of Sukarno in 1965. Unlike that of the Philippines, Indonesia's colonial experience left it without a large landowning class, an indigenous middle class, or even a cohesive peasantry or working class.[53] Chinese merchant capital had expanded under the Dutch in credit and trade occupations. But the Chinese community's relatively small size (less than 5% of total population), its lack of assimilation into Indonesian society, and the threat of indigenous (*pribumi*) resentment over Chinese economic strength precluded a Chinese-based political movement.[54] With no basis for coherent political parties following independence from the Dutch, "power virtually gravitated into the hands of the state and its officials by process of default."[55] Under Sukarno this meant the development of a politico-bureaucratic elite, a system in which politico-military factions took monopoly control of access to production and trade (such as the lucrative import of cars). Fundamental to this process was the gradually expanding role of the military, starting with the armed forces' dominance of Dutch enterprises confiscated by the state in 1957.

The second period, from 1965 through the mid 1970s, was marked by early economic reform, military consolidation, and the gradual emergence of new economic groups. During the initial years of the New Order, Western-trained technocrats with military backing shifted to more orthodox macroeconomic policies. Despite its autonomy from domestic forces, the country's economic deterioration forced the New Order state to accept an open-door policy toward foreign investment. As one senior minister noted, all sources of foreign capital were welcome. "We did not dare to refuse; we did not even dare to ask for bonafidity of credentials."[56]

Simultaneously, the need for political consolidation and the armed forces' own financial shortages (military budgets were cut to ease inflation) propelled military officers into the country's civil and economic administration.[57] With government enterprises contributing roughly 50 percent of value-added for large firms by the mid 1970s, the state was being "appropriated by its own officials."[58]

Yet two new categories of business groups gradually emerged. Several indigenous (*pribumi*) entrepreneurs sprang from the higher echelons of the civil and military bureaucracy, including Pertamina, the national oil company.[59] Even more important in terms of eventual economic power, budget cuts forced the military to promote Chinese business groups.

> Political patronage and state protection afforded privileged access to state bank credit, forestry concessions, trade and manufacturing monopolies, official distributorships of basic foodstuffs, and state contracts for supply and construction. The bulk of these new corporate groups were Chinese-owned; their directors generally had had long associations with the military, acting as financiers for army commands and individual generals, and de facto managers for corporations owned by the military.[60]

This nascent partnership between the still dominant state and new business groups expanded significantly during a third period of state-led industrialization from the mid 1970s through the early 1980s. As the economy recovered by the early 1970s and economic nationalism reasserted itself (most violently in the 1974 Malari riots), restrictions on foreign investment were tightened.[61] As noted in chapter 6, the new regulations stipulated that special preferences be granted to private *pribumi* firms. But the core objective of Indonesian economic policy had become "national resilience" through an integrated industrial base, not ethnic redistribution. The role of large private groups in the nationalist thrust was to grow through the 1970s.

In a sense, prominent Indonesian officials had espoused this goal since 1965.[62] But it took on new salience in the early 1970s for several reasons. Rising oil revenues made it feasible by reducing the state's dependence on foreign funds and by financing massive state infrastructure investments in which local firms participated to the extent of their capacities. The goal of "national resilience" also gained coherence and political credibility. A group of what Richard Robison calls "bureaucrat nationalists" advocated a "nationally integrated economic unit," "a state-coordinated economic structure within which finance and production could be coordinated to achieve national planning goals."[63]

This coalition included officials from the state oil company and the state intelligence center, Chinese intellectuals, and Chinese businessmen involved, or soon to be involved, in various economic arenas, including automobiles.[64] They espoused a corporatist economic vision designed explicitly to expand Indonesia's bargaining leverage with foreign capital. Previous efforts to make use of foreign capital had been too fragmented, they asserted, leading only to squabbling over economic spoils by local firms. But there was no need to exclude foreign firms.[65] The system required was a corporatist one "combining state power and resources with private business interests and building 'national giants' in an attempt to counterbalance the power of the 'foreign giants.' "[66]

No such organized partnership between the state and large-scale capital actually emerged during this period. The Indonesian economic policy process was instead relatively dualistic.[67] One component was an authoritarian corporatist arrangement involving smaller existing businesses.[68] The source of this arrangement lay in New Order efforts to undermine the extensive political mobilization that occurred in the final years of Sukarno's rule. Government officials established a strict system of functionally based organizations that covered previous sources of radicalism (e.g., labor, peasants, youth) as well as categories such as civil servants, teachers, and business. Formally, business demands were channeled by a highly developed and differentiated corporatist structure, with the Indonesian Chamber of Commerce and Industry, KADIN, at the apex. But this was a top-down process, supplemented by the establishment of a government party, Golkar, and the consolidation of existing parties into two heterogeneous groupings. To the extent that the associations supported the aims of government officials (e.g., GAAKINDO in the early-to-mid 1970s), they were involved in advice and consultation. More generally, they were excluded from the policy process and confined to the containment and absorption of demands by smaller firms.

The second component of this dualistic policy process was a more particularistic set of alliances involving government officials with the newer groups mentioned above. These were the actual core of Indonesia's industrialization drive, with the state oil company, Pertamina, initially considered to be the first among equals. Pertamina used access to the country's oil reserves as bargaining leverage to obtain funds for major petrochemical and gas projects.[69] It also used its vast funds to establish subsidiaries in related fields.[70] Finally, Pertamina provided the basis for several of its officers to become significant private capitalists in their own rights. In addition to eight auto assembly, import, and distribution operations, Ibnu Sutowo's business group included firms involved in property and construction, manufacture and shipbuilding, finance, forestry, architecture, travel, insurance, and trade. As noted in chapter 6, these firms also maintained links to the growing Chinese groups of Astra and Liem.[71]

Pertamina turned out to be an unreliable source of industrial growth. In 1975, owing to a temporary oil recession, the state oil firm was unable to meet its short-term debt-servicing obligations. A subsequent investigation discovered extensive corruption and led to the replacement of Sutowo and his assistants by officials more sympathetic to foreign capital and free-market policies.[72] But Sutowo's fall did not entail a repudiation of "national resilience." Officials advocating second-stage import substitution, such as Suhartoyo, Soehoed, and Habibie, kept their policy posts.

Reinforcing the state-led industrial drive were large Chinese groups such as Liem and Astra. Rising oil revenues during the 1970s had facilitated government investments in infrastructure and production, through which these groups expanded to the point where they "could effectively exploit protective policies and state subsidies and credit."[73] This growth had important implications for the position of local capital in relation to foreign firms: leading business groups such as Liem and Astra used state protection to develop their own financial and managerial bases, to exert greater influence in joint ventures, and to expand from import and distribution into manufacturing. This occurred in pharmaceuticals, chemicals, the milk industry, metal fabrication, engineering, banking, and, of course, auto manufacturing (e.g., Astra's decision to initiate the building of commercial vehicles despite Toyota's opposition).[74]

These firms did not operate through associational structures. Their links to government officials were more particularistic "alliances of individual capitalists with specific centers of politico-bureaucratic power."[75] Some of these alliances tended more toward the functional concertation discussed earlier, while others took on more clientelist features. Taken as a whole, however, they reflected an "increasing fusion of politico-bureaucratic power and corporate capital ownership."[76] It was this state-led fusion that drove the country's industrialization process during the 1970s and early 1980s.

Oil revenues made this fusion and the resulting industrialization process possible in the first place. But oil prices dropped and have remained low during the fourth and most recent period, 1982 to the present.[77] Ensuing budget deficits forced the state to reduce investments and intensify the search for non-oil revenue sources, especially manufactured exports. The impact of these developments on the actors and relations driving Indonesian economic policy is not yet clear. But a few important trends can be identified.

First, the new economic situation has reduced the state's autonomy vis-à-vis business as whole. Government deficits have forced officials to rely on the private sector for new investments. Squeezed by the economic downturn, increasingly broad sections of business have become more active in communicating their problems to policymakers. Business associations have become the locus of these activities. KADIN has become an arena in which increasingly dynamic associations attempt to expand their channels of influence.[78]

Second, the new economic situation has especially strengthened opponents of state-led industrial deepening.[79] This category includes economic planners in the World Bank and various Indonesian planning agencies; foreign firms; and domestic downstream producers forced by protection and/or import monopolies to purchase foreign inputs at high prices. This last group includes (but is not limited to) entrepreneurs with little inclination or capacity to move into upstream operations. Probosutejo is a case in point.

Attempts by the above groups to regularize policy and reduce corruption have been relatively effective. In 1983 several contracts involving Suharto's friends and supporters were rescheduled.[80] Beginning in 1982–83, efforts were undertaken to restrict Pertamina's financial autonomy and generally regularize the oil industry.[81] Perhaps most striking, in 1985 Suharto initiated a major effort to cut the cost of low-wage exports through a radical reform of Indonesia's notoriously corrupt Customs Department.

Third, efforts to weaken the policies and forces supporting state-led industrial deepening have been somewhat less successful.[82] The government did devalue the overvalued rupiah in 1983, initiated a deregulation of the banking system and even allowed downstream producers to circumvent certain import monopolies with independent imports when inputs were required for export production and not available domestically.[83] The whole trend has certainly lent backing to the *pribumi* opponents of full-scale automobile manufacturing such as Probosutejo.

But industrial deepening still has its public and private sector supporters. Importers of intermediate and capital goods (e.g., Liem for steel) remain politically powerful. So do private and state-owned firms in upstream operations such as cement, plastics, tin plate, airplanes, ships, and automobile engines.[84] A striking illustration of this is Suharto's support for Liem's inefficient cement and steel operations through loans and equity buy-ins.[85] Finally, throughout the 1980s these forces have had their supporters leading the Department of Industry and the BKPM.

It should come as no surprise that Indonesia's shift toward compliance with free-market forces and sensitivity to the needs of downstream producers has been halting and incomplete. These changes threaten the political-economic alliance that has dominated Indonesia. But the country's loss of oil revenues and the "space" this has provided for smaller producers suggest that the movement for change will continue.

This shifting policy framework provides a useful context in which to understand the evolution of major forces in the auto industry. "Growing up" at the top end of a dualistic and protected industry, the larger firms are having to adapt to a more competitive economic environment and a more fluid political one. This does not suggest that auto industrialization will be rolled back; the forces for industrial deepening remain strong. But it does point to increasing pressure on auto firms to meet two somewhat contradictory aims: efficiency on the one hand and side payments to, or incorporation of, the inefficient, but politically influential, smaller firms on the other.

One explanation for Astra's steady expansion in the auto industry has been its ability to reconcile these goals. In terms of efficiency, it has initiated export efforts while pressing its TNC partners for greater standardization and commonization. Politically, it has sided with the forces of industrial deepening, while avoiding the label of corruption generally applied to its major local rival in auto manufacture, Liem. To the extent that the emerging forces of Indonesian politics facilitate this combination of expansion and efficiency while discouraging the more rentier efforts of Liem and others, the country's ability to make use of foreign capital in manufacturing would seem to be enhanced.[86]

Malaysia

In both Indonesia and Malaysia Chinese minorities have dominated business while indigenous majorities controlled the state. In both countries these hierarchically ordered ethnic cleavages have spawned states more autonomous from dominant business interests than is the case in either the Philippines or Thailand. Yet state-society relations in Indonesia and Malaysia have evolved in somewhat different directions. In Indonesia there has been a gradual (albeit still incomplete) shift away from state autonomy toward the interdependence of *pribumi* political power and Chinese economic strength. In Malaysia, on the other hand, the Malay-dominated state's ability to formulate and implement policies independently of Chinese business has grown. But as the following examination shows, it is far from complete.

State-society relations in Malaysia have evolved in three stages. An intercommunal bargain was the primary political characteristic of Malaysia during the first decade or so following independence from Britain in 1957. Malay, Chinese, and Indian organizations formed a governing coalition, the Alliance party, in which each pledged cooperation through control of its communal base. Politically, the United Malay Nationalist Organization (UMNO) dominated this "consociationalist" arrangement by virtue of the Malay's numerical dominance, the concept of Malay "special rights" enunciated by the British, and the central role played by top Malay civil servants in the independence movement.[87] But if UMNO dominated the Alliance party, the Malaysian Chinese Association (MCA) financed it.[88]

This political arrangement reflected the economic division of labor encouraged by the British. The Malays emerged as food producers and civil servants, their employment as tin miners or rubber tappers having been discouraged to avoid disruption of the peasant-based agricultural economy. The Chinese dominated non-European commerce and the small industry of the towns and cities. And the Indians (represented in the Alliance party by the Malaysian Indian Congress) performed the tasks of both rural proletariat and professional class.

Laissez-faire economic policies during the first period reinforced this economic alignment. It should be noted that the creation of a Malay capitalist class through "special rights" was recognized in the constitution.[89] During the early 1960s, demands by incipient Malay entrepreneurs led to the establishment of state agencies to strengthen the Malay economic position. These had little impact, apart from some Malay gains in the transport industry, where, as we have seen, government preferences encouraged some Malay participation in assembly. Led by a Bumiputra Economic Congress demanding a Japanese, Meiji style of state-capital relations, pressure for government backing of Malay capitalists intensified during the second half of the decade.[90] But despite more substantial pro-Malay measures, government expenditures mainly targeted the rural infrastructure, and industrial choices were left in the hands of private (largely Chinese) firms. Manufacturing led the economy in growth, but few Malays entered the industrial sector and those who did were influential politicians or former senior civil servants. Chinese strength grew not only in the economy but in technical positions within the civil service as well.[91]

The interracial riots of May 1969 initiated a second period of increased state regulation under the New Economic Policy (NEP). Signifying a strong reaction against Malay-Chinese accommodation, the riots compelled the Malay political elite leading UMNO (and thus the government) to pay greater attention to its ethnic base. The state was transformed into a proxy and primary source of pressure for Malay capital accumulation. The NEP promised a growth of Malay corporate equity from 2 to 30 percent by 1990, in part through public enterprises in areas such as transportation and wholesaling. Along with a rise in public sector spending, the number of state firms jumped from ten in 1957 to eighty-two by the end of 1974.[92] Through the Industrial Coordination Act (ICA) of 1975, the NEP also aimed to expand Malay economic opportunities by imposing compulsory ownership and employment targets on private firms.

This radical extension of the state's economic role reflected what one observer called the end of a marriage between Malay political power and Chinese economic power.[93] UMNO moved from a position of first among equals to one of clear domination of a new governing coalition, the National Front, established in 1974. But this shift required a Malay economic as well as political base. This was achieved through NEP contracts and the Fleet Group, a set of banking, insurance, leasing, and mass communications firms established in the mid 1970s as the commercial arm of UMNO.

But UMNO's resources provided Malay leaders with an autonomy that was more instrumental than structural. That is, while Malays were able to formulate policies at odds with Chinese interests, the Chinese had the economic capacity to water down and otherwise obstruct the implementation of those policies. One component of the Chinese response was the "corporatization" of the mass of small, family-run Chinese firms through the creation of Multi-Purpose Holdings, a conglomerate with interests in major sectors of the country's economy.[94] The Chinese also reduced their investments.[95] The pressure resulted in 1979 amendments to the Industrial Coordination Act exempting small- and medium-sized firms from its provisions, thus protecting the majority of Chinese enterprises.

The NEP did lead to a growth of *bumiputra* corporate ownership from 2.4 percent in 1970 to 12.5 percent in 1980. But the reduction of Chinese dominance and creation of a Malay business class were still far off. Chinese holdings grew from 33 to 45 percent of the total, and over 80 percent of Malay holdings were in the hands of "Malay interests"—that is, government entities.[96] In addition, the state did not attempt to determine what was to be produced. Firms and state-firm relations in existing manufacturing sectors such as automobiles were left untouched. Thus, while the communal bargain was shaken at the peak level by the state's new regulations, it seemed to remain fairly stable in particular sectors.

In 1980 Mahathir, then minister of trade and industry, initiated a third stage, a still sharper departure from laissez-faire policies and intercommunal cooperation. State agencies such as HICOM were to have a major role in creating a new group of large-scale, capital-intensive, import-substituting industries using indigenous resources, especially cheap energy, to manufacture intermediate industrial goods and consumer durables for the domestic market.[97] Operations in iron and steel, cement, internal combustion engines, pulp and paper, and, of course, automobiles were established with support from foreign firms and massive injections of government funds.[98]

These enterprises were accompanied by campaigns extolling the virtues of the Asian NICs, especially South Korea and Japan. Malaysians were encouraged to "Look East" and create "Malaysia Inc." in which public and private sectors would share responsibility for national growth.[99] Emulating the NICs' work ethic and corporatist relations, Mahathir believed, would help Malaysia's heavy industries policy move the country out of its economic doldrums. Indeed, structural economic problems were one source of the new policy. The economy remained heavily dependent on a handful of primary commodities for much (61 percent) of gross exports.[100] Manufacturing growth rates at the beginning of the 1980s were just over 3 percent compared to rates of roughly 10 percent in the late 1970s and projections of 11 percent for the 1980s.[101] Despite some move away from the simple assembly of imported components during the 1970s, industry was narrowly concentrated in the foreign-owned, import-dependent electronics and textile industries while the contribution of large-scale capital-intensive industries to manufacturing output remained minimal.[102] Malaysia needed to move up the technology ladder. If private investors were unwilling to move into such areas, Mahathir argued, the government would have to lead the drive.

But Malaysia's economy had appeared to be structurally depressed ten years before without provoking anything like a heavy industries policy.[103] The more central explanation for Mahathir's initiative was ethnic politics. In 1980 UMNO's leadership was under "considerable political pressure from the Malay community to meet NEP objectives by using direct state action to overcome business intransigence."[104] Thus, the new policies were designed as a direct challenge to the domination of ethnic Chinese entrepreneurs. The new heavy industries were to serve as "training grounds for a new class of bumiputra industrial managers and skilled blue-collar workers."[105]

Ethnic politics provided the means as well as the motivation for this effort. The UMNO-dominated National Front government had strong rural Malay support and sufficient continuing backing from Chinese voters not to fear an electoral challenge. "Thus, because of its ethnic 'cast,' the state was effectively autonomous from those groups which in any other society might have been able to obstruct economic initiatives such as those of the heavy industries policy."[106] But again, this autonomy was largely instrumental. State contracts and profits from the Fleet Group could not provide the technology and funds required by this ambitious assault on Chinese strength. Replacing, as opposed to regulating, Chinese capital demanded resources available only from abroad. Each of the heavy industries projects involved the extensive participation of foreign capital.[107] As Martin Brennan suggests, state autonomy from Chinese business interests may require increased dependence on foreign capital.[108]

A review of the problems encountered by the new projects suggests the validity of this point. First, the government has had to increase its foreign indebtedness simply to maintain the projects under difficult external conditions. A commodity price slump and deteriorating terms of trade led to reduced government revenues in the early 1980s.[109] Rather than cut spending for the heavy industries projects, the government increased its borrowings from international capital markets. Federal debt as a percentage of GNP jumped from 10 percent in 1980 to 23 percent in 1982, while the country's balance of payments as a percentage of GNP shifted from a surplus of 5 percent in 1979 to a 13 percent deficit in 1982.[110] As of 1988 the government had incurred a public debt of M$41.6 billion, of which M$15.3 billion was attributable to public loans for the heavy industries projects.[111] Such debt levels "rendered the Malaysian economy and related policymaking far more vulnerable to foreign economic policy influence, especially by multilateral agencies, such as the IMF and the World Bank."[112]

Second, the government's operational control of the projects has deteriorated. Even with foreign borrowings, the projects have done poorly. As of March 1987 HICOM had net losses of US$111.9 million, an increase of 13 percent over 1986. Operating losses were recorded for each of its units, including Proton.[113] Although macroeconomic conditions accounted for much of the difficulty, the Malaysian finance minister stressed the responsibility of inefficient government officials.[114] As a result, HICOM lost control of its auto and steel projects. Proton's management, as noted in chapter 3, reverted back to Mitsubishi, while the steel project came under control of a company headed by Eric Chia, the local Chinese entrepreneur responsible for the marketing of the Proton.

These developments may be interpreted as reflecting one of three scenarios of state-society relations. In the first (Mahathir's view), a Malay-dominated state is using foreign capital as a temporary expedient to replace an outmoded industrializing coalition (Chinese capital and Malay political power) with one involving private as well as public Malay forces. The second suggests that, absent a feasible alternative to Chinese capital, such an alliance between the state and foreign capital is likely to be more permanent and less beneficial to Malaysia than Mahathir acknowledges. According to the third, local Chinese participation in the steel and auto projects (see chapter 5) indicates that the state–foreign capital alliance may be vulnerable to attack from Chinese businessmen willing to work with foreign firms but attempting to expand their own manufacturing activities. Given Mahathir's goal of encouraging *local* manufacturing and the overall economic power of Chinese business, the industrial goals of the latter carry weight.

Which scenario is "correct" remains uncertain. Varying combinations of the three are probably being played out in different sectors. What is clear is that the national car project has evolved in a period featuring a de facto coalition of Malay political power and Chinese business interests that is weaker than previous arrangements but certainly more durable than that envisaged by Malay leaders.

Thailand

Thailand exhibits a level of ethnic integration similar to that in the Philippines. But we also find there a bureaucracy whose expertise and independence exceeds that of its ethnically integrated Philippine counterpart. Like Indonesia, Thailand is shifting away from a bureaucratic polity.

But in Thailand that shift is much more pronounced. Indeed, only in Thailand do we find a relatively equal distribution of power among economic elites, a state more efficient than dominant, high levels of private sector organization, and extensive institutionalization of state-business ties. The result has been an extensive degree of functionalist concertation at the national as well as sectoral level, an arrangement that one observer labels "societal corporatist."[115] Here we do find a "growth coalition," but one whose state component is not highly insulated from elite pressures.

This arrangement has evolved in four general stages. From the end of World War II through the late 1950s, Thailand had the state-centered and politically weak private sector characteristics of a bureaucratic polity. Led by a nationalist military, the country pursued "haphazard, state-led development."[116] This involved the promulgation of anti-Chinese policies, the reservation of some petty trading and service-sector roles for Thai nationals, and the establishment of semigovernmental monopolies in several sectors.[117] This was a form of limited state capitalism, designed in part to subsidize Thai political activities and in part to prevent Chinese domination of Thai economic life.

But this arrangement did provide avenues of economic and associational growth for Chinese economic and political resources. Anti-Chinese policies merely engendered a particular form of alliance between Chinese business interests and the Thai bureaucratic elite: Chinese entrepreneurs operated under Thai political protection, while the Thai officials depended heavily on Chinese capital and management, a pattern similar to the one still found in Indonesia.[118]

But unlike in Indonesia, ethnic nationalism did not preclude organizational development of the Chinese business community. On the contrary, Chinese businessmen established a wide range of associations through which they exchanged information and formulated concerted and largely unpolitical responses to government harassment.[119] Economic factors encouraged associational growth as well. Thailand's commodity exports surged between the end of World War II and 1954, leading to excessive competition and bankruptcies.[120] This competition often took the form of product adulteration and breach of contracts with foreign importers. Because such practices might damage the country's reputation and reduce the inflow of foreign exchange,[121] the government moved to regulate commodities exports and avoid cut-throat competition by creating a

Board of Trade responsible for setting norms and minimal export prices. Originally (1954) a state agency, the board soon became a private association composed of the major private sector chambers of commerce.

A 1957 coup led by Field Marshal Sarit Thanarat ushered in a second stage running through the 1960s. During this time, a military-dominated authoritarian state improved the conditions of private capital accumulation and organization, thereby undermining its own authoritarianism. Anxious to stabilize the country's political life, Sarit abrogated the constitution and ruled without an elected legislature.[122] Concerned with the inefficiency of state-run enterprises, he also proclaimed a policy of non-competition with private business and radically changed the state's role from direct producer to provider of infrastructure and incentives.[123] Under a policy of import substitution, the private sector was to become the engine of economic growth. Foreign investment was to be welcomed, and Chinese or Sino-Thai businesses were to be encouraged and assimilated rather than repressed. Through a set of institutions created between 1959 and 1963—the Board of Investment, the Industrial Finance Corporation, and the National Economic and Social Development Board (NESDB)—the state would support the growth of local private capital.

The World Bank encouraged these changes but pressures from domestic firms and the nature of the Thai military elite were more central to them. Several Sino-Thai business groups had expanded their capital bases, especially in banking and commerce, and were anxious to move into the manufacture of consumer goods for the domestic market.[124] A reduction in the state's role would do away with competition and regularize the policy process. Local firms viewed foreign investment less as a threat than as a source of capital and technical skills. And because foreign firms enjoyed the right to own land and protection from threats of nationalization and government harassment, joint ventures with TNCs also provided a solid political base for the growth of domestic capital. If an expanded TNC presence was one of the costs of Thai government policies promoting the growth of domestic business, "Thai capitalists were prepared to pay the price."[125]

The policy influence of local capital was facilitated by the fact that Sarit's power base lay in the private sector rather than in state enterprises.[126] More generally, Thai firms confronted a military with little of the ethnic base, shared ideology, or nationalist tradition so prominent in

the Indonesian and Malaysian cases. The country had faced serious foreign threats and avoided colonization. However, Thai independence had
been maintained not by military conquests but through Thai monarchs'
relatively adroit use of rivalries among the imperialist powers. During the
nineteenth and early twentieth centuries, the Europeans eliminated
the threat of Thailand's traditional regional foes while constituting a
sufficient threat themselves to provoke a self-strengthening of the Thai
monarchy and bureaucracy.[127] Deprived of a clear role, the Thai military
was thus vulnerable to factionalization across service, patron, and academic class lines.

Military rule was further undermined during the 1960s by increasingly
assertive societal forces.[128] An economic boom, itself encouraged by foreign assistance and spending,[129] led to a sharp growth in the numbers and
influence of students, workers, professionals, and executives.[130] Manufacturing grew at an 11 percent annual rate during the 1960s, and "banking
capitalists... took advantage of ISI policies to expand into industry,
greatly enhancing their corporate power."[131]

Business associations grew as well. Although links to political and
military patrons remained important, associations further institutionalized connections with their bureaucratic counterparts. By the late 1960s,
representatives of peak associations such as the Board of Trade, the
Thai Bankers' Association, and the newly created Association of Thai Industries were regular participants in policy subcommittees of the
NESDB.[132] And, unlike their Indonesian counterparts, Thai associations
"were largely independent of the government in their operation. Almost
all of them had been organized by businessmen themselves."[133] As
reflected in auto manufacturing, relations of a functional concertationist
nature were thus beginning to replace the more clientelist links of a
bureaucratic polity.

Direct pressure on the state by organized business intensified in the late
1960s as ISI exhausted the limits of the Thai market and excess capacity
became a major problem. In 1969 the Association of Thai Industries
urged more export incentives and increased protection of domestic
industries.[134] The ATI's campaign in favor of more extensive, efficient
auto manufacturing was part of this general effort. Organizationally, sectoral peak associations also lobbied for the creation of a Federation of
Economic Organizations of Thailand (with compulsory membership) and
an institutionalized process of state-business consultation.[135]

But political instability blocked such efforts, at least temporarily. By the end of the decade, new popular forces demanding constitutional rule confronted the repressive rule of Generals Thanom Kittikachorn and Prapas Charusathien, Sarit's successors. This movement was reflected first in an increasingly assertive parliament, established in 1969. The military's 1971 dissolution of this parliament, it will be recalled, led to the gutting of the auto rationalization scheme created by the Ministry of Industry and the ATI. Temporarily set back, the democratic movement succeeded in overthrowing military rule in 1973 and ushering in a new period of state-society relations.

This third stage was a halting transition toward a more clearly open and bourgeois polity. Its first three years were marked by a succession of four unstable civilian governments. As seen in chapter 8, the political fragility of these governments in the face of strong popular demands precluded long-term bureaucratic planning and a strengthening of functional ties between state and organized business.

These conditions did, however inadvertently, encourage an organizational strengthening of bourgeois forces and clear the way for more solid long-term state-business concertation. This shift was illustrated in 1974 when the Bangkok Bank accepted the resignation of General Prapas, one of the deposed military leaders, as the bank's president. The bank then appointed a professional banker as its president for the first time.[136] Private-sector associations first represented Thai business in ASEAN regional meetings and subsequently, under a more liberal Prime Minister, General Kriangsak Chamanand, began consultations with government officials over the country's worsening current account deficits.[137]

During the fourth stage of Thai politics, from 1979 to the present, state-society concertation in Thailand intensified. The emerging system was "marked by the coexistence of state leadership and the initiative, autonomy and efficacy of interest groups. It is a model of collaboration between two relatively equal partners, not of domination by one partner over the other."[138] Institutional manifestations of this pattern include extensive links between sectoral associations and relevant bureaucratic agencies; a proliferation of provincial business associations since 1984; and the establishment of an active Joint Public and Private Sector Consultative Committee (JPPCC) in 1981. The latter body is composed of representatives of the three peak associations, economic ministers, and the prime minister, with a secretariat led by the NESDB.[139]

These developments have had important policy impacts. Business associations have played central roles in the adoption and implementation of an export thrust, while acting to ensure that local firms benefit from such a strategy.[140] At the national level, this has involved public-private sector promotion of domestically produced intermediate inputs for manufactured exports, and the reform of taxation, anachronistic laws, and customs procedures (a move that required an outside contractor in Indonesia and the Philippines).[141] These national efforts have drawn on pressures by export-reliant firms and associations at the sectoral level.[142] At the provincial level joint efforts have focused on promotion of industry and agriculture, infrastructure development, and administrative decentralization.

What factors account for the persistence of this move toward corporatist arrangements? A background condition, Thailand's relative dispersion of economic ownership, merits note here. By the 1980s several large economic groups controlled much of the nation's wealth. Yet these elites were "more diverse and competitive than their Filipino or Indonesian counterparts."[143] Because no firm or group of firms could dominate the system as they did twenty to thirty years ago, businesses have found associations to be increasingly useful in their responses to changing market conditions.

Worsening economic conditions also encouraged corporatist tendencies. By 1978–79 deteriorating trade and budget deficits[144] were creating political "space" for Thai entrepreneurs and their associations. This can be seen in business's response to the Kriangsak government's initial (1978) trade-deficit reduction efforts, which involved bans on certain items (such as CBU automobiles) and higher tariffs on others. Major business groups preferred a greater emphasis on export promotion, and the newly established Joint Standing Committee on Commerce, Industry and Banking proposed a cabinet-level public-private committee to explore an export strategy.

The proposal was willingly accepted by the Kriangsak government, which was anxious to find solutions to the country's economic squeeze.[145] While the joint committee was dissolved at the end of the Kriangsak government in early 1980, it was significant for several reasons. First, its very adoption reflected a reopening of the political arena to business. The chief lobbyist for the committee's creation was Ob Vasuratna, head of the Thai Chamber of Commerce, and close friend of Kriangsak's. Ob became minister of commerce in the second Kriangsak government following (April 1979) elections in which other business association leaders emerged as major opposition figures.

The joint public-private committee was also significant as a step in a movement begun in the early 1970s toward institutionalized state-business concertation. The committee's 1980 demise was followed by an informal government-business forum operating from 1980 to 1981 under a new government headed by General Prem Tinsulamond. Focusing on export promotion, the committee was formed by the new deputy prime minister, Boonchu Rojanasathien, formerly head of the Thai Bankers' Association.[146] In 1981 this informal arrangement was succeeded by the JPPCC.

Finally, the committee (and more specifically the activities of business in it) reflected the willingness of ISI-based entrepreneurs, including those in the auto industry to support at least a moderate export strategy. Ob, as seen in his subsequent support for auto localization, was a strong advocate of industrial deepening. So, for that matter, was Taworn Pornprapa, then president of the ATI, an active supporter of greater attention to exports and head of Thailand's largest automotive group, Siam Motors.[147] Both of these men viewed exports as building on, rather than negating, second-stage import substitution. They thus clashed with the more ardent advocates of EOI found in the IMF, the World Bank, and, as seen in the auto-manufacturing case, the NESDB and the Industrial Finance Corporation of Thailand.[148] But their understanding of the need for increased exports constituted "common ground" critical to ongoing links and policy cooperation between ISI-based firms and "free-market" officials in the NESDB and IFCT. The development of the diesel engine project and its eventual incorporation of an export component exemplify such cooperation.

If deteriorating market conditions provided impetus for increased business organization and greater opportunities for business influence in the policy process, they also strengthened the agency most active in the promotion of public–private sector ties—the National Economic and Social Development Board. The NESDB's chief during the entire span of General Prem's tenure as prime minister (1980–88) was Sanoh Unakul, a former head of the Bank of Thailand. Confronted with continuing budgetary problems, Prem relied heavily on Sanoh to ensure that the country's development efforts fit its fiscal constraints. With strong backing from Prem, the NESDB served as secretary and agenda-setter for inter-agency bodies. The agency also had the authority to review large capital projects, and frequently shot down those that were politically motivated and/or ill-advised.[149]

Prem's protection thus allowed for a depoliticization and increased efficiency of the NESDB, a tendency seen elsewhere in the Thai bureaucracy, albeit not so extensively.[150] The NESDB's relation to the country's political leadership during the 1980s is consistent with what Chalmers Johnson has called a separation between reigning (politicians) and ruling (bureaucrats) in the Asian NICs.[151] But Thailand does not exhibit the degree of insulation often assumed to be necessary for such a separation. While the NEDB under Sanoh was able to ignore more particularistic, rent-seeking types of business influence, it actively solicited the input of organized sectors and business as a whole.

Measured by changes of governments, Thailand has experienced greater political instability over the past twenty years than its ASEAN neighbors. Yet running beneath these changes are more constant features of Thai political economy: the strengthening of business associations, of the civil bureaucracy, and of institutionalized, policy-based consultation between state and private actors.

Can we say that a growth coalition exists in Thailand? Yes, in the sense that (1) increasingly integrated public and private entities have been responsible for shaping the country's economic strategies and incentives over the past twenty years or more, and (2) that these policies have encouraged an economy that "is justly famous for being 'fast on its feet,' that is, quick to seize new market opportunities," and a private sector that "is already bigger and arguably more dynamic than those of the other agriculture-based economies of the region—Indonesia, Malaysia, and the Philippines."[152] This dynamism is reflected in the growth of Thailand's manufactured exports during the 1970s and early 1980s (table 9.4), its GDP growth rate in the 1983–87 period, and the consistently strong role of local capital.[153]

But the core of this growth coalition is functional concertation rather than an "insulated developmentalist state." It involves considerably more negotiated authority than do the arrangements observed in the Asian NICs. The Thai state is autonomous enough to avoid colonization, but it

Table 9.4.   ASEAN Export Growth

	Average Annual Growth Rates of Exports (%)		Manufactured Exports as Percentage of Total	
	1960–70	1970–82	1960	1982
Indonesia	3.5	4.4	0.8	4.2
Malaysia	6.1	3.8	6.0	27.8
Philippines	2.3	7.9	3.2	23.6
Thailand	5.2	9.1	1.4	35.3

SOURCES: World Bank, *World Development Report*, 1984; Asian Development Bank, *Key Indicators of Developing Member Countries*, 1984, cited in Hirono Ryokichi 1988, 256.

is sufficiently weak to require (organized) private sector input in both policy formulation and implementation. The essential point here is that this lack of insulation from extra-bureaucratic forces has not impeded local growth. On the contrary, it seems to have resulted in relatively strong economic performance at the national as well as auto sectoral levels.

10

Conclusion: Taking
Third World
Capital Seriously

This book has explored the ways in which businessmen, bureaucrats, and politicians in Southeast Asia have sought to expand local manufacture in the face of opposition from foreign firms. With its emphasis on private actors and on coalitions of negotiated authority in sectoral development, this study raises some critical issues for development theory more generally. Specifically, I believe it suggests the need for a concertationist framework of development.

Both structuralist and product-cycle bargaining frameworks belong to broader tendencies within the literature on development. Both views have built on traditional dependency theory's analysis of conflict between LDC industrialization efforts and the interests of core capital.[1] But they have done so in sharply different ways. Fundamental to their divergence are contrasting assessments of the developmental potential of Third World capital. Here I wish to emphasize that the structuralist bargaining school is part of a more general tendency that has married what Stephan Haggard has termed "revisionist dependency" to a statist emphasis.[2]

Reactions to the deficiencies of traditional dependency theory are well known and need be noted only briefly here. Recognizing the reality of industrialization in certain LDCs, analysts allowed that development was occurring but emphasized its persistent reliance on core capital. The essential feature of this "revisionist" trend for our purposes is its maintenance of the traditional dependency belief in the inherent weakness of Third World capital. While local entrepreneurs are conceded to have asserted themselves in limited niches, their basic weakness is perceived to have required an assertive state to lead the development process.[3]

At least two factors accelerated the shift toward a more explicit view of development as necessarily a state-led process. One was the impact of foreign capital on the state. It was recognized that the challenges of transnational economic linkages could generate new state organizational capacities and enhance a government's leverage over private domestic actors.[4] The stunning economic performances of Japan and the Asian NICs was the second and more central impetus toward an explicitly statist perspective. Analyses of these experiences showed the critical developmental role of strong states—that is, those with high autonomy and capacity. Political leaders independent of popular and other elite forces insulated bureaucratic planners. The latter were in turn capable of steering their economies through crucial transitions, such as the shift from ISI to EOI.

Let me emphasize that this statist approach does not deny the importance of private entrepreneurship in the development process.[5] Nor does it ignore the ways in which state-led industrializing coalitions strengthen national capitalist classes over time.[6] Rather it relegates local firms to a distinctly subordinate policy role. This is especially true with regard to the shift from ISI to EOI.[7] An autonomous state is presumed necessary to ensure that entrepreneurship develops into productive coalitions rather than rent-seeking distributional ones. Strong governments have to nurture, reform, and channel local capital while avoiding the policy influence of indigenous capitalists. The NICs are thus presumed to have been successful because their governments were "shielded also against direct pressure from business groups, their policies being determined more by bureaucrats and technocratic specialists than by clamorous politicians or parties representing sectional interests."[8]

There can be little disagreement with the state's central role in the rapid economic growth of the Asian NICs. Nor is there any doubt as to the need for a focus on the "autonomy of the political,"[9] that is, on the state as a developmental actor with its own interests. But the extrapolation of a general statist development framework from these cases suffers from several weaknesses.

There are, first of all, problems in generalizing the model. The unique domestic and external conditions of Northeast Asia and Singapore suggest that few other countries have governments with the capacities and autonomy of the Asian NICs.[10] To the extent that industrial growth has occurred in countries with weaker governments one must question the broad analytical utility of the framework. In addition to Thailand, discussed in chapter 9, mention must be made here of Hong Kong, where private actors "assumed a role of economic tutelage" in the colony's development.[11]

Similar problems of generalizability may occur in applying a statist model to one country over time. It is clear, for example, that the South Korean government's policy of encouraging economic concentration and export growth facilitated the strengthening of the Federation of Korean Industries and thereby reduced the state's own control over financial resources.[12] To the extent that South Korea is able to sustain its growth, one must wonder, not whether state action was responsible for prior growth, but whether some functional equivalent has since developed that is not accounted for in the statist framework.

Problems of generalizability reflect two other limitations. One is a lack of systematic attention to the economic and political growth of Third World bourgeoisies. Unlike the product-cycle school and neo-Marxist critiques of dependency theory,[13] for example, the statist approach provides little sense of whether and how exposure to foreign capital can encourage what Nigel Harris has termed the maturation of local firms.[14] This neglect of Third World firms translates into an implicit view that "the bureaucrats are the good guys and the societal actors are the bad guys."[15]

A second and related problem is the failure to allow for gradations of state strength. Because the terms *autonomous, strong,* and *hard* lack clear definitions and empirical referents, the statist approach suggests a more clear-cut dichotomy between "strong" and "weak" states than is actually the case. It is not, for example, sufficiently nuanced to account for the beneficial impact of private sector opposition to the South Korean government's ISI policies in the early 1960s.[16] We are left with a choice between the "Latin American tradition of the caudillo" and the "East Asian style of bureaucratic authoritarianism."[17] This may help account for the problems of the Philippines under the caudillo-like Marcos. But it does little to explain growth where neither the state nor private capital clearly dominates.

The preceding observations suggest several components of an alternative, poststatist development framework. With regard to the characteristics of governments, it must first of all acknowledge variations in actual degrees of autonomy not simply cross-nationally but within particular countries. As shown in chapter 9's discussion of the ASEAN political economies, a state's ability to act independently of private elites often changes significantly over time. Levels of autonomy also vary by sector of capital (as reflected in Marcos's contrasting relations with different Philippine entrepreneurs), by industry, and by issue.[18]

A concertationist framework should also recognize variance in the developmental *utility* of autonomy and other aspects of state strength as well. As suggested in chapter 2, there may be a general tendency for the optimum degree of state strength to decline over time. What was initially set up to speed capital accumulation may become "an inhibition to growth as capital develops, as output diversifies, as businessmen are increasingly drawn to participate in the world economy."[19]

This general tendency does not preclude the need for a reassertion of strong state involvement at subsequent strategic turning points of a nation's economy. Shifts from import substitution to export-led growth or moves into high technology and heavy industry often involve changes in wage rates, credit allocations, and exchange rates. The weight of a strong state may be critical in overcoming societal opposition to such changes. However, a concertationist framework must also be sensitive to the possibility that the impetus for such shifts comes from particular sectors of capital, which then enlist the state on their behalf. As in the Thai case, this implies not so much a strong state but a more clearly coalitional one.

Finally, this alternative framework must allow for variation in the utility of state strength by issue. For example, the ASEAN and South Korean auto cases highlight the fact that vigorous state intervention has been essential to market rationalization, less so for increasing local content.

An alternative framework must also balance its understanding of the "autonomy of the political" with more systematic evaluation of Third World capital in the development process. Criteria for measuring the economic and political "maturity" of local capitalists must be developed. These certainly include quantitative measures such as composition of output, shares of gross domestic capital formation, and so on. But they must also incorporate a view of the bourgeoisie as a social movement, not unlike labor, whose development is reflected in the growth of institutions such as business associations.[20]

An appreciation of the factors encouraging such maturation is also required. One is clearly the state itself, although here again we must be sensitive to changing historical circumstances. Whereas early capitalist growth in the NICs (and most LDCs) required—and requires—a strong state, subsequent expansion may be facilitated more by "a supportive government, not one with a will and direction of its own."[21]

Foreign capital can also spur the maturation of local capital. Richard Sklar's "postimperialist" paradigm of capitalist development provides a starting point on this question. Its utility lies in its integration of cooperation and conflict between core and Third World capital. The two are clearly partners in that they share a basic interest in the structures and institutions of international capitalism. But they are also market rivals in that the leading strata of LDC capital "[yield] to no other class in the intensity of [their] nationalism."[22]

Yet, as discussed earlier, capitalists vary with regard to nationalist motivations and/or capacity to pursue such motivations. Peter Evans has explored the impact of foreign investment on Third World states, but we require greater specification of the factors mediating the influence of core capital (in its various forms) on local firms. Several issues merit further research for this purpose: industry-specific entry barriers (summarized in chapter 9); the particular strategies pursued by different TNCs;[23] the availability of foreign debt versus equity capital; the differing impacts of various colonial rules;[24] the opportunities provided to local firms by military-related commercial transactions;[25] and the information provided to local firms through transnational ties between nonprofit private organizations such as trade associations, educational institutions, and so on.[26]

The core of the development framework proposed here is a more explicit exploration of, and openness to, the developmental roles of private–

public sector linkages. There are empirical reasons for such a focus. Recent research has highlighted the extensive presence of networks, coalitions, and tacit alliances even in Japan and the strong-state Asian NICs.[27] Even more important is the functional role of such linkages. Whether bargaining with foreign capital at the sectoral level or responding to broader external market shifts, the more developed countries are those whose factors of production are more mobile. Mobility requires "flexible domestic structures" such as labor markets, capital markets, or information networks.[28] At the minimum, these structures in turn demand a combination of the state's provision of property rights and the more specific, market-based resources of private firms. Economic diversification and exposure to new external pressures increase the organizational requirements for overcoming resource scarcities and information complexities. All of these factors encourage (but clearly do not determine) the growth of public-private arrangements loosely termed networks or coalitions.

What guidelines can help us study these arrangements? We should begin with the assumption that they reflect what Richard Samuels calls "the politics of reciprocal consent." This refers to "plastic, imperfectly structured, often informal" arrangements in which private industry grants the state some jurisdiction over industrial structure in exchange for the use of public resources.[29] The continually negotiated character of such formations, which are analogous to what I have earlier termed *functional concertation*, means that the a priori identification of patron and client within them is impossible.

Given this fluidity, how is one to study such arrangements? The sectoral emphasis of this book supports Samuels' suggestion that they be examined through the market transformations they seek to effect. Better than an emphasis on state or private structures per se, a market focus can reveal how each competing group defines its view of the national interest while attempting to reduce its own cost of pursuing that interest.[30] This focus also allows classification of coalitions with regard to several important questions: What is the relative power of the participants? What are the sources of their power? Through what specific channels and structures are the participants linked? Is the coalition in question highly sector-specific or more reflective of nationwide patterns? What developmental tasks does the coalition perform?

The preceding constitutes only the beginnings of a concertationist approach to development. But the framework does help us move toward a more thorough response to the central question of this book: Can countries with weak states exploit opportunities for industrialization despite significant external obstacles? Put another way, are growth coalitions possible if we modify the assumption of state autonomy and acknowledge the utility of private elite influence?

The ASEAN auto cases suggest that the answer to both these questions is a qualified yes. Strengthened host country leverage and improved performance did not in these instances reflect fundamentally pluralist arrangements. Nor, given the relative inefficiency of the four ASEAN states, did state autonomy promise long-term bargaining leverage. ASEAN achievements instead resulted from coalitional arrangements involving regular exchanges of authority and resources between organized business interests and the government officials responsible for the sector in question. The concertationist framework encourages us to explore such arrangements more systematically. In so doing, I would suggest that the developmental options for most LDCs extend beyond the caudillo system of Marcos's Philippines and the authoritarianism of South Korea.

NOTES

Chapter 1

1. See, e.g., Moran 1974.
2. See Krasner 1985 and Doran et al. 1983.
3. ASEAN also includes Singapore and, since 1985, Brunei. Neither of these two countries is covered in this study: Singapore because it abandoned efforts to develop full-scale automobile manufacturing in 1980; Brunei because it has never pursued industrialization.
4. See Packenham 1983 and Grieco 1984. That shifts in bargaining power are not unidirectional is stressed in Encarnation 1989.
5. See, e.g., Deyo 1987b and White and Wade 1985.
6. "Much research . . . minimizes the importance of [local business groups] relative to government institutions and foreign enterprises. Or, even worse, it excludes local business groups from the bargaining process entirely" (Encarnation 1989, 24).
7. For recent exceptions see Higgott and Robison 1985 and Robison et al. 1987.
8. During the 1980–83 period, 18 percent of Japanese foreign investments were in the four Southeast Asian countries covered here, compared to 9 percent for South Korea, Taiwan, Hong Kong, and Singapore, 12 percent in Western Europe, and 21 percent in the United States (Japanese Ministry of Finance, cited in Abegglen and Stalk 1985, table 10.3).

Chapter 2

1. For a critical overview of these perspectives, see Grieco 1986, 35–39.
2. Such cases include Tugwell 1975, Goodsell 1974, and Moran 1974.
3. E.g., Stepan 1978, 235–36.
4. See Kindleberger 1979 and Encarnation 1989, 24.

5. This paragraph draws on the following: Vernon 1971, 47; Vernon 1977, 80–82; Krasner 1985, 182; Kobrin 1987, 619–27.

6. Bergsten et al. 1978, 380.

7. Baldwin 1979 and Moran 1978, 84.

8. See Goodman 1987, 124–27.

9. Poynter 1982, 13.

10. See, e.g., Bennett and Sharpe 1979 and Coronil and Skurski 1982.

11. The structuralist approach to measuring leverage suffers from some major methodological weaknesses. For a discussion of the structuralist view, see Grieco 1986, 41–44. Structural views are synonymous with what Richard S. Newfarmer has termed the "conglomerate power" view. See Newfarmer 1985a, 13–63, and also Gereffi and Newfarmer 1985.

12. This and the following paragaph draw on Newfarmer 1983, 185–86; Bennett and Sharpe 1985, 262; and Gereffi and Newfarmer 1985, 432.

13. See Bennett and Sharpe 1979.

14. See also Gereffi 1983, 160, and Stepan 1978, 237 n. 12. For a critical view of this assumption, see Harris 1988, 241–42.

15. Nordlinger 1987, 361–62.

16. My notion of orientations is adapted from Bennett and Sharpe's concept of "interests" (Bennett and Sharpe 1985a, 42–47). See also Haggard 1989, 203–5.

17. Zysman 1983, 76.

18. The "product cycle" approach is analogous to what Grieco terms the "bargaining school" (Grieco 1986, 41–44). See also Newfarmer 1985a, 26.

19. Moran 1978, 86; Vernon 1966; Wells 1971; and Vernon 1979.

20. Subsequent developments have shown that a "shortcutting of the traditional product cycle" often occurs through which TNCs skip other advanced countries and invest first in certain developing countries. This shift only intensifies the presence of foreign investment in LDC host countries. See Gilpin 1987, 255.

21. Moran 1978, 87 and 94.

22. Ibid.

23. This point is emphasized by Grieco 1986, 44. This and the following two paragraphs draw on Gereffi and Newfarmer 1985, 431–34, and Newfarmer 1985a, 27.

24. One study of TNC–host country bargaining in the ASEAN region found no close relationship between a TNC's percentage equity ownership and effective control of its subsidiary (Lecraw 1984, 38).

25. For a similar view, see Packenham 1983, 33.

26. See Bennett and Sharpe 1985a; Gereffi 1983; Coronil and Skurski 1982; the cases in Newfarmer 1985b; Lall and Bibile 1977; Fleet 1978. Several cross-national statistical analyses also confirm a positive correlation between an invest-

ment's technology requirements and the investor's leverage. However, these studies are static and therefore do not test the direction in which leverage shifts over time. See Kobrin 1987; Poynter 1982; Lecraw 1984.

27. See Bennett and Sharpe 1985a and the cases in Newfarmer 1985b. On autos in Latin America, see also Jenkins 1984, 65–69.

28. See Grieco 1984; Adler 1986, 674–705; Evans 1986; Amsden and Kim 1985.

29. See Vernon 1979, 263. This is consistent with cross-national studies according to which foreign firms in the middle range of technology were found to be most vulnerable to host country demands (measured by TNC ability to resist expropriation). TNCs at the highest end were the most powerful. See Fagre and Wells 1982, 12.

30. Hyundai spent six years producing a single model—the Ford Cortina—and then advanced to more sophisticated vehicles (see Shin 1984). Hyundai's connections with Ford during the 1968–73 period resulted in the mastery of assembly-line design, tool selection, and general worker education necessary to the subsequent absorption of technologies concerning engine blocks, transmissions, and rear axles, as well as factory construction and layout (Kim Young Kim 1984, 90). On Sri Lankan production of generic drugs, see Lall and Bibile 1977.

Computer firms in Taiwan and South Korea have shown that LDCs may also concentrate on more recently developed but still more manageable products. Taiwan firms, having developed the capacity to produce clones of first-generation IBM PCs, feared that their products would become obsolete when IBM came out with a new (PS/2) system in late 1986. Instead, consumers continued to demand the older technology that IBM no longer manufactured, thus leaving Taiwan with a major market segment. See Sanger 1988. On South Korea, see *The Economist*, November 27, 1985, 20. On Indian computers, see Grieco 1984.

31. See, for example, the discussions of paper manufacturing in Pakistan, pharmaceuticals and car bodies in the Philippines, molded plastic parts in Hong Kong, and capital equipment in Taiwan in Wells 1983, 20–25.

32. Vernon 1979, 263.

33. Mitsubishi's desire to bolster its weak position in the Japanese market encouraged it to be more amenable to South Korean auto measures than other Japanese firms. For other automobile cases, see Muller and Moore 1978; Bennett and Sharpe 1985a; Coronil and Skurski 1982; Fleet 1978. In electronics, it was Fairchild and Motorola, anxious to gain an overseas advantage over other U.S. companies and emerging Japanese firms, who trained South Korean firms in semiconductor production from 1964 on (Minor 1986, 11).

34. On "moments of transition," see Evans 1986. The development of the microprocessor and a move to smaller machines encouraged the entry of new foreign

firms with no proprietary interests in final demand sales. These firms were thus willing to transfer technology without maintaining ownership or organizational control. See also Grieco 1984. In pharmaceuticals this has involved new Swedish firms and independent testing units. See Gereffi 1983, 249, and Lall and Bibile 1977.

35. For a general discussion of this "miniature replica" phenomenon, see Evans 1977, 375.

36. See Newfarmer 1985b. On automobiles specifically, see Jenkins 1984, 217–20.

37. Fagre and Wells found that "none of the other independent variables . . . associated with bargaining success provides even a partial explanation for the bargaining power held by the pharmaceutical and cosmetic firms" (Fagre and Wells 1982, 13). For support, see Lall and Bibile 1977.

38. See, e.g., Goodman 1987, 121, and Kobrin 1977, 614.

39. For Venezuela, see Coronil and Skurski 1982; for Colombia, see Fleet 1978. Sri Lankan efforts to rationalize pharmaceuticals drew opposition from the TNCs' local importers, distributors, and many doctors (Lall and Bibile 1977, 685). And see the case of the Argentine tire industry in Newfarmer 1983, 186.

40. Bennett and Sharpe 1985a, 225. See also 208–9. For a similar case in which smaller domestic producers backed Sri Lanka's effort to rationalize finished drugs (while TNC subsidiaries opposed the policy), see Lall and Bibile 1977.

41. Grieco 1984.

42. Government officials viewed the merger as an opportunity to make South Korea a major production site for auto TNCs. Hyundai blocked the plan by demanding complete control over vehicle design and manufacture. Hyundai's control involved maintaining Japanese production methods, which, according to Amsden and Kim, were more efficient than those proposed by GM. Indeed, Daewoo eventually adopted the Japanese conditions for that reason. See Amsden and Kim 1985, 5, 6–15.

43. See Dominguez 1982.

44. Haggard 1989, 189.

45. Adler 1986, 699.

46. In Colombia, for example, Chrysler's local supporters backed a horizontal production structure in which assembly firms would purchase standardized parts produced in volumes large enough to allow effective economies of scale for local parts firms. Chrysler's support of this plan reflected opposition to Renault's plan for a vertically integrated structure involving the manufacture of nontransferable components. Fleet 1978. For a similar situation in Mexico, see Bennett and Sharpe 1985, ch. 7.

47. Hyundai's emphasis on developing an independent industrial capacity may reflect its traditional base in construction and producer goods, whereas Daewoo was originally based in the export trade. Hyundai's resistance to state pressure for a merger with GM-Daewoo was also bolstered by the firm's ability to draw on funds from within the broader Hyundai group (*chaebol*). Similarly, vertical integration helped the major South Korean semiconductor manufacturers, Samsung and Gold Star, to escape bankruptcy in the face of dumping by Japanese producers. Gold Star Telecommunications purchased unsold chips for telephones, while Samsung Electronics bought unsold chips for digital watch manufacturing. On the contrast between Hyundai and Daewoo's corporate roots, see Jones and Sakong 1983. I am grateful for suggestions from Soek-Jin Lew on the utility of Hyundai's corporate funds and from Chung-Yin Moon on Samsung and Gold Star.

48. Moran 1978, 94.

49. Mexican parts firms used their association to press for government support against the assemblers' vertical integration efforts and more informal maneuvers—abrupt changes of orders, demands for new components with little advance notice—that seriously threatened independent local firms. See Bennett and Sharpe 1985, 236. On the role of local hardware and peripheral producers' associations in Brazil, see Evans 1986, 801.

50. Gereffi 1983, 159–60.

51. Encarnation 1989, 223.

52. For cases illustrating both of these patterns, see Coronil and Skurski 1982 and Evans 1986, 795.

53. On government incentives for South Korean auto firms, see Kim Chuk Kyo and Lee Chul Heui 1984, 291–92.

54. Autonomy "is not sufficient to ensure that once goals are selected, they are accomplished" (Crone 1988, 256).

55. Evans 1987b, 340.

56. On licensing, see the studies of the Brazilian and Indian computer cases already noted; Evans 1982; and Kim Young Kim 1984. On the concept of "breakaway managers," see Vernon 1988, 13.

57. Grieco shows that Indian national objectives were realized only in the late 1970s, when privately owned firms overtook and changed the government's approach toward foreign technology (Grieco 1984, 154–55). Similarly, Mexican auto parts firms, politically inconsequential ten years before, pressured the state to strengthen its constraints on foreign assembly firms in the late 1970s (Bennett and Sharpe 1985, 236). In Brazil, private computer firms led the fight to restrain new state actors from weakening support for local manufacture in the early 1980s,

whereas ten years before, government officials had led the nationalist fight "on its own, while capital had sat largely disinterested on the sideline" (Evans 1986, 801).

58. Harris 1988, 239.

59. Gourevitch 1986, 230. Gourevitch terms such arrangements *corporatist*. In view of the usual connotation of corporatism as incorporating labor and business associations with compulsory membership, I prefer the term *concertation*. However, as elaborated in chapter 9, my use of the term includes interest intermediation as well as joint consultations. For a discussion emphasizing only the second component, see Schmitter 1982, 262–63.

60. Samuels 1987, 260–62. On the differences, see Milward and Francisco 1983, 281.

61. Along similar lines, Encarnation argues that while private sector innovations were central to Indian bargaining success, specific political arrangements (public–private sector ties) helped give rise to these innovations (Encarnation 1989, 224–25).

62. Evans 1982, 242.

63. Katzenstein 1978b; Bradford 1986, 123; Lynn and McKeown 1988.

64. Adler 1986, 686. The Mexican state also developed a nationalist strategy that avoided depiction as "against the interests of 'capital in general' " (Bennett and Sharpe 1985a, 258). See also Stepan 1978, 254.

65. On the problems of ISI see Encarnation 1989, 221. On the disadvantages of EOI, see Tauile 1987, 168–69, and Bennett and Sharpe 1985a, 208–9, 263–65.

66. See Kim Chuk Kyo and Lee Chul Heui 1984.

67. The Mexican case provides the negative evidence. See Bennett and Sharpe 1979, 76.

68. Grieco 1984, ch. 5; Bennett and Sharpe 1985a, 40, 111–14; Muller and Moore 1978; Fleet 1978; Mark Bennett 1986, 89.

69. See Evans 1986. For example, divisions between the pro-TNC policies of the South Korean Economic Planning Board and Ministry of Finance on the one hand and the more nationalist Ministry of Trade and Industry on the other provided Hyundai with room to oppose the government's merger plan. Personal communication from Soek-Jin Lew; and Kerns 1981, 41–42.

70. See Encarnation and Wells 1985.

71. In 1971 Brazilian officials drew on capital made available by the "economic miracle" of prior years to promote local computer production (Adler 1986, 686). In South Korea the state successfully promoted higher localization levels through preferential loans to firms investing in auto parts and component manufacture (Kim Chuk Kyo and Lee Chul Heui 1984, 292). The harmful impact of financial shortages is described in Fleet 1978, 248–50. See also Encarnation 1989, ch. 2.

72. Bennett and Sharpe 1985a, 274–75. On how a state's domestic weakness can translate into a strong position for bargaining with foreign capital, see Putnam 1988, 449.

73. See Eckstein 1975.

74. The quotation is from Haggard 1989, 193. Kobrin asserts that available case studies are limited to one sector in one country (Kobrin 1987, 615). There is, however, one other study covering the auto industry in several countries, although this does not analyze bargaining per se—see Jenkins 1977. See also the works listed in Gereffi 1983, 46–47, n. 43.

Chapter 3

1. For the 1970–82 period, the figures were even higher: Indonesia, 7.7 percent, Malaysia, 7.7 percent, Philippines, 6.0 percent, and Thailand, 7.1 percent, for an average of roughly 7.1 percent. See Asian Development Bank, *Key Indicators of Developing Member Countries of ADB*, April 1984.

2. Malaysia was no. 7, the Philippines no. 10, Thailand no. 11, and Indonesia no. 12. See World Bank, *World Development Report, 1987*, 49.

3. For the period 1970–80, the ASEAN rate was 9.5 percent compared to 10.3 percent for the Asian NICs. See Hong 1987, 130.

4. As a group, these four countries are the world's leading producers and exporters of seven primary commodities: natural rubber, tin, palm oil, tapioca, coconut products, tropical hardwoods, and pepper.

5. See Drysdale 1986, 14.

6. Hong 1987, 134–35.

7. Meier 1986, 15.

8. Asian Development Bank, *Key Indicators of Developing Member Countries of ADB*, April 1982, cited in Naya 1987, 33.

9. Meier 1986, 21.

10. See Lim and Gosling 1983.

11. Weinstein 1976. The concept of "soft" and "hard" states came first from Myrdal 1970.

12. On South Korea and Taiwan as "hard" developmental states, see Johnson 1987.

13. Duffey 1984, 297.

14. Thailand ranked next to the lowest of thirty-one selected LDCs on the World Bank's Price Distortion Index. Malaysia and the Philippines ranked third, along with South Korea, while Indonesia placed eleventh. World Bank, *World Development Report, 1983*, 60–61.

15. Kobrin 1984, 222.

16. For a discussion of "assertive" versus "accommodationist" regimes, see Grieco 1984, 7–8.

17. The summary here draws on United Nations, Expert Group on ASEAN and Pacific Economic Cooperation 1982, 6–13, and Crone 1983.

18. For the 1973–85 period, the World Bank classified Thailand and Malaysia as "moderately outward oriented" and Indonesia and the Philippines as "moderately inward oriented." World Bank, *World Development Report, 1987*, 83.

19. Linda Lim 1986, 4.

20. *FEER*, June 12, 1986, 72.

21. The United States, in contrast, takes 18.6 percent of the region's exports and contributes 13.6 percent of its imports. See Japan, Ministry of Foreign Affairs 1983, 8.

22. World exports of industrial goods grew sixfold, while ASEAN industrial exports to Japan grew about elevenfold (computed from UN, OECD, and individual country data in Shinohara 1985, 72–73).

23. Japan has been the most important source of investment in the ASEAN countries on a cumulative basis; between 1969 and 1981 it accounted for 48 percent of the investments from countries belonging to OECD, compared to 28.8 percent for the United States (Japan, Ministry of Foreign Affairs 1983, 11). The same source notes that the five original ASEAN members constitute Japan's second largest investment market, taking 21.7 percent of Japan's investments, compared to 24.7 percent going to the United States. Japan was the leading investor in Indonesia, Malaysia, and Thailand, and was second to the United States in the Philippines and Singapore. Indonesian data exclude petroleum and the banking sector. If these sectors were included, U.S. investments would exceed those of Japan. See United Nations, Expert Group on ASEAN and Pacific Economic Cooperation 1982, table 8. From 1977 to 1981 an annual average of 32 percent of Japan's worldwide overseas development assistance (ODA) went to the five ASEAN countries. See Japan, Ministry of Foreign Affairs n.d.

24. See, e.g., the essay on Malaysian Prime Minister Mahathir's "Look East" policy in Jomo 1985b.

25. See Weinstein 1982.

26. ASEAN's share of Japanese imports is second to that of the United States, which accounted for 18.3 percent. Figures from Japanese customs clearance and IMF trade statistics, cited in Japan, Ministry of Foreign Affairs 1983, 8.

27. Japan, External Trade Organization, *White Paper on International Trade* (Tokyo, 1979), 45, cited in Elsbree and Hoong 1985, 121.

28. ASEAN's share of total Japanese imports declined from 16.1 percent in 1984 to 13.1 percent in 1986, while the region's share of Japan's total external

trade fell from 12.7 percent in 1982 to 10.3 percent in 1985 and 8.5 percent in 1986. Japan Customs Clearance Statistics, cited in Oriyama 1987, 14–15.

29. Indonesia's role is critical. In most recent years Japan's bilateral trade deficit with Indonesia has been equal to over 100 percent of its trade deficit with the region as a whole (Smith 1986b, 62).

30. Computed from UN, OECD, and individual country data in Shinohara 1985, 73.

31. Smith 1986b, 63.

32. And even then, the flow of Japanese funds to the ASEAN Four has not expanded smoothly. Japanese investment from the fall of 1985 through mid 1986 grew mainly in the Asian NICs. Only as labor rates in those countries rose did Japanese investment in the ASEAN Four grow (Shimada 1987, 22).

33. See Weinstein 1982, 184.

34. Oriyama 1987, 14.

35. MITI terms the relationship "complementary" (MITI 1983, 1–2).

36. The discussion of the Philippine auto industry prior to the PCMP draws on Tolentino and Ybanez 1984; Mangahas 1970; and Sta. Romana 1979.

37. Program Implementation Agency 1965, 67.

38. Some of these were brought in by paying off customs officers; but probably more important was the increase in surplus U.S. jeeps and trucks passing through U.S. bases that were rebuilt and sold without any state taxation or other forms of control. Around 150,000 such vehicles are estimated to have been sold from the end of World War II through the late 1960s. Interviews.

39. World Bank figures cited in Bello et al. 1982, 129–30.

40. See Francia 1971.

41. *Daily Express* (Manila) (hereafter *DE*), December 1, 1979, 10.

42. Incentives included extensive exemptions from duties and business taxes on imports of raw materials. Effective rates of protection for passenger and commercial vehicles assembled in Thailand were approximately 573 percent and 121 percent respectively, whereas the average rate for all import-competing industries was 50 percent (Nawadhinsukh 1984, 181, 227). Total auto *sales* in Thailand rose from 26,489 in 1965 to 50,657 in 1967 and 71,120 in 1969. Ibid., 184.

43. Organ 1968, 8. This report constitutes the best overall review of the Thai auto industry's early weaknesses.

44. By 1969 twelve Japanese parts firms had also established Thai operations, compared to only one each in Indonesia and the Philippines, and none in Malaysia and Singapore (Dodwell Marketing Consultants 1984, 13).

45. Thai Ministry of Industry figures, cited in Nawadhinsukh 1984, 184.

46. Wichitwong 1977, 571.

47. Those firms in operation for several years were due to lose promotional incentives and thus operate at a disadvantage with respect to newly established firms enjoying the same incentives. The BOI consequently came under pressure by some firms to extend the incentives and by others to adhere to the original five-year limit. See Organ 1968.

48. Unless otherwise noted, information on the auto industry prior to 1967 is drawn from Lim Chee Peng and Onn 1984, 86–92.

49. One critical element in the initial merger of Singapore and Malaysia was Singapore's belief that the island required a broader market for its entrepreneurial economy. This led to a strong demand by Singaporean leaders for a common Malaysian market. The second element was the belief that the threat of civil disorder along left-centrist lines in Singapore could be contained only through merger with the larger and strongly anticommunist Malaya to the north. The separation was initiated by the Malaysian leader Tunku Abdul Raman in part because of Malaysia's reluctance to serve as a common market for Singapore's rapidly developing economy. Also important was Malay insistence on special privileges for Malays in opposition to Lee Kuan Yew's policy of a "Malaysian Malaysia," i.e., a policy of multiracialism negating special treatment for a particular ethnic group. See Milne 1966, 175–84.

50. Witoelar 1984, 18.

51. In 1965 shortages of imported raw materials had reduced industrial production to less than 20 percent of capacity, inflation was running at about 500 percent a year, and transport and communications were in disarray. See Palmer 1978, ch. 2.

52. See McCawley 1978a.

53. This paragraph draws on Hansen 1971, 51, and Witoelar 1984, 18.

54. By 1983 the Japanese market shares were 92 percent in Thailand, 90 percent in Indonesia, 80 percent in the Philippines, and 81 percent in Malaysia. GM and Ford continue to operate in ASEAN, but largely through their links to Suzuki, Isuzu, and Mazda. In 1983 the two U.S. firms accounted for only 2 percent of the Thai market, 5 percent of the Indonesian market, and 10 percent of the Malaysian market, but almost 48 percent of the Philippine market (of which over 60 percent came from Mazda and Isuzu). See Toyota Motor Corp. 1984.

55. Unless otherwise noted, information on original PCMP objectives draws on Philippines, BOI 1972, 12–22.

56. See Philippines, BOI 1977. The PMADE was designed to manufacture engines for commercial vehicles not included in the PCMP.

57. AMII 1976, 4.

58. Philippines, BOI 1972, 22.

59. Philippines, BOI 1972, 12.

60. Paterno 1972a, 11.

61. See, e.g., Annex G, 1 (f) of the "BOI Guidelines," 23.

62. Philippines, BOI 1977, appendix 3, p. 20.

63. The "two and a half" refers to two basic models each with one variant, and one basic model with no variant. A model was assumed to include a common engine, wheel base, and chassis. Variants would share those elements, but differ, for example, in terms of being two-door or four-door. Philippines, BOI 1983, no. 3.2.

64. The figure of under 30 percent in 1978 is from Susumu Watanabe's exhaustive study of the Philippine auto parts industry (Watanabe 1979, 56). I have inferred no more than 35 percent since from interviews and from EIU 1985, 37, which cites official LC levels as 43 percent in 1983, but notes that actual levels were probably lower.

65. AMII, *Annual Report, 1978.*

66. Watanabe 1979, 14, from which the rest of the information in this paragraph is drawn.

67. Ibid., 56. According to "Car Pricing Explained," *Times Journal* (Manila) (hereafter *TJ*), September 2, 1977, the assemblers' own production accounted for about half of the real domestic content.

68. Chrysler sold its 5 percent equity in Carco soon after the PCMP began. By the late 1970s GM's operations were 30 percent owned by Isuzu and most of GM's products were Isuzu vehicles; Ford was largely assembling Mazdas. For a discussion of Toyota's purchase of Delta, see *FEER*, June 9, 1988, 104.

69. AMII, *Annual Report,* 1979–83; *DE,* March 31, 1980.

70. An estimated 3,000 units per year were smuggled into the Philippines during the late 1970s and early 1980s. EIU 1984, 69.

71. This figure represents the average of 55 percent for passenger cars and only 28 percent for commercial vehicles cited in EIU 1985, 38.

72. Ibid., 42.

73. In a recent effort to revive local auto manufacture known as the Car Development Programme (CDP), debate has erupted within the BOI "on how many firms should be allowed to participate. . . . Some believe the PCMP's problem was that—through political influence—too many participated. They want membership limited to two. Others say the Philippines cannot afford to turn down sorely needed foreign investment and the jobs it would create" (*Asiaweek*, September 13, 1987, 59). More recent reports suggest that the CDP will limit the number of participants to three: Toyota, Nissan, and Mitsubishi (Galang 1988, 104).

74. Auto part exports for the ASEAN countries for 1975, 1976, 1977, and 1978 (in U.S. $m) were as follows. Indonesia: .12, .10, .17, 1.0; Malaysia: 3.37,

2.68, 2.62, 1.53; Philippines: .75, 1.29, 11.14, 18.56; Thailand: .72, 2.75, 2.33, 4.04 (United Nations, *Yearbook of International Trade Statistics,* 1975–78).

75. The 1976 and 1982 export and import figures are from Philippine foreign trade statistics, cited in Cororaton 1984, 4. Cumulative export revenue totals from EIU 1984, 66.

76. Author interview, Manila, March–April 1985; and *Asiaweek,* October 26, 1986, 54.

77. Marcos's call for a revamping of the PCMP is found in Executive Order No. 906, Manila, August 4, 1983.

78. Different LC levels were to be applied to different types of commercial vehicles. Information on the 1971 reforms is drawn from Nawadhinsukh 1984, 187–89.

79. The 1978 measures are reviewed in Nawadhinsukh 1984 and in Thailand, MOI 1984c, 2. Discussion of the 1978 measures below is drawn from these sources.

80. See Thailand, MOI 1984a, 1984b, 1985, and "NESDB Supports Local Content Plan," *Bangkok Post* (hereafter *BP*), July 14, 1987, 28. For a review, see EIU 1987, 37.

81. Interviews with BOI officials and Dr. Siriboon Nawadhinsukh of Thammasat University; and "Mitsubishi, Mazda, Join Isuzu in Race for Diesel Project," *Nation Business,* Agusut 31, 1985. Unless otherwise noted, information on the diesel engine project provided below is drawn from these sources.

82. This is based on interviews with the architect of the 1971 reforms, Dr. Wichitwong Na Pomphet, with members of the Thai Auto Parts Manufacturers' Association, and with a senior BOI official. See also Wichitwong 1977.

83. An assembly plant could produce (1) either CVs or PVs, but not both; (2) a limited number of models and engine sizes, depending on whether the plant was new or long-established, and whether production was of passenger or commercial vehicles. Nawadhinsukh 1984.

84. EIU 1987, 40.

85. As of July 1987 each producer was to export engines worth B150 million in the first three years of operation with an increase to B500 million for the next three years. In the sixth year the export value would be fixed at B100 million (U.S. $5 million) annually. See "BOI to Alter Conditions for Engine Producer," *BP,* July 30, 1987, 13.

86. On the question of LC credits, see "ATI Seeks Clear Cut Policy on Car Exports," *World* (Bangkok), September 6, 1986; "Local Content Law Must Apply for Exports as Well," *BP,* October 24, 1986. On lower LC for exports, see Handley 1988b, 74.

87. The figures for 1973 are from "Chaos Reigns in the Automobile Industry,"

Financial Post (Bangkok), October 26, 1973. The figures for 1977 are from interviews.

88. *Business in Thailand* (hereafter *BIT*), April 1981, 46, 78.

89. The 45–54 percent figure represents differences of opinion as to physical local content achieved, and variation in LC levels among makes and models. See "YMC Exceeds Local Content Requirement," *BP*, December 9, 1987, 19.

90. EIU 1985, 49. While comparable data for the other three countries are not available, it is safe to assume that the percentages are at least as high as in the Thai case. One indicator is the percentage of intermediate inputs necessary for a unit increase in automobile production that is purchased domestically. The figures were 57 percent for Thailand, 56 percent for the Philippines, 54.5 percent for Malaysia, and 31 percent for Indonesia. Japan Automobile Manufacturers' Association (JAMA) 1983, cited in EIU 1985, 59.

91. The estimate of "several dozen" is in Ritter 1987, 44. The only account of early Thai parts firms is a partial listing with only twelve firms established before 1970 (Ithijarakun 1977). A reliable listing of the 150 OE producers is found in Thailand, MOI 1986.

92. There has been no report on Thai auto firms on the scale of the 1979 Watanabe study of the Philippines. My assertions with regard to stability of operations are based on interviews and a comparison of the earlier partial listing found in Ithijarakun 1977 with the list in Thailand MOI 1986, and a photocopied 1983 "List of Auto-Parts Manufacturers in Thailand" provided by the Thai Auto Parts Manufacturers Association. The earlier listing contains thirty-one firms, of which at least twenty-five, or 89 percent, are still operating.

93. Handley 1988c, 76.

94. Interview.

95. Precise data on the portion of exports coming from locally owned firms are not available. However, of the roughly B27 million worth of applications for promotional incentives submitted to the BOI by auto parts firms between July 1985 and March 1987, Thai capital accounted for B20 million and foreign capital for B7 million (see Association of Thai Industries 1987, 7–14). Mitsubishi intends to import to Japan body-stamping dies from Summit Auto Seats, a Thai-owned and managed firm; these dies are up to 30 percent cheaper than the equivalent Japanese product (*JMB*, no. 14 [December 1987]: 69). On the increasing complexity of Thai auto exports, see *JMB*, no. 12 (June 1986): 42, no. 12 (June 1987): 67, and no. 14 (December 1987), 69. On Thailand's attraction for Japanese investors, see *FEER*, April 30, 1987, 75.

96. In 1985 the Thai auto industry's imports exceeded exports by roughly U.S. $227 million. The industry's trade deficit averaged a growth of almost 11 percent

from 1965 to 1976, but was around 3 percent from 1977 to 1984. Furthermore, the growth rate of auto parts imports fell from almost 13 percent in the 1965–76 period to 7 percent in the 1977–84 period, while the growth rate of exports rose from almost 6 percent in the earlier period to 25 percent in the latter period. Thai Customs Department figures in ATI 1987, 22.

97. EIU 1985, 45.

98. "Automotive Assemblers and Manufacturers Club," *Business in Thailand*, September 1986, 41; and Wright 1985.

99. Toyota Motors Thailand, "Monthly Sales Reports," various issues.

100. "SCG Expected to be Largest Engine Producer," *BP* September 9, 1985; and "Siam Nawaloha Strengthens Base," *Nation*, September 13, 1985.

101. The government acted on the basis of a report by the consulting firm of Arthur D. Little. See Lim and Onn 1984, 86–92, from which the rest of this paragraph is drawn.

102. *Bumiputra* literally means "son of the soil" and refers to the indigenous Malays. In 1969 Chinese owned 34 percent of corporate equity, compared to roughly 2 percent for Malays, with the rest belonging to foreigners. See Sundaram 1988, 256–68.

103. Make and model figures from AFM 1984, appendix 12. LC levels from *Asian Business and Industry (AB&I)*, February 1979, 74. Segal 1982, 33, says local content was 10 percent by value in 1979 and 11 percent in 1981.

104. AFM 1984, 2.1.

105. Information on numbers and nationality of ownership of parts firms in this paragraph draws on Lim and Onn 1984, 132–34. Only six out of the fifty firms studied had majority foreign equity, and the majority of those were Indian-owned. Information on ethnic ownership draws on interviews, there being, to my knowledge, no ethnic data available on parts firms.

106. See Lim and Onn 1984, 112.

107. See AFM 1984, p. 2.4, and also reports in the *New Straits Times* (Kuala Lumpur) (hereafter *NST*), July 22, 1979.

108. The figure of two hundred parts firms represents those licensed by the government to manufacture auto parts. Slightly over half had reportedly begun production of some fifty types of component parts by 1983. These included engine, electrical, drive, transmission, steering, suspension, brake, and body parts, as well as accessories. See AFM 1984, pp. 3.30–3.35.

109. Lim and Onn 1984, 93. In 1983 Malaysians owned 73.2 percent of equity in the assembly sector, and probably much more in the auto parts sector. AFM 1984, pp. 3.20, 3.28.

110. The three assembly firms with majority *bumiputra* equity were ranked nos. 8, 10, and 11 of eleven firms in terms of output. And even where Malays held dom-

inant equity, the staff was dominated by ethnic Chinese. See AFM 1984, pp. 3.23 and appendix 10.

111. On numbers of makes and models, see AFM 1984, pp. 3.23–3.26; and Ghazali 1985, 3. On failure of standardization, see MIDA 1985, 15.

112. After an annual growth rate of 7.8 percent during the 1970s, GDP growth slowed to 4.2 percent from 1980 to 1984 (World Bank, *World Development Report, 1982*, 112). As late as 1985 over 70 percent of exports were primary commodities (ibid., table 1.4).

113. The other projects were a sponge-iron and steel-billet plant, a cement plant, a motorcycle-engine plant, a pulp and paper mill, and a heavy engineering complex including a foundry and metal-machining plant to support automotive parts production. Pura 1985, 377–82.

114. On loans, see Aznam 1988, 97. For general information on the car project, see Raphael Pura, "Mitsubishi to Build Autos in Malaysia, Aiming for 60% Market Share by 1990," *Asian Wall Street Journal* (hereafter *AWSJ*), December 13, 1982, 8; Khoo Hock Aun, "Finding a Head Start," *Malaysian Business*, March 1983, 13.

115. The Saga began with a tariff exemption of 40 percent and by the summer of 1985 sold for almost M$4,000 less than competitors, with the state foregoing roughly M$4,500 on each vehicle sold. See "Malaysian Car's Success Is Mixed Boon," *AWSJ*, December 19, 1985.

116. Pura 1985, 380.

117. These figures are based on interviews with a leading official of MACPMA.

118. Seward 1987, 94.

119. See, e.g., Clad 1984b, 80–81; "Nissan-Proton Link Up Sought," *Business Times* (Kuala Lumpur), October 4, 1985; "UMW Plans Cushion against HICOM Car," *NST*, June 15, 1983; and "Malaysian Dealers Criticize Exports of 'National Car,'" *BP*, April 18, 1987, 16.

120. In 1985, sales were down 50 percent from 1984. "Car Sales Have Dropped by 50pc, Say Traders," *TS*, December 21, 1985. Capacity rates in 1986 were 18 percent (Seward 1987, 94) and 16 percent in 1987 and 1988 ("Malaysian Dealers Criticize Exports of National Car," *BP*, April 18, 1987, 16). Proton lost $17 million by the end of March 1986 and accounted for $80 million of the $132 million allocated to HICOM in 1988. See Duthie 1987a, 2. Capacity-utilization rates for other assemblers were not available for the period following the Saga's introduction.

121. On Mahathir's export push and resistance to it within the government, see "First Shipment of Sagas Abroad Begins This Week," *Business Times*, October 21, 1985.

122. *TS*, June 16, 1989; Aznam 1988, 97.

123. "Misfiring Saga," *Asiaweek*, July 8, 1988, 47; *TS*, April 1, 1989, and June 9, 1989.

124. Seward 1988, 118.

125. Local content included sixteen locally made parts, fourteen of which were already listed for mandatory deletion under the July 1979 measures and thus presumably produced by Chinese-owned parts firms. The other parts came from Proton's own stamping plant. See "Stamped Parts for the Proton by Mid '86," *TS*, November 21, 1985.

126. Aznam 1988, 97. The same source notes that while Proton sustained huge losses, its marketing arm, run by a Chinese with significant auto interests, made a good profit from sales commissions and installation of accessories.

127. Information on the 1969 measures is drawn from Witoelar 1984, 18–19; Hansen 1971, 49–51; and Chalmers 1988, ch. 5.

128. By the mid 1970s it had become obvious that CVs would constitute most of Indonesia's large and expanding auto market. CVs accounted for 59 percent of Indonesia's 59,800 vehicles sold in 1974, 68 percent of 75,500 in 1976, 86 percent of 108,600 in 1978, 87 percent of 174,782 in 1980, and 84 percent of 188,554 in 1982. Figures from *Kompas* (Jakarta), March 20, 1984, cited in Hill 1984b, 15.

129. See, for example, Witoelar 1984, 31.

130. "Malari" is short for Malapetaka Januari ("January disaster"). For a discussion of Chinese dominance in the auto industry, see *Indonesian Commercial News* (Jakarta) (hereafter *ICN*), no. 80, June 27, 1977, 33; no. 162, November 17, 1980, 1.

131. Indonesia, MOI, "Confirmation on Re-Applying Decree of Minister of Industry No. 307/M/SK/8/1976"; and interviews.

132. Indonesia MOI 1982.

133. Interviews with Department of Industry and Capital Investment Coordinating Board (BKPM) officials. A European auto official believed that the original plans involved three plants with a geographical balance: one independent (Perkins), one Japanese (Mitsubishi), and one European (Daimler Benz).

134. In the long run, the minister of industry intended to reduce the eight to four groups (interview).

135. Indonesia, MOI 1983, and EIU 1985, 55.

136. Chalmers 1988, ch. 7, 7.

137. *ICN*, no. 113, November 6, 1978, 38.

138. *ICN*, no. 265, March 11, 1985, 14; and Swaminathan 1982, 26.

139. Friedland 1988, 100.

140. EIU 1985, 55.

141. Interviews with officials of the Astra group. For figures as of late 1984 see

Astbury 1984, 84. LC levels for passenger cars are 20–25 percent (EIU 1985, 52).

142. EIU 1985, 54, cites forty local firms engaged in the manufacture of the items scheduled for mandatory localization. The figure of fifty original parts firms comes from Sabransjah and Soekandar n.d., 13. The figure of one hundred comes from the Department of Industry cited in *ICN*, no. 233, November 7, 1983, 13. The two hundred body parts firms mentioned earlier presumably include general metal fabricators, one of whose activities is the production of body parts.

143. Thee 1984, 25.

144. Further evidence for this assertion will be provided in subsequent chapters. On the Liem group, see Robison n.d. and 1987b. On Astra, see Astbury 1982.

145. Interviews with Astra officials. These sources also reported expanded ethnic Chinese control over Krama Yudha's dealerships in the mid 1980s.

146. Witoelar 1984, 19.

147. Pawitra 1985, 339.

148. Capacity-utilization rate (c.u.r.) drawn from EIU 1985, 53. CVs' better c.u.r. is indicated by the fact that Pawitra identifies fourteen makes of PVs compared to an average of seven makes for each category of CV (Pawitra 1985, 355). On the larger number of makes and models for *pribumi* firms, see Swaminathan 1982, 17–18; and "Car Manufacturing Capability is Next," *Asian Business*, June 1982, 24, which notes that compared with its rivals, Astra "has fewer models in its stable, but a worthwhile share in each of the market segments."

149. Chapter 6 discusses one ill-fated proposal for an export thrust in the Indonesian auto industry.

150. "Astra, a Booming Conglomerate, Sets the Pace for New Exports," *AWSJ Weekly*, August 22, 1988, p. 5B.

151. *JMB*, no. 14, December 1987, 20, 73; *JMB*, no. 15, March 1988, 72.

152. I am assuming that the stated problems cancel each other out and/or reflect developments in the auto industry itself. For example, the Philippines' market dropped in 1984 in large part because of general foreign-exchange shortages. But the auto industry itself strongly contributed to those shortages. Furthermore, while the Philippines' decline was especially drastic, each of the ASEAN Four suffered sharp drops in automobile demand during the mid 1980s.

153. The data in this chapter do not provide a full picture of uneven growth within countries, which will be addressed more fully in chs. 5–8.

Chapter 4

1. JAMA, *Motor Vehicle Statistics of Japan*, various years.

2. O'Brien and Lobo Allen 1984, 23.

3. On U.S. auto exports, see Bennett and Sharpe 1985b. Japanese figures from MITI, cited in Ozawa 1985, 170, table 5.3.

4. There is no accepted level of local content above which assembly becomes manufacture. The problem is complicated by the fact that not all assembly relies on CKD kits. A 1983 UN study, for example, notes that in 1980 Hyundai produced its own model, the Pony, by packaging a diverse set of imports cum local parts. Yet Hyundai was clearly also, to some extent, a manufacturer. The problem is reflected in the study's listing of South Korea as both a manufacturer and an assembler. See UNCTC 1983, 12–14.

5. "Administering the Traffic," *Asiaweek,* October 26, 1986, 63.

6. Japan Tariff Association figures cited in MRI 1987, 24–25, from which the twofold increase is also drawn.

7. Vernon 1966.

8. Bennett and Sharpe 1985b, 206–11.

9. Cole and Yakushiji 1984, 131.

10. Ibid., 138.

11. Altshuler et al. 1984, 180.

12. Cole and Yakushiji 1984, 56.

13. Livesay 1983.

14. Altshuler et al. 1984, 181.

15. The following discussion draws on Altshuler et al. 1984, 182–84.

16. This is contrary to the assertion in Bennett and Sharpe 1985a that "on the whole, concentration has been increasing in the world industry" (p. 73).

17. Gilpin calls such practices the "new protectionism" (Gilpin 1987, 204). For a different view, see Dunn, Jr. 1978, 232.

18. This is especially true of Japanese parts suppliers. See MRI 1987.

19. On surplus capacity see Cowhey and Long 1983.

20. On "defensive investment," see Knickerbocker 1973. For a summary discussion of U.S. firms in Latin America, see Jenkins 1977 and Bennett and Sharpe 1985b, esp. 206–8.

21. Developing countries include those outside the OECD, South Africa and Israel. See UNCTC 1983, 17, 19.

22. Interviews with officials from Southeast Asian parts firms.

23. Both of these points will be discussed in the course of this chapter.

24. Altshuler et al. 1984, 194.

25. The auto industry uses over 50 percent more physical capital per worker than the household appliance industry and 500 percent more than the clothing industry (Turner 1982, table 1.1). Investment for a fairly comprehensive styling re-

vision in the competitive European market is around $300 million, and costs for a new engine and transmission run at $450 million per plant (Bannock 1985, 66).

26. "Helping Each Other Along," *Economist*, October 15, 1988, 22.

27. In 1959–60 fiscal and exchange measures provided 89 cents of every dollar invested in the Brazilian auto industry (NACLA 1979, 12).

28. O'Brien and Allen 1984, 125.

29. In 1980 the average number of models produced in the major Latin American industries was thirty-two (UNCTC 1983, 110).

30. Goldstein 1988, 69.

31. These figures are drawn from Jenkins 1985, 65–67. Jenkins does not specify the localization levels he considers to be significant.

32. Ibid., 72.

33. Figures on trade in automotive products (vehicles and parts) from ibid., 67; figures on auto parts exports from United Nations, *Yearbook of International Trade Statistics, 1988,* 232.

34. This is the case if one assumes that the "world car" strategy emphasized imports of auto components to the OECD countries from developing areas. While imports of cars and parts to the OECD countries both increased, car imports have grown faster than parts imports. Moreover, parts imported to the OECD countries from lower-wage countries were well outweighed by the parts produced within the OECD countries. The United States has been the most important importer of non-OECD parts, yet these were less than 7 percent of total U.S. parts imports in 1980. See Dankbaar 1984, 238–40.

35. Jenkins 1985, 64; and UNCTC 1983, 104.

36. Adachi 1985.

37. Toyota Motor Corp. 1982, 26–27.

38. *Journal of Japanese Trade and Industry* 1 (1985): 29, and *Digest of Japanese Industry and Technology* 237 (1987): 23. The percentages are approximate since it is not clear whether the 1987 figures count CV and PV plants as separate operations.

39. Thailand had the second highest number of companies, twenty-two. Taiwan had the highest, thirty. Indonesia had twelve, the United States ten, Brazil nine, and South Korea eight. Cole and Hervey 1984, table 15.

40. Interviews with Japanese assemblers. Only five of the sixty-eight Japanese parts firms investing in the ASEAN Four from 1964 through 1983 began ASEAN operations before 1970, i.e., before LC programs were initiated (Dodwell Marketing Consultants 1984).

41. By 1965 plant and equipment investment for four-wheel-vehicle production represented 2 percent of total Japanese domestic investment in plant and

equipment. Figures on production increases are from Uneo and Muto 1974, 20. Investment data are from Duncan 1973, 79.

42. *Kan ban* refers to a production system developed by Toyota in which each station in the production process "pulls" parts from the preceding station as they are needed. Manufacturing stages are tightly coupled, thus reducing the need for work-in-process inventories. Because the system "pulls" parts along, suppliers must be capable of delivering parts "just in time" to assembly plants. See Cusumano 1985.

43. Duncan 1973, 89.

44. Yoshino 1978, 23.

45. Toyota and Nissan are independent firms but have close relations with the Fuji and Mitsui groups, respectively. Toyo Kogyo or Mazda is part of the Sumitomo group. Mitsubishi is, of course, part of the Mitsubishi group. Hino and Daihatsu are partly owned by Toyota. Honda is probably the most independent, with foreign trusts and individuals holding 20 percent of its stock. "There's Unity in Diversity," *Asiaweek*, September 28, 1984, 54.

46. Profit rates on total assets for the transport equipment industry (not including shipbuilding) were 11.7 percent from 1956 to 1960, 8.7 percent from 1961 to 1965, and 8.7 percent from 1966 to 1970, in all the fourth highest average profit rate for Japanese major industries during the 1956–70 period (Ueno 1980, 406).

47. Johnson 1982, 206.

48. Under pressure from the United States and Western Europe, the country renounced exchange controls in 1964 and lifted quantitative restrictions on finished automobile imports in 1965 (Genther 1986).

49. As Mitsubishi's president stated, the smaller firms had no wish "to capitulate to Toyota and Nissan." The firms also resisted MITI's suggestion that they reduce prices to meet the onslaught of foreign capital. See Duncan 1973, 88–95 (the quoted phrase is from p. 93).

50. From 1965 to 1973 the transport equipment industry had an average of two cartel violations per year compared to an average of six for all manufacturing sectors (Ueno 1980, 422). On product differentiation, led by Nissan and Toyota, see Koichi 1981, 524, and Ueno and Muto 1974, 36–43.

51. OECD 1983, 85.

52. This point was first suggested to me by Kei Ono of Keio University and subsequently affirmed in interviews with auto firm officials.

53. The view of Japan as a "middle country" is found in Wells 1971, 14.

54. JAMA, *Motor Vehicle Statistics of Japan*, various years. This is an approximate figure since after 1979 motor vehicle export figures exclude "non-countable KD sets." These are sets of components with less than 60 percent of the complete

vehicle by factory sales value. In 1985 such "non-countable" sets totaled just over 1 million, compared to 6.7 million complete vehicle exports.

55. Indonesia was seventh, Malaysia eighth, and Thailand fifteenth (JAMA, *Motor Vehicle Statistics of Japan, 1983*).

56. Figures for 1980 and 1981 from Cole and Hervey 1984, table 14; 1983 figures from *Digest of Japanese Industry and Technology* 197 (1984): 15.

57. Southeast Asia accounted for 7.5 percent of exports; Latin America for 3.7 percent; the Middle East for 3.2 percent; Africa for 2.3 percent. JAMA 1988, 4–6.

58. In 1982 automobile production accounted for 22 percent of the monetary value of Japan's exports, 11 percent of its manufacturing output, and 11 percent of its employment (Long Term Credit Bank of Japan study on the future of the auto market cited in Kobayashi n.d., 5, 6).

59. This has involved providing local partners with expanded technological and managerial support. "Toyota seeks closer ties with Southeast Asian firms," *AWSJ*, September 27, 1982, 19. On the persistence of Japanese auto firms' focus on Southeast Asia, see Hood and Young 1985, 107.

60. Pawitra 1985.

61. Author interview, Tokyo.

62. "MMC's winning design," *Investors' Digest* (Kuala Lumpur), mid-November 1988, 5–6; and Smith 1989, 73.

63. JAMA, *Motor Vehicle Statistics of Japan*, various years.

64. Lim 1982, 53.

65. Yanaga 1968, 212–22.

66. Kuntjoro-Jakti 1985, 9.

67. EIU 1985, 14; Chee 1988, 51.

68. The conscious distinction between developed and developing markets, with specific plans for the latter, is discussed in a MITI report cited in *The Investor* (Bangkok), May 1978, 13.

69. EIU 1985, 14. For examples, see the four tables listing "major auto assemblers" in chapter 3.

70. Sato 1982.

71. These include the Japan External Trade Organization (JETRO) and the Institute for Developing Economies (IDE).

72. Personal interviews. For a general assessment of the Japanese opportunities provided by the "Look East" policy, see Saravanamuttu 1985.

73. Author interviews, Bangkok.

74. Hood and Young 1985, 156.

75. There are, to my knowledge, no published discussions of Japanese payments specifically geared to auto policy. For a brief general discussion of the Indonesian

case, see Palmer 1978, 165. Documents uncovered following Marcos's departure show that Japanese trading and heavy engineering firms probably paid hundreds of millions of yen in "commissions" to Marcos or his close associates to gain contracts under Japan's Philippine aid program. See Smith 1986b, 64.

76. Based on interviews with Nissan officials in Tokyo.

77. Pawitra 1985, 526 n. 2. Western failures along these lines are illustrated by the inability of Ford (1973) and GM (1974) to promote sales of a basic utility vehicle (BUV) in Thailand. See "Crowded Auto Industry Poses Problems for General Motors Thailand," *Business Asia*, September 16, 1977, 292–93, and "Lessons from Ford's Fiero Flop in Thailand," *Business Asia*, October 15, 1976, 335, confirmed by author interviews in Tokyo, Manila, and Bangkok. For a description of Toyota's success in this area, see Tanaka n.d.

78. Pawitra 1985, 530.

79. Ozawa 1986. Ozawa notes in a personal communication that these figures exaggerate the auto industry's reliance on such funds since they include shipbuilding, a sector receiving extensive state financial support. Exim Bank loans have, nevertheless, clearly facilitated the overseas auto activities of Japanese firms.

80. At one end is cash-rich "Bank Toyota"; at the other is Toyo Kogyo (Mazda), whose desperate financial position in the mid 1970s required a major rescue operation led by Sumitomo Bank. See Pascale and Rohlen 1983.

81. Zysman 1983, 236. See also Altshuler et al. 1984, 153.

82. Martin Anderson 1982, 3, 9. The same source (pp. 3–4) notes that the debt levels of Ford and GM have risen steeply as those of the Japanese have declined. By 1981 GM's debt reached 17.7 percent of long-term capital, with that of Ford reaching 26.9 percent. Honda's levels were 19.7 percent, but those of Toyota and Nissan were zero. The Japanese and U.S. firms also differed with regard to liquid reserves (p. 5) and general operating performance (p. 9). Note that disparities along the latter dimension stemmed in part from reduced Japanese inventory costs owing to just-in-time production techniques. U.S. firms in 1980 had more than $6 billion above Japanese levels tied up in parts on the shelf (p. 11).

83. Interview.

84. The Europeans have traditionally been stronger in product technology, whereas American firms have been best positioned for worldwide sourcing and selling operations. Dankbaar 1984, 243–44.

85. Friedman 1983, 360.

86. Calton and Krumme 1984, 206; "Japanese Cars at the Crossroads," *The Economist*, July 11, 1981, 77; and "Japan Car Makers Eye Third World," *Wall Street Journal*, July 7, 1981, 25.

87. Information on Toyota Thailand operations is drawn from the author's interviews with Japanese engineers at Toyota's assembly plant outside Bangkok. Toyota is probably the fastest of the Japanese firms with regard to changes in passenger car models. Hino officials in Thailand claim the capacity to change models (defined by wheelbase) every ten units and sometimes every four units (author interview).

88. "Hard Drive from the East," *The Economist*, October 15, 1988, 7.

89. Altshuler et al. 1984, 159.

90. MRI 1987, 14.

91. Author interviews, Bangkok.

92. Hood and Young 1985, 152. The above-noted cost differences are drawn from the same source, p. 150.

93. This assertion is largely impressionistic. The only reference I have is an internal document of a Philippine assembler referring to "the huge amounts for advertising (notice the frequency in the papers) and promotions spent by car manufacturers" (anon., "A Status Report," 14).

94. For complaints on this issue by Thai parts firms, see Sentusuphon 1984, 7.

95. Watanabe 1979, 33.

96. According to one source, there were almost 15,000 jeepneys in Manila alone in 1976, with many more in the countryside. Enami and Takayama 1976, 8.

97. In 1977 Francisco also built a modern plant for body and chassis frame construction. The modern machinery used in the plant reduced much of the work to the mere feeding of materials into machines and supplanted many of the older skills such as welding and bar cutting. "Workers need slightly greater degees of discipline but little technical training" (Watanabe 1979, 75).

98. The Japanese response is that low deletion allowances are necessitated by the costs of actually removing certain parts from the CKD packs and procuring them locally, as well as by the inferior quality of local parts.

99. Interview with Toyota officials heading the firm's Philippine operations during the early PCMP period.

100. Hood and Young 1985, 156.

101. This characterization of JAMA is based on author interviews with auto assembler officials and JAMA staff.

102. These efforts pit engineers against the sales/marketing staff, which "is attempting to supply specifications to suit each local distributor" ("Nissan Motors Explores New Markets," *Asian Business and Industry*, December 1977, 62).

103. Charles Smith 1988, 71.

104. In Japan, for example, Mazda has agreed to collaborate with Mitsubishi

on the development and manufacture of auto parts. Abroad, Toyota and Mitsubishi were linking subsidiaries in Australia in line with the Australian government's policy of reducing the number of manufacturers. See *JMB*, no. 10 (December 1986): 73, 77.

105. On plans for Thailand, see *JMB*, no. 14 (December 1987): 20; on plans for Indonesia, see *JMB*, no. 14 (December 1987): 73.

106. See *JMB*, no. 12 (June 1986): 42.

107. See the previous discussion of Japanese parts firms' overseas activity for instances of investment from 1964 through 1983. Between 1983 and 1986, Japanese parts makers established 59 overseas "manufacturing affiliates" for a total of 187; 11 "affiliates" for a total of 66; and 77 "technical license" agreements for a total of 261 (MRI 1987, 26).

108. For examples, see *JMB*, no. 9 (September 1986): 6.

109. Charles Smith 1986, 56–57. See also Morris-Suzuki 1984.

110. See the discussion of anti-Japanese activities in chapter 3. For a review of Japanese aid efforts, see Atarashi 1984–85.

111. Bennett and Sharpe 1985a, 111.

112. Almost no mention is made of an official Japanese role in the work most sensitive to such a role (See Weinstein 1976). Tsurumi does argue that Japanese firms use "the unstated and unspecified attitudes or rulings of the Japanese government as convenient and overriding excuses for their not being able to accommodate the wishes, bargains and licensing agreements of foreign businesses," but he offers no concrete examples of this practice (Tsurumi 1976, 267–68).

113. The only published mention I have found of any cooperation between a particular firm and the Japanese government involved a 1972 Toyota loan of $100 million to Indonesia, which reflected Japanese factional politics and a general effort to strengthen the Suharto regime (Robinson 1985, 203).

114. See Cole and Yakushiji 1984, 82. More influential than any government policies was the Korean War, which boosted Toyota's production 40 percent. See the statement by Toyota's then president in Borden 1984, 146–47.

115. Altshuler et al. 1984, 232.

116. Author interviews, Tokyo.

117. In 1977 ASEAN supplied 30 percent of Japan's low sulphur crude, 37 percent of its imported copper, 19 percent of imported iron ore, 99 percent of imported tin, 30 percent of imported bauxite, 34 percent of imported nickel, 97 percent of imported natural rubber, and 100 percent of imported tropical timber. The shipping lanes running through the ASEAN region transport 80 percent of Japan's total oil imports and roughly 40 percent of its commodity trade. See Ikema 1980, 459–60.

118. For examples, see the discussion of Yazaki, Nippondenso, and Fuji Serina

Valve in *JMB*, no. 12 (June 1987): 41, and "Implications of the Higher Yen," *JMB*, no. 9 (September 1986): 3–4.

119. The United States "graduated" the NICs from GSP status in 1988.

120. See, e.g., Handley 1988b, 74.

121. As Haggard notes in his criticism of Bennett and Sharpe, this implies that a bilateral monopoly bargaining model is inappropriate. Haggard 1989, 194.

122. See, e.g., Treece 1988, 20.

123. The following discussion stresses cross-national rather than temporal variation. Because the economic conditions examined below tend to be longer-term, it is difficult to identify their relationship to performance variations over time within one country. This issue will be addressed in subsequent chapters.

124. In some cases, of course, these two views overlap; the Japanese may be attracted to those features that also facilitate host country exploitation of potential opportunities.

125. In support of this argument, Bennett and Sharpe cite the export successes of Brazil and Mexico compared with Colombia, Venezuela, and Peru (Bennett and Sharpe 1985b, 223).

126. For a different view, see EIU 1985, 71.

127. It may even be the case that smaller host countries have a better chance of compelling Japanese support for automotive export. According to one study, overseas production for export by Japanese auto firms has grown out of saturated local markets (Takeda 1980, 47). However, this study covered only the auto firms' export operations from developed countries.

128. Kobrin 1984, 230.

129. Rayfield 1984, 239.

130. JAMA, "Automotive Industry in Developing Countries and Their Policies" (in Japanese), March 1983, cited in EIU 1985, 72.

131. Follosco 1985, 1.

132. Castro 1975, 165.

133. On a scale of 1 to 5, with 5 the strongest, the Philippines and Singapore were ranked 4, Thailand and Malaysia 3, and Indonesia 1. A similar pattern emerges with respect to the supply of skilled workers: Philippines and Singapore both 4, Malaysia 3, Thailand 2, and Indonesia 1; and with respect to technicians: Philippines and Singapore 4; Malaysia 3; Thailand and Indonesia both 2. These rankings are drawn from a survey of foreign firms operating in the ASEAN countries published in Allen 1979, 140–41.

134. Kobrin 1984, 222.

135. This is not to deny that at some point in the development and bargaining process, shortages of trained people eventually impose limits on national leverage. Thailand, for example, may be approaching such a limit. The country reportedly

graduates 2,500 engineering students per year, while the car industry alone requires some 200 per year (Handley 1988a, 96).

136. Since debt is more a political phenomenon (i.e., a reflection of government policy) than a structural economic feature, it will be covered in subsequent chapters.

137. Indonesia is the Pacific Rim's largest exporter of crude oil, while Malaysia has the region's largest natural gas reserves. In 1985 Indonesia earned over $10 billion from energy exports; Malaysia roughly $5 billion. The Philippines and Thailand have been energy importers. These figures are rough estimates based on each country's percentage of exports accounted for by fuels, minerals, and metals. See World Bank, *World Development Report, 1987.*

Chapter 5

1. This and the following three chapters draw on, but do not repeat, details of the ASEAN Four's auto industries and policies. For specific references, figures, and policy details, readers should consult ch. 3.

2. Chan 1984, 25.

3. Unless otherwise noted, information about MACPMA is drawn from interviews with MACPMA's director. The level of organization was also encouraged by the auto parts industry's oligopolistic structure: three firms at most, usually fewer, dominated the production of each component (*Asian Business and Industry,* February 1979, 74). It should be noted that firms of 100–150 employees were not especially large in the Malaysian context. As of 1980 roughly 23 percent of Malaysian businesses were classified as "small-scale," i.e., presumably with fewer than 50 employees (Sinclair 1987, 123).

4. The group's director noted the effectiveness, for example, of a clause in MACPMA's constitution requiring office holders to be Malaysian citizens.

5. Firms were also to sell at a cost not to exceed the imported CKD price by 20 percent. See Paul Low, "Local Content Programme—The Manufacturers' Experience" (paper presented at the Seminar on Automotive Components Manufacturing—Technologies and Trends, Kuala Lumpur, April 15, 1985), 1–2; and "Mitsubishi Team Here to Assess Local Capabilities," *Business Times* (hereafter *BT*), March 17, 1983.

6. The ASEAN Automotive Federation set up a technical committee in 1976 to recommend packages of automotive parts for regional complementation and special tariff treatment. By 1978 the committee had identified several such products, those of Malaysia being the simplest.

7. Such local capacity reflected local firms' prior manufacture of these items for the replacement market.

8. The JTC initially reviewed LC issues and made recommendations to MVAC, which in turn made recommendations to the Minister of Trade and Industry. As this proved to be a long and tedious process, MVAC agreed to abide by JTC decisions in the spring of 1985.

9. At least until the mid 1980s, when research for this book was completed.

10. Chan 1984, 37.

11. Ibid., 30.

12. See ibid., 37, for strong criticism of the parts firms.

13. Some of these charges, however, reflected dissatisfaction with government policy more than anything else. Assemblers' charges of overregulation, for example, at least in part reflected MIDA's fairly efficient control of auto prices. For criticisms, see, e.g., Ghazali 1985.

14. Ibid., 2.

15. See, e.g., *Malaysian Business* (hereafter *MB*), December 1, 1984, 18.

16. For a useful review, see Kanapathy 1981.

17. The industry's total sales rose from M$160 million in 1975 to M$418.3 million in 1983. Total imports of the assembly sector alone grew from M$484.4 million to M$1.2 billion during the same period. The industry's (parts and assembly) total contribution to total manufacturing output and GDP actually declined from 2 percent to 1.63 percent and 0.79 percent to 0.62 percent respectively. See AFM 1984, 3.9–3.13.

18. *MB*, December 1, 1984, 20.

19. The statement is from a UNIDO Report, *Japan and Malaysia's Car: Rising Sun or False Dawn of Economic Cooperation*, quoted in Clad 1985b, 82.

20. Information on the early negotiations is based on author interviews. Although Mahathir reportedly had prior business ties with Daihatsu, it is unclear who approached whom and why Daihatsu was the first firm considered.

21. "Malaysia Gambles for Growth with Car," *AWSJ*, July 8, 1985.

22. "Nation Car Project: Industry Seeks Details," *BT*, February 1, 1983.

23. This paragraph draws on John Berthlesen, "Malaysia's UMW Tries to Avoid Collapse," *AWSJ*, December 30, 1985; Pillai 1983; and *TS*, February 1, 1983.

24. The deputy prime minister privately emphasized that the national car project was not his but Mahathir's. Author interviews, Tokyo and Kuala Lumpur.

25. Clad 1985a, 78. Most damaging to Mahathir was a report from the state-backed Institute for Strategic and International Studies (ISIS) (Tan 1985). See also Lim Chee Peng 1984 and Jomo 1985a.

26. Pura 1985, 382.

27. While those interviewed acknowledged that this was probably the case, I spoke to no one who could provide actual evidence that it was.

28. "Malaysian Car: Mitsubishi to Help," *TS*, October 30, 1982.

29. Author interview.

30. Author interviews.

31. *MB*, December 1, 1984, 19.

32. The profit prediction was cited in Raphael Pura, "Mitsubishi to Build Autos in Malaysia, Aiming for 60% Market Share by 1990," *AWSJ*, December 13, 1982. Toyota quotation from author interview in Kuala Lumpur.

33. Toyota knew of Mahathir's early negotiations with Daihatsu since Daihatsu's head during those talks was a former Toyota director. Author interview.

34. These campaigns are discussed in ch. 9.

35. Clad 1985b, 80.

36. The government gave a Saga to the Malaysian king, placed one in the National Museum, and focused extensive publicity on the car as part of the 1985 National Day celebrations. On government efforts to placate critics, see "Proton Goes Down to the People," *New Straits Times* (hereafter *NST*), September 29, 1984.

37. "Gov't Will Act to Protect Proton Saga, says Razaleigh," *NST,* September 17, 1984.

38. Information on informal government pressure was drawn from author interviews.

39. "Car Plants May Have to Close: Razaleigh," *TS*, October 22, 1984.

40. See "It's Out—Assemblers' Misgivings about Car Project," *TS*, June 16, 1983; "Good for the Country, Good for the Industry," *NST,* October 30, 1982; and AFM 1984.

41. Clad 1984b, 80–81; "Nissan-Proton Link Up Sought," *BT,* October 4, 1985; and "UMW Plans Cushion against Hicom Car," *NST,* June 15, 1983.

42. MIDA officials charged with price regulation said they generally allowed profit levels of roughly 16 percent on imported CKD packs. Author interviews.

43. Information for this and the following paragraphs were drawn from author interviews.

44. Author interview.

45. Author interviews.

46. This account draws on author interviews. And see "Car Parts Deals Awarded," *BT,* February 8, 1985.

47. Author interview.

48. See the statement by MMC's chief advisor to Proton in *BT,* October 22, 1984.

49. Author interviews in Tokyo; and "On Rubber and Local Car Market," *NST,* May 16, 1985.

50. The JCC was chaired by a senior MTI official and included representatives of Proton, MIDA, SIRIM, the Malaysian Development Bank, the Malaysian Industrial Development Finance Corp., and the Prime Minister's Office.

51. "147 Local Parts Groups for PS Listed," *BT,* May 15, 1985.

52. "Problem in Increasing Car Local Content," *NST,* May 15, 1985.

53. Author interviews and reports from SIRIM 1985.

54. Proton refused, for example, to provide MIDA with any automotive information for the government's Industrial Master Plan.

55. Author interviews.

56. It is unclear who made this decision.

57. Clad 1985b, 82.

58. "Proton Car to Have 40% LC," *NST,* September 11, 1984.

59. "Reason for Low Local Component Content," *NST,* May 15, 1985. For even earlier government efforts along these lines, see "Proton Saga for Britain Deal Signed," *TS,* October 27, 1984; "Dr. M Urges More Korean Investments," *NST,* August 15, 1983.

60. Unless otherwise noted, information on these cases is drawn from author interviews.

61. The source of this information, a HICOM engineer, would not or could not specify who made the decision.

62. Equity in the venture is 80 percent Malaysian, 10 percent Thai, and 10 percent Filipino. "PS to Get German Expertise," *NST,* May 25, 1985.

63. "Joint Venture to Make Vehicle Lights," *NST,* July 22, 1985. The Philippine interest was Joe Concepcion, a leader of the Philippine parts association and subsequently minister of industry in the Aquino administration.

64. "Proton Explains Protection Moves," *BT,* December 11, 1984.

65. Unless otherwise noted, information in this section is drawn from interviews.

66. "Tariff on Motor Parts for Saga to Be Lifted," *BT,* July 19, 1985.

67. "Mixed Reaction over Proton Request," *BT,* July 24, 1985.

68. Author interview.

69. "Car Sales Have Dropped by 50pc, Say Traders," *TS,* December 21, 1985. For further figures see ch. 3.

70. These firms accounted for about 10 percent of new car sales by the early 1980s. (The majority of new vehicles sold in Malaysia were assembled from CKD packs.) See "Saga Dealership Issue: Common Sense Prevails," *BT,* March 25, 1985.

71. "What They Say," *TS,* March 15, 1985. See also "Making Sure the Saga Will Sell," *NST,* March 22, 1985; "Row Over the Saga," *BT,* February 15, 1985; and "Saga: EON to Be Urged to Move Dealers," *BT,* March 15, 1985. Unless otherwise noted, information in this and the following paragraph is drawn from these sources.

72. "Saga Dealership Issue: Common Sense Prevails," *BT,* March 25, 1985.

73. Mahathir himself asserted that EON in fact upheld NEP principles while

denying Pekema claims that EON was controlled by rich "towkays" (Chinese entrepreneurs). See "PM Denies Saga Claim," *TS*, March 28, 1985.

74. For early intentions to promote Malay parts firms, see "Malaysia's First Step into the Car Industry," *BT*, June 4, 1983; "National Car: HICOM Spells out Local Content Position," *BT*, November 8, 1983.

75. Information in this paragraph is drawn from author interviews in Tokyo as well as Malaysia.

76. At the time of writing, it was unclear whether the government had complied with this request.

77. These included up-front capital requirements; no credit arrangements between EON and its dealers—transactions strictly by cash before delivery; a requirement that dealers sell at least five units per month or be terminated; and, depending on location, dealer commitments to minimum monthly purchases, level of sales force, and working capital. See "EON moves to quell discord," *BT*, March 19, 1985.

78. "Bumi Car Dealers Want to Compete with EON," *TS*, April 7, 1985.

79. "10 Bumiputra Motor Firms Squeezed Out," *TS*, October 9, 1985.

80. Proton finally decided to install cassette players and air conditioners at its own factories, thus reducing its losses per unit (Aznam 1988, 97).

81. Author interviews. Mitsubishi's chief advisor to Proton, Hiroshi Kakehi, noted that his firm's agreement with Proton "left unmentioned matters regarding the export of the car" ("First Shipment of Sagas Abroad Begins This Week," *BT*, October 21, 1985.

82. One MIDA official, for example, argued that private sector representatives would have raised the option of a "buy back" plan in which MMC would purchase those vehicles not sold domestically. Author interview.

83. The commodities slump led to reduced government revenues. Mahathir then incurred the resentment of the usually progovernment civil service by resisting pay increases (*FEER*, January 2, 1986, 20–27). Resource constraints and differences over the feasibility of the major industrial projects also intensified factionalism and profit-seeking within UMNO. The government's ability to promote Malay interests was thrown into doubt with the huge losses incurred by state-backed Bumiputra Malaysia Finance. Instead of promoting local enterprises, the bank tendered questionable loans to Hong Kong real estate speculators.

84. Mahathir ordered ten Sagas shipped to China to coincide with his visit to the PRC in November 1985.

85. Proton reported losses of $17.7 million in 1986 despite producing the country's largest-selling car ("Malaysian Dealers Criticise Exports of 'National Car,'" *BP*, May 18, 1987, 16). In November 1987 Mahathir said that the interest on Japanese loans to Proton had been reduced from 8.3 to 5.7 percent, but Mit-

subishi officials denied any such agreement had been concluded. Proton also accounted for $80 million of the $132 million allocated to HICOM for heavy industry projects in 1988 (Duthie 1987a, 2).

86. The debate is described in "First Shipment of Sagas Abroad Begins This Week," *BT*, October 21, 1985.

87. The assertion that Kushairi broke the stalemate is drawn from ibid. and an interview.

88. "6,000 Sagas for Britain in Two Years," *TS*, December 6, 1985.

89. "Proton Saga for Britain Deal Signed," *TS*, October 27, 1984; "UK firm Contracts to Buy PS," *BT*, March 27, 1985.

90. "First Shipment of Sagas Abroad Begins This Week," *BT*, October 21, 1985.

91. Ibid.

92. "Tariff on Motor Parts for Saga to Be Lifted," *BT*, July 19, 1985. Under the GSP, Malaysia could import the first 3,000 Sagas into England duty free, with the rest at only 15 percent of normal duty rates.

93. Seward 1986 and Berthelsen 1985, 1.

94. A confidential telex from K Line's Singapore office to Edarlaus warned the Malaysian firm to cease price-comparison discussions with a rival shipping company, NYK Line, "as NYK belongs to the Mitsubishi group and had been relaying every move made by Edarlaus back to its parent." Seward 1986, 71.

95. Proton announced hopes of exporting 10,000 units to Britain during 1989 ("Malaysia Expands State Car Maker," *FEER*, February 9, 1989, 67).

96. Mitsubishi was reportedly "stunned" by the agreement. Duthie 1987.

97. Seward 1987.

98. As of March 1987 competing Mitsubishi products were being sold in the United States by Hyundai, Chrysler, and Mitsubishi itself. See Smith 1987, 136–37.

99. Necessary modifications would include shifting the steering wheel to the left side of the dashboard, as well as installing new bumpers, headlights, and emission-control systems (Duthie 1987b, 22).

100. According to one estimate the Saga would have to be subsidized at 30 percent to be price competitive in the West, even with GSP status (Seward 1987, 95).

101. Ibid., and Duthie 1987b.

102. Such negotiations took place during a March 1987 visit to Japan by a senior Proton delegation (Seward 1987, 95).

103. "Misfiring Saga," *Asiaweek*, July 8, 1988, 46. Proton reportedly hoped to export 30,000 vehicles to North America in 1988.

104. Goldstein 1989, 40–41.

105. Aznam 1988.

Chapter 6

1. These differences are examined in detail in ch. 9.

2. Hansen 1971, 47. In 1959 a presidential decree on "party simplification" reduced a previous multiplicity of contending parties and ushered in a period of "guided democracy" under Sukarno. But a large number of parties continued to operate until Sukarno was overthrown in 1965.

3. For descriptions of the early *pribumi* entrepreneurs, see Robison 1978, 28, 35, and Robison 1986a, ch. 3. The following discussion draws heavily on these two works.

4. The Liem group is involved in trade, logging, tin, property and construction, manufacture (textiles, nails, flour milling, cement, steel), and finance, as well as auto assembly and distribution. The group has assets of over $1 billion, controls the largest private domestically owned bank in Indonesia, and has informal credit networks linking major overseas Chinese groups in Southeast Asia. See Robison n.d.

5. The following account is drawn from Astbury 1982, 20; and *Asian Finance*, November 15, 1983, 105–6.

6. Astra is known as Indonesia's best-managed group and is the largest non-financial corporation in Southeast Asia. In 1985 Astra ranked eighty-fourth among the developing world's top six hundred firms in terms of sales. See *South Magazine*, July 1985, 67.

7. Kostrad was also involved in banking, forestry, airlines, and trading (Robison 1987, 263).

8. See ibid., 277–93; Chalmers 1988, 198; author interviews.

9. Robison 1986a, 140.

10. Chalmers 1988, 153. More generally, see Robison 1986a, 140.

11. Thus, in 1969 the first development plan (Repelita I) made no mention of the role of market forces. On economic nationalism in Indonesian political thought, see McCawley 1982 and Myint 1984.

12. "Ir." is short for *Insinyur* ("engineer"), a respectful term of address for someone with a higher degree.

13. Chalmers 1988, chs. 5 and 6.

14. The measures divided assemblers into seven "general assemblers" and fifteen "local assemblers," with the latter designated to serve as subcontractors for the former. This favored larger firms such as Ning and Eman, which were among the first designated general assemblers. Chalmers 1988, ch. 6.

15. On the growth of this nonethnic nationalism, see Robison 1986a, 146–47. The directorate assumed authority for the auto industry under Presidential Decree No. 45.

16. *Tempo* (Jakarta), April 10, 1971, cited in Chalmers 1988, 164.

17. Chalmers 1988, 173.

18. Author interviews.

19. Witoelar 1984, 32.

20. Chalmers 1988, 182.

21. Ibid., 173.

22. Crude oil prices jumped 430 percent between 1972 and 1974. Government oil revenues rose from Rp140 billion in 1971–72 (25 percent of total government revenues), to Rp957 billion in 1974–75 (48 percent of total revenues). See McCawley 1978b.

23. This was reflected by the fact that between 1974 and 1977, Japanese components firms established nine manufacturing subsidiaries in Indonesia, compared to two during the previous four years. Dodwell Marketing Consultants 1984, 13. On the general defensive investment pattern among Japanese firms in Indonesia at this time, see Tsurumi 1980, 300.

24. There are no figures on the percentage of Indonesia's auto sales accounted for by Pertamina and other state purchases. According to interviews, Astra, Mercedes Benz, Volvo, and Mitsubishi sold large numbers of vehicles to Pertamina. Volkswagen and Mazda also profited from government contracts, with state sales at one point in the 1970s accounting for 40–50 percent of Mazda's production

25. *Kompas* (Jakarta), August 10, 1971, cited in Chalmers 1988, 163.

26. The following discussion is drawn from Robison 1987, 160–72, and Suryadinata 1976.

27. In absolute terms, government oil revenues rose from Rp150 billion in 1971–72 to Rp957 billion in 1974–75, to Rp8,575 billion in 1981–82 (Robison 1986a, 171).

28. Based on estimates cited in Robison 1986a, 276.

29. Chalmers 1988, 179.

30. "Astra Begins to Smile Again," *Asian Finance*, January 15–February 14, 1977, 32, and Chalmers 1988, 200. Chalmers notes that Astra's support for localization also resulted from a corporate restructuring induced by a mid-1970s' financial crisis.

31. Witoelar 1984, 32.

32. Chalmers 1988, 165–67.

33. *Indonesia Letter* (Hong Kong), no. 126 (1981).

34. Chalmers 1988, 199.

35. *Indonesian Commercial Newsletter* (hereafter *ICN*), no. 57 (July 12, 1976): 11–13.

36. Chalmers 1988, 165–67.

37. Taxes on CVs were removed while those on passenger cars were raised to

encourage a CV/PV sales ratio of 80/20, a ratio that was surpassed by 1977. See *Business News* (Jakarta) (hereafter *BN*), March 8, 1978, 6.

38. This paragraph is based on author interviews.

39. Hansen 1971, 51.

40. Chalmers 1988, 183.

41. *BN*, July 18, 1976, 5, July 23, 1976, 1, and author interviews. According to *BN*, September 22, 1976, 6, only ten makes were expected to have the capacity to fulfill LC requirements.

42. For similar networks in forestry and the milk industry, see Robison 1987, 186–88.

43. *Insight,* August 1979, 21.

44. Pertamina's financial problems are discussed in ch. 9.

45. Figures from GAAKINDO.

46. The degree of vertical integration is reflected in a 1977 finding that of the twenty-three members of the Indonesian Automobile Components Industrial Association, only four actually supplied original equipment to the assemblers. Only three members had over fifty employees. Nor did any parts firms unaffiliated with the Association sell original equipment. See Witoelar 1984, 35–36.

47. For background see *BN*, August 30, 1978, 9.

48. Author interviews.

49. Author interview.

50. For a description of this plan, see Chalmers 1988, 195.

51. Ibid., 191; *BN*, July 6, 1977, 9.

52. Author interview.

53. *BN*, July 6, 1977, 9.

54. Suhartoyo's autonomy was based in part on institutional tradition (Directorates were independent under Sukarno) and in part on the fact that the minister of industry until 1978, Mohammed Joesoef, paid little attention to the details of auto policy.

55. Unless otherwise noted, the discussion of differences between Soehoed and Suhartoyo is based on author interviews.

56. Indonesia, MOI 1982, 10.

57. Armed with extensive (and presumably off-budget) financing, as well as presidential support, Habibie pushed the BPPT into aircraft and ship manufacturing. And while he has drawn heavily on foreign capital and technology, Habibie has relied largely on Western firms. See Nasir 1987, 113, and Hill 1984a, 54.

58. *ICN*, no. 162 (November 17, 1980): 1.

59. *ICN*, no. 80 (June 27, 1977): 33; no. 112 (October 23, 1978): 1; no. 162 (November 17, 1980): 1. The issue was to grow politically more volatile, eventually (1980) taking the form of direct attacks on the New Order by retired senior

military officers. The government responded with a series of measures reserving certain government contracts for indigenous economically weak firms. See Sumantoro 1984, 33; Robison 1986a, 185.

60. Supplies of local wheel rims and leaf springs were still unsatisfactory, and only 30 percent of CV assemblers seemed willing to comply with the LC schedule for that year. See *BN*, August 30, 1978, 9; June 16, 1978, 6.

61. Chalmers 1988, 217.

62. Author interviews.

63. Chalmers 1988, 213.

64. Author interviews; *BN*, February 7, 1979, 4.

65. The only member not an official was a representative of the Society of Automotive Engineers. Author interviews.

66. Witoelar 1984, 31. The decision also reflected the government's concern with the rising costs of vehicles and parts owing to Indonesia's 1978 devaluation.

67. This would probably include GM and Toyota, the world's largest firms; Mercedes-Benz, one of Europe's strongest companies; and Mitsubishi, a medium-sized firm with a leading position in Indonesia. See BPPT/SRI 1979, 48–50, and BPPT/SRI 1982.

68. Author interviews.

69. In the long run, Soehoed intended to reduce these groups to four, with each group specializing in the standardized production of a particular engine size. Author interviews.

70. Author interviews.

71. Author interviews.

72. Author interviews and Pawitra 1985, 479.

73. In 1979 Nissan accused its partners, the Afaan brothers, of mismanagement and default. Claiming that the Afaans owed over U.S. $15 million in loans and had failed to promote Datsun sales, the Japanese halted shipments of CKD packs to the Afaans' firm, PT Indokaya, and demanded that new majority Indonesian partners be brought in. Nissan sweetened the demand with an offer to invest in an engine plant proposed as part of Decree No. 168.

The Afaans responded that Nissan's charges covered up its real concern—namely, that the Afaans had purchased a steel-pressing firm in cooperation with a German company that could threaten Nissan's vertical control of its subsidiary. The case rapidly took on the overtones of a nationalist struggle. For while the Afaans' management faults were well known (reportedly involving Afaan family and friends taking over and bleeding dealerships), they were defended in the press by a *pribumi* coalition.

Soehoed, who wanted to use German capital to bolster *pribumi* firms, but was also concerned with drawing Japanese investment into the country's upstream industrialization plans, prevailed on the Afaans to accept a restructuring of the management. The issue then became finding a new partner for Nissan. The two major contenders were (1) a firm owned by the Association for Retired Army Officers (Perabri), whose head was also the chair of the government political party, and (2) a firm owned by a group of leading *pribumi* businessmen, which included Afaan, Ning, Eman, and Probosutejo. Soehoed felt that the latter group was preferable because of its automotive and general business experience. In the event, however, the decision was made by President Suharto, and the choice was Perabri.

Nissan may have been pleased to have avoided "a pribumi group which was more likely to move toward full manufacture at a rate beyond the ability of Nissan to control." But the firm had hoped for a local partner more efficient and capable of aggressive sales promotion than Perabri. Two developments partially alleviated this concern. First, through special import duty and tax exemptions, the Indonesian State Secretariat promoted the sale of Nissan Stanzas to taxi cooperatives in which Perabri members were active. Second, at the time this research was completed, the Liem group was gradually taking over control of the assembly of Nissan passenger vehicles from Perabri and offsetting the latter's poor management practices (according to a Nissan executive, Perabri officials ordered more CKD packs than could be sold, since each pack yielded a commission).

This account is based on Chalmers 1983, 11–14, from which the above quotation is drawn; Robison 1987, 333–34; Awanohara 1983, 69–72, and author interviews.

74. Witoelar 1984, 21.

75. Author interviews.

76. Pawitra 1985, 355.

77. Author interviews.

78. Author interviews.

79. Swaminathan 1982, 26.

80. The DOI was to formulate and guide the implementation of industrial policy, including the issuance of factory licenses. The BKPM was to design terms of reference for participation of foreign capital, allocate promotional incentives, and decide when a sector was overcrowded.

81. Author interviews.

82. Author interview.

83. As construction of the Mitsubishi (Krama Yudha) engine plant began in late 1981, Said challenged the other firms to "fully support the government's progressive manufacturing program" despite the then prevailing business slump. See "Indonesia Travels a Local Road," *Asian Business,* September 1984, 84.

84. *Indonesia Letter,* no. 136 (1981).

85. Author interviews. A European auto official also asserted that the original plans involved a balance of foreign firms managing each plant: one independent (probably Perkins), one Japanese (Mitsubishi); and one European (Daimler Benz).

86. Author interviews.

87. Mitsubishi was probably hoping for precisely that, since its 1981 proposal specified a capacity sufficient to produce for other brands. See *Indonesia Letter,* no. 136 (1981).

88. See, e.g., Suharto's comments on industrial deepening in his 1982 State Address, in Gray 1982, 36.

89. The principal bureaucratic opponents to second-stage ISI policies such as automotive localization were found in the Indonesian Ministry of Finance, backed by the World Bank. See, e.g., Sacerdoti 1981, 44–47, and Kaye 1985, 68–71. There has not been any evidence of a strategic coalition between these forces and Japanese auto firms.

90. It is unclear whether Suhartoyo or Soehoed conducted negotiations with MITI. Government oil revenues rose from 2,308 billion rupiahs in 1978–79 to 4,260 billion in 1979–80, 6,430 billion in 1980–81, and 8,575 billion in 1981–82 (Robison 1986a, 171).

91. Ibid., 314.

92. Author interview. According to one source, the Japanese later pledged a $600 million untied loan for forging operations. Swaminathan 1982, 40.

93. Part of this effort involved a government request that the U.S. Trade and Development program provide a technical consultant on potential for Western participation in parts production. The consultant's report is found in Swaminathan 1982, 23.

94. Thee 1984, 38.

95. The following discussion of the Dana-Spicer and Probosutejo case is based on author interviews.

96. With little political background on Indonesia, Dana reportedly acted in part on U.S. Embassy advice. Joesoef (as noted earlier, an ally of Ibnu Sutowo's) had become embroiled in a public fight with Sutowo over control of a jointly owned Hilton hotel. The fight resulted in Sutowo taking full ownership of the hotel in return for ceding Star Motors (Mercedes-Benz) to Joesoef. See Robison 1987, 358. The fight reportedly resulted in a significant loss of presidential support for Joesoef.

97. Indonesian government efforts in support of Dana should also be noted. These involved advice on alternative partners and requests that Japan's MITI pressure its firms to back Dana's participation.

98. See the overall assessment of U.S. parts firms in Swaminathan 1982, 35–36.

99. There were also reports that Peugeot was discouraged by demands that 20 percent of the venture's shares be offered to particular state officials. Author interviews.

100. Chalmers 1988, 225.

101. Ibid., 226.

102. "Car Manufacturing Capability Is Next," *Asian Business*, June 1982, 24.

103. For evidence, see Robison 1987, and Jones and Pura 1986.

104. For example, in January 1985 a visiting Toyota official expressed open doubt that depressed market demand would permit further localization ("Auto Manufacturing Scheme Runs as Scheduled," *Jakarta Post*, January 21, 1985, 7).

105. Unless otherwise noted, information on opposition to local content is drawn from author interviews.

106. PT Indo Mobile Utama, producer of Suzuki vehicles.

107. Author interviews.

108. Hill 1984b, 13, and Kaye 1985, 68.

109. See for example *ICN*, no. 265 (March 11, 1985): 14–15.

110. Author interview.

111. Based on author interviews. The State Secretariat, which includes a State Procurement Team with the power to scrutinize all state expenditures on major public projects, gradually took some critical functions away from the Department of Industry.

112. Information on the changing institutional context of auto policy is drawn from author interviews.

113. The DOI also reportedly provided information to the press identifying firms that failed to submit reports, and sent out screening teams equipped with cameras to check on project implementation. Author interviews.

114. According to one source, as of 1984 there had "never been any reports of sanctions because of a company's failure to adhere to the schedule for use of locally manufactured components" (*ICN*, no. 257 [December 5, 1984]: 19).

115. See, e.g., Army Chief Benny Murdhani's 1984 ban on the use of the terms *pribumi* and *non-pribumi* to allay Chinese fears of a *pribumi* reaction against moves to privatize certain industrial sectors. Hill 1984b, 17.

116. Astra, in the words of one Western specialist, is the "good Chinese," while the Liem group is closer to the "bad Chinese." In my interviews, Astra officials were open in their concern that Liem's (and especially his son's) flaunting of ties to Suharto could provoke serious outbreaks. The potential for such outbreaks was confirmed in late 1984 and early 1985 when government forces opened fire on Moslem protestors in Jakarta demanding the release of arrested youths. Between

thirty and one hundred people died. In the following six months, a wave of fires, shootings, and bombings rocked Jakarta and other cities. Most of the targets were Chinese, including a branch of the Bank Central Asia, part of the Liem group. See Brannigan 1985.

117. Author interviews.

118. Personal communication from Ian Chalmers, 1985. The existence of such centers was also confirmed in my own interviews.

119. As noted earlier, Astra has had ties to Sutowo and Probosutejo. Also, 7.5 percent of PT Federal Motor, one of the major Astra firms, is owned by Kostrad and PT Pakarti Yoga, a firm belonging to several generals. Liem Bien Koen (Indonesian name, Sofyan Wanandi), head of one of the Astra group's component firms, is chief manager of the Kostrad foundation and Pakarti Yoga, as well as general manager in a business conglomerate controlled by the Department of Defense and Security.

120. The following discussion is based on author interviews.

121. See, e.g., the statement by an Astra spokesman in *Asian Finance*, November 15, 1983, 116.

122. Friedland 1988, 100.

123. Information on Astra's efforts to increase efficiency is drawn from author interviews with Astra officials.

124. In addition, the Japanese "still view Astra as a ticket to the import-substitution market, not as an equal partner in the sale of exports" (Friedland 1988, 101).

125. TDD officials were aware that Taiwan's "depackaging" of Japanese technology was facilitated by the high level of technical skills among a large number of smaller Taiwanese producers. Astra felt compelled to pursue an in-house approach to such technology transfer.

126. This exchange was originally recounted to me in interviews. Accounts are also to be found in "Kendoraan Niaga Produksi Indonesia Termurah di ASEAN," *Berit Yudha*, June 1, 1985, and "Industri Otomotif Tak Dapat Dihindari Di Negara Berkembang," *Merdeka*, June 1, 1985.

Chapter 7

1. On racial sensitivity, see Snow 1983, 26. As of 1989 there was a Federation of Filipino-Chinese Chambers of Commerce incorporating some 150 Filipino-Chinese chambers as affiliates (Franklin D. Lim 1989, 7).

2. Golay 1987a.

3. Steinberg 1982, 24.

4. Ocampo 1971.

5. Paterno 1972, 20.

6. Unless otherwise noted, information on Philippine assemblers is drawn from Schutte 1982, 127–28, and Yoshihara 1985.

7. Silverio had learned of a ship loaded with CKD Toyotas floating in the South China Sea after having been refused entry to Taiwan, and he bought the cargo at a token price (Schutte 1982).

8. Information on these objections from interviews. Information on the loan and foundry from interviews and from *Manila Chronicle* (hereafter *MC*), May 4, 1971, 6; May 23, 1971, 7.

9. By 1978 the Guevarra family was connected to at least eighteen firms, five of which were among the Philippines top thousand (Tsuda 1978, 137).

10. Author interview.

11. Information on the Yulos is drawn from Yoshihara 1985, 137 and interviews.

12. Yoshihara 1985, 130.

13. The Sycip family has connections with at least forty-two companies, of which sixteen are among the country's top thousand. David Sycip himself is president of the Rizal Commercial Banking Corp., chairman of the Council for Economic Development (the counterpart of the Keizai Doyu-kai, the Japanese Council for Economic Development), and co-chairman of the Philippines-Japan Economic Cooperation Committee. His brother, Washington Sycip, is chairman of Sycip, Gorres, Velayo and Co. (the SGV Group), a regionwide accounting and management consulting firm whose advisory activities make it one of the area's most important, albeit least publicized, private interests (Tsuda 1978, 125–26).

14. He was also concerned that GM would gut Yutivo's strength in its distributorships. Had the Yutivos maintained overall control, Sycip believed, they could have bargained with GM on car prices and conditions of distribution and, if necessary, moved to Nissan. Author interviews.

15. PAA 1969.

16. I am grateful to David Wurfel for bringing these points to my attention. On the nonpolitical nature of these groups, see "The Entrepreneur as a Conglomerate," *FEER*, September 12, 1986, 108.

17. This emerges from interviews and a comparison between Paterno's 1970 "Letter to President Marcos" and the final 1972 BOI Guidelines.

18. Author interview.

19. Unless otherwise noted, the following discussion draws on author interviews.

20. See, e.g., *MC*, August 9, 1972, 6.

21. PAA Information Memo no. 68-07, March 12, 1968, cited in Mangahas 1970, 53. My characterization of Sycip differs sharply from that presented by

Ohara, the only other political analysis of the PCMP and Sycip's role of which I am aware. He argues that "by virtue of his extensive business and marriage relations," Sycip is "an integral part of the international network of monopoly capitalists" (Ohara 1977, 174). I do not share Ohara's assumption that policy positions are necessarily a function of business and family ties.

22. Author interviews and Philippines, BOI 1972.

23. The 1969 PAA position paper noted that a minimum production of 300,000 units a year was necessary to achieve world market prices, whereas the Philippine market accounted for only 30,000 (PAA 1969, 3).

24. Author interviews.

25. *MC,* August 13, 1971, 6. Author interviews.

26. *MC,* January 23, 1972; February 15, 1972.

27. *MC,* February 15, 1972, 6.

28. Ibid.

29. See, e.g., *MC,* March 3 and March 4, 1972.

30. *MC,* March 17, 1972, 7; March 16, 1972, 7.

31. *MC,* March 4, 1972, 8.

32. *MC,* March 7, 1972, 7.

33. Forty points for LC excess; twenty for the creation of manufacturing activity in the industry; twenty for upgrading of engineering skills; ten for contribution to the regional complementation effort; and extra points to be given for horizontal supply sources, Philippine ownership, and other policies in line with national goals for firms within five points of each other. See *MC,* March 15, 1972.

34. Indeed, Ford's Philippine officials viewed the firm's original PCMP application as so weak that they took it on themselves to make the proposal more acceptable to the BOI at the last minute. The highest ranking Filipino in the firm stressed Ford's general arrogance and noted that "headquarters assumes that all the countries need us." Unless otherwise noted, information on Ford's activities are based on author interviews.

35. *MC,* March 31, 1972, 7. Paterno subsequently acknowledged Ford's importance to the viability of the EPZ. See *Business Day* (Manila) (hereafter *BD*), August 1, 1972.

36. *MC,* June 9, 1972, 8.

37. *MC,* June 14, 1972, 7.

38. A senator accused the NEC chairman of accepting a two million peso bribe, presumably in return for supporting the admission of UMC (Nissan) into the PCMP. Paterno accused Nissan of attempting to wreck the car program and wondered if UMC and its Filipino counsel (who happened to be a highly respected nationalist leader) might "unwittingly be the agents of a big Japanese business enterprise seeking to destroy the PCMP." See *MC,* July 14, 1972, 7.

39. Author interview.

40. *MC,* August 17, 1972, 6.

41. Ohara 1977, 188.

42. *MC,* June 20, 1972.

43. *MC,* July 13, 1972.

44. *MC,* July 6, 1972, 6.

45. *MC,* August 13, 1972, 4.

46. *MC,* July 6, 1972, 1.

47. This involved a sharing of facilities and export credits with three of the firms selected for the PCMP. Author interviews.

48. *Times Journal* (Manila) (hereafter *TJ*), January 28, 1981, 9.

49. Two other reasons have been raised, neither of which seems very plausible. In interviews, certain BOI officials cited their concern that closing down the firms would displace large numbers of workers. But these workers could have been absorbed by the PCMP firms, since the 1976–78 period was one of market expansion. Paterno reportedly cited another factor: the fear that the exclusion of UMC/Nissan would upset ASEAN regional plans, since Nissan operated in the other countries. This does not seem very plausible given Paterno's earlier criticisms of Nissan. Author interviews, from which the rest of this paragraph draws.

50. It is also possible that the Japanese trading company Marubeni helped UMC. Japanese auto firm officials interviewed in Tokyo spoke of Marubeni's influence with the presidential palace as one reason Nissan assumed it would be accepted as a PCMP participant even without a strong proposal.

51. Watanabe 1979, 7.

52. Ono 1973.

53. Many of the firms anxious to begin production of seat and trim items, for example, had heretofore functioned as upholstery makers of one sort or another.

54. Author interview.

55. Moreover, even if the approved firms limited themselves to the number of models stipulated in their proposals, he doubted that the existing level of demand (5,000 units per model) would sustain local production (*MC,* September 18, 1972, 6).

56. Author interviews.

57. Officials of Carco drew up the first drafts of the monitoring and reporting system. Carco and Delta officials developed subsequent drafts. A Delta official with SGV representatives prepared the audit program and procedures. Author interviews.

58. When Paterno was asked what kind of leverage the BOI had had in its early struggles over the PCMP, he replied flatly, "None." Author interview.

59. See Follosco 1985, 5–9.

60. Paterno 1970.

61. Author interviews.

62. Villegas 1984, 11–12.

63. Tolentino and Ybanez 1984, 239–40.

64. *MC*, May 12, 1972, 10, and author interviews, from which the rest of this paragraph draws.

65. Krarr 1981, 37.

66. Tolentino and Ybanez 1984, 240.

67. Krarr 1981, 37.

68. From 168 million pesos to 630 million (EIU 1985, 39).

69. Author interviews.

70. The problem is discussed in an unpublished study undertaken by various assemblers during the early 1980s ("A Status Report on the Philippine Automotive Industry" [mimeo, Manila, n.d.], 14). See also *BD*, March 30, 1979, 1.

71. *TJ*, February 24, 1978, May 27, 1978.

72. *TJ*, March 19, 1970, 6.

73. Author interviews.

74. Paterno was also concerned that such a measure would conflict with the programs of other ASEAN states and thus undermine the regional complementation program (*Evening Mail* [Manila], April 23, 1979).

75. The discussion of CAPPA is based on author interviews.

76. These links are presumably supported by the listed companies by the Presidential Council for Good Government established after Marcos's fall. These are listed in Aquino 1987.

77. This account draws on author interviews, especially with CAPPA staff.

78. *Nation's Journal* (Manila), Jan. 30, 1980, 13.

79. *Evening Mail*, April 23, 1979. The ILO study was Watanabe 1979.

80. *BD*, March 14, 1980, 1.

81. *BD*, August 5, 1980, 1.

82. *BD*, August 25, 1980, 8. These requests stemmed in part from declining auto sales (*TJ*, April 6, 1980, 10), but also from conflicts among the assemblers as to the exact LC percentages attributable to various components (author interviews).

83. *BD*, April 20, 1981, 2.

84. This paragraph draws on author interviews.

85. *BD*, May 8, 1981, 11.

86. This was especially difficult with regard to electronics parts. The key problem here had to do with the particular Japanese auto parts firms operating in the Philippines. The only "local" producer of electrical components was a subsidiary of Nippondenso, part of the Toyota group. Carco, along with Ford (Mazda), pur-

chased its electrical parts from Mitsubishi, which did not have a Philippine presence in electrical parts production. The vulnerability of Carco, as well as Ford, was reflected in the publicly stated concern of a Ford official that his firm would "be at the mercy of these automobile components makers and there's nothing we can do" (*BD,* July 8, 1981, 31).

87. Author interviews.

88. Unless otherwise noted, the discussion of the Compliance Committee draws on author interviews.

89. And, in fact, Concepcion's successor as CAPPA president took what some members considered irresponsible stands against the assemblers, in part because his strong nonautomotive business interests protected him from possible assembler retaliation. These positions were not only anathema to the BOI; they also did not sit well with many CAPPA members, whose commitment to the auto industry forced them to be somewhat more conciliatory in their individual dealings with the BOI and assemblers.

90. Author interviews and *Daily Express* (Manila) (hereafter *DE*), March 14, 1983, 16.

91. Indeed, when feasible the other assemblers availed themselves of the same methods used by Delta. Carco, for example, also took advantage of the high LC percentage granted to Delta for assembly operations.

92. Unless otherwise noted, this discussion of Silverio is based on author interviews with former Delta officials.

93. Known as the Delta Explorer, this four-wheel-drive general utility vehicle was manufactured for and with the Armed Forces of the Philippines and was beginning to compete in some export markets with a vehicle produced by Toyota, Silverio's Japanese partner. Delta had obtained orders for the Explorer from Colombia, Italy, the Middle East, and Papua New Guinea. Author interviews and Cororaton 1984, 3.

94. According to one source, the bank itself was anxious to make the loans, since it had recently lost the coconut and sugar industries as major customers. Author interview.

95. For a discussion of technocratic opposition to the cronies, see Bello et al. 1982, ch. 7.

96. Throughout most of the 1970s the Japanese had three major consultants in the firm, one each for finance, manufacturing, and marketing. These men were not in line positions, and, as one source said, "Filipinos are highly ingenious and can hide any number of things." Author interviews.

97. Unless otherwise noted, this account draws from Schutte 1982.

98. Silverio's natural partner, Toyota, did not produce large commercial vehi-

cles or engines, and initial contacts with Hino, the commercial vehicle firm linked to Toyota, fell through for reasons as yet unclear.

99. Philippines, BOI 1977, appendix 3, p. 20. Besides MAN, the other applicants included Fiat, Isuzu, Hino, Perkins, Leyland, Cummins, and Detroit Diesel (GM).

100. The Herdis group was led by Herminio Disini, another Marcos crony. Bello et al. 1982, 188–89.

101. See Schutte 1982, 5; "BOI Awaits Good Offer to Take over M.A.N. Job," *BD*, November 25, 1981; "M.A.N. Stresses Project Interest," *BD*, December 11, 1981, 9.

102. See Philippines, BOI 1977.

103. Schutte 1982, 6.

104. Delta's debt/equity ratio grew to 12:1 (ibid., 9).

105. By the end of 1981, these amounted to roughly U.S.$9 million in suppliers' credits ("M.A.N. Stresses Project Interest," *BD*, December 11, 1981, 9).

106. Philippines, BOI 1983, 2.

107. Author interviews in Tokyo.

108. *TJ*, October 26, 1977.

109. *TJ*, February 13, 1976.

110. Interviews.

111. One of the PCMP provisions allowed assembly firms that exceeded LC requirements, whether through physical sourcing or export earnings, to import CKD sets for vehicles larger than the four-cylinder/2,000 cc category permitted by the PCMP (*BD*, April 29, 1976, 5). Ford's move was legal, since the firm had exceeded LC requirements through export earnings. But other assemblers, especially GM, were worried that Ford's new model would cut into the large car market (*TJ*, November 16, 1977).

112. *BD*, November 28, 1979, 1.

113. In addition, registered models were not to be replaced within three years, and two extra models were allowed if they met prescribed LC standards through *physical* sourcing and used all components scheduled for mandatory deletion (Philippines, BOI 1983).

114. Ibid., no. 3.2.

115. *Financial Times of Manila*, March 23, 1981.

116. *TJ*, April 9, 1981, 12.

117. GM's share went from roughly 8 percent in 1980 to 15 percent in 1981 (*Financial Times of Manila*, April 14, 1981, 1).

118. *Manila Journal*, August 4–10, 1980, 1; *DE*, April 13, 1981, 10.

119. *BT*, February 17, 1982, 12.

120. Author interview.

121. *TJ*, April 30, 1981, 11.

122. *BD*, July 6, 1981, 9.

123. Interviews and published materials suggest no role for the parts firms in this issue.

124. Author interviews.

125. *BT*, June 23, 1982, 2.

126. *TJ*, May 9, 1983, 10.

127. Philippines, BOI 1983, 1.

128. The country's total debt outstanding rose from $9.81 billion in 1979 to $17 billion in 1982. By 1982 close to a quarter of this was short-term debt. Debt-service ratios had risen from 18.3 percent in 1979 to 33.9 percent in 1982. World Bank figures cited in Haggard 1990, table 2.

129. *TJ*, March 30, 1983, 6; *DE*, April 30, 1983, 9.

130. Author interviews.

131. Author interviews.

132. *BT*, August 11, 1983, 22; *BD*, July 11, 1983, 20.

133. *BD*, July 19, 1983. See also *BD*, July 18, 1983, 2.

134. Some months earlier the BOI chief had reminded Marcos to bring up the car price issue with Japanese Prime Minister Nakasone in the context of trade imbalances. *TJ*, April 30, 1983, 6.

135. *TJ*, July 19, 1983, 8.

136. *BD*, July 18, 1983, 2.

137. Anxious to avoid involvement that might imply favoritism, the embassy responded to JAMA's requests for help by saying that the debate was a "technical and an economic issue, not a political one that would require government interception [*sic*]" (*DE*, July 17, 1983, 1).

138. *BD*, August 1, 1983, 20. It remains unclear whether the BOI has in fact been able to enforce the 85 percent rule. A 1985 report strongly implied that the auto TNCs have convinced the government to accept the fact that locally assembled vehicles must cost more than Japanese manufactured cars "because of a whole range of differential cost factors." The survey also notes, however, that the Philippine authorities "examine all costs in detail every time a manufacturer wishes to instigate a price rise for all its models" (EIU 1985, 37).

139. The merged companies would then bid for PCMP slots on the basis of four criteria: self-sufficiency in foreign exchange; reasonable prices; local content; and willingness to buy out those firms not accepted for the program (*AWSJ*, August 22, 1983, 5; *BD*, August 29, 1983, 5).

140. *TJ*, August 20, 1983, 6.

141. *TJ*, September 17, 1983, 6.

142. Interview with BOI and AMII officials.

143. Author interviews; *DE*, September 23, 1984, 20.

144. Silverio owed the bank some 1.8 billion pesos (*Metro Manila Times*, April 3, 1984, 14).

145. Nissan's Philipinas Nissan was a joint venture between Nissan, the Marubeni trading company, and the First Manila Management Corp. (FMMC). Mazda's firm, MPI, was formed in July–August 1984 by Mazda, Sumitomo, and Genasia Management (GMMC) with an eye to taking over Ford's stamping plant. Both GMMC and FMMC are owned by a business group led by the Romualdez family. Author interviews, from which this paragraph is drawn. See also Aquino 1987.

146. *BD*, May 2, 1985, 13.

Chapter 8

1. Siam Motors (Nissan), for example, has close ties to the Bangkok Bank; United Development (Mitsubishi) to the Bangkok Metropolitan Bank through the Techapaipul family; Karnasutra (Fiat, Ford) to the Krung Thai Bank. See *Business in Thailand* (Bangkok), September 1983; Suehiro 1985; Phipatseritham and Yoshihara 1983.

2. Of those established between 1962 and 1975, eighteen out of twenty-nine were at least 90 percent Thai-held (Ithijarakun 1977).

3. The report suggested a stringent definition of CKD assembly, a sensible, progressive increase in LC requirements with rewards provided to firms exceeding minimum LC levels, revised import duties to make localization economically attractive, and a gradual limitation on CBU imports (Organ 1968, 10–20).

4. Ibid., 11, 16.

5. Nawadhinsukh 1984, 187. Unless otherwise noted, the following account is drawn from ibid., 187–89, and interviews in Bangkok.

6. The seminar took place in March 1970. Information on the private sector's role in this process is drawn from Thanamai 1985, 124–26.

7. Ibid., 125.

8. Author interviews.

9. Author interviews.

10. See, e.g., "Local Car Assemblers Laud Plans," *Bangkok Post* (hereafter *BP*), July 23, 1971; "Car Plants Agree to Proposals," *BP*, August 3, 1971.

11. See "Auto Parts Industry in the Offing," *BP*, May 9, 1970; and Dodwell Marketing Consultants 1984, 13.

12. The Ministry of Finance refused to support increased tariffs on CBUs (because they had recently been raised) or reduced tariffs on CKDs (because of con-

sequent revenue losses). The Ministry of Commerce opposed a ban on CBUs for fear of contravening GATT and damaging Thai agricultural exports. See Thanamai 1985, 129.

13. Na Pomphet 1977, 575.

14. The paper (*Daily News*, February 10, 1972, cited in Thanamai 1985, 137), noted the Philippines' success in this effort. As a further example of broad political support for the new auto measures, see the article by the prominent critic of government policy Kukrit Pramoj, *Siam Rath* (in Thai), July 24, 1971. This discussion also draws on author interviews.

15. Thanamai 1985, 131.

16. The coup was largely a military attempt to expand its own cohesion. But it also drew support from local business groups highly critical of the legislature's corruption and inability to pass budgets. See the articles in Segaran et al. 1973.

17. Thanamai 1985, 141–42.

18. Author interviews. See also "Car Assembly Plan to Be Revised," *BP*, January 4, 1972.

19. Author interview.

20. "Car Assembly Firms Oppose Pote's Move," *BP*, January 8, 1972.

21. "Auto Plants Seek Equal Rights," BP, February 9, 1972.

22. Thanamai 1985, 143–44.

23. *Business in Thailand* (herefter *BIT*), March 1975, 59.

24. "Components and Parts: Widening the Range," *BIT*, October 1977.

25. Ratanachaichanan 1977, 203–4.

26. The BOI stopped granting promotional privileges for new assemblers, but there was no move to stop the licensing of non-promoted plants. Ratanachaichanan 1977, 203–4.

27. "Chaos Reigns in Local Automobile Industry," *Financial Post*, October 26, 1973.

28. *BIT*, March 1975, 59.

29. Because the formula was calculated as a percentage of the price of a total CKD set and therefore sensitive to foreign-exchange fluctuations, it was difficult to calculate the real value of localized parts. The formula also allowed assemblers to understate the value of CKD kits on invoices and shipping documents, thereby inflating the value of local parts. Conversely, assemblers often overstated the value of local purchases by using false invoices ("Assembly: No Will No Way for Thai Components," *BIT*, August 1978, 48). Also, because LC regulations mandated 25 percent for *each* model, there was no attempt to exceed the requirement in any one model (Nawadinsukh 1984, 189–90). And, finally, Thai LC efforts were plagued by a problem seen in our other three cases—low deletion allowances by Japanese assemblers (*BIT*, March 1975, 65).

30. Not only were tariff differentials between CBUs and CKD packs fairly narrow, there was little reduction in tariffs on raw materials required by local parts producers (*Investor* [Bangkok], March 1976, cited in Thanamai 1985, 147).

31. Author interview.

32. Thai governments shifted from military rule (Thanom and Prapas until October 1973) to largely democratic rule (Sanya, Seni, Kukrit and Seni, October 1973–October 1976), and then back to various degrees of military rule (Thanin, October 1976–October 1977; Kriangsak, October 1977–February 1980).

33. "Growth Despite Chaos," *BIT,* October 1977.

34. Thailand became the third largest investor in Hong Kong during the mid 1970s (Stockwin 1976, 11).

35. "Assembly: No Will No Way for Thai Components," *BIT,* August 1978, 48–49.

36. Thanamai 1985, 146–47.

37. Nawadhinsukh 1984, 223–24.

38. "Components and Parts: Widening the Range," *BIT,* October 1977.

39. This is the number cited by Thanamai, based on Bangkok Bank reports (Thanamai 1985, 146). A different source states that the firms totaled roughly 140 in 1975 and 400 in 1978, of which 130 had actually registered with the MOI (*BIT,* March 1975, 65, and April 1981, 59–60).

40. The following discussion is based on author interviews.

41. For a review, see Tawarangkoon 1984, 40.

42. *Business Review* (Bangkok), June 1979, 414; "Import Ban Slapped on Cars, Luxuries," *BP,* February 1, 1978.

43. "Government Policy: Intransigent or Far Sighted," *BIT,* April 1981, 58.

44. *BIT,* April 1981, 61.

45. Siam Motors (Nissan) began work on a general pickup truck plant in 1977, and Toyota initiated a body parts operation in March 1978 (*Business Review,* June 1978, 457–58).

46. Information on local content and rationalization measures is drawn from Nawadhinsukh 1984, 190–91, and Thailand, MOI 1984c.

47. The old formula gave the assemblers extensive flexibility by basing local content on the value of the parts as a percentage of a vehicle's total value.

48. *Asian Business and Industry,* February 1979, 72.

49. The quotation is drawn from an author interview. On the assemblers' role in designing the formula, see *BIT,* August 1978, 48.

50. SNF began as a foundry in Siam Cement's Siam Iron and Steel Co. As demand increased the foundry was upgraded and established as a separate entity to produce quality castings. The foundry has operated at a loss borne by Siam Cement. Author interviews.

51. Author interviews and Sato 1982, 51.

52. After the capital scarcity of the democratic period, the new Thanin government was attempting to attract foreign investments through a streamlined and stronger BOI, now headed by the prime minister himself. See "Thais Hitched to a Resource Boom," *FEER*, September 9, 1977, 9.

53. General information on the diesel engine projects is to be found in "Diesel Engines: Five Offers to Manufacture," *BIT*, October 1977, and "Thai Diesel Projects: Why Some Have Stopped Pouring," *Asian Business*, October 1980.

54. "Ban on New Models Triggers Appeals," *BIT*, October 1978, 28.

55. *BIT*, April 1981, 46, 78.

56. In some cases meeting LC levels became a legal game (*BIT*, March 1982, 57).

57. Awanohara 1979, 41–42.

58. *BIT*, January 1979, 86.

59. Support for EOI came primarily from the country's planning agency, the National Economic and Social Development Board (NESDB), and the quasi-governmental Industrial Finance Corporation of Thailand (IFCT).

60. Ho 1980.

61. "Dispute Still Lingers over Local Car Content," *BR*, October 24, 1979. The parts firms also encouraged the new Thai prime minister, Prem Titsulamond, to press the Japanese government for support during one of his trips in late 1981. Author interviews.

62. "ATI Bids to Mediate Feud over Car Parts," *BP*, August 23, 1979.

63. This view is based on interviews with Hino officials. Note, too, that Isuzu was also at the time pressing to develop engine manufacturing in Indonesia and the Philippines (*ICN*, no. 112 [October 23, 1978]: 27).

64. "Diesel Engines: Five Offers to Manufacture," *BIT*, October 1977, and author interviews.

65. *Investor* (Bangkok), May 1978, 8.

66. "Diesel Engines: Five Offers," *BIT*, October 1977, 98; and "Trucks: Japanese Forced to Compete," *BIT*, August 1978, 56.

67. The European proposals were sent to the BOI from overseas home offices, whereas the Nissan proposals were submitted directly by both a major Thai industrialist and the chairman of Nissan Diesel ("Trucks: Japanese Forced to Compete," *BIT*, August 1978, 53).

68. *Investor*, May 1978, 8.

69. Author interview.

70. "Trucks: Japanese Forced to Compete," *BIT*, August 1978, 56.

71. The discussion of Hino strategy is based on author interviews.

72. As early as 1978 it was estimated that production of no engine model would exceed 1,500 units per year ("Trucks: Japanese Forced to Compete," BIT, August 1978, 56). Sales of six- and ten-wheel trucks rose 60 percent in 1977, to 11,200, over 1976 figures, but dropped to 7,900 in 1978, 7,300 in 1979, and 7,000 in 1980. The market also became more crowded, as Nissan gained 15 percent of it, leaving Isuzu and Hino with a combined share of 75 percent and others with 10 percent. ("Thai Diesel Projects: Why Some Have Stopped Pouring," *Asian Business*, October 1980, 39).

73. Author interviews and "Trucks: Japanese Forced to Compete," *BIT,* August 1978, 56.

74. "Thai Diesel Projects," *Asian Business*, October 1980, 39.

75. By 1986 the three approved manufacturers were producing approximately 130,000 engines per year at reasonable prices, generating work for eighty parts firms, and moving toward 76 percent localization ("Prem Urges Revisions on Diesel Engine Tax," *BP,* March 20, 1986).

76. Author interviews and Ho 1981, 41–42.

77. This account is based on personal interviews and Hock 1983.

78. Author interviews.

79. *Bangkok Bank Monthly Review,* May 1984, 186.

80. See the position paper by the head of Toyota Thailand, Sato 1982; and Vasurat and Sato 1983.

81. See, e.g., "Auto Policy Team Urged to Block Local Contents Rise," *BP,* September 6, 1983; "Call for Freeze on Truck Parts Rule," *BP,* March 2, 1984; "Ob Firm on LC Car Plan," *BP,* September 5, 1984.

82. Thailand, MOI 1984a, 1984b, 1985.

83. Ramsay 1986, 36.

84. Sricharatchanya 1984a, 54.

85. Trade deficits had risen from $333 million in 1973 to $1.6 billion in 1983. Sricharatchanya 1984c, 49. See also Sricharatchanya 1984b, 70.

86. Ob noted that imports of Japanese auto parts for trucks alone during the first eight months of 1983 amounted to B3,207 million, up 62 percent from 1982. The import total for buses and passenger cars was up 36 percent. See *Thailand Business*, April 1984, 49.

87. "The Basic Proposal," *BIT,* March 1985, 186; "Thais Need Efficiency Boost," *Asian Business*, September 1984, 85.

88. "Yontrakit Plan Irks Assemblers," *BP,* December 28, 1984.

89. *Bangkok Bank Monthly Review,* May 1984, 186–87; "BOI Rejects Bid to Make Mitsubishi Vehicles," *BP,* July 18, 1985.

90. While not against localization, Toyota does not have a local partner push-

ing it to localize. Toyota's local base is dominated by financial interests, not commercial-industrial entrepreneurs anxious to expand local manufacturing.

91. *Bangkok Bank Monthly Review,* May 1984, 186. The same official urged TNCs to comply with the ASEAN regional plan and set up parts plants in the region, asserting that "they have no choice. They must come in or give up this territory. They ought to understand that although at the beginning ASEAN may have looked like a paper tiger, actually it has really started something" ("Approaching the Multinationals," *BIT,* March 1984, 27).

92. *BIT,* March 1985, 44.

93. This discussion draws on author interviews and a presentation by the president of TAPMA to the Automobile Development Committee (Sentusophon 1984).

94. For example, the Japanese introduced plastic bumpers into the Thai market even though local capacity could supply only metal bumpers (Sentusophon 1984 and author interviews).

95. Sentusophon 1984, 2.

96. But another component of the tax structure discourages local manufacture: tariff rates on ready-made parts are often lower than those on the raw materials used by parts firms to manufacture those parts. See the TAPMA complaints in "Automobile Groups Oppose Scrapping Local Content Plans," *World,* (Bangkok), November 13, 1986.

97. Author interviews.

98. On Chinese dominance, see Suehiro 1985, p. 4/75, and Fish 1978, 23. On the large number of smaller and informal institutions, see World Bank 1983).

99. Until 1985, for example, the Industrial Finance Corporation of Thailand had almost no exposure in the auto industry (IFCT, *Annual Reports,* various years).

100. A case in point concerns one of the larger local assembly groups, Siam Motors (handling Nissan products). Siam Motors is also part of a major Thai conglomerate involved in finance, real estate, mining, tourism, and other sectors. When Siam Motors encountered severe financial difficulties a few years ago owing to excessive diversification, the Bangkok Bank reduced its exposure and pressed the firm's founder to rationalize the group's activities. Author interviews.

101. We shall examine these broader political arrangements in ch. 9.

102. Assembling Peugeots, Citroens, BMWs, and Lancias for Thailand's expanding elite, Yontrakit benefited from strong parent firm support (in the form of generous deletion allowances) and favorable exchange rates to bounce back from serious financial trouble in 1981 and take almost 20 percent of passenger car sales in 1983. Author interviews.

103. "Ob to Drive Plan for Fewer Car Models," *BP,* October 7, 1983.

104. "Ob to Table Plans on Local Car Contents," *BP,* February 10, 1984.

105. Author interviews.

106. Author interviews.

107. "Assemblers: Postpone Limit on Car Models," *BP,* June 21, 1985. The government reportedly rejected the appeals, but those interviewed stated that no action was taken to enforce the MOI's decision.

108. Author interviews and "Government to Launch New Auto Policy," *World* (Bangkok), January 16, 1986.

109. "Makers of Auto Parts Call for Urgent Meeting," *BP,* March 12, 1986. Yontrakit also asked its foreign principals for tooling equipment at no cost or at low rental ("Yontrakit Takes Action to Comply with Regulations," *BP,* April 10, 1986).

110. "Request for LC to Be Reversed," *BP,* March 28, 1986.

111. "Ministry Sets New Revised Rules," *BP,* August 6, 1986.

112. "Auto Parts Firms Split over Ruling" *BP,* March 18, 1987, 13.

113. Author interviews.

114. Most of the parts firms supported this modified formula, since some of them were simply not ready to produce parts previously listed for mandatory deletion. ("Six Months Deadline on LC Request," *World,* June 21, 1986). For information on the new formula, see "Ministry to Use New Local Content Concept," *BP,* April 16, 1986; "Local Car Content Set at 54%," *World,* April 16, 1986; "Car Industry to Produce Components," *BP,* April 11, 1986.

115. "Hyundai to Market Car, Bus, Truck, Here," *Business World,* January 25, 1986; "New Company Plans to Assemble Renault Car," *BP,* March 11, 1986. For reports on government problems in enforcing rationalization measures, see "Car Assemblers to Face Stricter Rules," *BP,* April 11, 1986.

116. " 'National' Pick-Ups and Trucks in the Making," *BP,* April 14, 1986.

117. Unless otherwise noted, the discussion of the engine project's recent phase is based on author interviews.

118. By 1985 the Siam Cement–Kubota joint venture was manufacturing 70 percent of the parts used in agricultural diesels. These parts reportedly reached international standards. SNF introduced new products such as disc brakes for pickups and introduced centrifugal casting for the first time in Thailand ("Siam Cement Co. Ltd.," *Business Review* May 1985, 71).

119. The following discussion draws on author interviews and the terms of reference for the automotive diesel engine project examined in BOI offices, Bangkok.

120. Author interview.

121. " 'National' Pick-Ups and Trucks in the Making," *BP,* April 14, 1986.

122. "Toyota Assures PM of Maximum Benefits," *Nation,* September 9, 1985.

123. In 1984 SNF acquired 75 percent equity in the Thai Industrial Forgings Co. for production of engine components. Siam Cement established a new subsidiary, Thai Engineering Products, for the production of aluminum die castings and machining of castings from SNF. The subsidiary concluded a technical cooperation agreement with Fuso Light Alloys of Japan for aluminum-casting production. See "SCG Expected to Be Largest Engine Producer," *BP,* September 9, 1985; "Siam Nawaloha Strengthens Base," *Nation,* September 13, 1985; "Siam Cement Co. Ltd." *Business Review,* May 1985, 72.

124. "IFCT Expects to Lend B3,000m by Year End," *Nation,* September 9, 1985.

125. "Tax Decisions Hit Diesel Engine Plan," *BP,* January 23, 1986; "Government Likely to Scrap Engine Project," *BP,* April 11, 1986.

126. On SNF pressure, author interviews. On motorcycles, see "BOI Sets Deadline for Engine Scheme," *BP,* May 2, 1986.

127. "Siam Cement to Produce Motorcycle Spare Parts," *World,* September 18, 1986.

128. "Isuzu Asks BOI to Aid Its Export Programme," *Nation,* December 13, 1986.

129. Nissan pledged that its Thai operation would export pickups to South Korea, Malaysia, Australia, and New Zealand as part of the company's global plan ("Siam Motors to Launch B1200m Engine Project" *BP,* October 29, 1986). Isuzu announced a three-step export plan involving first parts, then engines, and eventually the export of CBUs ("Isuzu Asks BOI to Aid Its Export Programme" and "Isuzu Unveils Ambitious Auto Export Project—Investment up to B2,000m," both in *Nation,* December 13, 1986). Isuzu also pledged to provide technical and marketing assistance for the export of brake drums and discs made by SNF to Japan; of wooden rear bodies made by another local firm, Thai Rung, to Egypt and Chile; and of auto seats made by Summit, still another local producer, to Egypt and Chile as well ("Japanese Firms to Relocate Here," *BP,* December 8, 1986). Honda pledged to shift all its manufacture of multipurpose motorcycle engines from Japan to Thailand ("Japanese Firms to Relocate Here"). And Mitsubishi pledged to export CBUs from Thailand to Canada ("Sittipon Car Exports to Begin Soon," *BP,* November 19, 1986).

130. Roscoe 1987, 75.

131. SNF is the obvious example. Another is Summit Auto Seats, a highly active TAPMA member that originally produced motorcycle seats and then moved into other components. The firm is now investing in die production in cooperation with Mitsubishi for export to Australia. See "Firms to Export Press Dies to Australia," *World,* April 4, 1986; "Auto Firm to Invest B80 Million in New Plant," *BP,* April 11, 1986; and further references in ch. 3.

132. "Car Engine Makers Get BOI Privileges," *BP*, September 26, 1987, 13.

133. See *JMB*, various issues.

134. Bennett and Sharpe 1985a.

135. "ATI Seeks Clear Cut Policy on Car Exports," *World*, September 6, 1986; "Local Content Law Must Apply for Exports as Well," *BP*, October 24, 1986.

Chapter 9

1. Cohen 1989, 48.

2. The following points draw on material presented in chs. 5–8, as well as author interviews not directly used in those chapters.

3. The same pattern, although to a lesser degree, seems true of the Liem group. The fact that it does not hold for a firm such as Thailand's Bangchan suggests that the number of allied makes provides only the potential for leverage, in the same way that interfirm competition provides host countries only with potential strength.

4. But as seen in the Philippine case, this diversification of buyers also translates into a lack of reliable financial and technical backing from the assemblers. It thus ironically also encourages parts firm support for a reduction of makes.

5. It remains to be seen whether ISI-based Malaysian parts firms will be strong enough to maintain and expand local control as plans for the Proton Saga's export proceed.

6. The methodological weaknesses of testing this argument must be acknowledged. The number of cases is limited, and none of the four countries fully conform to what I term a concertationist system. In addition, the empirical distinction between concertationist and other state-societal arrangement is not always clear. Finally, there are problems inherent in testing coalitional arguments. As Haggard notes, since "the relevant coalition is hard to identify . . . and the number of possible winning coalitions is often large . . . the temptation to post hoc analysis is particularly high" (Haggard 1988a, 95). Still, because some clearly fall closer to the concertation pole of the continuum than others, we can identify general relations between performance and concertationist arrangements at the sectoral level.

7. See Gourevitch 1986, 230, and the discussion in ch. 2.

8. My decision to eschew the label of corporatism is based in part on my excluding serious treatment of other dimensions often assumed to be part of corporatist orders, such as linkages among associations, the level of internal discipline, resources within associations, and the important role of organized labor. Second, the "state corporatism" variety of corporatism (see Schmitter 1974) connotes a degree of state leverage over societal actors that I prefer to reserve for what I term

state autonomy. The general tendency of analysts to focus on the "societal" form of corporatism suggests the utility of such a distinction. Finally, I want to avoid provoking questions as to whether certain of the processes I describe are truly "corporatist." Such discussions inevitably require the use of detailed taxonomies focusing on distinctions not critical for present purposes.

9. This passage is drawn from Schmitter's description of private interest governments in Schmitter 1985, 48.

10. See Cawson 1986, 33. On the problem of distinguishing a state's own preferences from those imposed by powerful private actors, see subsequent discussion.

11. Schmitter 1985, 49.

12. Streeck and Schmitter 1985, 21.

13. As Nordlinger notes: "To find that public officials are making public policies that derive from their own preferences is patently significant. And their doing so with societal support behind them is not necessarily less significant than their doing so in the face of societal opposition. Both intuitively and analytically, the former kind of state may be seen to be at least as 'strong' as the latter—all the more so if . . . it succeeds in . . . reinforcing . . . the beliefs of those private actors whose societal preferences converge with its own" (Nordlinger 1987, 365).

14. Cawson 1986, 76. As will be noted shortly, the concept of microcorporatism itself is a fuzzy but useful one.

15. Schmitter 1982, 263.

16. Streeck and Schmitter 1985, 15. The ability to depoliticize wage bargaining through compensation has been emphasized in this regard for the Western European cases, but as seen in the case of Japan, concertation "without Labor" can lead to similar outcomes (Pempel and Tsunekawa 1979, 25).

17. Streeck and Schmitter 1985, 15.

18. Ibid., 22. On Japan, see also Lynn and McKeown 1988 and Pempel 1978, 151. On South Korea, see Moskowitz 1984c and Cheng 1988.

19. See the information provided in ch. 6, which is supported by a personal communication from Kenosuke Ono of Keio University, Japan.

20. There was little or no personnel turnover in staff positions among those responsible for auto policy in the MOI. Wichitwong Na Pomphet's departure did not modify the staff's basic policy positions. Author interviews.

21. These institutional ties were enhanced by personal links between the TAPMA president, whose father had served in the Ministry of Industry, and MOI officials.

22. Necessary but not sufficient. Also important was a split among the assemblers.

23. Astra was a prime target of the Malari riots. But unlike Liem, it has not to my knowledge been attacked since.

24. Mackie 1988. This concept is analogous to "tacit alliances," as used by Haggard and Tun-jen Cheng 1987, 102.

25. Mackie 1988, 305.

26. Marcos's proposal for a "Philippines Inc." was reportedly suggested by one of his ghostwriters. See Villegas 1984, 11.

27. Overholt 1988.

28. Wolters 1984, 3. Note, however, that in many areas of the country, the "political leadership of the old leading families was overthrown by professional, career politicians," resulting in intense conflict as rural patrons were pressed to abdicate their traditional roles (Hawes 1987, 43, 44). The critical point is that rural power remained within an elite resistant to both national and peasant control.

29. Overholt 1986, 1138.

30. In 1969 the number of persons employed in manufacturing was approximately the same as in 1963 (Bello et al. 1982, 129).

31. Hawes 1987, 44.

32. Ongpin succeeded Paterno in 1979. *Business Day*, January 19, 1981, quoted in Broad 1988, 262–63.

33. On "constitutional authoritarianism," see Bello et al. 1982, 29, and Paterno 1973, 27.

34. Stauffer 1979, 194.

35. Sycip 1975, 4–6.

36. For a review, see Overholt 1986, 1140–41.

37. Villegas 1984, 12.

38. Hawes 1987.

39. Another is the career of Herminio Disini. Through presidential tariff exemptions, Disini monopolized the local market for tobacco filters. With Marcos's support, he obtained domestic and external funds to expand into logging, construction equipment, and construction contracts. See Aquino 1987.

40. "The Marcos Empire: Gold, Oil, Land, and Cash," *New York Times*, March 16, 1986.

41. Overholt 1986, 1146.

42. Jaime Ongpin, subsequently minister of finance in the Aquino government, cited in Ibon Databank 1983. From 1981 to 1983, corporate equity investments for bailouts by state firms, including the Philippines National Bank's support for Silverio, were the single most important government capital outlay, surpassing even infrastructure spending. The figures were 46 percent compared to 35 percent (Villegas 1984, 11).

43. Stauffer 1979, 203–4.

44. Haggard 1990.

45. *FEER*, January 1, 1982, 8–10; Overholt 1986, 1148. Policy consensus

among all technocrats should not be assumed. Those in the National Economic Development Authority (NEDA) advocated a less statist and protectionist approach than those in the Board of Investments. The latter agency was, however, the center of industrial promotion.

46. Haggard 1990.

47. Author interview.

48. Marcos and the technocrats had forced a merger of existing peak organizations resulting in a more heterogeneous and weaker group, the Philippine Chamber of Commerce and Industry. Author interviews. During the 1950s and 1960s, "rising young industrialists," dissatisfied with the mercantile orientation of the existing Chamber of Commerce of the Philippines, formed the more industrial Philippine Chamber of Commerce, as well as "various industry groupings such as the textile, cement, fertilizer and petroleum institutes" (Castro 1975, 165–66).

49. Haggard 1990.

50. Lindsey 1983, 490–92.

51. For the original concept, see Riggs 1966. On Indonesia as a bureaucratic polity, see Girling 1981. The term is also applied to Indonesia by Mackie 1988, 317.

52. Robison 1988, 73.

53. See Kahin 1952.

54. On the poor assimilation of Indonesian Chinese, see Skinner 1973 and Coppel 1983.

55. Robison 1986, 28.

56. The minister went on to say: "We needed a list of names and dollar figures of intended investments to give credence to our drive. The first mining company virtually wrote its own ticket" (Palmer 1978, 100). For a review of early investment incentives, see Hill 1988.

57. By 1978 generals, rear admirals, or air vice marshals held thirty-one of the top ninety-six departmental positions; generals filled the posts of two dozen of the country's twenty-seven governorships; and military men acted as either secretary general or inspector general under civilian ministers (David Jenkins 1978, 22).

58. Robison 1986, 28. Figures for contributions of state enterprises from McCawley 1978a, 74.

59. Also included here were government firms involved in tin mining, forestry, general mining corporations, fertilizer, steel, aluminum, banking, construction, and distribution and pricing of basic commodities (Robison 1986a, chs. 7, 8).

60. Robison 1988, 62.

61. Certain fields were closed off to new foreign investments; new investments were to be joint ventures; Indonesian equity was to be gradually raised; tax incentives were reduced and the number of foreign personnel was restricted (Hill 1988, ch. 3).

62. Robison 1988, 63.

63. Robison 1986a, 149.

64. The coalition included the director of the state oil company (Ibnu Sutowo), the leaders of a special army intelligence unit, and Chinese intellectuals associated with a think tank known as the Centre for Strategic and International Studies (CSIS). Both Soehoed and Suhartoyo had close ties to CSIS. One of CSIS's major officials is Jusuf Wanandi, brother of Sofyan Wanandi and head of one of Astra's component firms noted in ch. 6. Sofyan is reported to be the key to financial links between the Chinese business community and CSIS.

65. Indeed, one of the main proponents of state-led industrial deepening "had, by 1974, become the focal brokerage point for Japanese capital investment in Indonesia" (Robison 1986a, 156).

66. Ibid., 151. For examples of this approach, see Panglaykim 1974.

67. Although not in the sense of the Philippines discussed earlier.

68. The following discussion is drawn from MacIntyre 1988. See also Reeve 1985.

69. On Indonesia's efforts to procure Japanese funds in this manner, see Robinson 1985.

70. Pertamina borrowed heavily on the international money market to finance investments in shipping, petrochemicals, fertilizer, and steel (e.g., the Krakatau complex).

71. Liem and Sutowo's personal assistants were reportedly partners in the sale of 5,000 jeeps to the Indonesian army by Liem's Volvo agency and the Chrysler agency owned by Suharto's brother, Probosutejo and Hashim Ning (Robison 1986a, 241). The same source provides a general review of the Sutowo group (pp. 352–53).

72. McCawley 1987b.

73. Robison 1986a, 171.

74. Ibid., 196. Astra's decision to move into commercial vehicle production is noted in ch. 6.

75. Robison 1988, 65.

76. Ibid.

77. In 1982 oil prices fell from $38 to $28 per barrel, and in early 1986 slipped to $12 before moving back to $18. On the resulting declines in government oil revenues and rise in budget deficits, see Robison 1986a, 44–45.

78. Robison 1988 and MacIntyre 1988, esp. 227–28.

79. The following outline of forces draws on Robison 1988, 68–69.

80. Interviews.

81. Robison 1986a, 32–34, from which the rest of this paragraph draws as well.

82. Most of those complaining about corruption are part of the attack on industrial deepening as a policy. While the two are closely intertwined in the Indonesian case, they are not necessarily so. Collapsing the two precludes consideration of less corrupt nationalist industrializers like Astra.

83. Robison 1988, 67, 72–73.

84. Ibid., 68.

85. Financial support for the steel operation came even as the government raised electricity rates by 25 percent, claiming it could not afford to subsidize a state company (Vatikiotis 1989, 64).

86. As of 1989 Liem was reportedly trying to get rid of some of his Indonesian interests and concentrate on international operations, perhaps rebasing in Singapore (ibid.).

87. On consociationalism, see Lijphart 1969. On Malay political dominance, see Sundaram 1988, ch. 10, and Puthucheary 1978, 40–41.

88. Lim Mah Hui 1985, 45.

89. Means 1972 and Sundaram 1988, 248–49, from which the rest of this paragraph is drawn unless otherwise noted.

90. Lim Mah Hui 1985, 44.

91. On Chinese economic strength, see Sundaram 1988, 252–53. On Chinese (and Indian) domination of technical positions, see von der Mehden 1975, 260.

92. Lim Mah Hui 1985, 46. Public development expenditures rose from $4.2 billion in 1966–70 to $9.8 billion in 1971–75 an estimated $24.9 billion in 1976–80, and a projected $42.8 billion for 1981–85 (Sundaram 1988, 266).

93. *The Guardian* (Kuala Lumpur), cited in Milne and Mauzy 1978, 346.

94. The initiative for this move came from the Malaysian Chinese Association (Heng 1986, 14).

95. Halim 1982, 269. Capital outflows were estimated at M$7.57 billion in 1979 as compared to original expectations of M$2.45 billion (Ho 1979, 36–39).

96. Sundaram 1988, 264–65.

97. As minister of trade and industry and deputy prime minister (posts he held concurrently from 1977 to 1981), Mahathir had relatively free rein over industrial policy and was able to establish the basic institutions and policies linked to the heavy industries strategy. The heavy industries approach did not become the core of state economic efforts until Mahathir became prime minister in 1981. See Bowie 1988, 3, 47.

98. Between 1981 and 1986 public sector investment in the projects was roughly equal to the entire government development budget for all social programs (ibid., 2).

99. Jomo 1985b, 305–412.

100. Lim Mah Hui and Canak 1981, 220.

101. Bowie 1988, 15–16.

102. Kanapathy 1981, 10, 22.

103. Bowie 1988, 21.

104. Ibid., 22.

105. Pura 1985, 380.

106. Bowie 1988, 23.

107. In steel, a sponge-iron and steel-billet plant and a cold-rolling mill are joint ventures with Nippon Steel-led Japanese consortia. The cement plant is a joint venture with Nichirin of Japan. Motorcycle engine production involves Honda and Suzuki. The pulp and paper operation involves a French consortium. Pura 1985, 381–82.

108. Brennan 1985, 112.

109. The country relies on a handful of primary commodities such as rubber, tin, and palm oil for 60 percent of its gross exports. Clad 1984; Lim Mah Hui and Canak 1981, 220.

110. Federal debt figures from Sundaram 1987, 128. Deficit figures from *Asia Yearbook, 1982,* 197.

111. Bowie 1988, 35.

112. Sundaram 1987, 146–47.

113. Seward 1988a, 66; Duthie 1987c, 14.

114. Aznam 1988, 97, from which the rest of this paragraph is drawn.

115. Laothamatas 1989.

116. Hewison 1985, 275.

117. On Thai-ification, see Ayal 1970.

118. Skinner 1958, esp. chs. 5 and 9.

119. Skinner 1957, 255.

120. This discussion is drawn from Laothamatas 1989, ch. 2.

121. Central to this concern was the growing importance of export revenues to state finances. Government revenues from export duties rose from B3.38 million in 1944 to B170.56 million in 1950. See Ingram 1971, 185.

122. Wilson 1962, ch. 2.

123. Hewison 1985, 270.

124. On the growth of local capital, see Suehiro 1985.

125. Hewison 1985, 286.

126. Chaloemtiarana 1979.

127. Since Thailand did not experience colonization, it also did not experience the rise of an all-powerful political party or armed force in the course of an independence struggle; this left the civil bureaucracies with a full share of authority (Overholt 1988). On the military, see Ben Anderson 1977, 21. On the growth of centralized administration in response to foreign threats, see Wilson 1979, 288–89.

128. This point is emphasized in Girling 1984, 390.

129. From 1951 to 1967 Thailand received over $1 billion in U.S. economic and military assistance. By 1965 the country also received over $180 million from the World Bank, a sum accounting for roughly 10 percent of the country's first development plan. See Hewison 1987, 63–64.

130. Ben Anderson 1977.

131. Hewison 1987, 56. It is important to emphasize the persistently dominant role of domestic capital: foreign investment grew considerably in absolute terms during the 1960s, but it declined in percentage terms (ibid., 59).

132. In addition, the Third National Plan (1971) was the first of its kind to solicit information and opinions from business associations (Laothamatas 1989, ch. 2, p. 22).

133. Ibid., 21, 26, from which information on business participation in NESDB meetings is also drawn.

134. Hewison 1987, 56.

135. Laothamatas 1989, ch. 2. p. 27.

136. Ibid., ch. 6, p. 14.

137. Thailand's trade deficit jumped from $60 million in 1976 to $114 million in 1977 (*Asia Year Book, 1979*, 313).

138. Laothamatas 1989, ch. 7, p. 25.

139. A summary of these developments is to be found in Laothamatas 1988, from which the rest of this and the following paragraph is drawn.

140. According to the head of the NESDB, Thailand's increased export emphasis "is to a great extent the result of meticulous work by business representatives in the national JPPCC" (ibid., 462).

141. The same Swiss firm was hired to take over Philippine customs during Marcos's last years. Unlike in Indonesia, however, vested Philippine interests succeeded in limiting the range of goods and countries of origins under the firm's jurisdiction. I am indebted to Gary Hawes for this information.

142. Laothamatas 1989, ch. 5, p. 38.

143. Overholt 1988, 7. For a similar perspective, see Mackie 1988, 303.

144. The country's trade deficit rose from 6 percent of GNP in 1977 to 8.3 percent in 1979 and 8.6 percent in 1980 (Laothamatas 1989, ch. 2, p. 36). The budget deficit rose from B8,114 million in 1975 to B18,511 million in 1980. Thai government figures cited in Hewison 1987, 68.

145. Laothamatas 1989, ch. 6, p. 15.

146. Ibid.

147. The roles of both these men in promoting the joint public-private committee are discussed in ibid., ch. 6, p. 14.

148. The conflict between the more "free-market" backers of export promotion and those based in import substitution is highly complex and unresolved as of this writing. For an account, see Hewison 1987.

149. Handley 1989, 71.

150. "Within the civil bureaucracy, on vital policy issues technocratic calculations outweigh patronage issues" (Overholt 1988, 46).

151. Johnson 1987, 152.

152. The first quotation is from Overholt 1988, 8; the second is from "Holding Back the Private Sector," *Economist*, October 31, 1987, 9. It is, of course, possible that Thai economic success is the result of other factors, such as natural resources, historical circumstances, and "getting the prices right." But Thailand's natural resources do not differ significantly from those of its ASEAN neighbors. Varying historical circumstances, such as Thailand's particular experiences with colonial powers, are clearly important. But such conditions are best understood as background variables promoting particular types of state-society linkages (for an analogous argument, see the discussion of how early or late industrialization help account for policy networks in the advanced industrialized states in Katzenstein 1978a, "Conclusion"). Finally, "getting the prices right" requires a particular arrangement of interests that is no more natural than an arrangement leading to market failure.

153. Thailand's growth rate rate was 5.2 percent, compared to rates of 0.5 to 4.2 percent for the other ASEAN countries (Bowring 1987, 69). Foreign investment as a percentage of manufacturing value-added in 1978 was 5 percent for Thailand, compared to 13 percent for Indonesia (1977), 17 percent for Malaysia (1977), and 9 percent for the Philippines (1978) (Hill 1988, 49). For more anecdotal accounts of the strength of Thai capital, see the numerous articles by Philip Bowring and Paul Handley in *FEER*, various issues, 1987–88.

Chapter 10

1. Evans 1989, 210. For an earlier elaboration, see Moran 1978.

2. Haggard 1986.

3. On the role of local capital, see Evans 1979, ch. 3. On the broader sources of the tendency to downgrade Third World entrepreneurs, see Harris 1988.

4. Evans 1985, 206.

5. See, e.g., the discussion of the role of business groups in Johnson 1987, 160–62.

6. Haggard and Cheng 1987, 102.

7. "Import-substitution in the Third World usually has deep political roots,

while those efficient firms which could be internationally competitive are unaware of the fact, and thus politically 'unavailable' to act as a counterweight to inward-looking policies" (Haggard 1988b, 264).

8. Mackie 1988, 293.

9. Kohli 1986.

10. On state origins, see Cumings 1984 and Haggard and Cheng 1987.

11. Deyo 1987a, 243–44.

12. On this shift, see Cheng 1988.

13. Warren 1980.

14. Harris 1988. See also Evans 1979, ch. 3.

15. Binder 1986, 17.

16. Government planners were "groping, learning about market conditions" and endorsing the traditional measures of ISI in cement and fertilizer along with exports of primary goods. Private exporters took the initiative in exporting unskilled labor-intensive products in which Korea had a comparative advantage. In the process, government planners learned the necessity for flexibility and "market augmenting" planning. See Kim Youngil 1981, 18.

17. Evans 1987a, 211–12.

18. For other cases of increasing or decreasing autonomy, see Hamilton 1982, Pempel and Tsunekawa 1979, and Amsden 1985. Variation of autonomy by industry is reflected in the literature on the Japanese state's role in various economic sectors. See, e.g., Samuels 1987 and Friedman 1988. On autonomy by issue, see Encarnation 1979.

19. Harris 1988, 247.

20. Becker 1988, 7.

21. For Harris, support involves maintaining exchange rates, making available public sector assets, and allowing the market to select directions of growth rather than imposing other priorities. This is not a laissez-faire strategy, but "an external market-oriented opportunism which does not at all exclude important elements of protection" (Harris 1988, 238–39).

22. Sklar 1976 and Becker 1988, 5.

23. I find too general the assertion in Sklar 1976 that a "corporate doctrine of domicile" will lead TNC subsidiaries to comply with host country policies and thereby reconcile corporate group interests and those of the host country.

24. Cumings 1984.

25. This was clearly important in the Philippines, Thailand, and South Korea. On Thailand, see Ben Anderson 1977. On South Korea, see Moskowitz 1984b, 15–16.

26. For a discussion of these issues in the context of U.S.–South Korean rela-

tions, see Moskowitz 1984c and Lee 1984. On support provided by private U.S. organizations for Thai business associations, see Laothamatas 1988.

27. See the references to this research in ch. 2.

28. Krasner 1985, 58.

29. Samuels 1987, 292, and see pp. 8–9 for an elaboration of the concept of reciprocal consent.

30. Ibid., 9.

INTERVIEWEES

The positions listed below are those the interviewees had held relevant to the automobile industry, not necessarily the ones held at the time of the interviews.

Japan

Fumihiko Adachi	Faculty of Economics, Nanzan University
Takeshi Fukuda	Toyota Motor Corp.
Ryozo Fukushiro	Mitsubishi Motors Corp.
Koji Hasegawa	Toyota Motor Corp.
Ryokichi Hirono	Department of Economics, Seikei University
Hiroshi Karu	Japan Committee for Economic Development
Hiroshi Kakehi	Proton
Kanichi Inoue	Toyota Motor Corp.
Kiyohiko Miura	Toyota Tokyo Corolla Co.
Tatsuaki Mohri	Nissho Iwai Corp.
Konosuke Odaka	Hitotsubashi University
Keichi Oguru	Japan External Trade Organization
Torajiro Ohashi	Hino Motors, Ltd.
Keinosuke Ono	Graduate School of Business Administration, Keio University
Shiro Saito	Nissan Motor Co.
Toshio Sasaki	Honda Motor Co.
Shinji Shimabara	Toyota Motor Corp.
Akira Suehiro	Institute of Developing Economies
Takeo Takemi	Honda Motor Corp.
Setsuo Tanaka	Nissan Motor Co.
Teruji Tsuji	Japan–ASEAN Investment Co.
Shozo Uchio	Nissan Motor Co.
Shigehira Yoshioka	Japan Automobile Manufacturers Association (JAMA)

Thailand

Kanokphan Chancharaswat	Industrial Economics and Planning Division, Ministry of Industry
Narongchai Akrasanee	Industrial Finance Corporation of Thailand
Chira Panuphong	Board of Investments
Saneh Chamarik	Department of Political Science, Thammasat University
Vichit Chantracharoen	Yontrakit Motor Co.
Saroj Dhitikiatipong	Siam Nawaloha Foundry Co.
Jakamon	NESDB
Sitachai Jeeratanyaskul	Toyota Motor Thailand Co.
Kyoichi Kazizaki	Nissan Motor Co. (Thailand)
Sadahiro Koshimizu	Nissan Motor Co. (Thailand)
Wichitwong Na Pomphet	Chief, Department of Industrial Economics, Ministry of Industry
Siriboon Nawadhinsukh	Economics Department, Thammasat University
K. Nagura	Toyota Motor Thailand Co.
Yukitoshi Ooi	Thai Hino Motor Sales, Ltd.
Noppadon Pimonmarn	Auto Parts Industries Co.
Ajarin Sarasas	Thai Hino Industry Co.
Ichiro Sato	Toyota Motor Thailand Co.
Suriyan Setthasawad	Toyota Motor Thailand Co.
Lek Sindusopon	Pressure Container Industry Co., TAPMA
Prakitti Siripraiwan	Thai Radiator Mfg Co., TAPMA
Takeshi Takahashi	Toyota Motor Thailand Co.
Suchart Uthaiwat	Summit Auto Seats Industry Co., TAPMA
Kauee Vasuwat	Siam Motors, Association of Thai Industries
Vicharat Vichit-Vadakan	Bangkok Nomura International Securities

Philippines

Lillia Bautista	Board of Investments
Caesar B. Cororaton	Center for Research and Communications
Victor O. David	RFM Corp., CAPPA
Ceferino Follosco	Ford Philippines
George Francisco	Francisco Motors
Hilarion Henares	National Economic Council
Harry Hoffman	Carco (Mitsubishi)
Kazuo Kobayashi	Carco (Mitsubishi)
Arturo R. Macapagal	Delta
Danny Maling	Honda Philippines, Inc.
Vincente T. Mills	Pilipinas Hino, Inc.
Fernando A. Ramillano	P and R Parts

Carlos D. Sazon   Delta Motors and Ford (Philippines)
David Sycip   Northern Motors (GM)
Quintin Tan   Ministry of Trade and Industry
Angelo Tonson   Delta
Bernardo Villegas   Center for Research and Communications

Indonesia

James W. Castle   Business Advisory Indonesia
Bruce Glassburner   Associate, Agricultural Development Council
                           (Bogor, Indonesia)
Ir. Ridwan Gunawan   Operations Director, PT Federal Motor (Astra)
Irawan Ibrahim   Agency for Research and Application of Tech-
                           nology (BPPT)
A. Kemal Idris   President, Griyawisata Hotel Corp., former
                           Kostrad member
Hitoshi Imamura   Export Department, Asia and Australia, Nissan
                           Motor Co.
Jeffrey C. Jones   Arthur Young International
J. R. Koesman   Director, PT Panaragan Motors (Hino/Mazda)
Dorodjatun Kuntjoro-Jakti Faculty of Economics, University of Indonesia
Sisdjiatmo Ksumusuwidho   Assistant to Finance Director, PT Federal Motor
                           (Astra)
Franklin J. Kline   Managing Director, PT Sarna Komputer Utama
Soebronto Laras   President Director, PT Indo Mobil Utama;
                           GAAKINDO
A. Noor Luddin   PT Menamas
Ir. Rudyanto   Vice President, PT Toyota-Astra Motor
Mohammad Sadli   Secretary General, Indonesian Chamber of Com-
                           merce and Industry (KADIN Indonesia)
Peter Senger   Director, Finance and Administration, PT Star
                           Engines Indonesia
Ir. Soehoed   Minister of Industry
Ir. Suhartoyo   Minister of Industry and Chairman of BKPM
Ir. Rikiyanto Tanamas   Technology Development Division Manager,
                           Astra
Thee Kian Wie   Senior Research Associate, National Research
                           Council

Malaysia

Darwis Bin Mohd. Daek   Malaysian Industrial Development Finance
John Berthelsen   *Asian Wall Street Journal*
Chua Eng Seng   Malaysian Industrial Development Authority
                           (MIDA)

Chee Peng Lim	Faculty of Economics, University of Malaya
Abdul Muis Hassan	Malaysian Industrial Development Finance
Johnny Hoo	UMW Auto Parts
Phillip Khoo	Cycle and Carriage, Inc.
Joseph Ling	Sejati Motors (UMW Toyota)
Paul Low	Malaysian Sheet Glass, MACPMA
Kol Mohamad Bin Munip	Proton
Shohei Nishimoto	Sejati Motors (UMW Toyota)
M. T. S. Phung	Heavy Industries Corporation of Malaysia (HICOM)
Raphael Pura	*Asian Wall Street Journal*
A. B. Sim	Sejati Motors (UMW Toyota)
Mohd. Noordin Sopiee	Institute of Strategic and International Studies, Malaysia
Jomo Sundaram	Faculty of Economics, Universiti Malaya
Ghazali Bin Dato' Yusoff	Automotive Federation of Malaysia

REFERENCES

All references cited in the notes are included below, with the exception of anonymous newspaper and magazine articles.

Abegglen, James C., and George Stalk, Jr. 1985. *Kaisha: The Japanese Corporation*. New York: Basic Books.
Adachi Fumihiko. 1985. "Trade, Growth and International Economic Conflicts." University of Nagoya. Photocopy.
Adler, Emanuel. 1986. "Ideological 'Guerrillas' and the Quest for Technological Autonomy: Brazil's Domestic Computer Industry." *International Organization* 40 (Summer): 673–705.
Allen, T. W. 1979. *The ASEAN Report*. Hong Kong: *AWSJ*.
Altshuler, Alan, Martin Anderson, Daniel Jones, Daniel Roos, and James Womack. 1984. *The Future of the Automobile: The Report of MIT's International Automobile Program*. Cambridge, Mass.: MIT Press.
Amsden, Alice. 1985. "The State and Taiwan's Economic Development." In Evans et al., eds., *Bringing the State Back In*.
Amsden, Alice, and Linsu Kim. 1985. "The Role of Transnational Corporations in the Production and Exports of the Korean Automobile Industry." Working paper. Boston: Harvard University Graduate School of Business Administration.
Anderson, Ben. 1977. "Withdrawal Symptoms: Social and Cultural Aspects of the October 6 Coup." *Bulletin of Concerned Asian Scholars* 9 (July–September): 13–30.
Anderson, Martin. 1982. "Financial Restructuring of the World Auto Industry." Cambridge, Mass.: Future of the Automobile Program, MIT.
Aquino, Belinda. 1987. *The Politics of Plunder: The Philippines under Marcos*. Occasional Paper no. 87–1. Manila: University of the Philippines, College of Public Administration.
Asian Business and Industry. Various issues.
Asian Development Bank (Manila). *Key Indicators of Developing Member Countries of ADB*. Various years.

343

Asia Yearbook (Hong Kong). Various issues.

Association of Thai Industries [ATI]. 1986. *Newsletter,* no. 2.

———. Parts Producers' Club. 1987. *Newsletter,* no. 2.

Astbury, Sid. 1982. "Jakarta's First Contender for International Stardom." *Asian Business,* June.

———. 1984. "Indonesia Travels a Local Road." *Asian Business,* September.

Atarashi, Kinju. 1984–85. "Japan's Economic Cooperation Policy toward the ASEAN Countries." *International Affairs* 61 (Winter): 109–27.

Automobile Development Committee [ADC]. 1984. "Saphawa pachupan leh neew thang anakhot khong udsahakam yan yon" (Present conditions and future trends of the motor industry). Ministry of Industry, Bangkok.

Automotive Federation of Malaysia [AFM]. 1984. "Submission of AFM on the Industrial Master Plan." Organizational Resources Sdn. Bhd., Kuala Lumpur.

Automotive Manufacturers' Institute, Inc. [AMII]. *Annual Report.* Various years.

———. 1976. "Progressive Car Manufacturing Program 1976." Manila: AMII.

Awanohara Susumu. 1979. "Japan's Cautious Look at Thailand." *FEER,* June 15.

———. 1983. "Nissan Hails a Cab." *FEER,* March 3.

Ayal, Eliezer B. "Thailand." In Golay et al., eds., *Underdevelopment and Economic Nationalism.*

Aznam, Suhaini. 1988. "New Man at the Wheel? Malaysia Looks to Japan for Help at Proton." *FEER,* July 7.

Baldwin, David. 1979. "Power Analysis and World Politics: New Trends versus Old Tendencies." *World Politics* 31 (January): 161–94.

Bangkok Bank. *Bangkok Bank Monthly Review.* Various issues.

Bannock, Graham. 1985. "The Motor Industry and Its Massive Investment Requirements." London: Economist Intelligence Unit.

Bauer, Peter. 1976. *Dissent on Development.* Cambridge, Mass.: Harvard University Press.

Becker, David. 1983. *The New Bourgeoisie and the Limit of Dependency: Mining, Class, and Power in "Revolutionary" Peru.* Princeton: Princeton University Press.

———. 1988. "Business Associations in Latin America: The Venezuelan Case." Paper presented at the Annual Meeting of the American Political Science Association, Washington, D.C., September 1–4.

Bello, Walden, David Kinley, and Elaine Elinson. 1982. *Development Debacle: The World Bank in the Philippines.* San Francisco: Institute for Food and Development Policy.

Bennett, Douglas C., and Kenneth E. Sharpe. 1979. "Agenda Setting and Bargaining Power: The Mexican State vs. the Transnational Automobile Corporations." *World Politics* 32: 57–89.

———. 1985a. *Transnational Corporations versus the State: The Political Economy of the Mexican Auto Industry.* Princeton: Princeton University Press.

———. 1985b. "The World Automobile Industry and Its Implications." In Newfarmer, ed., *Profits, Progress and Poverty.*

Bennett, Mark. 1986. *Public Policy and Industrial Development: The Case of the Mexican Auto Parts Industry.* Boulder, Colo.: Westview Press.

Bergsten, Fred, Thomas Horst, and Theodore H. Moran, eds. 1978. *American Multinationals and American Interests.* Washington, D.C.: Brookings Institution.

Berthelsen, John. 1985. "Malaysian Car's Success Is Mixed Boon." *AWSJ* December 19.

Bhatia, V. G. 1988. "Asian and Pacific Developing Economies: Performance and Issues." *Asian Development Review* 6, no. 1: 1–21.

Binder, Leonard. 1986. "The Natural History of Development Theory." *Comparative Studies in Society and History* 28 (January): 3–33.

Bittlingmayer, George. 1983. *World Auto Demand.* Ann Arbor: Joint U.S.–Japan Automotive Study.

Borden, William S. 1984. *The Pacific Alliance: United States Foreign Economic Policy and Japanese Trade Recovery, 1947–1955.* Madison: University of Wisconsin Press.

Bowie, Alasdair. 1988. "Industrial Aspirations in a Divided Society: Malaysian Heavy Industries, 1980–1988." Paper presented at the Annual Meeting of the Association for Asian Studies, San Francisco, March 25–27.

Bowring, Philip. 1987. "While Others Falter." *FEER*, June 25.

BPPT [Agency for Research and Application of Technology] / SRI [Stanford Research Institute]. 1979. "Strategic Plan for the Indonesian Automotive Industry." Jakarta.

———. 1982. "Rationalization of the Indonesian Automotive Industry." Jakarta.

Bradford, Colin. 1986. "East Asian Models: Myths and Lessons." In John P. Lewis and Valeriana Kallab, eds., *Development Strategies Reconsidered.* New Brunswick, N.J.: Transaction Books.

Brannigan, William. 1985. "Dissidents Once Suharto's Comrades." *Sunday Star* (Kuala Lumpur), October 20.

Brennan, Martin. 1985. "Class, Politics and Race In Modern Malaysia." In Higgott and Robison, eds., *Southeast Asia.*

Broad, Robin. 1988. *Unequal Alliance: The World Bank, the International Monetary Fund, and the Philippines.* Berkeley: University of California Press.

Calton, Jerry M., and Gunter Krumme. 1984. "The Political Economy of U.S.–Japanese Automotive Competition." In Moxon et al., eds., *International Business Strategies* (Part B).

Campbell, Burnham O. 1987. "Asian and Pacific Developing Economies: Performance and Issues." *Asian Development Review* 5, no. 1:1–43.

Castro, Amado A. 1975. "Import Substitution in the Philippines, 1954–1961: A Historical Interpretation." In Nagatoshi Suzuki, ed., *Asian Industrial Development.* Tokyo: Institute of Developing Economies.

Cawson, Alan. 1986. *Corporatism and Political Theory.* London: Basil Blackwell.

Chaloemtiarana, Thak. 1979. *Thailand: The Politics of Despotic Paternalism.* Bangkok: Thai Kadi Research Institute.

Chalmers, Ian. 1983. "The Third World State: Epicentre or Epiphenomenon? The Motor Vehicle Industry in Indonesia." Paper presented at the Annual Meeting of the Australian Political Science Association, August.

———. 1988. "Economic Nationalism and the Third World State: The Political Economy of the Indonesian Automotive Industry, 1950–1984." Ph.D. diss., Australian National University.

Chan, Paul. 1984. "Economics of Regulation in Malaysia with Reference to the Motor Vehicle and Component Industry." University of Malaya, Kuala Lumpur. Photocopy.

Chee Teoh Chew. 1988. "MMC's Winning Design." *The Investor* (Kuala Lumpur), mid-November.

Cheng Tun-Jen. 1988. "Business Interest Associations in Export-Oriented Industrializing Economies: Theoretical Observations and a Korean Case Study." Paper presented at the Annual Meeting of the American Political Science Association, Washington, D.C., September 1–4.

Clad, James. 1984a. "The Profit of the East." *FEER*, June 14.

———. 1984b. "Off the Road, into Orbit." *FEER*, June 28.

———. 1985a. "Captain of Industry." *FEER*, February 14.

———. 1985b. "The Proton in a Nuclear Automobile Family." *FEER*, February 14.

Cohen, Margot. 1989. "The Car Cartel." *FEER*, April 20.

Cole, Robert E., and Richard P. Hervey. 1984. *Internationalization of the Auto Industry: Its Meaning and Significance*. Ann Arbor: University of Michigan Joint U.S.–Japan Automotive Study.

Cole, Robert E., and Taizo Yakushiji, eds. 1984. *The American and Japanese Auto Industries in Transition: Report of the Joint U.S.–Japan Automotive Study*. Ann Arbor: University of Michigan, Center for Japanese Studies.

Coppel, Charles A. 1983. *Indonesian Chinese in Crisis*. Kuala Lumpur: Oxford University Press.

Coronil, Fernando, and Julie Skurski. 1982. "Reproducing Dependency: Auto Industry Policy and Petrodollar Circulation in Venezuela." *International Organization* 36 (Winter): 61–94.

Cororaton, Cesar B. 1984. "Can We Still Crank Up Our Automotive Industry?" Staff memo. Manila: Centre for Research and Communication.

Cowhey, Peter F., and Edward Long. 1983. "Testing Theories of Regime Change: Hegemonic Decline or Surplus Capacity." *International Organization* 37 (Spring): 157–83.

Crone, Donald K. 1983. *The ASEAN States: Coping with Dependence*. New York: Praeger.

———. 1988. "State, Social Elites, and Government Capacity in Southeast Asia." *World Politics* 15 (January): 252–68.

Cumings, Bruce. 1984. "The Origins and Development of the Northeast Asian Political Economy: Industrial Sectors, Product Cycles and Political Consequences." *International Organization* 38 (Winter): 1–40.

Cusumano, Michael A. 1985. *The Japanese Automobile Industry: Technology and Management at Nissan and Toyota*. Cambridge, Mass.: Harvard University, Council on East Asian Studies.

Dankbaar, Ben. 1984. "Maturity and Relocation in the Car Industry." *Development and Change* 15 (September): 223–50.

Deyo, Frederic C. 1987a. "Coalitions, Institutions and Linkage Sequencing—Toward a Strategic Capacity Model of East Asian Development." In Deyo, ed., *Political Economy*.

———, ed. 1987b. *The Political Economy of the New Asian Industrialism*. Ithaca: Cornell University Press.

Dodwell Marketing Consultants. 1984. *The Japanese Auto Parts Industry*. Tokyo: Dodwell Marketing Consultants.

Dominguez, Jorge I. 1982. "Business Nationalism: Latin American Business Attitudes and Behavior toward Multinational Enterprises." In Jorge I. Dominguez, ed., *Economic Issues and Political Conflict: U.S.–Latin American Relations*. London: Butterworth Scientific.

Doran, Charles F., George Modelski, and Cal Clark, eds. 1983. *North/South Relations: Studies in Dependency Reversal*. New York: Praeger.

Drucker, Peter F. 1985. "Multinationals and Developing Countries: Myths and Realities." In John Adams, ed., *The Contemporary International Economy: A Reader*. New York: St. Martin's Press.

Drysdale, Peter. 1986. "The Pacific Basin and Its Economic Vitality." In James W. Morley, ed., *The Pacific Basin: New Challenges for the United States*. New York: Academy of Political Science.

Duffey, Gunter. 1984. "Banking in the Asia-Pacific Region." In Moxon et al., eds., *International Business Strategies*.

Duncan, William C. 1973. *U.S.–Japan Automobile Diplomacy: A Study in Economic Confrontation*. Cambridge, Mass.: Ballinger Publishing.

Dunn, James. 1978. "Automobiles in International Trade: Regime Change or Persistence?" *International Organization* 41 (Spring): 225–52.

Duthie, Stephen. 1987a. "Malaysia Is Preparing Its National Car for an American Debut Next November." *AWSJ*, November 23.

———. 1987b. "Bricklin Unit Wins U.S. Rights to Proton Saga." *AWSJ*, November 30.

———. 1987c. "Malaysia's Hicom Reports Heavy Losses for Fiscal Year." *AWSJ*, December 28.

Eckstein, Harry. 1975. "Case Study and Theory in Political Science." In Fred I. Greenstein and Nelson W. Polsby, eds., *Strategies of Inquiry*, vol. 7 of Greenstein and Polsby, eds., *Handbook of Political Science*, 79–137. Reading, Mass.: Addison-Wesley.

Economist Intelligence Unit [EIV]. 1984. *International Motor Business*, no. 120 (4th quarter).

———. 1985. *The ASEAN Motor Industry*. London: *The Economist*.

————. 1987. "Thailand: Japan's Components Satellite?" *JMB*, no. 12 (June): 36–45.

————. *Japanese Motor Business* [*JMB*]. Various issues.

Elsbree, Willard, and Khong Kim Hoong. 1985. "Japan and ASEAN." In Robert S. Ozaki and Walter Arnold, eds., *Japan's Foreign Relations: A Global Search for Economic Security*. Boulder, Colo.: Westview Press.

Enami Kimio and Yuichi Takayama. 1976. "The Role of Motor Vehicles in the Countries of Southeast-Asia." *The Wheel Extended* (Tokyo: Toyota Motor Corp.).

Encarnation, Dennis J. 1979. "The Indian Central Bureaucracy: Responsiveness to Whom." *Asian Survey* 19 (November): 1126–45.

————. 1989. *Dislodging Multinationals: India's Strategy in Comparative Perspective*. Ithaca: Cornell University Press.

Encarnation, Dennis J., and Louis T. Wells, Jr. 1985. "Sovereignty en Garde: Negotiating with Foreign Investors." *International Organization* 39 (Winter): 47–78.

Evans, Peter B. 1977. "Direct Investment and Industrial Concentration." *Journal of Development Studies* 13 (July): 373–86.

————. 1979. *Dependent Development: The Alliance of Multinational, State, and Local Capital in Brazil*. Princeton: Princeton University Press.

————. 1982. "Reinventing the Bourgeoisie: State Entrepreneurship and Class Formation in Dependent Capitalist Development." *American Journal of Sociology* 88 (Supplement): S210–S247.

————. 1985. "Transnational Linkages and the Economic Role of the State: An Analysis of Developing and Industrialized Nations in the Post-World War II Period." In Evans et al., eds., *Bringing the State Back In*.

————. 1986. "State, Capital, and the Transformation of Dependence: The Brazilian Computer Case." *World Development* 14 (August): 791–808.

————. 1987a. "Class, State and Dependence in East Asia: Lessons for Latin Americanists." In Deyo, ed., *The Political Economy*.

————. 1987b. "Foreign Capital and the Third World State." In Weiner and Huntingon, eds., *Understanding Political Development*.

————. 1989. "Declining Hegemony and Assertive Industrialization: U.S.–Brazilian Conflicts in the Computer Industry." *International Organization* 43 (Spring): 207–38.

Evans, Peter B., Dietrich Rueschemeyer, and Theda Skocpol, eds. 1985. *Bringing the State Back In*. New York: Cambridge University Press.

Fagre, Nathan, and Louis T. Wells, Jr. 1982. "Bargaining Power of Multinationals and Host Governments." *Journal of International Business Studies*, Fall, 9–23.

Fish, Peter. 1978. "Children the Key to Thai Integration." *FEER*, June 16.

Fleet, Mark. 1978. "Host Country–Multinational Relations in the Colombian Automobile Industry." *Interamerican Economic Affairs* 32 (Summer): 3–32.

Follosco, Ceferino. 1985. "Developing the Engineering and Metalworking Industries in the Philippines." Paper presented at the Symposium on Engineering Industries, Manila, April 25. Photocopy.

Francia, Julio B. 1971. "Hard Realities for Philippines Industry." *Industrial Philippines,* July.

Friedland, Jonathan. 1988. "An Engine of Growth." *FEER,* November 17.

Friedman, David. 1983. "Beyond the Age of Ford: The Strategic Basis of the Japanese Success in Automobiles." In John Zysman and Laura Tyson, eds., *American Industry in International Competition: Government Policies and Corporate Strategies.* Ithaca: Cornell University Press.

———. 1988. *The Misunderstood Miracle: Industrial Development and Political Change in Japan.* Ithaca: Cornell University Press.

Galang, Jose. 1988. "Just Ticking Over." *FEER,* June 9.

Genther, Phyllis Ann. 1986. "The Changing Government-Business Relationship: Japan's Passenger Car Industry." Ph.D. diss., George Washington University.

Gereffi, Gary. 1983. *The Pharmaceutical Industry and Dependency in the Third World.* Princeton: Princeton University Press.

Gereffi, Gary, and Richard Newfarmer. 1985. "International Oligopoly and Uneven Development: Some Lessons from Industrial Case Studies." In Newfarmer, ed., *Profits, Progress, and Poverty.*

Ghazali Bin Dato Yusoff. 1985. "Keynote Address." Speech to the Automotive Federation of Malaysia, Kuala Lumpur, July 2.

Gilpin, Robert. 1987. *The Political Economy of International Relations.* Princeton: Princeton University Press.

Girling, John L. S. 1981. *The Bureaucratic Polity in Modernizing Societies: Similarities, Differences and Prospects in the ASEAN Region.* Singapore: Institute of Southeast Asian Studies.

———. 1984. "Thailand in Gramscian Perspective." *Pacific Affairs,* Fall, 385–403.

Golay, Frank. 1970. "The Philippines." In Golay et al., eds., *Underdevelopment and Economic Nationalism in Southeast Asia.*

Golay, Frank, Ralph Anspach, and Ruth Farmer, eds. 1970. *Underdevelopment and Economic Nationalism in Southeast Asia.* Ithaca: Cornell University Press.

Goldstein, Carl. 1988. "Manufacturers See a Future Outside Japan." *FEER,* October 13.

———. 1989. "Saga of Recovery." *FEER,* August 3.

Goodman, Louis W. 1987. *Small Nations, Giant Firms.* New York: Holmes & Meier.

Goodsell, Charles. 1974. *American Corporations and Peruvian Politics.* Cambridge, Mass.: Harvard University Press.

Gourevitch, Peter A. 1986. *Politics in Hard Times: Comparative Responses to International Economic Crises.* Ithaca: Cornell University Press.

Gray, Clyve S. 1982. "Survey of Recent Developments." *BIES* 18 (November): 1–51.

Grieco, Joseph M. 1984. *Between Dependency and Autonomy: India's Experience with the International Computer Industry.* Berkeley: University of California Press.
————. 1986. "Foreign Investment and Development: Theories and Evidence." In Theodore Moran, ed., *Investing in Development: New Roles for Private Capital.* Washington, D.C.: Overseas Development Council.
Haggard, Stephan. 1986. "The Newly Industrializing Countries in the International System." *World Politics* 38 (January): 343–70.
————. 1988a. "The Institutional Foundations of Hegemony: Explaining the Reciprocal Trade Agreements Act of 1934." *International Organization* 42 (Winter).
————. 1988b. "The Politics of Industrialization in the Republic of Korea and Taiwan." In Hughes, ed., *Achieving Industrialization.*
————. 1989. "The Political Economy of Foreign Direct Investment in Latin America." *Latin American Research Review* 24:184–208.
————. 1990. "The Political Economy of the Philippine Debt Crisis." In Joan Nelson, ed., *Economic Crisis and Policy Choice: The Politics of Adjustment in Developing Countries.* Princeton: Princeton University Press.
Haggard, Stephan, and Tun-jen Cheng. 1987. "State and Foreign Capital in the Asian NICs." In Deyo, ed., *Political Economy.*
Halim, Fatimah. 1982. "Capital, Labour and the State: The West Malaysian Case." *Journal of Contemporary Asia* 12:259–80.
Hamilton, Clive. 1984. "Can the Rest of Asia Emulate the NICs?" *Third World Quarterly* 9, no. 4 (October): 1225–56.
Hamilton, Nora. 1982. *The Limits of State Autonomy: Post-Revolutionary Mexico.* Princeton: Princeton University Press.
Handley, Paul. 1988a. "Share and Share Alike." *FEER,* January 28.
————. 1988b. "Long Road to Success." *FEER,* January 28.
————. 1988c. "Engineering Trained Workers." *FEER,* September 29.
————. 1989. "A Planner Quits." *FEER,* May 4.
Hansen, J. F. 1971. "The Motor Vehicle Industry." *Bulletin of Indonesian Economic Studies* 7, no. 2 (July): 38–69.
Harris, Nigel. 1988. "New Bourgeoisies?" *Journal of Development Studies* 24 (January): 237–49.
Hawes, Gary. 1987. *The Philippine State and the Marcos Regime: The Politics of Export.* Ithaca: Cornell University Press.
Heng Pek Koon. 1986. "Chinese Business Elites of Malaysia." Paper presented at the Social Science Research Council Conference on Industrializing Elites in Southeast Asia, Sukhothai (Thailand), December 9–12.
Hewison, Kevin. 1985. "The State and Capitalist Development in Thailand." In Higgott and Robison, eds., *Southeast Asia.*
————. 1987. "National Interests and Economic Downturn: Thailand." In Robison et al., eds., *Southeast Asia in the 1980s.*
Higgott, Richard, and Richard Robison, eds. 1985. *Southeast Asia: Essays in the Political Economy of Structural Change.* London: Routledge & Kegan Paul.
Hill, Hal. 1984a. "High Time for High Tech—Or Is It." *FEER,* July 12.

———. 1984b. "Survey of Recent Developments." *BIES* 20 (August): 1–38.

———. 1988. *Foreign Investment and Industrialization in Indonesia*. New York: Oxford University Press.

Hirono Ryokichi. 1988. "Japan: Model for East Asian Industrialization?" In Hughes, ed., *Achieving Industrialization in East Asia*.

Ho Kwon Ping. 1979. "Savouring the Sweet Smell of Oil." *FEER*, April 13.

———. 1980. "The Price of Credibility." *FEER*, December 12.

———. 1981. "Thailand Faces a Hard Choice." *FEER*, February 13.

Hock, William. 1983. "Policy Proposals for the Restructuring of the Automobile Industry in Thailand." Industrial Management Co., Bangkok. Photocopy.

Hong Moong-Shin. 1987. "Competition between NICs and ASEAN." In *East Asia: International Review of Economic, Political and Social Development*. Boulder, Colo.: Westview Press.

Hood, Neil, and Stephen Young. 1985. "The Automobile Industry." In Stephen E. Guisinger and associates, *Investment Incentives and Performance Requirements: Patterns of International Trade, Production, and Investment*. New York: Praeger.

Hughes, Helen, ed. 1988. *Achieving Industrialization in East Asia*. New York: Cambridge University Press, 1988.

Ibon Databank (Manila). 1983. "State in Distressed Business." *Ibon Facts and Figures* 118 (July 14): 1–8.

Ikema Makato. 1980. "Japan's Economic Relations with ASEAN." In Ross Garnaut, ed., *ASEAN in Changing Pacific and World Economy*. Canberra: Australian University Press.

Indonesian Commercial News [ICN]. Various issues.

Indonesia. Ministry of Industry [MOI]. 1979. "Decree of the Ministry of Industry No. 168/M/SK/9/1978." Jakarta: MOI. Mimeographed.

———. 1982. *Development of Basic and Key Industries in Indonesia*. Jakarta: MOI.

———. 1983. "Decree of Minister of Industry, No. 371/M/SK/9/1983 re the Obligation to Use Local Components in the Commercial Assembling Car [*sic*]." Jakarta: MOI. Mimeo.

Industrial Finance Corporation of Thailand [IFCT]. *Annual Reports*. Various years.

Ingram, James C. 1971. *Economic Change in Thailand, 1850–1970*. Stanford: Stanford University Press.

Ithijarakun, Suchada, ed. 1977. *Manufacturing in Thailand*. Bangkok: Business Information and Research.

James, William E., Seiji Naya, and Gerald M. Meier. 1989. *Asian Development: Economic Success and Policy Lessons*. Madison: University of Wisconsin Press.

Japan Automobile Manufacturers' Association [JAMA]. *Motor Vehicle Statistics of Japan*. Various years.

———. 1983. *The Automotive Industry in Developing Countries and Their Policies* [in Japanese].

———. 1988. *The Motor Industry of Japan*.

Japan. Ministry of Foreign Affairs. n.d. *Japan's Economic Cooperation to ASEAN.* Tokyo: Ministry of Foreign Affairs.

———. Ministry of Foreign Affairs. 1983. *ASEAN and Japan: Dynamic Partnership for the Twenty-First Century.* Tokyo: Ministry of Foreign Affairs.

———. Ministry of International Trade and Industry [MITI]. 1983. *Economic Relations between Japan and the ASEAN Nations.* Tokyo: MITI.

Jenkins, David. 1978. "Where the Generals Reign Supreme." *FEER,* January 13.

Jenkins, Rhys. 1977. *Dependent Industrialization in Latin America: The Automotive Industry in Argentina, Chile, and Mexico.* New York: Praeger.

———. 1984. *Transnational Corporations and Industrial Transformation in Latin America.* London: Macmillan.

———. 1985. "Internationalization of Capital and the Semi-Industrialized Countries: The Case of the Motor Industry." *Review of Radical Political Economics* 17 (Spring/Summer): 59–81.

Johnson, Chalmers. 1987. "Political Institutions and Economic Performance: The Government-Business Relationship in Japan, South Korea, and Taiwan." In Deyo, ed., *Political Economy.*

———. 1982. *MITI and the Japanese Miracle.* Stanford: Stanford University Press.

Jomo, K. S. 1985a. "Project Proton: Malaysian Car, Mitsubishi Profit." In Jomo, ed., *The Sun Also Sets.*

———, ed. 1985b. *The Sun Also Sets: Lessons in "Looking East."* Kuala Lumpur: INSAN.

Jones, Leroy, and Il Sakong. 1983. *Government, Business, and Entrepreneurship in Economic Development: The Korean Case.* Cambridge, Mass.: Harvard University Press.

Jones, Steve, and Raphael Pura. 1986. "Suharto-linked Monopolies Hobble Economy." *AWSJ,* November 26.

Kahin, George M. 1952. *Nationalism and Revolution in Indonesia.* Ithaca: Cornell University Press.

Kanapathy, V. 1981. "Why Malaysia Needs an Industrial Policy." *UMBC Economic Review* (Kuala Lumpur) 17:5–22.

Katzenstein, Peter, ed. 1978a. *Between Power and Plenty: Foreign Economic Policies of Advanced Industrial States.* Madison: University of Wisconsin Press.

———. 1978b. "Domestic Structures and Strategies of Foreign Economic Policy." In Katzenstein, ed., *Between Power and Plenty.*

———. 1985. *Small States in World Markets: Industrial Policy in Europe.* Ithaca: Cornell University Press.

Kaye, Lincoln. 1985. "Sermon from the Bank." *FEER,* May 16.

Kerns, Hikaru. 1981. "The Climate Turns Chilly." *FEER,* February 19.

Kim Chuk Kyo and Lee Chul Heui. 1984. "Ancillary Firm Development in the Korean Automobile Industry." In Odaka, ed., *The Motor Vehicle Industry in Asia.*

Kim Youngil. 1981. *Government Policy and Private Enterprise: Korean Experience in Industrialization.* Berkeley: University of California, Institute of East Asian Studies.

Kim Young Kee. 1984. "American Technology and Korea's Technological Development." In Moskowitz, ed., *From Patron to Partner.*

Kindleberger, Charles P. 1979. *American Business Abroad: Six Lectures on Direct Investment.* New Haven: Yale University Press.

Knickerbocker, Frederick. 1973. *Oligopolistic Reaction and Multinational Enterprise.* Cambridge, Mass.: Harvard University Graduate School of Business Administration.

Kobayashi Noritake. n.d. "The Japanese Auto Industry and Its Relationship with the Worldwide Components Industry: Can an Appropriate Strategy Be Developed?" Keio University, Tokyo. Photocopy.

Kobrin, Stephen J. 1984. "Economic Nationalism in the Developing Countries of the Asia Pacific Region." In Moxon et al., eds, *International Business Strategies,* vol. 4 (Part A).

———. 1987. "Testing the Bargaining Hypothesis in the Manufacturing Sector in Developing Countries." *International Organization* 41 (Autumn): 609–38.

Kohli, Atul. 1986. "Introduction." In Kohli, ed., *The State and Development in the Third World.* Princeton: Princeton University Press.

Koichi Shimokawa. 1981. "Automobiles—Groping for Coexistence Rather than International Rivalry." *Japan Quarterly* 27 (October–December): 518–527.

Konglakai, Somsak. 1975. "Import Substitution by Way of Trade Protection: A Case Study of the Automobile Industry in Thailand." M.A. thesis, Thammasat University.

Krarr, Louis. 1981. "The Philippines Veers toward Crisis." *Fortune,* July 27.

Krasner, Stephen D. 1984. "Approaches to the State: Alternative Conceptions and Historical Dynamics." *Comparative Politics* 16 (January): 223–46.

———. 1985. *Structural Conflict: The Third World against Global Liberalism.* Berkeley: University of California Press.

Kuntjoro-Jakti, Dorodjatun. 1985. "Foreign Investment in Indonesia." Bangkok: U.N. Economic and Social Commission for Asia and the Pacific.

Lall, Sanjaya, and Senaka Bibile. 1977. "The Political Economy of Controlling Transnationals: The Pharmaceutical Industry in Sri Lanka, 1972–1976." *World Development* 5:677–697.

Laothamatas, Anek. 1988. "Business and Politics in Thailand: New Patterns of Influence." *Asian Survey* 28 (April): 451–70.

———. 1989. "No Longer a Bureaucratic Polity: Business Associations and the New Political Economy of Thailand." Ph.D. diss., Columbia University.

Lecraw, Donald J. 1984. "Bargaining Power, Ownership, and Profitability of Transnational Corporations in Developing Countries." *Journal of International Business Studies* (Spring/Summer): 27–44.

Lee Hak Chong. 1984. "The American Role in the Development of Management Education in Korea." In Moskowitz, ed., *From Patron to Partner.*

Lijphart, Arend. 1969. "Consociational Democracy." *World Politics* 21 (January): 207–225.

Lim Chee Peng. 1982. "International Rivalry: U.S.–Japanese Competition in the ASEAN Countries." *Contemporary Southeast Asia* 4, no. 1 (June): 35–57.

———. 1984. "The Malaysian Car Industry at the Crossroads." Paper presented at the Seventh Malaysian Economics Convention, Kuala Lumpur, January 18–20.

Lim Chee Peng and Fong Chan Onn. 1984. "Ancillary Firm Development in the Malaysian Motor Vehicle Industry." In Odaka, ed., *The Motor Vehicle Industry in Asia*.

Lim, Franklin D. 1989. "Channel for Community." *FEER*, February 23.

Lim, Linda Y. C. 1983. "Chinese Economic Activity in Southeast Asia: An Introductory Review." In Lim and Gosling, eds., *Chinese in Southeast Asia*.

———. 1986. "Economic Development in Southeast Asia: Retrospect and Prospect." *Southeast Asia Business*, Fall, 3–11.

Lim, Linda Y. C., and L. A. Peter Gosling, eds. 1983. *The Chinese in Southeast Asia: Ethnicity and Economic Activity*. Vol. 1. Singapore: Maruzen Asia.

Lim Mah Hui. 1985. "Contradictions in the Development of Malay Capital: State, Accumulation and Legitimation." *Journal of Contemporary Asia* 15:37–63.

Lim Mah Hui, and William Canak. 1981. "The Political Economy of State Policies in Malaysia." *Journal of Contemporary Asia* 11: 208–24.

Lindsey, Charles W. 1983. "In Search of Dynamism: Foreign Investment in the Philippines under Martial Law." *Pacific Affairs* 56 (Fall): 477–94.

Livesay, Harold. 1983. "The Philippines as an Example of the Ford Motor Company's Multinational Strategy." In Norman G. Owen, ed., *The Philippine Economy and the United States: Studies in Past and Present Interactions*. Ann Arbor: University of Michigan, Center for South and Southeast Asian Studies.

Lynn, Leonard H., and Timothy J. McKeown. 1988. *Organizing Business: Trade Associations in America and Japan*. Washington, D.C.: American Enterprise Institute.

McCawley, Peter. 1978a. "The Growth of the Industrial Sector." In Anne Booth and Peter McCawley, eds., *The Indonesian Economy during the Soeharto Era*. London: Frank Cass.

———. 1978b. "Some Consequences of the Pertamina Crisis." *Journal of Southeast Asian Studies* (Singapore) 9: 1–27.

———. 1982. "The Economics of Ekonomi Pancasila." *BIES* 18 (March): 102–9.

MacIntyre, Andrew J. 1988. "Business, Policy and Participation: Business-Government Relations in Indonesia." Ph.D. diss., Australian National University.

Mackie, J. A. C. 1988. "Economic Growth in the ASEAN Region: The Political Underpinnings." In Hughes, ed., *Achieving Industrialization in East Asia*.

Malaysian Industrial Development Authority [MIDA]. 1985. *Medium and Long Term Industrial Master Plan, Malaysia*. Vol. 2, *Transport Equipment Industry*. Part 9. Kuala Lumpur: MIDA/UN Industrial Development Authority.

Mangahas, A. C. 1970. "The Automotive Industry in the Philippines: Its Profile, Problems, and Prospects." Ateneo Graduate School of Business, Manila. Photocopy.

Marcos, Ferdinand. 1983. Executive Order No. 906, "Directing the Review of the Progressive Car Manufacturing Program." Manila, August 4. Photocopy.

Means, Gordon. 1972. " 'Special Rights' as a Strategy for Development." *Comparative Politics* 5 (October): 29–61.

Meier, Gerald M. 1986. *Financing Asian Development: Performance and Prospects.* New York: University Press of America.

Milne, R. S. 1966. "Singapore's Exit from Malaysia." *Asian Survey* 6 (March): 175–84.

Milne, R. S., and Diane K. Mauzy. 1978. *Politics and Government in Malaysia.* Vancouver: University of British Columbia Press. Rev. ed. 1980.

Milward, H. Brinton, and Ronald A. Francisco. 1983. "Subsystem Politics and Corporatism in the United States." *Policy and Politics* 11: 279–93.

Minor, Michael. 1986. "South Korea's Personal Computer Industry and Prospects in the American Market." Paper presented at the Annual Meeting of the International Studies Association–South, Atlanta, November 6–8.

Mitsubishi Research Institute [MRI]. 1987. *The Relationship between Japanese Auto and Auto Parts Makers.* Tokyo: MRI.

Mohamad, Mahathir. 1985. "The Second Opening of Japan." In Jomo, ed., *The Sun Also Sets.*

Moran, Theodore H. 1974. *Multinational Corporations and the Politics of Dependence: Copper in Chile.* Princeton: Princeton University Press.

———. 1978. "Multinational Corporations and Dependency: A Dialogue for Dependentistas and non-Dependentistas." *International Organization* 32 (Winter): 79–100.

Morrison, Charles E. 1988. "Japan and the ASEAN Countries: The Evolution of Japan's Regional Role." In Takashi Inoguchi and Daniel I. Okimoto, *The Political Economy of Japan: The Changing International Context.* Stanford: Stanford University Press.

Morris-Suzuki, Tessa. 1984. "Japan's Role in the New International Division of Labor—A Reassessment." *Journal of Contemporary Asia* 14: 62–81.

Moskowitz, Karl, ed. 1984a. *From Patron to Partner: The Development of U.S.–Korean Business and Trade Relationships.* Lexington, Mass.: D.C. Heath.

———. 1984b. "Issues in the Emerging Partnership." In Moskowitz, ed., *From Patron to Partner.*

———. 1984c. "Limited Partners: Transnational Alliances between Private Sector Organizations in the U.S.–Korea Trade Relationship." In Moskowitz, ed., *From Patron to Partner.*

Moxon, Richard, Thomas Roehl, and J. Frederick Truitt, eds. 1984. *International Business Strategies in the Asia-Pacific Region: Industry Studies.* Parts A and B. Greenwich, Conn.: JAI Press.

Muller, Ronald, and David H. Moore. 1978. "Case One: Brazilian Bargaining

Power Success in BEFIEX Export Promotion with the Transnational Automotive Industry." New York: UN Centre on Transnational Corporations.

Myint, Hyla. 1984. "Inward Looking Countries Revisited: The Case of Indonesia." *BIES* 20 (August): 39–52.

Myrdal, Gunnar. 1970. *The Challenge of World Poverty: A World Anti-Poverty Program in Outline.* New York: Pantheon Books.

Nasir, Anwar. 1987. "The Bonds of Friendship." *FEER*, June 11.

Nawadhinsukh, Siriboon. 1984. "Ancillary Firm Development in the Thai Automobile Industry." In Odaka, ed., *The Motor Vehicle Industry in Asia.*

Naya, Seiji. 1987. "Asian and Pacific Developing Countries: Performance and Issues." In W. Chan Kim and Phillip K. Y. Young, eds., *The Pacific Challenge in International Business.* Ann Arbor: UMI Research Press.

Newfarmer, Richard. 1983. "Multinationals and Marketplace Magic in the 1980s." In Kindleberger, Charles, and David Audretsch, eds. *The Multinational Corporations in the 1980s.* Cambridge, Mass.: MIT Press.

———. 1985. "International Industrial Organization and Development: A Survey." In Richard Newfarmer, ed., *Profits, Progress and Poverty: Case Studies of International Industries in Latin America.* Notre Dame, Ind.: University of Notre Dame Press.

Nissan Motor Co. 1987. *Handbook of Automobile Industry.*

Nordlinger, Eric. 1987. "Taking the State Seriously." In Weiner and Huntington, eds., *Understanding Political Development.*

North American Congress on Latin America [NACLA]. 1979. "Car Wars." *NACLA Research Report on the Americas* 12 (July–August).

O'Brien, Peter, and J. Felix Lobo Allen. 1984. *International Industrial Restructuring and the International Division of Labour in the Automotive Industry.* Vienna: UN Industrial Development Organization.

Ocampo, Romeo B. 1971. "Technocrats and Planning: Sketch and Exploration." *Philippine Journal of Public Administration* (January): 31–64.

Odaka Konosuke, ed. 1984. *The Motor Vehicle Industry in Asia.* Singapore: Singapore University Press.

Ohara, Ken. 1977. "Strategy for the [*sic*] Asian Regionalism: World Auto Industries and National Governments." *AMPO* (Tokyo).

Olson, Mancur. 1982. *The Rise and Decline of Nations: Economic Growth, Stagflation, and Social Rigidities.* New Haven: Yale University Press.

Ono Keinosuke. 1973. "Delta Motor Corporation." Tokyo: Keio University Business School.

Organ, J. B. 1968. "The Status of the Automotive Industry in Thailand, Together with Recommended Policies for Its Orderly Development." Bangkok: International Executive Service Corp.

Organization for Economic Cooperation and Development [OECD]. 1983. *Long Term Outlook for the World Automobile Industry.* Paris: OECD.

Oriyama Mitsutoshi. 1987. "Recent Trends in Japan-ASEAN Trade Relations." *Digest of Japanese Industry and Technology* 238: 13–16.

Overholt, William H. 1986. "The Rise and Fall of Ferdinand Marcos." *Asian Survey* 26 (November): 1137–63.

———. 1988. "Thailand: A Moving Equilibrium." In Ansil Ramsay and Wiwat Mungkandi, eds., *Thailand-U.S. Relations: Changing Political, Strategic, and Economic Factors*. Berkeley: University of California, Institute of East Asian Studies.

Ozawa Terutomo. 1985. "Japan." In John Dunning, ed., *Multinational Enterprises, Economic Structure and International Competitiveness*. New York: John Wiley & Sons.

———. 1986. "Japan's Largest Financier of Multinationalism: The Exim Bank." *Journal of World Trade Law* 20 (November–December): 599–614.

Packenham, Robert. 1983. "The Dependency Perspective and Analytic Dependency." In Doran et al., eds., *North/South Relations*.

Palma, Gabriel. 1978. "Dependency: A Formal Theory on Underdevelopment or a Methodology for the Analysis of Concrete Situations of Underdevelopment?" *World Development* 6 (July–August): 881–924.

Palmer, Ingrid. 1978. *The Indonesian Economy since 1965: A Case Study of Political Economy*. London: Frank Cass.

Panglaykim, J. 1974. *Business Relations between Indonesia and Japan*. Jakarta: Center for Strategic and International Studies.

Pascale, Richard, and Thomas P. Rohlen. 1983. "The Mazda Turnaround." *Journal of Japanese Studies* 9:219–63.

Paterno, Vicente T. 1970. "Letter to President Marcos." Manila, December 11. Photocopy.

———. 1972a. "The Philippine Progressive Car Manufacturing Program." *Industrial Philippines*, June–July.

———. 1972b. "Foreign Investments." *Industrial Philippines*, October.

———. 1973. "The BOI: Its Role in Philippine Industrial Development." *Philippine Quarterly*, June.

Pawitra, T. 1985. "The Automobile Marketing Channels in Indonesia: A Study of Its Significance towards [*sic*] the Distribution System." Ph.D. diss., University of Surabaya.

Pearson, L. B. 1969. *Partners in Development: Report of the Commission on International Development*. New York: Praeger.

Pempel, T. J. 1978. "Japanese Foreign Economic Policy: The Domestic Bases for International Behavior." In Katzenstein, ed., *Between Power and Plenty*.

Pempel, T. J., and K. Tsunekawa. 1979. "Corporatism without Labor? The Japanese Anomaly." In Philippe Schmitter and Gerhard Lembruch, eds., *Trends toward Corporatist Intermediation*. Beverly Hills, Calif.: Sage.

Philippine Automotive Association [PAA]. 1969. "Position Paper on Local Content Program." Manila, December 22. Photocopy.

Philippines. Board of Investment [BOI]. 1972. "BOI Guidelines for Progressive Car Manufacturing Program." *Industrial Philippines*, June–July, 12–22.

———. 1977. "Invitation for Submission of Proposals." BOI, Makati. Photocopy.

————. 1981. "Revised Guidelines for Progressive Car Manufacturing Program (PCMP)." BOI, Makati. Photocopy.

Phipatseritham, Krirkhiat, and Kunio Yoshihara. 1983. *Business Groups in Thailand.* Singapore: Institute of Southeast Asian Studies.

Pillai, M. G. G. 1983. "Ecstasy at UMW over Eric Chia's Toyota Coup." *Insight* (Hong Kong), December.

Poynter, Thomas A. 1982. "Government Intervention in Less Developed Countries: The Experience of Multinational Companies." *Journal of International Business Studies,* Spring/Summer, 9–24.

Program Implementation Agency. 1965. *Motor Vehicle Industry in the Philippines.* Manila: Program Implementation Agency.

Pura, Raphael. 1985. "Doubts over Heavy Industrialization Strategy." In Jomo, ed., *The Sun Also Sets.*

Puthucheary, Mavis. 1978. *The Politics of Administration: The Malaysian Experience.* Kuala Lumpur: Oxford University Press.

Putnam, Robert D. 1988. "Diplomacy and Domestic Politics: The Logic of Two-Level Games." *International Organization* 42 (Summer): 427–60.

Ramsay, Ansil. 1986. "Thai Domestic Politics and Foreign Policy." In Karl D. Jackson, Sukhumbhand Paribatra, and J. Soedjati Djiwandono, eds., *ASEAN in a Regional and Global Context.* Berkeley: University of California, Institute of East Asian Studies.

Ratanachaichanan, Choosak. 1977. "Excess Capacity in Automobile Industry in Thailand." M.A. thesis, Thammasat University.

Rayfield, Gordon. 1984. "Comments on Kobrin." In Moxon et al., *International Business Strategies* (Part A).

Reeve, David. 1985. *Golkar of Indonesia: An Alternative to the Party System.* Singapore: Oxford University Press.

Riggs, Fred. 1966. *Thailand: The Modernization of a Bureaucratic Polity.* Honolulu: East-West Center Press.

Ritter, Eric. 1987. "The Thai Auto Industry: Has the Import-Substitution Policy Worked?" Unpublished MS. Columbia University, Uris School of Business. September.

Robinson, Wayne. 1985. "Imperialism, Dependency and Peripheral Industrialization: The Case of Japan in Indonesia." In Higgott and Robison, eds., *Southeast Asia.*

Robison, Richard. n.d. "The Liem Group: From Domestic to International Corporate Operations in Asia—Some Theoretical Considerations." Photocopy.

————. 1978. "Towards a Class Analysis of the Indonesian Military Bureaucratic State." *Indonesia* 25 (April): 17–40.

————. 1986. "Into a New Phase Where Economic Laws Prevail." *FEER,* May 29.

————. 1986a. *Indonesia: The Rise of Capital.* London: Allen & Unwin.

————. 1987. "After the Gold Rush: The Politics of Economic Restructuring in Indonesia in the 1980s." In Robison et al., *Southeast Asia in the 1980s.*

———. 1988. "Authoritarian States, Capital-Owning Classes, and the Politics of Newly Industrializing Countries: The Case of Indonesia." *World Politics* 40 (October): 52–74.

Robison, Richard, Kevin Hewison, and Richard Higgott, eds. 1987. *Southeast Asia in the 1980s: The Politics of Economic Crisis*. London: Allen & Unwin.

Roscoe, Bruce, 1987. "Japanese Business Moves Offshore Slowly." *FEER*, April 30.

Rueschemeyer, Dietrich, and Peter B. Evans. 1985. "The State and Economic Transformation: Toward an Analysis of the Conditions Underlying Effective Intervention." In Evans et al., *Bringing the State Back In*.

Sabransjah, Simorangkir, and Soekandar. n.d. "Development of the Automotive Parts, Components and Supplier Industry in Indonesia." BPPT, Jakarta. Photocopy.

Sacerdoti, Guy. 1981. "Overdraft of Inefficiency: Indonesia's Industrial Development Comes under WB Attack." *FEER*, May 29.

Samuels, Richard J. 1987. *The Business of the Japanese State: Energy Markets in Comparative and Historical Perspective*. Ithaca: Cornell University Press.

Sanger, David E. 1988. "PC Powerhouse (Made in Taiwan)." 1988. *New York Times*, September 28.

Saravanamuttu, Johan. 1985. "The Look East Policy and Japanese Economic Penetration in Malaysia." In Jomo, ed., *The Sun Also Sets*.

Sato, Ichiro. 1982. "Localization Policy for Automobile Production." Bangkok Japanese Chamber of Commerce. Photocopy.

Schmitter, Philippe. 1974. "Still the Century of Corporatism?" *Review of Politics* 36 (January): 85–131.

———. 1982. "Reflections on Where the Theory of Neo-Corporatism Has Gone and Where the Praxis of Neo-Corporatism May Be Going." In Gerhard Lembruch and Philippe Schmitter, eds., *Patterns of Corporatist Policy Making*. Beverly Hills, Calif: Sage.

———. 1985. "Neo-Corporatism and the State." In Wyn Grant, ed., *The Political Economy of Corporatism*. London: Macmillan.

Schutte, Hellmut. 1982. "M.A.N. Philippines." Euro-Asia Centre, INSEAD, Fontainebleau. Photocopy.

Segal, Aaron. 1987. "Growing Pains: Latin America's Auto Industry." *Caribbean Review* 15 (Spring): 24–25.

Segal, Jeffrey. 1982. "Ambition on Wheels." *FEER*, December 24.

Segaran, Raja, Patrick Low, and M. Rajaretman, eds. 1973. *Trends in Thailand*, I. Singapore: Institute of Southeast Asian Studies.

Sentusophon, Laphli. 1984. "Khaw saneh khong khun laphli sentusophon." Thai Auto Parts Manufacturers' Association, Bangkok. Photocopy.

Seward, Nick. 1986. "Manufactured Success." *FEER*, July 31.

———. 1987. "The Proton Bomb." *FEER*, March 13.

———. 1988a. "Putting Its House in Order." *FEER*, January 14.

———. 1988b. "A Rethink on Rationalization." *FEER*, March 2.

Shimada Masahiro. 1987. "Toward the International Division of Labor between Japan and Southeast Asian Nations." *Digest of Japanese Industry and Technology* 237.

Shin, H. D. 1984. "Background of Development of All-Korean Car, Pony—A Suggestion on ASEAN Car." Hyundai presentation to ASEAN automotive delegation, Seoul.

Shinohara Miyohei. 1985. "Trends and Dynamics of East and Southeast Asian Economies." *Asian Development Review* 3:55–78.

Sinclair, Stuart W. 1982. *Motorizing the Third World: Prospects to 1990.* EIU Special Report no. 131. London: Economist.

———. 1987. *The Pacific Basin: An Economic Handbook.* London: Euromonitor.

Skinner, G. William. 1957. *Chinese Society in Thailand: An Analytical History.* Ithaca: Cornell University Press.

———. 1958. *Leadership and Power in the Chinese Community in Thailand.* Ithaca: Cornell University Press.

———. 1973. "Change and Persistence in Chinese Culture Overseas: A Comparison of Thailand and Java." In John T. MacAlister, ed., *Southeast Asia: The Politics of National Integration.* New York: Random House.

Sklar, Richard L. 1976. "Postimperialism: A Class Analysis of Multinational Corporate Expansion." *Comparative Politics* 9:75–92.

Smith, Charles. 1986a. "Tokyo's Neighbourly Urge." *FEER,* June 12.

———. 1986b. "Upset Equations Spark a New Look at Old Problems." *FEER,* June 12.

———. 1987. "Sleight of Hand." *FEER,* March 19.

———. 1988. "New Look, New Life: Nissan Finds New Fight to Hold Its Ground." *FEER,* July 14.

———. 1989. "Parts Exchange." *FEER,* September 21.

Smith, Patrick. 1983. "The Wrong Vehicle." *FEER,* June 16.

Snow, Robert T. 1983. "The Bourgeois Opposition to Export Oriented Industrialization in the Philippines." Boston. Mimeo.

Sricharatchanya, Paisal. 1984a. "Structural Unadjustment." *FEER,* February 2.

———. 1984b, "Now for Bangkok Rules." *FEER,* August 2.

———. 1984c. "Cultured Caution." *FEER,* August 16.

Sta. Romana, Leonardo. 1979. "Domestic Resource Costs in the Car Manufacturing Industry." In Romeo M. Bautista, John H. Power, and associates, eds., *Industrial Promotion Policies in the Philippines.* Manila: Philippine Institute for Development Studies.

Standard and Industrial Research Institute of Malaysia [SIRIM]. 1985. "Seminar on Automotive Components Manufacturing—Technologies and Trends." SIRIM, Kuala Lumpur, May 15–16. Mimeo.

Stauffer, Robert B. 1979. "The Political Economy of Refeudalization." In David A. Rosenberg, ed., *Marcos and Martial Law in the Philippines.* Ithaca: Cornell University Press.

Steinberg, David Joel. 1982. *The Philippines: A Singular and Plural Place*. Boulder, Colo.: Westview Press.

Stepan, Alfred. 1978. *The State and Society: Peru in Comparative Perspective*. Princeton: Princeton University Press.

Stockwin, Harvey. 1976. "Fuel for Doom and Gloom." *FEER*, July 23.

Streeck, Wolfgang, and Philippe C. Schmitter. 1985. "Community, Market, State—and Associations? The Prospective Contribution of Interest Governance to Social Order." In Streeck and Schmitter, eds., *Private Interest Government: Beyond Market and State*. Beverly Hills, Calif.: Sage.

Suehiro Akira. 1985. *Capital Accumulation and Industrial Development in Thailand*. Bangkok: Social Research Institute.

Sumantoro. 1984. *MNCs and the Host Country: The Indonesian Case*. Singapore: Institute for Southeast Asian Studies.

Sundaram, Jomo Kwame. 1987. "Economic Crisis and Policy Response in Malaysia." In Robison et al., eds., *Southeast Asia in the 1980s*.

———. 1988. *A Question of Class: Capital, the State and Uneven Development in Malaya*. New York: Monthly Review Press.

Suryadinata, Leo. 1976. "Indonesian Policies toward the Chinese Minority under the New Order." *Asian Survey* 16 (August): 770–87.

Swaminathan, S. 1982. "Definition Mission: Automotive Parts and Components—Indonesia." Riverdale, Md.: Sheladia Associates for the U.S. Trade and Development Program.

Sycip, David. 1975. "Foreign Trade Policy as It Bears on National Development and the Interests of Labor." Makati. Photocopy.

Taiwan. *Statistical Yearbook*. Various years.

Takeda Shiri. 1980. "How Japanese Corporations Develop International Markets: Product Differentiation and Marketing Efforts." *The Wheel Extended* (Tokyo: Toyota Motor Corp.).

Tan Bok Huai. 1985. "The Malaysian Car Project: A Financial Economic/Social Cost-Benefit Analysis." Institute for Strategic and International Studies, Kuala Lumpur. Photocopy.

Tanaka Masaharu. n.d. "Transportation and an Affluent Society: The Toyota Basic Utility Vehicle." *The Wheel Extended* (Tokyo: Toyota Motor Corp.).

Tang, Roger. 1988. "The Automobile Industry in Indonesia." *Columbia Journal of World Business*, Winter, 25–35.

Tauile, Jose Ricardo. 1987. "Microelectronics and the Internationalization of the Brazilian Automobile Industry." In Susumu Watanabe, ed., *Microelectronics, Automation and Employment in the Automobile Industry*. New York: John Wiley & Sons.

Tawarangkoon, Wuttipan. 1984. "Comparative Advantage and Protection in Automobile Parts and Components Industry in Thailand." M.A. thesis, Thammasat University.

Thailand. Board of Investment [BOI]. n.d. *Autoparts Industries in Thailand*. Bangkok: BOI, Office of the Prime Minister.

Thailand. Ministry of Industry [MOI]. 1984a. "Announcement concerning Permission to Assemble Motor Vehicles." MOI, Bangkok.

———. 1984b. "Industrial Policy for Assembly of Passenger Vehicles." MOI, Bangkok.

———. 1984c. "Saphawa patchuban leh neew thang anakhot khong utsahakam rot yon" (Present conditions and future trends of the motor industry). Automobile Development Committee, MOI, Bangkok.

———. 1985. "Industrial Policy for Assembly of Commercial Vehicles." MOI, Bangkok.

———. 1986. "Udsahakam phlit ch'in suan rot yon" (The auto parts industry). Industrial Economics Office, MOI, Bangkok.

Thanamai, Patcharee. 1985. "Patterns of Industrial Policymaking in Thailand: Japanese Multinationals and Domestic Actors in the Automobile and Electrical Appliance Industries." Ph.D. diss., University of Wisconsin—Madison.

Thee Kian Wee. 1984. "Subcontracting in the Engineering Sector in Indonesia: A Preliminary Survey." Lekmas-LIPI, Jakarta.

Tolentino, Arturo, and Roy Ybanez. 1984. "Ancillary Firm Development in the Philippine Automobile Industry." In Odaka, ed., *The Motor Vehicle Industry in Asia*.

Toyota Motor Corp. 1982. *The Automobile Industry: Japan and Toyota*. Tokyo: Toyota Motor Corp.

———. 1984. *Auto Markets of Southeast Asia and Oceania*. Tokyo: Toyota Motor Corp.

Treece, James B. 1988. "The Auto Onslaught That Never Was." *Business Week* (international ed.), January 16.

Tsuda Mamoru. 1978. *A Preliminary Study of Japanese-Filipino Joint Ventures*. Manila: Foundation for Nationalist Studies.

Tsurumi Yoshi. 1976. *The Japanese Are Coming: A Multinational Interaction of Firms and Politics*. Cambridge, Mass.: Ballinger.

———. 1980. "Japanese Investment in Indonesia: Ownership, Technology Transfer and Political Conflict." In G. Papanek, ed., *The Indonesian Economy*. New York: Praeger.

Tugwell, Franklin. 1975. *The Politics of Oil in Venezuela*. Stanford: Stanford University Press.

Turner, Louis, and Neil McMullen, eds. 1982. *The Newly Industrializing Countries: Trade and Adjustment*. London: Allen & Unwin.

Ueno Hiroya. 1980. "The Conception and Evaluation of Japanese Industrial Policy." In Kazuo Sato, ed., *Industry and Business in Japan*. New York: M. E. Sharpe.

Ueno Hiroya, and Hiromichi Muto. 1974. "The Automobile Industry of Japan." *Japanese Economic Studies*, Fall, 3–90.

United Nations. Centre on Transnational Corporations [UNCTC]. 1983. *Transnational Corporations in the International Auto Industry*. New York: UN.

———. Export Group on ASEAN and Pacific Economic Cooperation. 1982. *ASEAN Foreign Investment from Pacific Sources*. Bangkok: UN.

————. *Yearbook of International Trade Statistics*. Various years.

Vasurat, Kavee, and Ichiro Sato. 1983. "Report of Joint Thailand/Japan Working Group on Automotive Industry." Association of Thai Industries, Bangkok. Photocopy.

Vatikiotis, Michael. 1989. "Roll on Favours." *FEER*, April 27.

Vernon, Raymond. 1966. "International Investment and International Trade in the Product Life Cycle." *Quarterly Journal of Economics* 80: 190–207.

————. 1971. *Sovereignty at Bay: The Multinational Spread of U.S. Enterprises*. New York: Basic Books.

————. 1977. *Storm over the Multinationals: The Real Issues*. Cambridge, Mass.: Harvard University Press.

————. 1979. "The Product Cycle Hypothesis in a New International Environment." *Oxford Bulletin of Economics and Statistics* 41 (November): 255–67

————. 1988. "Introduction: The Promise and the Challenge." In Raymond Vernon, ed., *The Promise of Privatization: A Challenge for American Foreign Policy*. New York: Council on Foreign Relations.

Villegas, Bernardo M. 1984. "Another View of the Philippines Economic Crisis." Manila: Center for Research and Communication.

Von der Mehden, Fred R. 1975. "Communalism, Industrial Policy and Income Distribution in Malaysia." *Asian Survey* 15 (March): 247–61.

Warren, Bill. 1980. *Imperialism: Pioneer of Capitalism*. London: New Left Books.

Watanabe, Susumu. 1979. *Technical Cooperation between Large and Small Firms in the Filipino Automobile Industry*. Geneva: International Labor Organization.

Weiner, Myron, and Samuel P. Huntington, eds. 1987. *Understanding Political Development: An Analytic Study*. Boston: Little, Brown.

Weinstein, Franklin B. 1976. "Multinational Corporations and the Third World: The Case of Japan and Southeast Asia." *International Organization* 30: 373–404.

————. 1982. "Japan and Southeast Asia." In Robert A. Scalapino and Jusuf Wanandi, eds., *Economic, Political and Security Issues in Southeast Asia in the 1980s*. Berkeley: University of California, Institute of East Asian Studies.

Wells, Louis T., Jr. 1971. "International Trade: The Product Life Cycle Approach." In Louis T. Wells, Jr., ed., *The Product Life Cycle and International Trade*. Boston: Harvard University Graduate School of Business Administration.

————. 1983. *Third World Multinationals: The Rise of Foreign Investment from Developing Countries*. Cambridge, Mass.: MIT Press.

White, Gordon, and Robert Wade, eds. 1985. *Developmental States in East Asia* Brighton: Institute of Developmental Studies, Research Report no. 16.

Wibisanto, Christianto. 1984. "Strategi industri otomotif kita." *Kompas* (Jakarta), March 20.

Wichitwong Na Pomphet. 1977. "Nayopai phatana udsahakam rot yon" (Automobile industry development policy). In Wichitwong, *Nayopai saethakit: Khaw* khit leh kan wikhraw (Economic policy: thoughts and analysis). Bangkok: Pra-cacon.

Wilber, Charles K., ed. 1973. *The Political Economy of Development and Underdevelopment*. New York: Random House.

Wilson, David A. 1962. *Politics in Thailand*. Ithaca: Cornell University Press.

———. 1979. "Political Tradition and Political Change in Thailand." In Clark Neher, ed., *Modern Thai Politics: From Village to Nation*. Cambridge, Mass.: Schenkman.

Witoelar, Wimar. 1984. "Ancillary Firm Development in the Motor Industry in Indonesia." In Odaka, ed., *The Motor Vehicle Industry in Asia*.

Wolters, William. 1984. *Politics, Patronage and Class Conflict in Central Luzon*. Quezon City: New Day Publishers.

World Bank. 1983. *Thailand: Perspectives for Financial Reform*. Washington, D.C.: World Bank.

———. *World Development Report*. New York: Oxford University Press. Various years.

Wright, Michael. 1985. "The Motor Vehicle Industry." *Bangkok Bank Monthly Review*, October.

Yanaga Chitoshi. 1968. *Big Business in Japanese Politics*. New Haven: Yale University Press.

Yoshihara Kunio. 1985. *Philippine Industrialization: Foreign and Domestic Capital*. New York: Oxford University Press.

Yoshino, M. Y. 1978. *Japan's Multinational Enterprises*. Cambridge, Mass.: Harvard University Press.

Zysman, John. 1983. *Governments, Markets and Growth: Financial Systems and the Politics of Industrial Change*. Ithaca: Cornell University Press.

INDEX

Compositor:	BookMasters, Inc.
Text:	Galliard
Display:	Galliard and Friz Quadrata
Printer:	Braun-Brumfield
Binder:	Braun-Brumfield